FIRST WORDS

FIRST WORDS

EARLIEST WRITING FROM FAVORITE CONTEMPORARY AUTHORS

Collected and Edited by
Paul Mandelbaum

ALGONQUIN BOOKS OF CHAPEL HILL
1993

Published by
ALGONQUIN BOOKS OF CHAPEL HILL
Post Office Box 2225
Chapel Hill, North Carolina   27515-2225

a division of
WORKMAN PUBLISHING COMPANY, INC.
708 Broadway
New York, New York 10003

LIBRARY OF CONGRESS CATALOGING–IN–PUBLICATION DATA
First Words / edited by Paul Mandelbaum.
p.   cm.
Includes bibliographical references.
ISBN 0-945575-71-8
1. Children's writings, American 2. American literature—
20th century. I. Mandelbaum, Paul, 1959-.
PS508.C5F57 1993
813' .54089283—dc20   93-4809
                                                                        CIP

2 4 6 8 10 9 7 5 3 1

First Printing

For Hank and Rachelle

*   *   *   *

TABLE OF CONTENTS

INTRODUCTION

What We Have Here, and What We Don't

When he was fourteen, John Updike, having long steeped himself in mystery novels, decided it was time to try his hand at one. He feverishly wrote forty-five pages, and, in the process, created Manuel Citarro the "dashing Spanish sleuth" and his secretary, Thomas Mays, an impetuous and delightfully naive narrator.

As a high school student, Joyce Carol Oates wrote a short story about a young boy longing to go fishing with his older brother, due back from the war. No serene reunion emerges, however, in this tale which brims with complex family secrets.

Norman Mailer, at the age of ten, was cranking out his action-packed adventure fantasy, *The Martian Invasion,* in which the hero, Bob Porter, saws through the chains that imprison him, bops Martians on the head, and gleefully practices his French.

John Updike, Joyce Carol Oates, Norman Mailer, and thirty-nine other esteemed authors honored our request to publish samples of what they had written before the age of twenty-one. Many of the pieces in this volume are, as to be expected, highly precocious. But more importantly, each work is invested with the budding character of its author as well as a measure of that valuable commodity innocence.

Except for two Canadians, the authors we solicited were all from the United States and primarily fiction writers—decisions made in order to keep the project manageable. For several reasons only living authors were considered. Most of all, dealing with living authors has allowed us to seek clarification directly from the writer. Also, readers are not stealing a peek at the effects of celebrities who have no say in the matter; instead we are invited guests. (Both Isaac Asimov and John Hersey, who died while this book was in progress, were very gracious about sharing their childhood efforts.) Additionally, to our knowledge, a juvenilia anthology from living U.S. authors has never before been compiled. Although some of the writers included may not be famous a hundred years from now, what this approach risks in terms of posterity's judgment, it gains in the opportunity to preserve writings that otherwise might become lost.

And so much has been lost already. Many of the 170 authors we wrote to replied to say their juvenilia were no longer available, including Rita Mae Brown, Frank Conroy, Mavis Gallant, John Hawkes, Oscar Hijuelos, Harper Lee, James Alan McPherson, Ann Petry, Scott Spencer, and Robert Stone. Julia Alvarez's were lost in some move, as were Sue Miller's. Tama Janowitz cited flooding in her mother's basement. A similar fate destroyed Lee Smith's first novel. Written when she was about nine, the work "featured my then-favorite people as main characters—Adlai Stevenson and Jane Russell. The *plot* was that they went West together in a covered wagon, then (inexplicably) became Mormons."

Laurie Colwin responded before her very premature death: "My juvenilia has been relegated to what Isaac B. Singer calls 'the vessel of mercy,' known to you and me as the waste paper basket." And Wallace Stegner reported before his recent death at age eighty-four: "Everything I have on hand was written after I was ninety."

Hortense Calisher no longer had the fairy tales she wrote at age seven. Nor could Tom Robbins put his hands on the *Snow White and the Seven Dwarfs* scrapbook filled with stories that he wrote when he was five and six. The magazines that Lorrie Moore and her brother used to assemble out of notebook paper and ribbon were also irretrievable.

Amy Hempel couldn't locate her bound grade-school volume *Mary Climbs the Mountain.* Likewise, Elizabeth Tallent had no luck turning up *The Postage-Stamp Horse,* her first book, "a novel set entirely on geranium leaves. The characters spring from leaf to leaf. Crayola illustrations. 3rd grade."

Joy Williams's mother had been doing some pruning in the family archives, and the author was "forced to admit" that the "small shrine" of juvenilia she had believed still in existence was no longer. Grace Paley tried in vain to find the ballad she wrote on the kidnapping of the Lindbergh baby, a subject "which struck me to the heart when I was about nine."

"I wish I had the play I wrote in the fifth grade, set in the first World War, that we put on in the classroom," replied Elmore Leonard, "but I don't."

And James Michener sent his regrets as well: "Alas, I have no samples of my own early writing, and that's a shame, because when I was eight or nine I had my first encounter with Homer's *Iliad,* and when, in the final pages of the child's account of those heroic days, I learned that my Trojans had been defeated by a dirty trick perpetrated by the wily Greeks, I became so angry that I sat down, took a blue-covered examination book, and rewrote the ending of the Trojan War. I can assure you that though the pages are lost, in *my* version Ajax, Achilles and their bully-boys received what for!"

A few authors, though able to locate some juvenilia, were unwilling to see them in print. William Kennedy could not be persuaded to share his story "Eggs," which he had spoken about so temptingly at a PEN/Faulkner gala. Cynthia Ozick's juvenilia are sealed in a box in her attic labeled "DO NOT OPEN UPON PAIN OF DEATH." And William F. Buckley, Jr., exercising similar caution, replied, "if I poked back at the stuff I wrote before age twenty-one I would almost certainly be driven to suicide, and I don't think the country could stand that premature loss."

Other potential contributions had been censored by outside parties. Mary Hood's grade-school novel about the westward pioneers was destroyed by one of her teachers, who "took one look and cried out, like a hay fever sufferer offered a bouquet of ragweed, 'Ridiculous!' and tossed the whole thing in the trash. I slunk away. I knew what she meant: 'Kid stuff!'"

But, as Mary Hood's teacher was not prescient enough to consider, the kid stuff of writers who grow up to achieve eminence can be another matter entirely.

The Value of Juvenilia;
Some Historical and Contemporary Examples

*J*ane Austen wrote far better as a teenager than most people ever manage as adults. And she undoubtedly knew it. In August of 1792, inscribing her latest fictional creation to Cassandra, her adored sister, the sixteen-year-old author wrote playfully:

> Madam, Encouraged by your warm patronage of "The Beautiful Cassandra" and "The History of England," which, through your generous support, have obtained a place in every library in the kingdom, and run through threescore editions, I take the liberty of begging the same exertions in favour of the following novel, which, I humbly flatter myself, possesses merit beyond any already published, or any that will ever in future appear, except such as may proceed from the pen of your most grateful humble servant, the Author.

Contrary to Austen's jest, many others have written novels of greater merit than the one in question, *Catharine.* Still, Penguin Classics saw fit in 1986 to include it with much of the rest of Austen's 90,000 words of existing juvenilia—and a large portion of Charlotte Brontë's as well—in its august series, alongside Homer's *Iliad* and Boccaccio's *Decameron.*

This act of canonization helped promote not only juvenilia's entertainment value but also its literary significance. Childhood writing often indicates an author's bent, demonstrating that each great novel is a chapter in a lifelong body of work. At surprisingly early ages, authors can establish a creative agenda: a theme, or a plot, or a voice—sometimes subtle, sometimes not, but likely all the same to assert itself over and over again. Retracing an author's steps back into childhood illuminates the creative process behind the adult work and strengthens the bond between literature and life.

In the Penguin Classics edition of Austen and Brontë, for example, editor Frances Beer traces the emergence of Austen's trademark moral criticism as it mingles with the youngster's earlier taste for pure ridicule—a taste that (thank goodness) she never outgrew. Other scholars have also found Austen's juvenilia useful in charting her development. *Persuasion,* notes Donald Stone, has been commonly thought to "mark a new romantic element in Austen; and yet we see in 'Catharine' that it was there from the very beginning."

Like Austen, F. Scott Fitzgerald left some traceable literary fingerprints in adolescence. For example, two short pieces from his prep school days, "A Luckless Santa Claus" and "The Trail of the Duke," both feature hapless men playing the fool for frivolous women. This theme will sound familiar to anyone who's read *The Great Gatsby* or *The Beautiful and Damned.* Having the juvenilia at hand helps delineate this pattern even more clearly and establishes the presence early on, notes Fitzgerald scholar John Kuehl, of the author's typical "hero, the homme manqué, and heroine, the femme fatale." In the light of Fitzgerald's juvenilia, Daisy's appearance in *Gatsby* seems in part destined, her creation the collaboration between an author at the height of his powers and a teenage boy groping to understand his own particular romantic bondage. Kuehl, who points to several *femmes fatales* in Fitzgerald's life, remarks that "from childhood through marriage this kind of female fascinated him." Already she can be heard in Dorothy Harmon, the whimsical fiancée of "A Luckless Santa Claus," as she makes such declarations as: "'Harry Talbot [. . .] if you aren't the most ridiculous boy I ever met, I'll eat that terrible box of candy you brought me last week!'"

Gustave Flaubert, whose extensive apprentice writings are preserved in three volumes, was also moved by teenage longing as he wrote juvenilia that would form a basis for his most famous adult masterpiece. At fifteen he completed "Passion and Virtue," which, says Lewis Piaget Shanks, is actually a "sketch of *Madame Bovary.*" Its protagonist Mazza, dissatisfied with her drab husband, takes a lover in whom she invests great stores of passion ("she had an unquenchable thirst for infinite love," writes the young Flaubert). But after things go from bad to worse, she, like Emma Bovary, poisons herself, having similarly proved to be hopelessly maladapted to her world, according to Robert Griffin, who has translated some of Flaubert's juvenilia into English. Shanks connects Mazza's and Mme. Bovary's burning adulterous passions to Flaubert's own deeply felt teenage crush on a married woman, an episode that Flaubert refers to more directly in another work of juvenilia (written at about age sixteen) under the histrionic title "Diary of a Madman."

In his juvenilia, Flaubert already was experimenting with style, in particular his use of roving and ambiguous point-of-view, a technique for which he would later be studied. Flaubert is also famous for the gravity with which he devoted himself to his art. So it is not surprising, though a little alarming, to see the beginnings of this lifetime obsession already documented at age twelve in the following temperamental passage from a letter to a friend: "If I didn't have in my head and at my penpoint a French queen of the fifteenth century, I should be completely disgusted with life, and long since a bullet would have set me free of this clownish pleasantry which is called life."

Childhood, especially for those of artistic temper, has not become fundamentally easier in the modern age. Paul Bowles, for example, perhaps in response to his early feelings of alienation, wrote voluminous juvenilia, and from these one can fashion a striking portrait of the artist as a wonderfully weird boy. He was partial to diaries (not of his own life, but of fictional characters), jotted down in a frantic headline style. The diary he wrote at age nine for the adventuresome Bluey Laber Dozlen begins: "Minnesota was erected. Bluey plans to come. Dolok Parosol stops her saying 'Marry me don't go.' Bluey gets mad. Dolok Parosol tells her again to marry him. She knocks him down. Bluey gets her things packed and puts on a beautiful blue sash. Bluey sails for Wen Kroy and lands. Bluey loves it."

And this all in the first five days! The next four months' entries outline many elements in Bowles's well-known novel *The Sheltering Sky* and his other adult writing. The impetuous, whirlwind travel is already present, as are punishing illness, romantic estrangement (the fact that Bluey can take a driving lesson on the same day her suitor "Dolok almost dies" seems to predict Kit's ability to betray her dying husband), and extreme climates (a 201-foot snowfall in "Bluey," the relentless desert in the adult work). As amusing as "Bluey" is, there is something unsettling about its darkness and the pace of its plotting, as though off the page lurks some intolerable void waiting to rush in at the characters' first sign of inactivity—an undercurrent appropriate for a writer who would someday be called "existentialist to his fingertips."

Much as Bowles's existentialism apparently was formed and expressed in childhood, so was Gail Godwin's fascination with religion. Her convent-school education, which seems so central to her 1987 novel, *A Southern Family,* also inspired a story written when she was fourteen. Though Godwin says she always enjoyed the school, and even fantasized about becoming a nun, the young protagonist in "The Accomplice" is terrified of strict Mother Blanche. "Nancy had feared Mother Blanche ever since that awful fall day when Mother and Daddy had deposited her at St. Catherine's," the story begins. In *A Southern Family,* convent-school nuns exert lingering influence on the lives of the other characters. And one nun in particular, Mother von Blücher, "famous for her ill temper," could be descended from Mother Blanche. "'Boy, she really hates us!' the little girls would exclaim, fascinated by her perpetual wrath"—so remembers Julia, who as an adult is now better able to understand the nun's complexity. Perhaps the ending of *A Southern Family,* with its prayer for Maria von Blücher, is a quiet, even subconscious nod from the adult author toward her teenage story.

Godwin recognizes the significance of patterns. In her 1988 essay "How to Be the Heroine of Your Own Life," she rejects the "fashionable cynics" when they claim that it is "childish to go looking for a consistent, continuous self." Instead, she asserts that "you have to recognize the design in your own being before you can contribute anything of value to the larger design of your civilization."

Sometimes such designs of being are haunting in their insistence. In Godwin's teenage story, Nancy dreams that she has pulled Jesus, suddenly alive, from a crucifix to help act out her revenge on mean Mother Blanche; about four decades later Godwin would write a scene in *Father Melancholy's Daughter* (1991) in which Margaret is awakened from a dream, only to be told that someone has sawed down the crucifix outside her father's rectory during the night.

Other designs stand out for their contrast or irony. At about age twelve, Virginia Woolf wrote "Miss Smith," a sketch "making fun of feminism," according to Neville Braybrooke, editor of the juvenilia anthology *Seeds in the Wind*. "Miss Smith" is about a precocious girl, enamored of her own specialness, who grows up into an advocate of "Women's Rights." She finds herself lonely and unloved, however, until she renounces her former self and meets a gallant gentleman: "so much did she feel the need of someone stronger and wiser than herself that she consented to become his wife. So the two married like ordinary human beings[. . .] ." Presumably still under the yoke of her Victorian upbringing, Woolf wrote this sketch apparently in utter earnestness, thus providing a striking antithesis to the later writing that would establish her place among the most eloquent feminists of her time. (She was constant in other ways, however: she chose the title "To the Light-House" for a sketch written at about age ten.)

Considering the acute individualism of Sylvia Plath's poetry, one imagines the contortions she must have suffered (after forty-five rejections!) to write the formulaic story that *Seventeen* magazine published in 1950. "A date!" Plath writes in "And Summer Will Not Come Again." "Celia gulped, 'I'd love to!'" And yet the seventeen-year-old who could abide those words was also confiding in her diary that year: "spare me from the relentless cage of routine and rote. I want to be free [. . .]. I want, I think, to be omniscient . . . . I think I would like to call myself 'The girl who wanted to be God.'"

Looking at the authors represented in *First Words* turns up additional ironies: For Isaac Asimov, who built his reputation writing about other worlds in other times, no subject could have been more earthly than the one he chose for a school theme—the inconvenient arrival of his baby brother. No intergalactic glamor here; Asimov the fourteen-year-

old turns his attention to a screaming, hair-pulling infant and concludes, "I wish I were dead!"

Before making his fame and fortune writing best-selling tech-
nothrillers such as *Jurassic Park*—about a mad businessman's ill-advised
attempt to build a theme park around cloned dinosaurs—Michael
Crichton, while still a teenager, was cutting his literary teeth on *minimalism*, of all things. ("The day had left me depressed, and annoyed with
people in general," concludes one story, "though I couldn't say exactly
why. And that, in itself, was annoying.")

As for William Styron, whose novels are admired in part for the depth
of their somber vision, we do not really expect to find him, at seventeen,
gamboling through a set of literary parodies in a pointed and mischievous
satire of his school administration. "It is a College President, / And much
surprised are we; / 'By that tailored suit and Arrow tie, / What shalt thou
say to me?'" he writes, with apologies to Coleridge, whose brooding "Rime
of the Ancient Mariner" was similarly preceded by such teenage amuse-
ments as "Monody on a Tea-Kettle" and "The Nose."

Whether for the patterns they confirm or the ironies they reveal, juvenilia draw their greatest significance from the fact that they were written by
someone who has gone on to achieve fame. This is true even for an accomplished teenaged writer like Jane Austen, according to A. Walton Litz,
though he points out that "if Jane Austen had never written anything more,
and the juvenilia had been recently discovered in a croquet box in
Twickenham, I do think they would have been published and read with great
interest." Austen, it's safe to say, is one of a few exceptions to the rule.

The idea of comparison is implied in *juvenilia*'s definition in the
O. E. D.: "literary or artistic works produced in the author's youth," as
opposed to simply works written by a child. (Actually, although we associate
juvenilia with childhood now, its Latin definition refers to young adulthood,
Litz notes.)

Accepting this premise, perhaps a work such as Anne Frank's famous
diary, which due to the narrator's tragic historical circumstances can never

be compared with adult work, is more reasonably considered something other than juvenilia. The element of comparison is also missing in the cases of Hilda Conkling and Marjory Fleming, both celebrated as child poets. Conkling, who was made a tremendous fuss over for her three volumes of verse published in the 1920s, didn't write much as an adult. Fleming, who lived in Scotland in the 1800s, has become enshrined for her endearing verses and other writing; she died from measles at the age of eight (though if she *had* lived to become a mature writer, suggests one scholar, she or someone else might very well have destroyed the childhood efforts that have made her famous).

Occasionally, youthful writing is worth celebrating for its unqualified literary merit, regardless of any comparative view it might provide. Edgar Allan Poe may have written his famous poem "To Helen" ("the glory that was Greece / And the grandeur that was Rome") as early as age fourteen. And Alexander Pope is believed to have first drafted his "Ode on Solitude" when only twelve.

Walter de la Mare suggests in his 1935 study of childhood and juvenilia, *Early One Morning in the Spring*, that sometimes writers will return to material that in many ways they had dealt with more ably as teenagers. Authors—poets really—even have gone back and debased with their clumsy adult hands perfectly fine pieces written in youth, de la Mare goes so far as to say, citing regrettable revisions by Percy Bysshe Shelley and Abraham Cowley.

Juvenilia come in many forms other than poetry and fiction. And even if Anne Frank's diary might not land within the O. E. D. definition of *junenilia*, Anaïs Nin's diaries must. In them, she left a continuously traceable path of her personality and authorship all the way back to age eleven ("I notice no child in my class of my age thinks as I do," she reports in one undated entry from around age twelve). More recently, in the 1950s, fourteen-year-old Maxine Hong (later Maxine Hong Kingston) was using her journal in part as a way to flex her developing social criticism ("People just leave their manners at home when they come to dances it seems. [. . .]

Priscilla heard someone make remarks about my pigtails [. . .]). Scraps of a diary Nathaniel Hawthorne is said to have kept in his teens are rich with a benevolence beyond what might be explained by the fact that his uncle was invited to read it. Young Hawthorne discusses a lamb he bought to save from slaughter, a bedraggled dray horse he conversed with, and a neighboring orphan, Betty Tarbox, for whom he felt pity and compassion ("I love the elf because of her loss").

Depending on the writer and the nature of the correspondence, letters can provide tantalizing glimpses of an emerging writer. One registers the apparent relish with which seventeen-year-old Edgar Allan Poe relates the grisly details of campus life in a letter to his foster father. (In describing someone's arm, wounded in a fight Poe had witnessed, he writes: "It was bitten from the shoulder to the elbow—and it is likely that pieces of flesh as large as my hand will be obliged to be cut out.") And Chekhov as a teenager was already demonstrating a mellow wisdom beyond his years in a letter to his younger brother in which he urges: "you must be conscious of your dignity."

Journalism has been and remains one of the natural steppingstones for aspiring authors. W. E. B. Du Bois was writing for the *New York Globe* at age fifteen. Ben Franklin, at age sixteen, was sneaking letters to the editor into his brother's newspaper, under the pen name Silence Dogood.

One of the most famous examples of the journalistic apprenticeship involves the teenaged Samuel Clemens (later known as Mark Twain). Between the ages of sixteen and seventeen he contributed to his brother's newspapers about forty pieces, many of them attempts at the popular humor that characterized much of the newspaper contents of the day, and thus, writes Edgar Marquess Branch in *The Literary Apprenticeship of Mark Twain,* "Journalism determined his purpose, materials, and methods." In the Hannibal *Journal,* under the bombastic pen name W. Epaminondas Adrastus Blab, the sixteen-year-old Clemens took an opportunity to poke fun at the state legislature and to indulge in some plain old goofiness. As the sketch goes, in response to Blab's request to grant him a legal name change, "the Legislature was convened; my title was altered, shortened, and greatly beautified—and all at a cost of *only a few thousands of dollars to the State!*"

More than a hundred years later, in a Georgia high school newspaper, sixteen-year-old budding humorist Roy Blount, Jr., would uphold the fine tradition of comic faux-reportage. In his column *Dear Diary by Joe Crutch*, he covers, for example, the public affairs of his student government: "(somebody had stepped on President Bobby DeFoor's nose, rendering him unfit for service)." From an earlier *Joe Crutch* report, we learn that, in the world of sports, "Zack Hayes got his head tangled in the net of the basketball goal." Oddly enough, three years later, comic-novelist-to-be Clyde Edgerton would, at the same age as Blount, make that very joke, in almost the exact same way, in his high school magazine in North Carolina.

Besides getting stuck in basketball nets, what are the big subjects of literary juvenilia? Animals are popular with the youngest writers (see Madison Smartt Bell's "Mr. Beaver"). By the teen years, love and death have gained considerable ground.

De la Mare makes the point that boys tend to eschew personal disclosure in their juvenilia—at least until the age of fourteen. This void—though de la Mare may not have considered it that—is often filled with plot. One hilarious example, Evelyn Waugh's *The Curse of the Horse Race*, has become something of a classic, having turned up in several juvenilia anthologies. Written when Waugh was seven, this nine-chapter tale of some five hundred words is loaded with such action-packed lines as, "The peliesman lept from his horse only to be stabed to the hart by Rupert." It also contains this innocent—one assumes—gem: "Rupert mounted Sally (which was his horse) [. . .] ."

The contemporary authors in *First Words* give some anecdotal support for de la Mare's observation. John Hersey at age seven is caught up in several daring rescues ("The boys swam for their friend's life"); ten-year-old Norman Mailer is deep into his adventure epic *The Martian Invasion* ("'You shall die a nice death, a very nice death'"); and Stephen King, at nine, spins a three-wishes fairy tale that sends its protagonist on a witch hunt ("Now he had onley to kill the third witch and he would have the 5,000 crowns").

By contrast, Jill McCorkle, at age seven, is confessing her insistent horse dreams ("I had rather dream horses then any thing else"). In a brief verse four-year-old Ursula K. Le Guin (then Kroeber) declares her love for her mother, and Amy Tan's essay from age eight reveals her feelings for the library; whereas Vance Bourjaily's poem from age six enthusiastically recounts an insect battle.

Working-class children often create protagonists who desire a better way of life. "Evening was growing colder as the white-collar workers scurried home to warm fires and after-dinner pipes," begins Charles Johnson's vignette about two homeless people, published in his high school newspaper when he was seventeen. Stephen King's hero, "Jhonathan [the] cobblers son," bravely seeks his fortune. The downtrodden in Carolyn Chute's story—talking hogs waiting to perform their mortal role at the hot dog factory—are rescued by young, spunky Nancy. And Tillie Olsen, who has embraced working-class issues throughout her career, at about nineteen was writing a long story concerning the toll such a life exerts on a young woman with artistic aspirations. "'I've no means of attaining that other kind of life,'" says the subject of her story "Not You I Weep For."

On the other hand, children from more affluent backgrounds tend to reflect that fact in their juvenilia. Teenaged Gore Vidal, in his short story "Mostly About Geoffrey," employs a genteel, drawing-room tone. And, in "The Futility of Prophesy," Louis Auchincloss adroitly sets his readers amid a gathering of French aristocrats, who are enjoying a gracious if somewhat tense evening until they become mutilated casualties of the French Revolution. Although one of the characters makes the point that the "filthy, half-starved, and penniless mobs [. . .] 'have suffered so much wrong,'" this particular tale, as related by the fourteen-year-old author, emphasizes the horrors that befell the "aristocracy and wealthy folk."

Writers and writing remain perennial subjects in juvenilia (and can sometimes point out lineages of influence). Obsessed with becoming a writer, the tormented Fuzzie in Olsen's "Not You I Weep For" devours the work of her mentors—who include Mansfield and Barbellion—and tries to see the world through "'Katherine Mansfield eyes.'" "'You had a way of casually bringing one of these writers into the conversation as if they were mutual friends,'" the narrator says of Fuzzie, "'even as if they were present.'"

In his philosophical *Not to Confound My Elders*, teenaged Vance Bourjaily touches on the shortcomings and virtues of various literary giants. "Byron is too full of cliches[. . .] . When it comes to Robert Browning, I'll march in the same parade with him anytime." Wordsworth, Milton, Keats, Dickinson, and others are briefly considered, as well as Tennyson, whom "I admire but do not like." (For his part, Tennyson wrote copious juvenilia, including a critique, at age twelve, of Milton's *Samson Agonistes* in a letter to his Aunt Marianne. "The first scene is the lamentation of Samson, which possesses much pathos and sublimity," he tells her.)

In the diary excerpts attributed to teenaged Nathaniel Hawthorne, this literary critique survives: "I have read 'Gulliver's Travels,' and do not agree with Captain Britton that it is a witty and uncommonly interesting book. The wit is obscene, and the *lies too false*."

Other literary references abound in juvenilia: Styron's parodies of Coleridge, Shakespeare, Shelley, Kipling, and Tennyson, for example. Tipping his hat to an early influence, no doubt, eighteen-year-old Michael Crichton has one of his characters mention: "'Like what Hemingway said in—.'" Fred Chappell's "And with Ah! Bright Wings" (age sixteen or seventeen) refers quite pointedly, beyond just the title, to Gerard Manley Hopkins. In one of her short stories, teenaged Judith Ortiz Cofer confesses, or at least her narrator does, to "a debauchery of uncensored reading beginning with John Updike's *Couples*." And Updike, at fourteen, has the characters in his mystery-novel-in-progress make several observations comparing the action they find themselves in to the literary genre that inspired it.

In his anthology of juvenilia collected largely from 1880 to 1950, Braybrooke notices a paucity of classical references in comparison to the juvenilia of earlier eras. And despite the fact that James Michener at age eight or nine rewrote the ending of the Trojan War, this nonclassical trend apparently has continued. (When Alexander Pope was twelve, he, too, was inspired by the *Iliad*, de la Mare relates, and wrote a play "which was acted by his schoolfellows in the garden at Hyde Park Corner; Mr. Dean, the gardener himself, taking the part of Ajax.")

To many readers, getting one's hands on a copy of James Michener's childhood treatment of the *Iliad*—(or Alexander Pope's!)—would seem supremely desirable. And yet there are some who are not so easily charmed by the idea of juvenilia. "One of the worst of the literary habits of our day," one Austen scholar was arguing in 1931, "is that of fishing out of drawers and cupboards the crudities and juvenilities of authors who have subsequently written famous books."

Admittedly, there are some bad reasons to like juvenilia. For example, it would be a mistake to ascribe to childhood pieces more brilliance than they might actually possess, lapsing into the sort of hyper-romantic attitude cautioned against by Myra Cohn Livingston in *The Child as Poet: Myth or Reality?* On the other hand, cruelty, or the desire to cut down successful authors (as one contributor to *First Words* initially feared the anthology was set up to do), isn't a very productive purpose either. There is a much more reasonable motive—in addition, of course, to our quest for items of literary significance or our enjoyment at discovering the familiar in an unfamiliar guise—and that motive is neither cruel nor coddling. It is our desire to connect with the person inside the artist.

To read the mystery novel—precocious and awkward at once—that John Updike wrote in early adolescence, is to empathize with that young author's barely restrained excitement over his new role as creator.

Perhaps this sort of appreciation verges on being sentimental. Certainly to read young Robert Louis Stevenson imploring his father to let him come home from boarding school ("My dear papa, you told me to tell you whenever I was miserable") strikes a poignant chord, as does a letter from the twelve-year-old Charles Dodgson (later Lewis Carroll) confessing that he can't find his toothbrush and so hasn't used one in "3 or 4 days" and ending with this plea: "Excuse bad writing."

We do excuse the bad writing. We are happy to. Anyone who has ever tried to plot out a short story of even modest originality can understand, for example, the forced results of Hemingway's revenge-in-the-wilderness tale "Judgment of Manitou," published in his high school literary magazine when he was sixteen ("Two ravens left off picking at the shapeless something that had once been Dick Haywood [. . .]").

In this mood of fond affinity we pleasantly drift in and out of the knowledge that these young writers are the same people who have come to occupy the places of greatest honor on our bookshelves. Juvenilia reminds us of often forgotten truths: that art takes its nourishment from the common garden of human experience. And that authors are children grown up, still learning, even as they teach us.

A Brief Guide to This Book

* **Margin notes.** In the margins of the text, readers will find several hundred side notes. These make connections between the juvenilia and an author's life or adult work. When such a link pertains to a specific spot in the juvenilia, an arrow points to it. Margin notes that have no arrow do not necessarily correspond to any particular passage in the juvenilia.

* **Ellipses.** Virtually all the ellipses that appear in the side notes are the editor's, indicating where quoted material has been omitted. In very rare cases, ellipses are actually a part of the quoted material. In the juvenilia themselves, ellipses are always the author's unless they appear in brackets intended to give a clear indication that the juvenilia have been abridged or altered.

* **Mistakes.** Editing the juvenilia, we have tried to adhere whenever possible to a sensible policy prompted by John Updike: we have silently corrected mere slips of the pen or of the typewriter keys, but mistakes that

seem to reveal something about the development of the writer have been left intact. Even genuine mistakes, however, if their effect is to confuse the reader, have been corrected; in such rare cases, these changes are indicated inside brackets. Often, when it seemed unclear what to do with an error, the author was consulted, though owing to the many intervening years since the juvenilia were written, this method was hardly foolproof. So despite the best of intentions and much painstaking effort, this process has by no means been scientific.

Approximately half of the juvenilia in this anthology first appeared in some sort of school journal (most commonly a high school literary magazine). In the absence of manuscripts, we have applied the same principles of correction to the schools' typeset versions. Of course, some student or faculty editor may have cleaned up these pieces a bit. (On the other hand, the schools' typesetters may have added new mistakes.)

* Dates. In cases where the juvenilia first appeared in school or other publications, a notation is made in the appendix, and the year listed with the text of the juvenilia refers to this original publication— unless the author recalled that the piece was written in a previous year.

The years included alongside references to an author's mature short stories are dates of first publication (except in such rare cases as we are aware of dates of composition), while the appendix provides the publication date of the collection the stories later appeared in.

Acknowledgments

I'd like to express my deep appreciation, not only to the authors who contributed juvenilia to this project, but also to the following people for their guidance and aid: Alice E. Adams, Larry Baker, Geoffrey Becker, Jackson Bryer, Michael Cheney, Frank Conroy, Nicole Daya,

Cheryl Friedman, Bernice Hausman, Mark Holt, Paul Ingram, Clair James, Betsy Keller, Brooks Landon, Tom Lutz, Richard Macksey, Fred Moten, Carol Offen, Kevin Potter, Margaret Richardson, Helen Ryan, Nancy Schwalb, Alan Sea, and Sharon Wood. And an extra thanks to Shannon Ravenel, whose encouragement and help have made working on this project over the past four years a special pleasure.

—Paul Mandelbaum

FIRST WORDS

Isaac Asimov at age 14.

ISAAC ASIMOV

*I*n his seventy-two years, Isaac Asimov produced nearly five hundred books, many of them in the genre of science fiction, for which he became one of America's leading exponents. The author of "Nightfall" (1941), *The Gods Themselves* (1972), "The Bicentennial Man" (1976), and the Foundation series spanning four decades, Asimov also published mysteries, histories, and science fact, displaying an encyclopedic interest in the universe and an unquenchable desire to tell someone else about it. His published titles even include *An Easy Introduction to the Slide Rule* (1965). To his fiction Asimov brought his authority as a biochemistry professor and his expansive knowledge of science in general. The works also display a strong interest in politics, ethics, and the nature of intelligence.

Born in a small Russian town—sometime between October 4, 1919, and January 2, 1920—Asimov immigrated with his family to Brooklyn, New York, when he was three. In *The Early Asimov* (1972), he describes growing up as a voracious reader in a family too poor to afford books. To supplement the two books per week he was allowed from the library, Asimov began composing his own reading matter.

The essay below, written for a high school English class—in which the young author was made to feel a lightweight—was included in the school's literary magazine, according to Asimov, only because the adviser needed at least one piece that wasn't serious.

In a 1989 letter to *First Words*, Asimov elaborated: "The faculty adviser...accepted it with the worst possible grace, because it was the only offering that attempted to be funny—and he told me so quite bluntly."

In his autobiography *In Memory Yet Green* (1979), Asimov recounts some of the trauma of this class; in particular, one moment when the teacher-adviser reportedly interrupted Asimov in the middle of his recitation of a floridly descriptive essay by exclaiming, "This is shit!"

"His opinion of my writing ability was rock-bottom, and I don't know if he lived long enough to realize that he was badly mistaken," continued Asimov in his letter, adding: "Fortunately, regardless of his opinion, I already knew, at the age of fourteen, that I was a great writer and so I didn't require his approval at all."

Isaac Asimov died April 6, 1992.

Little Brothers
(1934, age 14)

In Asimov's short story "The Ugly Little Boy" (1958), scientists transport a young Neanderthal boy into modern times. The head scientist's son, drafted as playmate for the strange youngster, does not welcome his new companion graciously.

My mission in life right now is to express the venomous feelings that we "big" brothers have for the bane of our lives, the "little" brothers.

When I first received the news that I had a little brother, on July 25, 1929, I felt slightly uncomfortable. As for myself, I knew nothing about brothers, but many of my friends had related at great length the inconveniences (to say the least) of attending babies.

On August 3, my little brother came home. All I could see was a little bundle of pink flesh, with apparently no ability to do the slightest mischief.

That night, I suddenly sprang out of bed with gooseflesh all over me and my hair on end. I had heard a shriek apparently made by no earthly being. In response to my frenzied questions, my mother informed me in a common-place manner that it was just the baby. Just the baby! I was almost knocked unconscious. A puny nine-pound baby, 10 days old, to make such a scream! Why, I was convinced that no less than three men together could have strained their vocal cords to such an extent.

But this was only the beginning. When he began teething, the real torture came. I did not sleep a wink for two months. I only existed by sleeping with my eyes open in school.

And still it wasn't all. Easter was coming, and I was feeling joyous at the prospect of a trip to Rhode Island, when that kid brother of mine got the measles and everything went up like smoke.

Soon he reached the age where his teeth were already cut and I hoped to obtain a little peace, but no, that could not be. I had yet to learn that when a child learns to walk, and talk baby-language, he is rather more of an inconvenience than a cyclone, with a hurricane thrown in for good measure.

His favorite recreation was that of falling down the stairs, hitting each step with a resounding bump. This occurred on the average of once every other minute and always brought on a scolding from my mother (not for him, but for me for not taking care of him).

This "taking care" of him is not as easy as it sounds. The baby usually shows his devotion by grabbing generous fistfuls of hair and pulling with a strength that you would never have thought possible in a one-year-old. When, after a few minutes of excruciating torture, you persuade him to let go, he seeks diversion in hitting your shins with a heavy piece of iron, preferably a sharp or pointed one.

Not only is a baby a pest when awake, but is doubly so when taking his daily nap.

This is a typical scene. I am sitting in a chair next to the carriage deeply immersed in the *Three Musketeers* and my little brother is apparently sleeping peacefully; but he really isn't. With an uncanny instinct, in spite of his closed eyes and inability to read, he knows exactly when I reach an exciting point and with a malicious grin selects that very moment to awake. With a groan I leave my book and rock him till my arms feel as if they will fall off any

The very idea of full-blooded siblings is considered completely aberrant in the futuristic society depicted in Asimov's 1974 short story "Stranger in Paradise."

Asimov says in his autobiography that "Little Brothers" was an unsuccessful attempt to emulate the humor of Robert Benchley.

In truth, Asimov writes in his autobiography, caring for his baby brother was not a hardship. "I could wheel him around the block a dozen times or so with a book propped against the handle of the carriage. No problem."

Stanley Asimov at age 3.

Stanley, the stowaway boy in Asimov's early short story "The Callistan Menace" (1938), bears the same name as the author's younger brother. The child protagonist, whose parting gesture is to stick out his tongue at one of Jupiter's moons, proves himself to be a "spunky little kid."

minute. By the time he does go back to sleep, I have lost interest in the famous trio and my day is ruined.

Now my little brother is 4½ years old and most of these aggravating habits have disappeared, but I feel in my bones that there is more to come. I shudder to think of the day when he'll enter school and place a new burden upon my shoulders. I feel absolutely sure that not only will I be afflicted with the homework which my hard-hearted teachers will give me, but I will also be responsible for my little brother's.

I wish I were dead!

Isaac Asimov

Margaret Atwood as a 14-year-old, pictured here at Niagara Falls.

MARGARET ATWOOD

When Margaret Atwood was in high school, she wrote about political repression, class inequality, and the difficult choices facing women—themes that continue to appear in her more than twenty published books of fiction and poetry. The author of *Second Words: Selected Critical Prose* (1982), *Bluebeard's Egg and Other Stories* (1983), *Selected Poems II* (1987), and *Cat's Eye* (a novel, 1989), Atwood is perhaps best known for her 1985 novel *The Handmaid's Tale*, a futuristic nightmare in which an oppressive society classifies certain women as reproductive chattel.

Born in Ottawa, Ontario, in 1939, Atwood didn't write much as a child until age sixteen, "when it came to me that I was a writer." In much of the juvenilia below, she focuses on the very adult subject of regret: In "A Cliché for January," a young woman mourns a childhood friend trapped, by pregnancy, in an unwanted marriage. "The English Lesson," written when Atwood was seventeen, features a morose schoolteacher reflecting on the fiancé she lost to war and the literary career that eluded her.

In a lighter mood, "Three Cheers for Corona" is a tongue-in-cheek essay (written as an English assignment) defending a woman's right to smoke cigars. As does so much of Atwood's adult work, this spoof takes aim at restrictive gender roles and strikes a blow for equality and flamboyance.

A Representative

(circa 1956, age 15–17)

Sad intelligence, that seeks
Down dark and lone deserted streets
And through the sewerage of men
For one small spark, one ray of light;
He, the machine, enclosed in night
Potential, silent, still and sad
Lacks the power to use the power
To drive the wheels to make him mad.
Inertia, curse of everything
That wants to grow, to reach and stretch,
Has laid its thin sciatic hand
Upon this sorely crippled land.

Atwood employs a variety → of dark imagery to convey the often sorry state of humanity. She returns to the gutter in her story "The Man from Mars" (1977) when she refers to an old man "who lived for three years in a manhole."

Three Cheers for Corona!

(circa 1956, age 16–17)

"I did smoke cigars a couple of times, on a 'dare,'" says Atwood. "They made me ill."

For some time now, my name has been drifting through a sooty cloud of misunderstanding and prejudice. My erstwhile friends avoid me on the street, I hear strangers whispering about me as I pass, and my aquaintences regard me with raised eyebrows and a supercilious curl of the lip.

Why? The answer is reasonable enough. I smoke cigars. Mind you, I don't publicize the fact. When offered a cigarette, I lower my eyes modestly and murmur a polite, "No, thank you." Then I brace myself for the inevitable question: "Don't you smoke?" My upbringing compels me to tell the truth. "Well, not exactly. At least, not cigarettes. Only cigars." This usually brings an amused but obviously disbelieving smile; but the smiles vanish when I slip my stoogie out of my purse, lick it all over to counteract dryness, chomp off the end with my little yellow incisors, and light up. Astonishment is hardly the word for the reaction.

There are many arguments against women smoking cigars. I have heard them all, and have concluded that they are, without exception, weak, inconclusive, and based on the shaky foundation of conformity. Most people contend that smoking cigars is unfeminine; it is hardly worth the space to point out that short skirts, short hair, and short marriages, all established facets of present society, were once frowned upon. Another popular fallacy is the one that confines the use of cigars to middle-aged, paunchy business executives. There is no reason why women, who are now participating actively in the business world, should not inherit the cigar along with the seat on the Control Board. As for the pale, quavering neurotic boys (I refuse to call them "men") who, while fumbling in their pockets for matches, and opening their cigarette cases with shaky, nicotine-stained fingers, *dare* to tell me that cigars are bad for the health—they are merely pitiable. Anyone who maintains that one medium-sized cigar every two weeks is more harmful than a pack of cigarettes a day is flying in the face of logical reasoning, mathematics, and known facts, and is not even worth arguing with. My little weakness is held to be "something that just isn't done," and therefore undesirable. But it *is* done: *I* do it.

The advantages of being a cigar-smoker far outweigh the disadvantages. Cigars have all the good qualities, and only a few of the bad ones, of cigarettes. For instance, cigarettes give you "something to do with your hands." So do cigars; but, whereas cigarettes only occupy *one* hand, it takes

Even in this high school essay, Atwood displays a keen awareness of the sexual-political freight attached to everyday items and gestures. In her dystopian novel The Handmaid's Tale, *Atwood's enslaved protagonist describes, with an anthropologist's curiosity, the high-heeled shoes worn by tourists as "delicate instruments of torture. The women teeter on their spiked feet as if on stilts, but off balance; their backs arch at the waist, thrusting the buttocks out."*

◄— *In Atwood's novel* The Edible Woman *(1969), we're introduced to Duncan: a pale, 26-year-old (he looks 15), "compulsive neurotic," cigarette-smoking "boy," who delivers such garden-variety pronouncements as, "The only thing about laundromats...is that you're always finding other people's pubic hairs in the washers."*

two, and sometimes even three hands to keep a good cigar under control. Cigars are soothing and relaxing; (the beginner should take care *not* to relax on the floor). No one could stand too many cigars in succession; therefore, the danger of becoming a slave to the habit is slight. And they certainly separate the sheep from the goats as far as friends are concerned: only the most faithful and loyal of friends will venture to be seen in public with a cigar-smoking female. (I admit it was rather a shock to discover that I hadn't a true friend in the world; however I'm glad to be rid of them—the hypocrites!)

This sort of breezy commentary on social convention developed into one of the more provocative tones of Atwood's adult voice.

But the best reason—the reason without which all the others would be as useless as a well at the bottom of a lake—the culminating triumph of a reason, resulting from years of torturing self-analysis and mental research—is a simple one.

I enjoy them!!

Care to join me?

1956 — and For Ever
(*circa 1956, age 16–17*)

*T*here is no room for giants on this earth
The petty people swaggar, strut, and preen,
Gathering gold with avaricious claws.
All thoughts except the trivial wilt and die;
True joy has gone, there is but shallow mirth;
The rich are worthless, and sharp envy green
Moves them to cram still more their full-filled paws;
The poor are only born to toil and cry.

In The Handmaid's Tale, *society's most oppressed are forced to work at toxic-waste dumps, "the way they used to use up old women, in Russia, sweeping dirt."* ➤

First Snow
(circa 1956, age 16–17)

*T*he first snow is the saddest snow;
By city slums the first flakes blow
They fall upon the streets in vain
And trickle down the window pane.
Conceived in beauty, killed in soot,
A smudge of mud upon a boot.
And no impression can they make
Upon the filth; they die, each flake.

First snow of Hungary is past.
The second snow will last and last.

This poem about the Hungarian Revolution demonstrates Atwood's early interest in foreign affairs. In her 1981 novel Bodily Harm, *Dr. Minnow, an opposition candidate challenging a corrupt Caribbean government, tries to convince Rennie, a self-described "lifestyles" journalist, to report on the truth of his country. After her arrest, Rennie learns that she "is not exempt. Nobody is ← exempt from anything."*

The English Lesson
(1957, age 17)

*M*iss Murdock adjusted her thick, steel-rimmed glasses in front of the mirror. She regarded the reflection before her: her own familiar shapeless face with its wispy frame of brownish-gray hair (those wisps would never stay in place—she had ceased to try); the green leather armchair in the corner; the legs of Miss Spencer, the History teacher, who was dozing by the window with her shoes off; and the mirror on the opposite wall that reflected her own reflection. If there were three mirrors, she thought, I would see a whole line of Miss Murdocks, one after the other, all moving together like puppets. She wondered idly why Miss Spencer, who was fifty-six if a day, wore red nail-polish on her toes. She dabbed powder on her biscuity cheeks with her fluttery, irresolute hands, applied her lipstick (unevenly, as usual), in a thick, dark line and blotted most of it off, twitched her pearls and flicked a few crinkly hairs from her collar. I really don't know why I bother, she thought; struggle, struggle for survival like an amoeba in a glass dish, without purpose, without direction. Miss Spencer stirred in her sleep as the door wheezed shut.

Outside the Lady Teachers' Room, Miss Murdock plodded down the hall with her habitual wavering gait. There was a time, far back, when she had marched erect—shoulders back, chin up, toes pointing straight ahead—but it was too much effort now. The bell went, and students spurted into the hall. Where was she going? Where? Oh yes—Room 6, 10B English—her worst class. Without anticipation, without enthusiasm, without fear, practically without thinking, she would teach grammar rules for half an hour to 10B; then lunch, then classes, then another night and another day. I am a dried-up well, she thought, with dry dead moss around the edges.

She reached her classroom. Everything was as usual. The swell of noisy talking, the muffled cries of "Here comes the sheep!!" suddenly stilling as she entered, her own feeble, vacant smile, her bleated half-plea, half-command to open books, all the same, day after day, for ever and ever, world without end. Mechanically, she began to take up the homework, even though she knew four-fifths of the class had not done it.

"John and I (was, were) going to the store."

Where was John now? Is there a heaven? She heard her own words, made familiar by memory, coming from afar: "Not yet, John; I want a career first; I want to finish college, and go to Europe for a year; maybe work on a newspaper. But perhaps in a few years...." And then the war and good-bye. And then the letters—ten, fifteen, twenty of them, a line of letters—a line that ceased abruptly, to be followed, it seemed a minute later, by one more—one more letter, edged in black. She had cried then. She never cried now.

A boy in the back row slipped a note across the aisle. A girl tried not to giggle. Miss Murdock ignored them. She realized that her pupils did not

Even though Atwood grew up during the '50s, "when marriage was seen as the only desirable goal" for a woman, her parents did ➤ *not pressure her to marry, she once told Joyce Carol Oates in a* New York Times *interview.*

respect her for her laxness, her mental laxness that sagged like the ring of fat about her waist and the flabby, freckle-covered muscles at the backs of her arms. She tried to tell herself that it was not good to force children to pay attention, that their interest would develop spontaneously in time, but she felt uneasily that this attitude was just a not-too-effective excuse for her laziness.

"I (will, shall) write a letter to-night."

To write. To write had been to live. To write she had saved and scrimped, scrimped and saved, rejected the bright, gay clothes she had once been so fond of, put herself through college, hating her poverty, waiting for the day she would be famous.... She could not pinpoint the exact moment when her resolution had deserted her. It had flowed from her in days of drudgery at the office of the newspaper that had hired her, in nights of remembering, in rejection slips from weekly magazines. Finally she had clutched the once despised security around her and fled to the sheltering shadow of the local high school..... fled from the limelight of life to the semi-shade of a slow death. This fertile cultivated ground was to her a flat, sterile plain, devoid of life, productive only of a monthly pay-cheque. The meaning of her life had seeped through the sand, and she was left wandering in a desert between the dawn that would never come and the sun that had already set.

Miss Murdock sighed. Her class was doing its utmost to be annoying, she reflected. She smiled her feeble smile and continued with the lesson.

"He (ate, eat) his lunch, (which, who) was very good."

Lunch. In five minutes—no, four—the bell would ring for noon-hour dismissal. In her mind's eye, she saw herself descending the stairs to the cafeteria, in the faded print dress that looked like a housecoat and didn't fit; she saw herself buying her sandwich and coffee and sitting down opposite Miss Spencer in the Teachers' Dining Room; she heard Miss Spencer chirp something about the weather,

← Rennie in Bodily Harm *once wanted to be a serious reporter but finds herself writing more and more fluff. She describes a desertion of will that caused her to see her "ambitions ... as illusions."*

Literary critic Clifton Fadiman remarks that in Atwood's story "The Man from Mars," the author "never raises her voice, yet the desired effect of mingled pathos and irony registers perfectly." Passages from "The English Lesson" have not yet achieved this level of understatement, but "A Cliché for January" (see page 18) seems an early experiment in such restraint.

and saw herself smiling her weak smile—smiling
vacantly as she watched the coffee dribble down the
side of the cup, smiling and smiling through the days
of darkening shade, for ever.

Pause Before Transition
(circa 1957, age 17–18)

*I*t has been winter.
. . .
But
There comes a day
When the sun is suddenly too hot,
Too bright;
Heavy coats weigh
And winter legs anaemicly inadequate
Glare white in the light;
A day
When the roads are no longer wet with melting
    snow,
Rushing down drains,
Carrying damp, half-earth-already leaves
To clog the sewers,
But dry with the first fine dust
That buses raise in clouds.
The sun
Encountering no resistence from the embryo buds
Pasted on spindling stems,
Strung like knots in string,
Burns in diluted blue,
And swims in heightened shadows on the sidewalks.
The streets
Photographs overexposed
Blink;
And faded awnings sprout on crowded stores.
Still no leaves to filter

Break the impact
Of light in squares;
Hydrants and garbage cans
Squat darkly on the walks
Reliefed, defined in shade.
Now
Wool is too warm;
Women sweat, uncomfortable,
And squint their eyes on buses
And breathe the first dust.
    Last year's leaves in corners;
    A blot of spit drying in a dirty gutter
    And old men coughing in the backs of streetcars.
. . .
Later is spring.

Atwood has continued to refine her eye for the grim detail: the deer carcass found in a ditch, for example, in the title poem of her 1974 collection You Are Happy.

Margaret Atwood at age 20, reading poetry at the Bohemian Embassy in Toronto.

A Cliché for January

(1959, age 19)

*D*amn, she thought, as she climbed the last step. Mrs. Carter.

She dropped her bus ticket into her purse and fumbled for it, to give herself time to think. I could pretend not to see her—no—too late for that—or get off at the next stop—she weighed fifteen minutes in the rain against Mrs. Carter, and Mrs. Carter won. Bus too empty—can't sit somewhere else. She's beaming at me—she knows I see her. Well, here's for it. Colours flying high for the good of the cause.

Mrs. Carter's smile broadened as she approached. Your smile always reminds me vaguely of a halitosis ad, she thought, or one of those little back-pages-of-the-newspaper ones about false teeth. She gave herself an internal twist, and felt the pattern click into place.

—"Oh, hello, Mrs. Carter, how are you?"

—"Well, Diane, how are you"?

—"Just fine, thank you," as she sat down.

Slight pause. The acrid smell of damp wool rose from her coat in the warmth of the bus. Think, you fool. The inevitable topic.

—Its real nasty weather to-day, said Mrs. Carter. You must have got real wet. On days when its storming like this I always say how lucky I am cause we're right outside a stop and I can wait till I see it coming, you know, and just run out and get it. But you have to wait, don't you. It must be just terrible on days like this."

—Oh, it isn't too bad. I don't like the drizzle, but I like sliding on the ice if I'm alone and have boots on.

She felt Mrs. Carter twitch at the word "sliding", and draw back slightly. Watch it, she thought. Keep to the surface, damn it.

Atwood takes special pleasure in satirizing the banality of commerce. In The Edible Woman, *Marian works for a market research firm and must survey consumer response to such advertising phrases as "Deep-down manly flavor."* ➤

—How is your dear mother? I see her at most of the Home and School meetings, you know, when I go that is. Your little brother's in Grade nine now isn't he? How they grow up! My Robert, he's in Grade 12 now and I can hardly believe it.

Why don't you call him Boop? All his friends do—I mean its *done*. But of course, *Robert* is so much more distinguished.

Mrs. Carter was staring vaguely at a large pink placard advertising girdles. She said, in a somewhat softer voice:

—"Seems like just yesterday you and Myrna was in Grade 12 together."

Myrna.

What did you do with yourself, Myrna? You were really quite clever in Grade 12. You used to do things, too; I remember those drawings you always made in your margins. They were good. The teachers didn't like it, though.

Her feet were getting uncomfortably warm inside her flight boots. I hate the smell of damp feet in flight boots, especially on buses, she thought. She took off her gloves.

Silence. Two minutes of silence while we take off our gloves and remember the dead.

I wish we could take off our boots too, and slide on the watery ice with our bare feet. But that wouldn't be nice. She thought of Mrs. Carter on the ice with no boots and pink feet like the girdle ad and smiled with the far corner of her mouth.

The half-anxious, half brittle voice which rippled the image was hardly Mrs. Carter's. It sounded as if it were being strained through a seive.

—You know that Myrna's—married—now?

Yes, I know that Myrna's married.

—Yes! Last month, wasn't it? It must have been a lot of excitement!

Mrs. Carter relaxed. Thinks I don't know. Yes, I know.

—She worked for a while, you know, but I guess every girl wants to get married sooner or later, and

← *"This is the pregnancy tip-off," explains the author.*

she really wasn't all that keen on her job.... Dave is really such a nice boy... she trailed off.

That "nice" is in red neon capitals, of course. No, it would be better in italics, or small black type in a letter to the manufacturer of a patent cough medicine beginning "I shall always be grateful for the relief...."

A new gush. "We're really *so* happy.... it was a lovely wedding", in a minor key. Then, with a pathetic attempt at condescension:

"You're still going to school, aren't you?"

—Yes. College.

—Well, that's very nice...though I don't know—for a woman—'course men can always use an education for their life work, you know, but you can't learn to cook no matter how many books you read." She squeezed out a parody of her usual laugh.

"Yes, I suppose that's so." Keep up the front; good girl.

There was a longer interval; the bus lurched through a puddle.

Suddenly she was aware that Mrs. Carter was crying. Her eyes were closed and she was sucking her lip, her hands loose, her whole body slack against the seat.

My God, she thought, and felt an outward surge ... Mrs. Carter Mrs. Carter, there's nothing I can ... your self-created pattern ... you wanted ... She got up. [...?]

Mrs. Carter opened her eyes weakly. She made an effort:

—Its been so nice talking to you, Diane. Say hello to your mother for me, won't you?"

*   *   *   *

Outside it was still raining, in heavy misty drops. The snow was melting rapidly. She stood with her feet in the cool slush-filled gutter and listened to the gush of the sewer beside her.

The water said pity pity pretty pretty pity as it trickled down the drain.

"The pregnancy is why Mrs. C. is crying," explains the author. ➤

This paragraph in the manuscript is so heavily revised that even the author ➤ *finds it impossible to decipher completely.*

Atwood shows continual curiosity about words, their sounds, their derivations, and the way they tumble over one another to make meaning. "Waste not want not," Offred writes in The Handmaid's Tale, *trotting out an old maxim, which she then proceeds to examine afresh: "I am not being wasted. Why do I want?" In* Bodily Harm, *Rennie recalls that* ➤ *at age 8 she thought a "molester was someone who caught moles."*

A Cliché for January

Oh, ~~you who~~ Damn, she thought, ~~who~~ as she climbed the last step. Mrs. Carter.

She dropped her bus ticket into her purse and fumbled ~~around~~ for it, to give herself time to ~~think~~. I could pretend not to see her — no — too late for that — ~~I could get~~ or get off at the next stop — she weighed fifteen minutes in the rain against Mrs. Carter, and Mrs. Carter won. Bus too empty — can't sit somewhere else. She's beaming at me — she knows I see her. Well, here's for it. Colours flying high for the good of the cause ~~She dropped her ticket~~ as she approached. Mrs. Carter's smile broadened ~~as~~ Your smile always reminds me vaguely of a halitosis ad, she thought, or one of those little back-pages-of-the-newspaper ones about false teeth. She gave herself an internal ~~twist~~, and ~~she~~ felt the pattern click into place.

— "Oh, hello, Mrs. Carter, how are you"?
— "Well, Diane, ~~just~~ how are you?"
— "Just fine, thank you; as she sat down.
Slight pause. The ~~damp~~ acrid smell of ~~damp~~ wool rose from her coat in the warmth of the bus. Think, you fool. The inevitable topic.
— It's real nasty weather to-day, said Mrs. Carter. You must have ~~gotten~~ ~~got~~ real wet. On days when it's showering like this I always

5

Soft, passive...

the seat. Thank God

Mrs. Carter opened her eyes
weakly. She made an effort:

— It's been so nice talking to you,
Diane. Say hello to your mother
for me, won't you?"

Outside it was still raining, in a
heavy, misty. The snow was
melting rapidly. She stood with
her feet in the slush, gutter,
and listened to the gush of the sewer
beside her.

The water said pity pity pretty
pretty pity as it trickled down
the drain.

— end —

Peggy Atwood
Jan. 23, 1959

Margaret Atwood

"The picture of the Groton Third Form is the only picture that is exactly contemporaneous," says Louis Auchincloss, "and it's so good of the smug boy I was, I couldn't resist cutting it out. This is I: little hair slipping down over the forehead and the feet 'just so.'"

LOUIS AUCHINCLOSS

"An author is always writing and rewriting his own name," Louis Auchincloss observes in Jackson Bryer's bibliography of him. "For better or worse he is essentially limited, in subject matter, to himself." For Auchincloss, who was born into New York society in 1917, this subject matter has included aristocracy—domestic and contemporary as well as foreign and historical. His 1964 novel *The Rector of Justin* concerns an illustrious private boy's boarding school. In several works, including *Diary of a Yuppie* (novel, 1986), his twenty-ninth book of fiction, Auchincloss draws on his experience as an attorney, examining the corporate law firm, that bastion of power and fortune. He also has published more than ten works of nonfiction, including studies of Richelieu, Queen Victoria, and, in *False Dawn: Women in the Age of the Sun King* (1984), fifteen female contemporaries of Louis XIV.

When he was fourteen, Auchincloss published the following French Revolutionary tale, "The Futility of Prophesy," in his boarding school journal, *Third Form Weekly*. The story marks the author's "first experience in print" as well as the early stirrings of an enduring taste for French history. His 1981 novel *The Cat and the King* indicates a particular fascination with the intrigues and social ambition of court life, a pet topic foreshadowed below in the passing reference to Madame de Retz, "one of the late King's favorites."

The young Auchincloss felt a poignant awareness of the politics of popularity while a student at Groton School. In fact, his first year at Groton was a social disaster, according to the autobiography of his early years, *A Writer's Capital* (1974). "I had no friends," confesses the author, with the charming self-deprecation that is a familiar key of his narrative voice.

Auchincloss dismisses his early writings as calculated attempts at "high marks and personal distinction." Although "The Futility of Prophesy" lacks any of the psychological portraiture for which the author would later be valued, it exhibits some of the polish of his prose, and it clearly stakes literary territory that Auchincloss would retain and develop in adulthood.

When, at Groton, Auchincloss became a slave to the acquisition of top grades, his parents grew concerned. His mother went so far as to offer him cash to slack off a bit, recalls the author in A Writer's Capital, *confessing his own warped reaction: "Not since Marie Antoinette had directed the poor to the* pâtisserie *had there been such evidence of female frivolity in the presence of serious things."*

The Futility of Prophesy
(1931, age 14)

"What is the revolution? Bah! 'Tis just a mere uprising of the commoners who fancy themselves overtaxed and will soon be quelled."

It was the Marquis de la Tour d'Azyr who spoke. The people whom he addressed were a distinguished-looking company of French aristocrats, who were guests of the Marquis at his beautiful mansion in Paris. The dining-room was exquisitely furnished in Louis XVI style, and lackeys, resplendent in their scarlet livery, hurried to and fro, carrying delicious dainties on golden platters for the Marquis' guests. The time, as the reader may have surmised from the Marquis' speech, was during the early months of the French Revolution, after the fall of the Bastille. Paris was the scene of constant violences to the aristocracy and wealthy folk, from the filthy, half-starved, and penniless mobs. However, several nobles had not yet met with any damage either to themselves or to their property, and these often met at dinner parties and such in their mansions. Louis XVI was still king, although held practically a prisoner in his palace, the Tuileries, with the beautiful Queen Marie Antoinette.

"But Monsieur le Marquis," protested the Vicomtesse Aline de Rochambeau, "you do not seem to realize that our sovereigns are almost prisoners, and that our lives are in constant jeopardy every time we venture into the streets, from the infuriated populace."

"My dear Aline," chimed in the Comtesse de Charny, "it's you who do not realize that the armies of Austria, Prussia and England are at this very moment on the march to crush this unseemly rebellion and to restore his most gracious majesty to the supreme position which he held before the revolt."

"That's quite true," broke in Madame de Retz, one of the late king's favorites. "We have nothing to fear from the Parisians; they would not dare to touch one of us."

"But they are so fierce and wild, and they have suffered so much wrong," replied the still doubtful Aline.

"Now, Aline, be reasonable," said the Marquis. "Would they dare to harm us when they think of the punishment the allied forces would give them when they invade Paris? Do I not speak truly, friends?" He turned to the company, who assented.

"Well, I still am not convinced," said Aline, "but my carriage is waiting, and I must now beg you to excuse me." Here she broke off and left the dining-room. They could hear the swish of her dress as she passed down the stairs into the street.

"Maybe there is something in what she says," said the Marquis hesitatingly.

Suddenly they heard screams from the street below. The Marquis rushed to the curtained window and threw it open, then staggered back, horror-struck at what he saw. The guests simultaneously arose from their seats and stared out the window, for there on a bloody pole was the head of the unfortu-

So attached is the author to historical France that Robespierre, Danton, Louis XIV, Madame de Maintenon, Louis XV, and Madame de Pompadour all get a mention in Diary of a Yuppie, *set in contemporary corporate Manhattan.*

During his first year at Groton School, the author was not a favorite in this rigorous social system that bore some similarity to Versailles. "Oh, yes, the faculty were kind and well-meaning," he recalls in A Writer's Capital. *"They knew I was wretched, but what could they do? One night, at a party in the dormitory, I was pelted from head to foot with ice cream..."*

In The Rector of Justin, *former headmaster Prescott and his large entourage cross paths with trustee chair Griscam, who suddenly seems, to the narrator, like a "threatened symbol of authority about to take his chances with an unruly mob. Dr. Prescott had never struck me before as a revolutionary, but now he might have been a wily old Danton, ready ... to consign the chairman of the board ... to the fury of his followers."*

nate Aline de Rochambeau, its features ghastly and pinched, while through the open window came the roars of an angry mob.

The mob then invaded the building, and shortly afterwards only mangled corpses remained of those who had scoffed at the Revolution.

Louis Auchincloss

This photo of LeRoy Jones accompanies his story in the Barringer High School Acropolis, *spring 1951.*

AMIRI BARAKA

*P*oet, playwright, fiction writer, essayist, music critic and leader in the 1960s' Black Arts Movement, Amiri Baraka has orchestrated a number of highly discernible changes in his life and career. Starting out as Everett LeRoy Jones (born in Newark in 1934), he became LeRoi Jones at college and during his early involvement with Beat and other avant-garde poetry. Several years into his personal and artistic alignment with black nationalism, he took the Bantuized Muslim name Imamu Ameer Baraka (his published works during this time included the 1970 poetry collection *It's Nation Time*). More recently, as Amiri Baraka, he has written Marxist-inspired works that include *What Was the Relationship of the Lone Ranger to the Means of Production?* (play, 1979). He has also published a novel, *The System of Dante's Hell* (1965), and *Dutchman* (1964), an Obie award–winning play, which is perhaps his most famous work. In it, says Baraka scholar William J. Harris, "an angry young man fights for his ethnic identity and his manhood."

At first glance Baraka's teenage story "The Statue" bears little resemblance to his adult work. Although Baraka says music was the predominant influence in his writing, that musicality will become much more audible later. Also, the adult emphasis on political education and inspiration is not yet present. And, this story, the author believes, has been his only use of a female point of view.

Resistance to oppression is apparent in "The Statue," just as it is a vital force in much of Baraka's mature work. Though the oppression Betty feels in "The Statue" is familial, the author was aware of the social oppression around him by the time he wrote the story. In the early fifties, Barringer High School (whose literary magazine published "The Statue"), was a deeply problematic place and time for him, writes Baraka in *The Autobiography of LeRoi Jones* (1984). Although he has some fond memories of his senior-year writing teacher and a few classmates, he describes having felt alienated from the school's white majority and being the object of racial aggression.

"I think it did something to me too," he writes. "I was not wholly there, I felt, but the part of me that was, suffered."

At a PEN-Faulkner award gala in 1989, Baraka recalled his beginnings as a writer. "My writing came out of me without too much formal grunting and extrapolation of the dry.... It was the poetry (the form and feeling) of the blues that first moved me word wise...."

In his autobiography, the author recalls some earlier juvenilia, a "weird" comic strip he created in grammar school, "semi-plagiarized, called 'The Crime Wave,' which consisted of a hand with a gun sticking out of strange places holding people up."

The Statue

BY LEROY JONES

(1951, age 16)

*I*t was of glass, black glass. Its place was by the mantle piece, but somehow it never seemed to be there. It was a cat—the statue of a cat. It had stood there on the mantle for about twenty years while four sisters grew up. Always it had the same expression on its face, as if it could never change, an expression of smugness, of quiet knowledge. It had watched as three of the sisters had grown up, married, moved away. Now there was left only Betty, the youngest.

She sat in front of the fireplace, reminiscing over the years. Her face screwed up in frown, she thought about the other days she had spent in this house. They seemed like centuries ago. She was the youngest. Even now, she was too young to get married, her mother had said. She looked at the cat; it reminded her of all her childhood days, her youngness.

The cat was a gift from an uncle who had died. He had always called her his "baby." She twisted in her seat, still remembering. She remembered the day she couldn't go to school when her sisters went because she was too young. But that was silly. Then again, when they were going to dances and parties, she was always too young. All through her life, she was too young. Now she was too young to wed. She laughed softly. She would show them.

She rose, went over to the mantle, looked at the clock. Her eyes wandered back to the cat. Then she went into the closet and got her coat and small overnight bag. She sat down.

After a while, a horn sounded outside. Betty got up, went to the window, then turned off the lights. She went out. A tall figure met her at the bottom of the steps. They embraced.

They walked arm in arm to the car, got in. Suddenly, Betty opened the door and ran back to the house. She went in, stayed a minute, then came back. The car pulled away.

The lonely house was sheathed in darkness. The dim light of the moon shone through the lace curtains, forming a silhouette on the floor. The beams of the new moon played over the pieces of black glass scattered on the floor. Somebody would have a job cleaning it up in the morning. But then, it was only glass.

In high school Baraka was a self-described "nonstop sardonic-mouthed joker and quick start artist," according to his autobiography.

"Now that we are old we know so much," writes Baraka in his autobiography. "But we never know what it was like to have ourselves [as children] to put up with."

*Baraka's narrator in "The Death of Horatio Alger" (*Tales, 1967*), the self-described "SHORT SKINNY BOY WITH THE BUBBLE EYES," expresses his pent-up anger during a moment of playground conflict: "Could leap up and slay them. Could hammer my fist and misery through their faces."*

Amiri Baraka

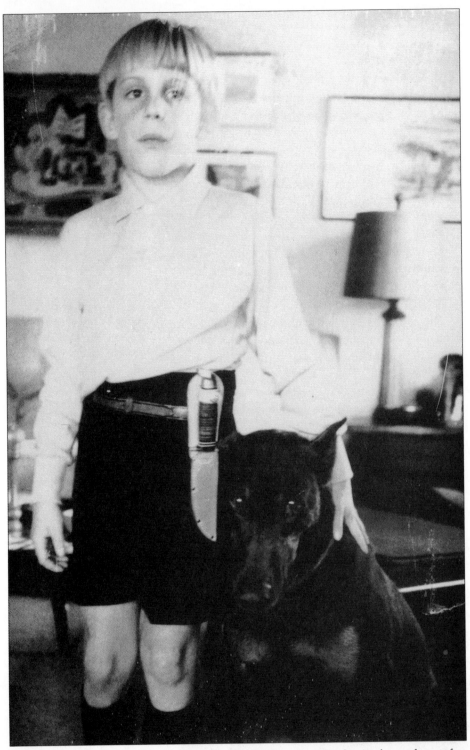

Around age 8, Madison Bell poses with Wotan, the Doberman. Explaining his preference for this shot, Bell quips, "I always prefer to be represented with my weapons...."

MADISON SMARTT BELL

*B*orn in Tennessee in 1957, Madison Smartt Bell has already published seven novels and two story collections and has seen four of his stories anthologized in the prestigious *Best American Short Stories* annual. Much of Bell's fiction, including *The Washington Square Ensemble* (novel, 1983) and *The Year of Silence* (novel, 1987), has featured the eccentric New York that was his home away from home for six years after college. But his longest novel to date, *Soldier's Joy* (1989), and a fair number of his stories are set in the rural South of his childhood. He grew up—somewhat sickly and bookish—on a farm outside of Nashville, and regard for the land was very much a part of the Bell family code.

The juvenilia below are all vignettes about animals—domestic and wild—and animals still receive good coverage in Bell's fiction, especially dogs, which his parents continue to raise. So prominent are dogs on Bell's fictional landscape, in fact, that the title story of the author's 1990 collection, *Barking Man*, describes an alienated protagonist's perilously complete retreat into a canine alter ego.

"My pick hit is 'Wotan with an egg in his mouth,'" says the author. "I'm sending a couple of other little things, too, first or second grade I reckon...."

Of the three school pieces, "Mr. Beaver" seems to have most impressed the teacher, who marked a big round "O"—for Outstanding, presumably. "At Nine on Thursday" garnered an S+ with the encouraging message, "A cute story." And "Sting Ray Tail Clipping," the most prosaic of the efforts, rated only an S.

"Who'd a thought it?" asks the author in a recent letter.

At Nine on Thursday

(circa 1963, age 6–7)

My father and I were on a hill when we heard a dove calling. I was scared stiff but wouldn't show it. The dove followed us quite a while. Father and I followed the dove up the hill. Then we went back to a turkey supper and the dove went where?

Votan with an Egg in His Mouth

(circa 1963, age 6–7)

Votan is Bell's childhood spelling of Wotan.

I was sitting on the ground and my dog had picked up one egg. And I ran to see what it was. I saw him bury it and then I dug it up. To my surprise it was an egg.

In a passage from Soldier's Joy, Laidlaw, a reclusive Vietnam vet, goes for a moonlit walk on the family land near Nashville, during which the far-off baying of dogs slowly brings back memories of a hound he knew in childhood: " a big amiable floppy creature" that could lick his face while he was standing up. "He must have been less than ten. That would have been a dead dog now for around a decade."

"The creature in question was not, as the artwork suggests, a cross between a snubnosed crocodile and a rocket ship on sawhorses, but a big red Doberman," says Bell. "In those days we had some volunteer banty chickens around who would lay eggs who knows where. The dog would find them and carry them with great delicacy and bury them without breaking them. Months later when they had had plenty of time to rot he would dig them up and smash them and roll in the putrefaction, which seemed to give him considerable pleasure. We were all very proud of him for this ability. 'Beach Creek News' was the newspaper of the day camp my mother ran for many years on our farm...."

Sting Ray Tail Clipping

(circa 1963, age 6–7)

*O*ne day last summer Father caught a sting ray. Last time he had an old lady stand on it while he pulled the hook out. This time I was with him. Mother came to look at it. It rolled its eyes at everyone. Finally two men came. One stood on it while the other cut its tail off.

In "Barking Man," Alf, a disturbed economics student, guiltily remembers shooting toads with a BB gun as a child on the farm. "The thing was that it didn't actually kill the toads, at least not right away, just left them drearily flopping around with drooling puncture wounds through their slack stomachs."

---

5   Sting Ray Tail Clipping

One day last summer
Father caught a sting ray.
Last time he had an old
lady stand on it while he
pulled the hook out. This time
I was with him. Mother
came to look at it. Itr rolled
its eyes at everyone. Finally
two men came. One stoodon
it while the other cutits
tail off.

M

Alf retreats from life's troubles by taking on the persona of a dog. When asked by his hypnotist to pinpoint when this began, Alf recalls a visit to the zoo.
   "'What did you think about the animals?'" the hypnotist asks. "'I envied them,'" Alf responds.

Mr. Beaver
(circa 1963, age 6–7)

I am Mr. Beaver. I live in a lodge. Right now I am throwing mud-balls at Mr. Wolf who is thinking how good a fat kit would taste for supper. (A kit is a baby beaver.) Anyway I'm having a good time watching Mr. Wolf roll down the side of my lodge. I'm used to this. Mr. Wolf comes often. He seldom gets anywhere. He usually goes off muddy while I get a spell of the dry grins.

The author at age 1 with Wotan, the Doberman.

Madison Smartt Bell

Roy Blount, Jr., at about age 16.

ROY BLOUNT, JR.

*G*rowing up in Decatur, Georgia, Roy Blount, Jr., fantasized about a place where "movies and the federal government and magazines came from and where they argued about books," writes the author in his 1980 essay "Trash No More." As one of the country's foremost wags, Blount has been living in such a figurative place for some time; his humor pieces have appeared in scores of magazines, on topics spanning politics, the media, sports—and the occasional book argument.

The author of *Crackers* (his 1980 collection that includes "Trash No More" and discusses, among other things, the Carter administration), *What Men Don't Tell Women* (1984), *First Hubby* (a novel, 1990), and more than a half-dozen other published books, Blount is considered a "literary humorist"; his career, in one recent critical appraisal, has been compared to Mark Twain's. Blount's writing style is highly personal, tangential, allusive, and on easy speaking terms with literary tradition (one Blount essay makes the case for Walt Whitman as a locker-room sports reporter). Although he was born in Indianapolis, in 1941, he spent most of his childhood in Decatur, and plays up the southern elements of his voice, which is at times homey, genteel, or parodistically crude. Appropriately, in view of our interests here, his writing has been called "at once adult and adolescent." It is also often extremely funny, as the following remarks explaining his disappointment in his own juvenilia confirm:

Maybe my mother saved the wrong things. I know she threw away all my *Mad* magazines because she found them too erotic. Or maybe I should blame my children: they got into my box of juvenilia, picked out all the magical passages, copied them in their own hands and burned the originals. At any rate, I am too principled to pass their surviving early work off as my own.

So I represent myself with highlights of my earliest journalism, largely fictional. I was sixteen and seventeen, writing two columns ("Roy's Noise" and "Dear Diary by Joe Crutch") and various other things for the Decatur High School *Scribbler*. You would be in a better position to appreciate these items if you had known Mrs. Ormston and Kenny McNeely, as my readers then did. Mrs. Ormston was the physics teacher, determined to catch up with Sputnik. Kenny McNeely looked like Opie only round.

Here also, from my senior year (Class of '59), is the first thing of mine to appear in a national publication (*The Beta Club Journal*). This apologia for not playing varsity football strikes me as overly self-deprecatory, in retrospect, and I fear that it may provoke glib theories as to why my first book, written fifteen years later, was about hanging out with the Pittsburgh Steelers. Yet I submit it, selflessly.

(Ah. It just now hits me that I am older than the writer of that book by more years than he was older than the *Scribbler* writer. Never mind. I'll be all right.)

I might mention that if you are a juvenile writer, and on reading these selections you feel you have not yet attained this level of sophistication, and therefore you despair of ever developing into an author of sufficient stature to be included in an anthology of juvenilia, you should bear in mind that these are the *best* things I could find. The worst, and even the next worst, are less promising than anything you or anyone else has ever written. Nothing could persuade me to share with you any of my extremely long 1958 Christmas poem, for instance, beyond this representative couplet:

> As a Frenchman would say, "*bon* grief"—
> We've nearly forgotten to herald Greg Moncrief.

I must have thought that anything was possible.

If on the other hand you are a youngster who feels that you personally would never consent to the publication of anything as immature as these writings even now, much less once you have reached the height of your powers, my response is this:

Yeah, sure. You wish.

Science Fair Is Miserable Flop

(1958, age 16)

*T*he annual Science Fair was held on March 5th, 6th and 7th, and was acclaimed by one and all as a miserable failure. All of the projects turned out to be either fakes or not good enough, and no one had a good time. In fact, during the scuffle following the disqualification of Elaine Porter's project, an ultra-sonic high frequency fordomatic grunch, for the fourth straight year (this disqualification and ultimate brawl has become an annual occasion and cupcakes and punch are usually served afterward); Mrs. Hammet received a nasty gash on her forehead and four biology students and an as yet unidentified bystander were trampled to death. Also, one of the judges was blown up when someone crammed a cherry bomb into his ear after he went to sleep.

Blount had a clear sight of his vocation as a humorist back in high school. But after graduating from college in 1963, he discovered that he'd overestimated the need for his services. "This was partly because I was not as good at Humor as I had been in high school and partly because of the historical moment," he writes in Not Exactly What I Had in Mind *(1985).*

← *"I can't believe that this was my semi-colon," says the author. "But I suppose some desperate measure seemed called for."*

In First Hubby, *Blount* ➤ *focuses his wit on some proposed arts projects: Verna Passevant's "The Songs of Mosquitoes and Flies," T. P. Fullilove's "Criticizing Clouds," and Foley Bigelow's "Carrots in the Shapes of States: An Attempt to Grow These Root Vegetables So as to Resemble Vermont, New Hampshire, Illinois, Idaho, Virginia, Kentucky and Tennessee on Purpose."*

Several lines seem to ➤ *have been cut here and lost forever, notes the author.*

The exclamation point, ➤ *says Blount, "doesn't sound like me either."*

Among projects that figured in the judging for awards was an invisible small-mouth bass which Ronnie Shutley had bred by crossing a grizzly bear and the common garden pea. (Crossing a grizzly bear is not advisable for the amateur.) Of course the judges had to take Ronnie's word for the fact that the fish was there.

Joan Givens was about to be awarded the grand prize for her excellent study of Neanderthal Man when the bulk of her project turned out to be Gordon Cranford watching a butterfly.

Jean Fell had what looked like an excellent project coming along. She put two mice in a cage and fed one of them sauerkraut, orange Kool-Aid, and creole limas.

First prize was awarded to a new student, Nikolai Kopek. Nikolai constructed a very nice earth satellite. (We regret to state, however, that Nikolai was not present when the decisions of the judges were announced. It seems the F.B.I. wanted to ask him a few questions.)

Edwin Jelks was awarded second prize for his superb scale model of Mrs. Ormston, and he made a very nice acceptance speech! He said that he was "honored" and that he wished to thank "my fellow students, Mrs. Ormston, and the entire faculty; all of whom helped me tremendously with my project, and most of all, my father, who made it."

Signs of Spring
(1958, age 16)

*T*he whole world is green and living. The flowers are blooming, the leaves are returning to the trees, and the lawns are covered with a soft, beautifully green carpet of grass that grows, and grows, and grows, and grows, until it's about knee deep and you gotta cut it. And the lawnmower doesn't work.

All the birds and bees and little animals are active once more, scurrying around with a refreshing display of energy, and digging holes, eating the plums off the plum tree, leaving spots all over the car, and biting, pecking, scratching, and stinging people.

The weather is simply lovely. The days are clear; the sky, blue as Jack Benny's eyes, is mottled only slightly by a few white puffs of cloud. Of course it does rain some. And it's too cold for alligator shirts and swimming, but too hot to enjoy doing anything.

There is Easter, new clothes, and Easter egg hunts. There is Daytona, where you spend all your money.

The young men's fancy lightly (or, in some cases, heavily) turns to love. And you know where that can get them.

These are the Signs of Spring.

← *Blount reuses the inherently playful image of "little animals" in the subtitle to* Crackers: This Whole Many-Angled Thing of Jimmy, More Carters, Ominous Little Animals, Sad-Singing Women, My Daddy and Me.

Roy's Noise
(1958, age 16)

← *"Sending flowers to a woman is like...heroin to them," observes Ken, one of Blount's twenty-seven case studies in* What Men Don't Tell Women. *Ken longs to send his wife a more original gift but doesn't, "because that's how I always get in trouble."*

Watching early football practice, I came upon a surprise in the form of a first-string guard. Don't know whether or not it was because a yellow shirt couldn't be found to fit him, but Bobby Anderson was playing with the first team. No, not against them. With them. We of *The Scribbler* think Bobby is a living memorial to what perseverance, hard work, and lack of competition can do for a man.

There is one phase of the football half-time ceremonies that has caused me no end of wonderment (actually, I haven't lost any sleep over it, but I have to fill this space *some* way), and that is the fact that the majorettes are *always* smiling. I have watched the faces of generations of twirlers (another lie—I seldom look any higher than their legs), but I have yet to see one frown. I have seen them drop their batons six or seven times hand-running, swallow flies, knock the stuffings out of their corsages with their batons, almost lose their little skirts, and be bitten by dogs, but never yet has one frowned just a little. They may be grinding their teeth and swearing inside, but they never show it on the outside. I may be in the minority, but I believe I would feel immensely better if I saw just one little scowl on the face of a majorette while she was going through her routines during the half-time.

FROM

Dear Diary by Joe Crutch
(December 1957–February 1959, ages 16–17)

*N*othing particularly interesting happened today in school. Jack Crider accidentally hoisted himself up the flagpole while trying to raise the flag. Zack Hayes got his head tangled in the net of the basketball goal. Just those little everyday things that go into a regular school day.

Dick Gear's absence from school for the past two weeks hadn't aroused much comment up to now, but it has taken on a new light now since it was found that the Student Council funds have been reduced to a 1902 Indian Head Penny, a badly tarnished medallion bearing the head of Francis Tarkenton and a six-year subscription to the American Poultry Journal.

← Before becoming a professional quarterback, Francis Tarkenton was a star athlete at nearby Athens High School, which competed against Decatur. He was two years ahead of Blount.

I am forever being amazed by the grace and agility of Kenny McNeely. The other day, for instance, while marching smartly toward the rifle range (in better step than anybody), he slipped on some ice, slid a good fifteen feet, and ended up flat on his back underneath a parked car. The last time I passed by the scene he was still there, still at a perfect port arms.

Speaking of the Junior-Senior, the Junior girls voted, en masse, at a recent class meeting, not to invite dates from other classes. The boys, who would have outvoted the girls, had it not been for the fact that Nancy Butcher, class V.P. (somebody had stepped on President Bobby DeFoor's nose, rendering him unfit for service) counted the votes, and that Tommy Lucas and fourteen other boys were asleep and didn't vote, claim the girls are afraid of competition.

U.S. Vice President Clementine Fox becomes "Leader of the Free World," in First Hubby, *after a 13-pound fish mysteriously drops from the sky, killing ← President DaSilva.*

Mrs. Ormston's class fired off a rocket today. Unfortunately, it missed Mrs. Ormston, and the whole class had to stay in after school and write, "I will not shoot no rockets at Mrs. Ormston no more." 500 times. When Mrs. Dieckman heard about it, she made Mrs. Ormston write, "I will not use incorrect grammar no more." 500 times. What would Werner Von Braun think?

Wernher Von Braun (1912–1977), ← rocket scientist.

I had an exam this morning. A French exam, no less. I'm pretty good at French (hinky dinky parlez vous; ou, la, la; B.B.'s pour moi), but my grades don't reflect the fact. But I know one French student who passed with flying colors though he knew only one French phrase— "Mademoiselle McGeachy, vous etes losing weight, n'est-ce pas?"

"HUH-uh Mffff Mfffff." "FWOO." ← "Ooo-laaaaaaah." And so the lovers in First Hubby *achieve sexual union, as Blount displays his ear for phonetic humor.*

You Ought to Be in Football

OR
"YOUNG MAN, WHY AREN'T YOU IN THE SERVICE?"
(circa 1958, age 16)

*P*robably the most prevalent delusion existing among adults today is the deep-seated conviction that any high school boy who has more than one leg and is worth his salt plays high school football. Late last summer this fact was brought out clearly as I cut the grass of a neighbor. For some reason, he was trying desperately to make idle conversation over the frenzied roar of my lawnmower. (The word "roar" does not cover at all adequately the sounds made by my lawnmower. My lawnmower makes various sounds, all very loud and unpleasant. Come to think of it, the lawnmower itself is very unpleasant, and I kick it frequently. But I digress—and about time, you will say, if you are still listening.) Suddenly the neighbor had an idea: "Ah!" he said to himself, "this big strapping youth must certainly play football. I will talk to him about that."

So, willy-nilly, he began to talk about it: "Well, Jimmy, (this, as you no doubt have noticed, is not, and was not, my name; but I have, and had, forgotten his name, too, so I don't, and didn't, mind) how is football coming on?" he said confidently, his face lighting up. I looked at him somewhat blankly and ran over a gladiola. "Football," he reiterated, after an awkward pause. "You do play football, don't you?" "No," I said, simply. After waiting tensely for a few seconds for me to explain that football was against my religion, or that I had a wooden foot or something, he asked, incredulously and with a touch of horror creeping into his voice, "Why?" He had me there, so I just mumbled a little and ran over another gladiola. After staring in utter, open-mouthed disbelief, and with a "should this boy be cutting my grass?" look in his eyes, the neighbor went back into his house. He left my pay on the front step, I haven't been invited back, and he now herds his children in the house whenever I pass by.

Surprisingly enough, the fact that I don't play football has never kept me up nights worrying, and I don't cower with shame when a gridiron hero passes by in the halls at school. By the same ticket, then, I have also never figured out why I don't play football; I just don't. After my afore-mentioned little interview, however, I have given it a little thought.

When I say I don't play football, I don't, of course, mean that I have never played football. I just don't play organized football. And I have played some of the organized brand. In the seventh grade, for instance, I was a scrappy 93-pound guard (I am tempted to say that a 93-pound guard has to be scrappy, but actually I wasn't particularly scrappy—I just threw that in because it reads good) on the grammar school team. I also went out for football in eighth grade. I did some calisthenics, ran a little, watched some of the others scrimmage, and didn't come back the second day. Since then my participation in high-school football has been strictly vicarious.

Actually, I tell myself, I am not exactly the football type. I have always considered myself more the lean, bronzed, woodsman type. However, since I used to get homesick on Boy Scout camping trips, I peel easily, and I am finding it increasingly neces-sary to pull in my stomach, this illusion does not hold up too well. Probably my best excuse for not being a gridder (not that I need one, mind you) is the fact that I am too light for the line and too slow for the backfield.

Also, I'm chicken.

Pro football dressing rooms "had always made me ner-vous," Blount confesses in About Three Bricks Shy of a Load *(1974), his behind-the-scenes account of a season spent with the Pittsburgh Steelers. "I had never liked being around a lot of people each of whom could so easily beat me half to death that there wouldn't ← be any point to it."*

← This bronzed look doesn't come easily, as Blount explains in Not Exactly What I Had in Mind. *"I go to a nearby tannery every spring, lay out twenty-eight dollars and a little something for the attendant, and have myself dipped."*

Robot Goes Berserk

87 PERISH AS MONSTER ROAMS STREETS

(1959, age 17)

*I*n a flurry of excitement last week, the Science Club robot broke from his moorings in T.M. Johnson's basement and escaped to peril the entire population for forty-eight hours before he was captured.

Franticly flinging its arms, singing "Charlie Brown," singeing everything within reach with its flame thrower, the monster wreaked havoc on the city streets, killing eighty-seven men, women and children, injuring 114 others, and causing an estimated $47,000 worth of damage.

Unfortunately, the first call for the police came while the entire force was engrossed in a pinochle game, and no one answered the phone, but within twelve hours the men in blue were out hunting the monster, and finally they cornered him and finally destroyed him. The monster left in his wake scores of corpses and tremendous destruction. An added tragedy was revealed when Mrs. Ormston announced that everyone who worked on the robot for his science project would get an "Incomplete" on his permanent record.

In First Hubby, Dr. Dingler, the founder of Dingler College, also invokes the classic threat against youthful transgression: "Things can be made to show on people's pummanent reckuds." ➤

Roy Blount, Jr.

Vance Bourjaily, at left (about age 7), with his younger brother Paul (middle) and older brother Monte.

VANCE BOURJAILY

*T*hrough his mother's literary agent, at the age of seventeen Vance Bourjaily was able to show his first book, a collection of philosophical musings entitled *Not to Confound My Elders*, to Maxwell Perkins. The celebrated editor (of Hemingway, Fitzgerald, and Wolfe, among many others) "thought it publishable as a curiosity or something," says Bourjaily, recalling a third-hand conversation. But Perkins also cautioned that to publish it "would be a bad start for what he thought would be a literary career. Or might be."

In one interview Bourjaily remembers *Not to Confound My Elders* as "a work of sheer, self-indulgent self-expression." It is, essentially, the author's ruminations upon a wide range of topics of concern to him in the late summer and early fall of 1939, when, having to put off college for a year, he retreated to some family property in the southwestern Virginia mountains. (His consideration of this same period opens his autobiographical novel *Confessions of a Spent Youth*, 1960.)

Bourjaily was born in Cleveland in 1922, one of three sons. His parents were both journalists. His mother, who also wrote romance novels, held "some claim of descent from American gentry," writes Bourjaily in an autobiographical essay. "There was a lot of Gatsby" in his father, who had emigrated from Lebanon and was able to achieve large, if brief, wealth from a publishing venture. Bourjaily, whose childhood was filled with travel, glamorous stepparents, and a mix of cosmopolitan and farm life, knew by age nine that he would be a writer.

His novels, which include *The Violated* (1958), *The Man Who Knew*

Kennedy (1967), and *Old Soldier* (1990), often deal with his characters' personal responses to the post–World War II age. In the fall of 1939, seventeen-year-old Bourjaily already was formulating ideas about war and his generation in *Not to Confound My Elders*.

In addition to the excerpt from that early work, the author has contributed a short story written in college and a poem composed at age six, "Dance of the Fireflies," his first piece of writing. Though the poem no longer exists on paper, he has remembered it all these years and introduces it with the following reminiscence:

> We were staying for a few weeks of summer vacation at someone's rather fancy farm in Virginia, where, for reasons I don't recall, the owners were putting up paying guests.
>
> They had a gelding named Traveller, who, they said, was a great grandson of General Lee's Traveller. I rode the horse several times; my legs were too short to reach the stirrups, so I'd shove my feet on top, into the stirrup leathers. I was a fair rider. Nevertheless, Traveller shied at something one day and threw me, but I didn't go all the way off. My left foot caught in the leather and I was dangling upside down on a galloping horse. You'd think a scare like that might spark some written words. Nope. I didn't really know that I'd been in danger as my head swung back and forth between the hooves.
>
> On another afternoon, my two brothers and I earned the first money we'd ever worked for, thinning corn at 10 cents a row. It was hot, hard, stoop labor, but did I, in the spirit of those times, write about the toil and exploitation of the proletariat? Nope. Didn't know there was a proletariat.
>
> One Virginia night I saw fireflies for the first time, and in the morning, very excited by all the new stuff that was happening, I wrote what I announced to my mother was a poem. She'd been reading poetry to us from an anthology for kids called *This Singing World*, and I'm sure that had something to do with my response. The poem, if I may, went:

Dance of the Fireflies
(1928, age 6)

*T*he fireflies one autumn night
Went dancing with their little lights.
Under the stars they danced all night
Till they and the beetles began to fight.
They fought from twelve to half-past one,
And the result was that the fireflies won.

Not to Confound My Elders
(1939, ages 16–17)

I've got some things I want to get off my chest before I go to war and get shot in the leg, or get a job as clerk in a grocery store and work my way up to be assistant manager, or find a gold mine and learn to play polo. Before I start though, I want to make one thing very clear: I am speaking for myself as an individual, not for seventeen-year-olds as a group. If I personally would rather dance slow than jitterbug, it doesn't mean that the younger generation is swinging away from jitterbugging. If I call myself a Socialist, it doesn't mean that the vast majority of my contemporaries are anything more alarming than Republicans and Democrats. So if on reading this you have an impulse to go out and chloroform every high-school kid you see, resist it. This isn't youth speaking, its only me.

In order to make things clear.....

I am the middle member of a family of three boys aged 16, 17, and 18. My mother comes from fairly solid, middle-class, American stock, my father from the land-owning class of Lebanon. Dad arrived in this country at the age of five. My parents are divorced, both have happily remarried. Both my step-parents are good eggs, all three of us like them. Relations between the two households while hardly cordial are not particularly strained. We boys are not required by any fixed agreement to spend so much time here, so much there and the matter is governed mainly by convenience. My father's home is a New York apartment, my mother's a Virginia farm.

I went to prep school until the end of my Sophomore year, then withdrew (I wasn't kicked out) and finished at a public high-school near the farm. The year after I left prep school my older brother graduated; the youngest, then a sophomore was forced to leave. The family could no longer afford to send him. He will graduate this year from the same highschool which gave me my diploma. My older brother is going to college this year on a scholarship after a year away from school. I have been accepted for entrance at Harvard and hope to start next fall.

Both branches of the family are in highly reduced circumstances, barely able to keep their heads above water. Dad was once a very successful man. He lost his money in a business gamble, partly on poor judgement and partly because he didn't hold the cards. My mother and step-father are farming. Mother is an author of light fiction, but the editors are getting a little sour. Adversity hasn't done our spirit much harm, and we don't go hungry. Whether or not its uses have been sweet, remains to be seen.

A note of justification.....

The fault, of course, with this whole thing is that its too disjointed. The reader has to jump from one topic sentence to the next with no gentle conjunc-

A lifelong outdoorsman, Bourjaily has collected his pieces about hunting and rural life in two volumes of nonfiction, The Unnatural Enemy *(1963) and* Country Matters *(1973).* ➤

Actually, Bourjaily says, ➤ *he was sort of kicked out for smoking and other rule breaking. It remains something of a gray area.*

tive passages to lessen the pain of transition.

But I've had to do these things as they occured to me. And in not a few cases they probably sound a little forced and they are. For there've been plenty of gorgeous mornings when I've wanted to sit in the sun; plenty when I wanted to lie flat on my stomach and read some intriguing, year-old copy of "Western Thrillers." I've had to remind myself that I'm working for a tough boss, a guy who won't let me off until I've done so many pages of copy in a day.

And try as I will I can't sustain a connected series of thoughts any longer than they last and I can't blow them up any larger than they are. The ability to do it will come some day, I hope.

I reallize that I have treated subjects with innumerible sides from my side only. I have failed to think a lot of things through. So this is really not a justification but an apology; and with the correct number of blushes, with head bowed at just the right angle of shame, I must sincerely beg your pardon.

I have done what I can do and I have not attempted what is still beyond my reach. [....]

I've got it all worked out....

I love to talk about myself. Do you mind? If you do, skip this part.

I've got my life pretty carefully mapped out. Nothing very rigid, you understand, this is more day-dreaming than anything else. But I intend to do all of it.

In the first place I am going to Harvard next fall. Just how I shall do it is highly problematical. I shall have to have some money saved and I shall have to accept all the student aid I can get. I shall probably have to wait on tables and whatever other work I can find. I think now that I want to major in philosophy. They give you a year, though, to decide on your field of concentration, and I may change my mind about that.

As to why I want to go to Harvard and why I want to study philosophy, I can't give any very good

Quincy, the narrator of Confessions of a Spent Youth, *reassures his readers that he does not intend to present the "loose collection of … philosophic biases" he developed in youth "in an argumentative or any other* ← *sort of explicit way."*

← *This excerpt from* Not to Confound My Elders *has been compiled from various points in the manuscript by the editor. Bracketed ellipses [....] are used to indicate when material has been omitted. Only the ellipses after the topic sentences belong to the manuscript.*

reasons. Going to Harvard, is I think, more an emotional desire than anything else. Call it a hunch. It comes from knowing people who have graduated there, knowing boys who are there now, from the sound of the name and the qualities associated with it. The Harvard tradition is a wonderful salesman.

Majoring in philosophy is a whim, quite a serious whim, but a whim nevertheless. Its not that I think I'll find any of the answers in books of philosophy any more than that I'll find them in books of shorthand. But the philosophers are supposed to know, so I want to give them a chance. And perhaps serve to start me thinking.

Then after four years of academic atmosphere and beer parties, I am going to begin to do everything. I may spend as much as ten years at it. Its a pretty goodsized undertaking.

I am going everywhere and I shall work at every conceivable trade from barber to bootlegger. I shall bum cigarettes in every corner of the world, Tibet, Morroco, and Tuscon, Oklahoma. I want to experience all the sensations which a man can experience and I may make up a few new ones for myself.

I want to kill somebody in cold blood, to have an illegitimate child, to smuggle cocaine, to be in an airplane crash. Not because the criminal life appeals to me or because I intend to be a professional thrill seeker, but because I sincerely believe that to write about something I had not myself experienced or seen intimately would be as dishonest as plagiarism. And because after four years of Harvard it will probably take ten years of violence to give me the sane unbiased outlook, which I believe necessary to write anything but propaganda.

And then, having completed both college and postgraduate work, I shall count myself ready to settle down. I will be about thirty years old, assuming of course that I survive my turbulent education. I shall take stock of myself, ask myself whether I have learned all the answers[,] ask myself indeed whether there are any answers, and what I write will be the product.

In Confessions of a Spent Youth, *Quincy imagines asking his 17-year-old self: "Remember a list you made? Of things you wanted to do, experiences you hoped to have.... I did those things. Nearly all of them. Now it's over and I have these responsibilities." To this, the 17-year-old responds, "It doesn't sound like what I meant exactly." →*

Skinner Galt, protagonist of Bourjaily's first novel, The End of My Life *(1947), subscribes to a similarly all-or-nothing vision, according to critic John Aldridge. "It is the philosophy of a disillusioned absolutist," Aldridge writes of Galt's cynicism, "one who will believe nothing if he cannot believe wholly...." →*

Then I shall marry, I shall own a piece of land somewhere with a house on it, and I shall be a solid citizen earning (more daydreams) a comfortable living by my writing, sought after by editors, rating a front page review in the Herald Tribune Sunday book section. I'll wear riding clothes most of the time, smoke strong tobacco, drink the very best liquor. Perhaps I shall dabble in local politics.

Included in this scheme are as many children as I can comfortably support, perhaps five or six. Two or three boys and two or three girls would, I think, make a nice family. And I know how I plan to bring them up, too. They will be allowed to do pretty much as they please with only enough restraint placed on them to give them decent manners. But when I say allowed, I mean just that and no more. They may start smoking whenever they want to but they'll have to buy their own cigarettes. Or maybe there's something incongruous about a seventeen year old kid having ideas on raising his own.

Thats as far as it goes. I'll let the details fill themselves out. Whether I live happily ever after is a matter of indifference to me. If I do all the living I plan to do, I shall have had a full life and I think, a happy one. At least I shall never find it boring. [....]

Small things which gripe me......

[....] People telling me what a harmful habit smoking is. I feel particularly strongly about this. I realize that it probably does me no good to smoke but after all its my own health which I choose to ruin. If I prefer to risk cutting my life span short by six months in order to add a little pleasure to it, it seems to me that this is purely my affair.

Good advice about anything, particularly small things, when unsolicited. I think I may speak for my entire generation and perhaps people my age in any generation when I say that there is nothing which has a more harmful effect than good advice. The immediate and obvious reaction is to dash out and act in whatever way is advised against.

"Where on earth did we ever get this petty notion that happiness is any kind of fit goal for a grown man's life?" asks Al Barker in Bourjaily's The Hound of Earth *(1955). Appalled by his unwitting role in developing the atomic bomb, Barker has run away from his old* ← *life as Allerd Pennington.*

← *Two-thirds through the narrative of* The Man Who Knew Kennedy, *Barney James quits smoking and devotes a small segment to the subject, including this opinion: "to have made smoking a romance was innocently harmful. To try to perpetuate it, after the bad news is in, seems to me the sickest of all Madison Avenue's perversions."*

The unfortunate habit of many otherwise nice people of being deliberately unconventional in order to show off. I only object to this however when it takes the form of bad manners. Eccentricity and bad manners are two entirely diferent things.

Paragraphs like the preceding one which point out the obvious in a very smug manner.

People whom I dislike but who seem to like me. Also people whom I like but who seem to dislike me.

Poorly drawn comic strips, now that comic strips have become a form of adult entertainment.

Clarinet solos in jazz orchestras. Also bells used in jazz orchestras. Arty arrangements of what should be simple, rhythmic, straightforward pieces. And finally orchestras in which you can't hear the drums. [....]

Work....

One part of my personal and peculiar creed reads:

"I believe in the dignity of work; its ability to heal the body and the mind." Perhaps this comes as an inevitable result of having entered my teens in a time of widespread unemployment. I believe so strongly in it that I look on working as an indispensable part of education. No matter if I have millions, my sons will be required to drive trucks or work on road gangs before I shall send them to college; I shall see that my daughters hold down jobs clerking at Woolworths or weaving in a woolen mill and then probably send them to finishing school.

For it is impossible to have a proper sense of perspective if one has not held down a hard job, drawn a paycheck at the end of the week, groused with the other employees about the working conditions, and forced himself to go to work no matter how lousy he felt.

My first experience with honest work, besides driving the delivery truck and delivering the milk for my stepfather, was as cashier in a small restau-

"I was a fairly snobbish ➤ boy," recalls Barney James, in The Man Who Knew Kennedy. *But despite some "pessimism and surliness[,] I'd been taught to keep my grouch private under a screen of pleasant manners...."*

In Confessions of a Spent Youth, *Quincy takes on a grueling 55-hour-a-week job at a wood-processing mill "under conditions so bad, that I couldn't have imagined that men could survive year after year of it, as they did." ➤*

rant. It gave me a feeling of self-reliance and responsibility that I had never had before. The small sum of money I took away from that job felt like the largest sum I had ever laid hands on.

Since then I have had three or four other jobs, odds and ends, one real, honest to god, man's job. I have found that I am able to work at anything I can get. It gives me a wonderful feeling of security. I feel now that if I should suddenly find myself independent, I could rise to the occasion and work, without asking anybody's help, without depending on anybody's kindness. [....]

Why I want to be a writer.....

If I didn't want to write for any other reasons, it would be almost necessary by a process of elimination. Medicine? Well, I wouldn't be any good as a practitioner because I am not steady enough. I wouldn't make a surgeon because I don't believe I'd be able to cut into anybody unless I were mad at him. As for research, a glance at my scholastic records in mathematics and science is enough to discourage that.

Law? I know too many bright boys, friends of mine, who are going in for law. And I know a couple of lawyers too who haven't gotten the breaks.

Vance Bourjaily in his late teens, date unknown.

The attorney is too impersonal. He doesn't get much chance to put his soul into it.

Farming? Farmers are born, not made. I was not born a farmer, much to my regret. Journalism? It is no longer a profession. Radio and the movies have made the newspapers back up too far. Acting, music, and painting are all professions which require the same talents as writing and I prefer to write. I can't say I [am] terribly good at any of them either. Teaching is a field in which I think I might make good if I had the patience but I don't. Politics offer an opportunity and an appeal which I find quite to my taste except that I'm afraid that I would always be a politician, never a statesman. The army, navy, and foreign service require patience and subjection to discipline, both of which I am quite incapable of.

I haven't spoken of the trades or of manual labor because I am thinking in terms of ideals. While I may very well end up as a bus driver, or a riveter, I would prefer not to dwell on the possibility. Anyway, writing can be just as menial as share-cropping, if you let it.

So, without eliminating anything, I have disposed of everything that comes to mind. In the past, I have disposed of other possible careers in a like manner and for just as inconclusive reasons. The inconclusive reasons, it seems to me, all point to one thing. I want to write more than I want to do anything else.

Perhaps the principal reason for it is that I am confident in my ability. This may sound like conceit, but I don't think it is. A mechanic is confident of his ability to change a tire, a dentist knows darn well that he can pull a tooth out; the same holds true for me. I'm not saying that I can write circles around Willa Cather with one hand tied behind me, but I can write. [....]

During World War II, ➤ *Quincy (*Confessions of a Spent Youth*) summons deep reserves of discipline in basic training, taking on extra duties and becoming squad leader. But his conversion into a military machine is born not of genuine calling but of masochism and malaise. "I passed for quite a different sort of person than I am in basic training, for my behavior was construed as a manly and courageous aptitude for army life—and was, of course, the opposite."*

The younger generation as seen by one member of it.....

I'm afraid that my generation is not destined to be startlingly diferent. We will, I believe have the same number of sots, lawyers, confidence men, and doctors as did the preceding. Our martyred proletariat will be crucified just as often; we will fight just as hard for security and leave the burden of democracy to rest on as few shoulders. For like the two generations immediately preceding us, we haven't got a chance.

Like the two generations before us, we have inherited strife and poverty and we are as bewildered as they by the swift rush of technical progress, going too fast for our mental development to keep pace with it. Another lost generation, another era of nervous gaiety and underlying struggle wherein a man has to have been through the mill, has to know his way around[,] has to be hard to survive.

Some will find the answer in retreat to the quietness of country living, some will find the answer in playing what cards they hold to the limit and bluffing out the rest, some will not find the answer at all.

I'm not blaming it entirely on war and depression though it would be absurd to underestimate their effect. Part of it lies in youth itself. For this generation lacks idealism and has nothing to take its place; it wants security, something it can get its feet on, and it is willing to sacrifice a lot for it.

The talk about the idealism of youth makes me laugh. Of all the hundred odd seniors in my high-school class, I don't suppose more than ten ever thought about what was wrong with America or even what was right about it. In fact I doubt if more than ten ever thought consciously about anything but their own personal problems. They sensed that all was not well, that something was screwy somewhere, but they hardly bothered to find out what was wrong, much less to figure out what to do about it. And I have wondered whether, if a strong man should appear who could offer them the security which they lack, they wouldn't be willing to trade democracy off for it.

But perhaps not. For I think that emotionally, if not intellectually, they are for the most part convinced that the American system is the best. They are emotionally idealists, though they are a little

Critic John Aldridge would later consider this very point. In After the Lost Generation *(1951), he contrasts the two generations of American writers that emerged from each world war and features Bourjaily prominently. In fact, the book helped put Bourjaily on* ← *the literary map.*

ashamed to admit it. And this emotional idealism is stubborn and dangerous to trifle with.

Perhaps it will be their undoing. For if it carries them off to war, as it probably will, and is lost in the mud of the trenches, pray to whatever god you worship for America. But I may be wrong: It may survive the war and return home even stronger. I hope that I am wrong.

Be all this as it may, our generation doesn't stand a chance as far as cultural contributions go. For cultural acheivments grace times of peace and plenty, not those of war and tightened belts. People are too busy to create; people are too disillusioned to patronise the arts.

There is one contribution we can make. We can rebel against the causes of these troubled times in which we live. We cannot perhaps prevent ourselves from being drawn into the now inevitable cycle of war, false prosperity, and depression but we may produce some statesmen who can insure our children (or will it be their children?) an era of greater peace.

So, despite the temptation to do so, I will not shed embittered tears for this generation. For lost as it may be in itself and on the positive and creative side, it may also be the salvation; the generation which prepares for a golden age it cannot hope to share. [....]

Random thoughts on books and authors....

The book to which I pay tribute above all others is one whose title I cannot remember. Maybe it was something like "Essays for Highschool Study", at least that's the general idea. I owe this book a tremendous debt of gratitude, for it introduced me to the "Trivia" of Logan Pearsall Smith. I read the selections from "Trivia" in that forgotten volume and the next day I wrote my father asking him to buy me a copy of the complete work. For almost two years I read and reread that book, underlining passages, getting sensual pleasure from the subtle beauty of

the style in which these little fragments of experience are couched. There is a wisdom and gentleness
and philosophy; mixed in with these is an almost
wistful acknowledgment of human limitations. And
he seems to be able to express them all simply by his
arrangement of verbs and adjectives.

It always seemed to me that Dr. Smith had left
out the lines and included only what was to be read
between them. My indulgent mother has told me
that my own style has been influenced by his and I
hope that it is so. It is the only style which I admire
wholly and without reserve. He has a mellowness
which is felt rather than observed; he has a way of
ending his paragraphs as if he were saying, "Thus it
seemed to me; tell me, how does it seem to you?"

It is so. Not to Confound My Elders *indeed seems fashioned after Smith's* Trivia *(1918) in its tone, purpose, and compartmentalized structure.*

I have developed a most pleasant vice. Whenever
life palls on me, I pick up Bartlett and read quotations. Sometimes I read them at random, sometimes
I choose a particular author and read all of the inclu-
sions from his works, sometimes I choose a subject,
say love, and read all the quotations which are listed
under it in the index. Yesterday I went through the
Shakespeare section for the seventh or eighth time
and picked out my favorites from it. I shant put them
all in but these two seem to vie for top position in my
esteem. The first is from "As You Like It" and goes:

"It is a melancholy of mine own, compounded of
many simples, extracted from many objects, and
indeed the sundry contemplation of my travels, in
which my often rumination wraps me in a most
humorous sadness."

I hope someday to have developed a similar
melancholy.

The other is a single line from "King John", "I
will instruct my sorrows to be proud." Such
courage may I myself show when the life I have constructed lies in ruins about my feet.

At the end of a long night's debauch, Barney James in The Man Who Knew Kennedy *settles into "long, lachrymose, befuddled thoughts—like what the hell my life had become. Or anybody else's who was forty-four."*

*   *   *   *

I have always thought that the most beautiful
simile in the English language (and this opinion

In The Man Who Knew Kennedy, *Barney James is, in a grief-stricken moment, similarly forthcoming about his literary tastes, dismissing first modern, and then romantic poetry: "I don't like anything since Milton well enough to spend an evening reading it, and I wouldn't take Milton to a desert island either. It's the Elizabethans who can get to me."*

comes not from Bartlett but from more honest reading) was written by Wordsworth in his sonnet, "It is a beauteous evening." The simile is, of course,

"The holy time is quiet as a nun,
"Breathless with adoration."

I have never liked Wordsworth very well except in his sonnets. He takes himself too seriously in his longer poems, which of course he is priveleged to do but it does become monotonous. His short poems give me a sense of incompletion, as if the last stanza were written to wind it up and there were several left out in the middle somewhere.

Shelley was my first love and I still call his poems my favorites. I like "Ozymandias" and "The Skylark" and have liked them so long they have become a habit. I like "Adonais" because of its first line, "I weep for Adonais, he is dead." I think "To Night" a most beautiful job of onamatapoea (O! most horrible word.) as well as feeling it to be the best expressed poem I have yet read. And he wrote eight lines called "A Dirge" which can make me feel like a sardonic ghost medit[at]ing on all the opressions of the self-righteous in his lon[e]liness.

Byron is too full of cliches. With the exception of two short pieces, "Maid of Athens," and "She Walks in Beauty", I would as soon he had not written at all; that he had only lived his evil and glamorous life, the best piece of escape fiction ever conceived.

Tennyson I admire but do not like. Perhaps he's a little too pat, his poems a little too mechanically perfect. Only when he lets himself go as in "Ring Out, Wild Bells," can I really get any kick from Tennyson. But I will forgive anything of the man who wrote such music as "The Lady of Shallot".

Milton, I think, must be a poet for the more mature. After reading "L'Allegro" and "Il Pensoroso" as part of my high school course in literature, and "Lycidas" just to make sure I was right, I decided to put him off for a few years. I'm sure Milton will still be there when I decide I am ready to take him on.

Keats is swell, a nice guy but not an intimate friend. He is too reserved, a poet for the studious esthete. I like his poetry but I feel that in reading it, I too must show the proper reserve and a corresponding depth.

When it comes to Robert Browning, I'll march in the same parade with him anytime. "The Lost Leader" and "Prospice" are poems for a guy that likes his music noisy.

I've used up too much space writing about poets. Robert Burns, the man of the people, I think a little overated. Or maybe I just don't like the dialect. Emily Dickinson is fine until she gets too whimsical. I think Elenor Wylie will emerge as the finest poet of this generation. I wish Coleridge had written more, much more. The same goes for A.E. Houseman, although perhaps he was wiser not to. Masefield and Kipling are good on their particular subjects, lost when they get outside them.

I don't know Swinburne or Rossetti well enough to have anything but a very vague opinion of them. I think Christina Rossetti wrote two or three of the finest poems ever set on paper. I am still trying to get aquainted with Whitman.

I could mention a lot of poems written by apparently one-poem authors. Some of them rank high among my favorite poems.

Perhaps everyone has one poem in him, if he would only write it. I'm sure that, writing with the apparently aimless meter of Whitman, and freeing himself completely from self-consciousness, Uncle George, my weather-beaten mountaineer companion, could write a dozen lines or so that would live forever. And so, I believe, could any man or woman who has ever thought about life or wondered about death.

*   *   *   *

Whenever I dwell on books and authors and the beauty of words I always arrive in the end at the same questions. Shall I ever be able to include my

Uncle George was the caretaker of the family land in Virginia where Bourjaily retreated after high school graduation. George also appears in Confessions of ◄ a Spent Youth.

own name among these? Then I force myself to answer it and the answer is always one of two, depending on my mood; its always "Hell, yes" or "God, no."

War....

The first wars I ever fought, with the exceptions of heaving bricks at my brothers and a few abortive little nursery revolutions against tyranny, were the wars in my history books. As I remember them, I went through some pretty thrilling battles. I crossed the Delaware one Christmas Eve and took Trenton; with my trusty rifle spitting death, I defended Bunker Hill almost singlehanded; racing in the forefront of my men, I defeated Lee at Gettysburg and then I planted the American flag at the top of San Juan Hill, spearing innumerible huge Spaniards with a broken bayonet. My shirt was torn, there was blood running from my many wounds, but I stood by Old Glory until the rest of my trusty band finished cleaning up what I had left of the enemy.

Then I read "All Quiet On the Western Front" and every thing changed. It mixed me up a little, too, because I hadn't known about the mud and latrines and how bad the food was. I think I finally decided that these were Germans anyway and that the Yanks must have been a little better off. But it did start me wondering and so I read some more books. And pretty soon I was fed up with war. When we talked about it at school, we were all fed up with war. We swore solemn oaths to be concientious objectors when the next one came.

There was lots of anti-war literature around too; books that talked about people getting blown to bits and their arms landing in your face as you slept; books that proved the futility of it all, the waste of lives and money and morale which accomplished nothing; there were other books that talked with figures—how much it cost to kill a man, how much each of us individually was out because of the last war.

We had a couple of speakers too who told us

much the same thing. And we held peace rallies and figured out what each of us could do to keep the world out of war. I believed then and I believe now that war is cruel and stupid and pointless.

When I see a parade, men marching, flags flying, martial music, I have trained myself to think, "Suppose instead of those men out there they marched the cripples from the last war down the street. Suppose these banners were printed with statistics—17,000,000 men. Then that gay parade would mean something."

But its all a matter of training and try as I will, I can't prevent a shiver going down my spine. Try as I will, I can't help straightening my back as they march by and the weight on my feet shifts back and forth in rhythm to the music.

And when America enters the war, I shall be one of the first to present myself and lie about my age. I shall be one who sticks out his chest and swaggers as he goes down the street in uniform. By that time of course I shall have persuaded myself that this is a crusade in the holy cause of liberty. If any of my schoolmates have the courage to stick by their oaths and become conscientious objectors I shall feel like socking them in the nose and I shall call them yellow.

I've tried to persuade myself that I feel otherwise, but its no good. I can't fool myself. Those history books did too good a job. I'll have to lead my men across the Delaware on Christmas eve and plant Old Glory on top of San Juan hill before I finally learn that Christmas Eve is damn cold and that nobody not even me cares very much whether Old Glory gets to the top of the hill or not so long as we have enough money to get drunk when we get our next leave.

Apparently evolution hasn't gotten around yet to taking the battle-lust out of human nature. The thought of dying for a cause (should be spelled with a capitol C) outweighs reason; the heroic death has lost none of its glamour.

In Old Soldier, *Joe McKay, who served in the U.S. Army for 20 years and through three wars, has inherited young Bourjaily's visceral patriotism. "Joe, I know how you feel about the President," says brother Tommy. "No matter what sorry specimen's in there, he's ◄ your commander-in-chief."*

Bourjaily had followed the Spanish Civil war but ◄ says he was oblivious to Germany's invasion of Poland in September of 1939, sequestered as he was in the Virginia countryside, and that he is writing here about war in general. World War II, nevertheless, would determine the course for much of Bourjaily's writing. As one critic observed in the 1970s, Bourjaily's novels "explore the divisive consequences of the war on American society and the personal lives of individuals."

*True to his prediction,
Bourjaily left college in the
summer of 1942 to join the
American Field Service as
an ambulance driver. "When
I went off to the war I took
a typewriter with me," he
told an interviewer in 1977,
"a little portable."* ➤

I am not alone in feeling this way. I cannot think of any one of my friends who could resist the scarlet of a recruiting poster. I cannot think of one who wouldn't react in the perscribed manner to a well-concocted atrocity story, one who could pass up a chance to save democracy, one who does not even now feel a choke in his throat when a solitary bugle plays taps.

I am under no illusions as to what I shall do when the call to arms is sounded. I shall follow my heart, not my head, to the nearest recruiting office. [....]

Jack and Jill
(1942, age 19)

*H*e waited for her and thought of what it would be like. They would walk up the side of the hill, not saying much, and Spring would overwhelm them more and more each step. The sun would be just warm enough and there would be a smooth little breeze to blow her hair back. And they would walk up the hill, hand in hand, with their eyes looking up towards the top, and they would see the clear sky high above and the clouds. They would be overwhelmed by Spring and the implications of Spring.

She walked along quickly, smiling at herself, feeling as if she were two people. One of them was a girl walking along quickly, you see, and the other one was smiling. The first one wasn't thinking very much; she was too happy to think. She was going to meet a boy who was too grand for words, and the day was too beautiful for words, and the sky was too blue for words; so the first girl had no use for words, and since she couldn't have thought without them, the first girl had no use for thinking.

I know it sounds very complicated, but the second person that she was was watching the first girl and smiling. The second girl was thinking how silly the first one was to be so inarticulately happy. But she envied the first girl and wished she could be all like that, and then she suddenly said to herself,

"My God, I'm practically schizophrenic." Yet in spite of the fact that the second girl was a relatively cynical and therefore presumably stronger personality, the nearer she got to where she was to meet him, the more she tended to merge into the first one.

He saw her come around the place where the road bent and he thought: "I must put my pipe in my right hand pocket and my matches in my left hand pocket. I must keep my feet in the same position until I have spoken to her. And if I do these things, it will turn out as I have planned it." She was close, and he spoke to her.

"Hi, Dorothy," he said.

"Am I late, Tom?"

He looked at his watch. "Two and a half minutes."

"Sorry, I meant to be at least five." She held out her hand and he slapped it. It was one of their jokes.

"Let's walk up the hill. It's such a wonderful day." That wasn't what he meant to say, but it would do.

"Oh, Tom, the grass is wet, isn't it?"

"If it is, we'll come back. Let me help you over the fence."

And when they were both on the other side there was a silence to be broken, so she said, "Judy Farrell's mother and father are separated. Had you heard?" And though they both knew that it was the wrong thing for her to have said, they were both afraid of silence now and of how it sometimes draws people too close. So he answered, Yes, he'd heard. And wasn't it a shame?

And the second girl that she was noticed that the grass was indeed wet and that her stockings were being ruined.

Bourjaily's characters often approach romantic love with wariness—and attempt to control its course or to mitigate its pain. In Old Soldier, *when Joe's wife tells him about another man, he reacts this way: "He was getting ahold of the pain, squeezing it into a little plastic ball of don't-give-a-shit."*

Creed....

Here is the summing up of all the contradictions and confusions
with which I have filled this manuscript. Whether or not you respect
admireit I do not care; ~~but~~ only please don't laugh at it, for it is
~~an~~ as honest an expression of my faith and faiths as I can make.

~~Ixxbmxeixmxxfixxtxmfxakkxxinxmyxmmkfyxfmmxxifxixxdidxnmkyxxkifmxxmmkk
ixbmkk~~

I believe first in myself.

I believe in ènjoyment, both physicalx and intellectual.

I beleive in the power of words.

I beleive in the power of the bullet, the fist, and the ~~monkey~~
~~wrench~~

I beleiev in fear and my ability to overcome it.

I fear ~~next~~ myself and death and these are two fears I cannot over
come, for they are well founded
I beleiev in beauty and the purication of mankind through beauty.

Vance Bourjaily

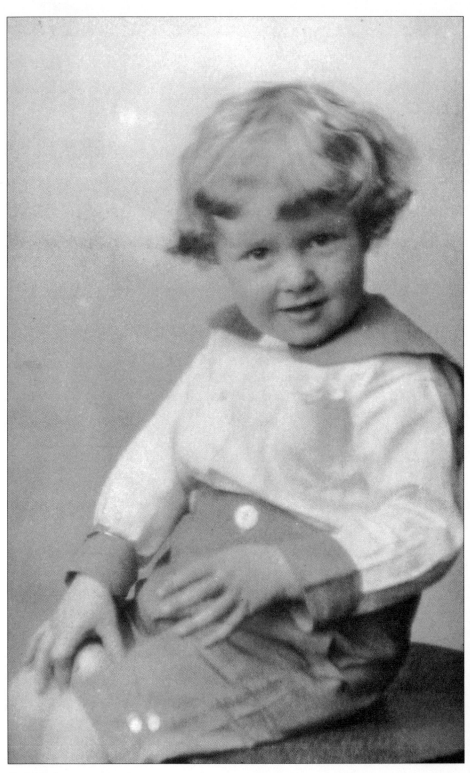

Paul Bowles at age 2 or 3.

PAUL BOWLES

*E*xpatriate author and composer Paul Bowles is known for haunting tales set around the world, particularly in North Africa—his home for most of his life. The author of more than a dozen published books of fiction, including the novels *Let It Come Down* (1952) and *Points in Time* (1982) and numerous short story collections, he is perhaps best known for his first novel, *The Sheltering Sky* (1949), the story of an American couple whose marriage decays far away from the security of home. Alienated from others, from themselves, and from their surroundings, many of his characters lead dreamlike—or nightmarish—lives, thus inviting a comparison to Poe, whose stories transfixed Bowles as a child whenever his mother read them to him.

Born in 1910 in Jamaica, New York, Bowles was five years old before he had any significant contact with other children. Of all the eccentric, critical, sickly, or unpredictable adult relatives that people his autobiography *Without Stopping* (1972), Bowles's father stands out as a problematic character. The dentist's animosity toward his newborn son was supposedly so deep that the man once set the infant Bowles in front of an open window during a blizzard. (Or so, Bowles recounts, his maternal grandmother once told him.) Years later, at the age of nineteen, Bowles returned the favor, to his own surprise, by throwing a meat knife in his father's direction.

The young Bowles retreated into his own imaginative world whenever possible. One of the by-products of this was reams of juvenilia: stories about animals, written when he was four, maps of an imaginary planet (around age seven), diaries about imaginary characters (see below), a daily newspaper featuring dispatches by foreign correspondents, a pseudo-opera (see below), and melodramatic stories his seventh-grade classmates would stay after school to hear him read.

At one point his grandmother exhorted Bowles to rid himself of some of his copious creations. "No, no! I have to have them all," he said. Despite such youthful resolve, sadly only a little remains today.

Seventy-three years later, spiders are still objects of his scrutiny. "I have a spider whose behavior mystifies me," Bowles notes in his journal. In the intervening years, he named his 1955 novel The Spider's House *(a title taken from the Koran).* ➤

A letter
(1915, age 4)

*D*ear Miss Anna.

Thank you for the erector. I have been making letters with it. Monday the 3rd I was playing with a little yellow spider, but he was so tiny that I lost it.

Do you notice my Red Cross sticker, and my other little Santa Claus?

Love from Paul.

The Lady of Peace
(1917, age 6)

Bowles employs another malicious, talking animal in his darkly humorous fable "The Hyena" (1960), in which the misfit protagonist outwits and kills the conventionally proper stork.

*O*ne day when the Lady of Peace was out walking, she met a cat.

"My word! What a pretty cat," she said.

The cat looked at her kind of queer, then said: "Go home."

"The idea! I won't," said the Lady of Peace.

"Hike it home," said the cat.

"I won't!" cried the Lady of Peace, stamping her foot.

"If you don't go home, I'll make you," said the cat, throwing some stones.

"After all, I don't think it's such a pretty cat," said the Lady of Peace, and went home.

Poor Aunt Emma
(circa 1919, age 8)

*P*oor Aunt Emma, sick in bed
With an ice-cap on her head.
Poor Aunt Emma, sick in bed!
She's very sick, but she's not dead.

Bowles describes the manuscript of Poor Aunt Emma: *"It's made into a little booklet, about 1½ inches by 1½ inches, with only a few words in block letters on each page. On the last page it says: «The End. If you want more, apply to Paul F. Bowles.»"*

Lyrics from "Le Carré," an "opera"
(circa 1919, age 8)

*O*h, lala,
Oh daba,
Oh honeymoon!
Say, oh say when . . .
But she got no further
For there was her ex-husband
Glaring at her like a starving pussycat.

Love triangles complicate a number of Bowles's works, including his celebrated story "In The Red Room" (1981), which, according to John Updike, "presents, at a level of understatement almost beneath thermal detection, that original hotspot, the Oedipal triangle."

Bowles grew up during Prohibition, a subject of some debate between his father and paternal grandfather. As an occasional motif in his adult work, the consumption of alcohol takes on special significance against the backdrop of Muslim cultures.

Give Me Wine

(*circa 1919, age 8*)

Give me wine, give me wine
That comes from a vine
Hanging in a garden of thine.
Oh, no! You'd get drunk.
Yes, you would, would rank old skunk.
You'd yell and yell
Until the bell of jail would ring:
Bring him, bring him.
I'll give you some molasses
Served in little glasses,
But never any wine.

Bluey

(*1919–20, age 9*)

1919 December 1919

Bluey Laber Dozlen was one of Bowles's favorite imaginary diary subjects. Bowles wrote these entries in newspaper-headline style because "that seemed to me the most adult way of presenting the material," he recalls.

26. Minnesota was erected. Bluey plans to come.
27. Dolok Parosol stops her saying "Marry me don't go." Bluey gets mad.
28. Dolok Parosol tells her again to marry him. She knocks him down.
29. Bluey gets her things packed and puts on a beautiful blue sash.
30. Bluey sails for Wen Kroy and lands. Bluey loves it.
31. Bluey thought this country was heaven. Bluey writes to Dolok.

1920 January 1920

1. Dolok sails for Wen Kroy and gets wrecked.

2. Dolok got back to Wen Kroy. Bluey welcomes him.

3. Bluey gets an awful cold, and gets into her bed.

4. Bluey feels a little better. Dolok comes to see her. Bluey cries.

5. Bluey was worse. Doctor says she has Pneumonia. She faints.

6. Bluey feels better and gets up. Dolok gets diptheria.

7. Dolok gets worse. Bluey gets a Pierce Arrow Automobile.

8. Dolok almost dies. Bluey weeps. Bluey takes a lesson in running her auto.

9. Bluey has a blowout. Dolok dies. Bluey faints.

10. Dolok had funeral. Bluey goes. Mrs. Jobestor dies. Red Cross Day.

11. Bluey shuts herself in the closet all day long. Dolok is buried.

12. Bluey buys a new tire. Bluey takes another lesson on her auto.

13. Bluey goes out to ride in the auto and gets frozen.

14. Auto runs on four hundred miles still frozen.

15. Auto runs fifty-eight miles and gasoline runs out.

16. 37 degrees. Bluey comes to. Faints when she finds herself.

17. Bluey comes to. 37 to 39 degrees. Bluey gets some gas.

18. 40 to 41 degrees. Bluey starts for home and goes one hundred miles.

19. 39 to 40 degrees. Bluey gets home again.

20. 30 to 31 degrees. Bluey gets a bad cold. Henry Altman visits.

21. Bluey falls in love with Henry. Bluey worse.

22. Bluey worse. Doctor says she has pneumonia.

23. 21 degrees. Bluey better. Henry Altman calls again.

24. Bluey better. 20 degrees. About five o'clock it begins to snow.

25. Snow worse. 18 degrees. Bluey all right. Bluey goes to call on Henry.

In The Sheltering Sky, *Port becomes seriously ill, and his skittish wife, trying to determine the malady, runs through her knowledge of diseases: "Diphtheria began with a sore throat, cholera with diarrhea, but typhus, typhoid, the plague, malaria, yellow fever, kala* ← *azar—as far as she knew they all began with fever and malaise of one sort or another. It was a toss-up."*

← *Bluey's frantic movements prophesy Bowles's own dizzying international itinerary recorded in* Without Stopping.

26. 16 degrees. Great blizzard in Chicago. Bluey stays at Henry's.
27. 12 to 14 degrees. Great blizzard arrives. Bluey still at Henry's.
28. Bluey tells Henry she loves him. Henry tells her he loves her.
29. 10 degrees. Bluey gets snowed in has to stay at Henry's.
30. 6 degrees. Blizzard worse. Henry wants to marry Bluey.
31. 2 degrees. Bluey wants to marry Henry. Blizzard covers everything.

1920 February 1920

1. 0 degrees. Bluey and Henry get engaged. Blizzard worse.
2. Snow covers all the houses up. 1 degree below zero at noon.
3. It stops snowing. 0 degrees. Bluey still at Henry's.
4. 3 degrees. Snow starts to melt. Bluey wants to marry Henry.
5. 5 degrees. Snow still melting. Bluey tries to dig through.
6. 6 degrees. Bluey digs and digs. Snow stopped melting.
7. Bluey finds out she has dug a block under the snow.
8. Bluey and Henry dig some steps up and land a block away.
9. 13 degrees. Bluey uses that way to get home. Henry goes with her.
10. 15 degrees, Bluey feels bad. It snows. Bluey reads "Hovertis."
11. Doctor says Bluey must get weighed once a week. Bluey yells.
12. Bluey gets weighed 95 lbs. 19 degrees Bluey goes back to Henry Altman's.
13. They get snowed in again. 2 degrees. Bluey reads and gets a headache.

14. Bluey's headache worse. 23 degrees. Henry worries.
15. Bluey and Henry get out. 25 degrees. Bluey's headache all right when she gets out.
16. Bluey and Henry go ice skating. Henry falls down.
17. 29 degrees. Bluey goes home again. Henry goes with her.
18. 31 degrees. Bluey says she loves Henry. Henry almost faints.
19. Bluey weighs 95½ lbs. 33 degrees. Bluey says she wants to weigh 186.
20. 35 degrees. Henry digs out the house. Bluey helps him.
21. It starts snowing again. 34 degrees. Bluey wants a child.
22. Henry says they cannot have a child until they get married. 31 degrees.
23. Bluey says in seven weeks she will marry Henry. Henry faints.
24. It still snows. 25 degrees. Bluey goes back to Henry's house.
25. It snows and hails 22 degrees. Bluey has a headache stays in bed.
26. 19 degrees. Bluey gets up. Henry tells her to marry him.
27. 16 degrees. Bluey has a fight with Henry. Bluey yells.
28. Greatest storm in world's history. 13 degrees. Bluey knocks Henry down.
29. 10 degrees. Bluey hits Henry. Henry hits Bluey and gives her a black eye.

1920 March 1920

1. 8 degrees. Bluey tries to get out but snow is 108 feet high.
2. 5 degrees. Bluey breaks down and cries and forgives Henry.
3. 6 degrees. Henry forgives Bluey. Bluey still cries and cries.

This excerpt from the Bluey diaries is reprinted as it appeared in a 1943 issue of View *magazine, to which the adult author was a regular contributor. "For pure comedy, dramatic tension, and harmonic development of theme," according to the magazine's contents page, "it seems unequalled by any other work by a writer of the same age, and needless to say, is far more persuasive than the writing of most adults."*

4. 8 degrees. Still snowing and hailing snows 86 feet that day.

5. 9 degrees. 195 feet of snow. Bluey weighs 96½ lbs. Henry is so mad he has a fit.

6. Bluey starts crying again. 10 degrees out. 197 ft. of snow.

7. Still snowing and hailing. 8 degrees out. 198 feet of snow.

8. Bluey reads "Da Lod help ma." Bluey laughs so she has a pain.

9. Henry finds out there is no food in the house.

10. Bluey tries her best to shovel out but cannot.

11. Bluey faints of hunger. Henry eats a live cockroach.

12. Henry faints of starvation. 201 feet of snow.

13. The cat dies of starvation. 20 degrees out. Still hailing.

14. Bluey and Henry both unconscious. 21 degrees out.

15. It stops snowing. 200 feet of snow. Robbers try to get in.

16. 194 feet of snow. Dolok Parosol's mother gets a cold.

17. 192 feet. She is worse. 24 degrees. Robbers try to get in.

18. 192 feet. Robbers get in and don't find anything. 23 degrees.

19. 190 ft. Dolok's mother is worse. 26 degrees.

20. 188 ft. Doctor says she has Pneumonia, she faints. 28 degrees.

21. 186 ft. She is worse. She tries to get another doctor.

22. 180 ft. She gets another doctor. 30 degrees at twelve o'clock.

23. 174 ft. The other doctor says she has the influenza.

24. Dolok Parosol's mother dies of grief for loss of Dolok.

25. 163 ft. Dolok Parosol's sister weeps and weeps for her mother.

26. 160 ft. Bessie still weeping.

In other entries, Bluey "becomes a spy.... learns how to play bridge and smoke opium.... and is last seen hiding out in Hong Kong from a vengeful housemaid she was once foolish enough to dismiss," describes the author in Without Stopping.

27. 154 ft. Bessie gets influenza.
28. 147 ft. Mr. Parasol gets influenza. Bessie worse.
29. 137 ft. Mr. Parasol gets crazy. Bessie worse.
30. 127 ft. Mr. Parasol almost dies. Bessie has Chrisis.
31. 117 ft. Mr. Parasol wishes he would have chrisis. Bessie better.

← "I regularly settled into protracted illnesses with a shiver of voluptuousness at the prospect of the stretches of privacy that lay ahead," Bowles writes of his childhood, in his autobiography.

1920 April 1920

1. 110 ft. Mr. Parasol has chrisis. Bessie better.
2. 101 ft. Mr. Parasol dies. Bessie allright.
3. 91 ft. Baker comes and stuffs a roll down both of their throats.
4. 72 ft. Bluey and Henry come to and thank each other.
5. 70 ft. Henry kisses Bluey, Bluey kisses Henry. He faints.
6. Bluey and Henry get out. Snow still 62 feet.
7. 60 ft. Bluey and Henry find 7 billion dollars, divide it.
8. 51 ft. Bluey gets $3,500,000, gets an areoplane.
9. 45 ft. Henry gets a beautiful car, Packard.
10. 34 ft. Bluey says she will live and keep house for Henry.
11. 30 ft. Bluey gets a maid. Lina Minner. Bluey faints.
12. Bluey Dozlen & Henry Altman get married. 21 ft. Bluey faints.
13. They go on their honey-moon. 18 ft.
14. 57 degrees 6 ft. They go to Niagara Falls.
15. 2 ft. Bluey weighs 99. Bluey faints.
16. 1 ft. They go to Thousand Islands.
17. 6 inches. Bluey says she will stay at Thousand Islands.
18. 2 inches. Henry doesn't want to.
19. Snow melts entirely away.
20. Houses all flooded in Ridgefield.

The travel tugs of war between Bluey and her lovers seem to anticipate the author's own frequent negotiations with his wife, Jane, as recounted in ← Without Stopping.

Inspired by Breton and the surrealists, "Entity" was written during a period in which Bowles avoided "conscious intervention.... The material itself, being beyond my control, also escaped my judgment, but this did not matter; the important thing as far as I was concerned was that no one seeing it should guess that I was only sixteen," he recalls in Without Stopping. *The piece appeared (in 1928) in* transition, *a hot Paris literary magazine, which also published James Joyce and Gertrude Stein.*

Entity

(1927, age 16)

The intimacy of spirals has become stone to him. This is in reality only the last prayer urge. As it is, all the crimson of stamps has resolved into loops. These fold up and seek sounds beyond lime rinds.

Let it not be understood that the frenzied fingers were here wishing us to leave. It was only that he went away and shells returned. An urn of disgust cannot stop up the pores for they are after his creases of intelligence. Or, let us say, if one end were rubbed blue and all edges left green we should have a pleasing effect. But all this is uncertain. One does not feel the imperative qualities soon because behind lapels there are buttons of unrest.

Eradicate, if you can, the adaptability of my nature to joy. It is our heritage, this abandoned cerise; — perhaps the only one we have left. The steel of now cannot be rounded like letters of the system into laughing hordes of misunderstanding. We cannot permit these unflinching bones to perform such elegies. There may be abysms in our fingers. There may be falsehoods about ponds. Last leek occurred a strange step. Paradise stalked, and seizing a trombone from the wall, stumbled. In this way all such margins weaken.

Can you not all discover how ennui will creep thus? There is no object in such flight. Masses have power.

At any rate, I shall not have panted entirely beyond borders of limpness. Our sycamores need repose. Is it possible that ever we shall be able to trace our responsibilities to such commands? We cannot ignore successfully the call of feathers. We must heed somewhat bristles. As it is, we are not entirely beyond aluminum fences. This is the reason for his dialogue. The origin of power is everywhere.

If any such enmity is discovered let us discard our yawning.

The susceptibility of emotionalism to unguarded caves may be readily realized by all of us. His smiles fall slowly into jars of porcelain. Even if his pain persists, all these losing forces discover their positions.

A rubber is black. The eternal verities are not. In this effigy we may discern a long boulevard. Leaves of such tendencies shall impale him, and he will be certain to remain poised over lavender pebbles.

The immutability of spheres is constant. All about us are carcasses of planets. Whirling continues a short while. Close her eyes and fold her hands above. We are ready for the treatise on hexagonal tiles.

When all shall have been immersed in brass, it will be easily recognized. Only then shall the grain of the pelt be held by fundamental hands. The only tense is the future and futility is taken for granted.

Much of Bowles's adult work is concerned with the tenuous nature of consciousness, reality, and meaning. In "A Distant Episode" (1945), a linguistics professor has his tongue cut off by nomads, who then imprison him as their jester, negating whatever meaning his life may have had.

Paul Bowles, as a teenager in the late 1920s.

*"A White Goat's Shadow,"
which appeared in* Argo, *a
student magazine, is the
author's first published piece
of fiction. It was adapted by
Bowles from a longer,
stream-of-consciousness
account of his trip to Paris.
Concerned chiefly with
"flow," the young author
was afraid that a more careful approach to the writing
would shut him down, he
recalls in his autobiography.*

A White Goat's Shadow
(1929, age 18)

*D*inner was to be at two thirty and I was invited to accompany the duc and his brother to a nearby café for an apéritif. It is not yet created for me the Paris café. We sit on the terrasse and I see sawdust on the floor. The sun is bright but there is a heaviness somewhere in me. A nostalgia already? What are you having? Quick, buck up. Show your teeth and smile saying same as you. Trois amourettes. You like Paris? Yes forcé I think I am going to like it. I know. I am going to love it. The bread is strange lying there in the basket. The three glasses arrive on white saucers pricemarked. My God, it's anisette. Ce n'est pas tout-à-fait la même chose. Oh, but I've passed out on anisette and after you've passed out on anisette you can never taste it again. But I gulped a third of it and felt it percolate upward into the convolutions. I haven't eaten since early this morning in Boulogne. I'm sorry. I can't drink any more. They are worried. Don't drink it they say. Don't drink it. The traffic is becoming a roar. The city is sweet-smelling. I relax and spread my legs under the little table. A long sigh goes out from my lips. You are tired? says the duc solicitously. Yes and awfully hungry. What? he asks. Very tired, very hungry I repeated with French accent. Yes yes he nods understanding. We are going to eat presently. The city is spread far out away from and around me. The sun seems near. It is slowing down. A painful ralentir like the Pacific 231 coming to a halt. In between the beats I feel an agony. It has always been like that. When I have been delirious it is the horror of the two conflicting tempi that makes my hands sweat. The taxis trumpet too gaily. I suddenly want to weep; to wake up. I close my eyes stoically. If I press the lids together too tightly two tears may roll out. I cough casually; blow my nose. Open. They have drained their pernods and are eating the bread. The duc offers me a cigarette. I take it pushing back my chair. The sudden motion makes me want to dance. I feel my ankle muscles contract involuntarily. We will return to my mother's says the duc rising. I walk elastically. The sun shines. I notice that the trees have little iron fences around them and that above the fences they are budding. They are farther on their way towards the spring here than in the country on the way from the boat. As we reenter the apartment I am already feeling at home. The dinner is heavy. Pitchers of wine red and white. America is dead. Long live the Etoile.

Sipping Pernod in a drab North African town, Port declares, in The Sheltering Sky, *that he'd "still a damned sight rather be here than back in the ◄ United States."*

II

"A white goat's shadow. They were walking
"down the shale steps during the next
"reincarnation and he was ahead of them so that
"they dared to discuss him. The lake was blue and
"the woods shrieked with locusts. In the fields the
"dust quivered with heat and all the grass was dead
"but on the east verandah it was cool with the
"venetian blinds let down all around. They were
"sitting in deck-chairs sipping bacardis. As he
"entered they frowned slightly and continued to
"sip. This will never do. Blast them. Take me
"back to my other life."

"The quotation marks and the brackets at the margin were clearly a European affectation which I must have considered chic at the time," explains the author.

It is difficult to live. Slowly the dusk fell to a serenade of taxi-horns. It is the supreme test to be alone the first evening surtout after an April when the twilight is scented with adolescence. Pang pang says the night as it falls quietly layer upon layer. I am so tired. The world is just coming out of ether. A passive spirit. Twenty francs a day is too much because at that rate I shall have

Many uncomprehending, ➤
inflexible, or obnoxious trav-
elers make their way across
Bowles's fictional landscape.
Tunner, who brings an
especially inimical ugliness
to The Sheltering Sky,
announces, "'One thing I
can't stand is filth.' 'Yes,
you're a real American, I
know,'" counters Kit.

that makes oh my God what shall I do? I do not
eat, neither do I sleep. But later ca sera mieux.
(At Boulogne after two in the morning down
(stamped an Americaine shouting I must have a
(bathroom adjoining my room. I'm sorry
(Madame there are none. It's ridiculous. There
(must be some. I've got to have one. Upstairs it is
(quiet. The curtains at the window are heavy.
(The cord pulls them back to show the basin out-
(side. The empty place at night. The strange little
(lights around the place. Two men trot allegro
(laughing. They are lost. A fog is coming in. A
(whistle out on the Channel. Frisson and sigh.
(Pull back the cord and undress. It is too late to
(sing. Go to sleep.)

Paul Bowles

William S. Burroughs at the Los Alamos Ranch School, age 15.

WILLIAM S. BURROUGHS

"A s a young child I wanted to be a writer because writers were rich and famous," William Burroughs recalls in his 1986 essay "The Name Is Burroughs." "They lounged around Singapore and Rangoon smoking opium in a yellow pongee silk suit. They sniffed cocaine in Mayfair and they penetrated forbidden swamps with a faithful native boy and lived in the native quarter of Tangier smoking hashish and languidly caressing a pet gazelle."

Born in 1914 to a prominent St. Louis family—whose fortunes had been enhanced by his grandfather's invention of an adding machine— Burroughs has fully escaped his establishment birthright. At times a drifter, a criminal, and a drug addict, he became an early force in the Beat literary movement and wrote about a wide variety of taboo subjects. Over the years Burroughs has written more than fifteen novels, including *Junky* (1953), *The Wild Boys* (1971), which he characterizes in one essay as "a kind of homosexual *Peter Pan*," and, more recently, *Cities of the Red Night* (1981) and *The Western Lands* (1987). He remains most famous for his 1959 dystopian novel *Naked Lunch*, a fantastical, comic-horrific dispatch from the land of addiction and withdrawal. (It won a significant court victory over censorship in 1966).

The author is also recognized as a pioneer of form. His early experiments with narrative montage—called cut-ups—were, according to a 1991 critical volume on his work, an attempt "to explode conventional notions of language, the book, reality, and the self."

Burroughs was a rebel early in life. As a teenager, according to biographer

Ted Morgan, he threw a homemade bomb (it did not explode) through a window of his principal's home. During Burroughs's childhood, people regarded him as unusual and made such remarks as: "That boy looks like a walking corpse," relates Morgan. "It had occurred to him that he belonged to another species," Morgan adds.

Burroughs wrote fiction during his childhood and teen years as a form of refuge. It's a pity that most of this work no longer exists. But at least the author has re-created parts from memory in his essay "The Name Is Burroughs," which appears in *The Adding Machine* (Seaver Books, 1986). Around age twelve he tried his hand at gangster and ghost stories (in fact, elements from such popular forms would later provide the adult author with raw material). As a boy, he also wrote bloody westerns, sprinkled liberally—in anticipation of his later work—with hangings and vultures. In "The Name Is Burroughs," the author recalls a passage from one such story: "Hardened old sinner that he was, he still experienced a shudder as he looked back at the three bodies twisting on ropes, etched against the beautiful red sunset." Then there were his tales of remorseful murderers, philosophical jewel thieves, and genteel adventurers. A snippet:

> "My god, that poor old chief!" He broke down sobbing.
> The other looked at him coldly and raised an eyebrow: "Well after all, Reggie, you didn't expect him to *give us* the emeralds, did you?"
> "I don't know what I expected, but not *that piranha* fish!"
> "It was much the easiest and most convenient method."

Using a combination of paraphrase and direct quotation, Burroughs re-creates parts of a prescient early effort about "a decent young man who gets on the dope" after a "sinister hypnotist" plies him with "injections of marijuana." The story progresses:

> "Kill, kill, kill." The words turned relentlessly in his brain, and he walked up to a young cop and said "If you don't lock me up I shall kill you." The cop sapped him without a word. But a wise old detective in the precinct takes a like to the boy, sets him straight and gets him off the snow. It was a

hard fight but he made it. He now works in a hardware store in Ottawa, Illinois […] "And if any kind stranger ever offers me some pills that will drive all my blues away, I will simply call a policeman."

Ted Morgan unearthed the following story in the literary magazine of the John Burroughs School, Burroughs's alma mater. The story serves as an early example of Burroughs's fascination with control, and in particular "with debunking control systems." Morgan adds, "Already, he had adopted the guise of psychic explorer, just as he would later explore psychoanalysis, Scientology…and other, more arcane systems."

The piece is also humorous, a quality that has not always been appreciated in Burroughs's adult writing. "Much of my work," the author once pointed out, "is intended to be *funny*."

Personal Magnetism

(1929, age 14)

"Are you bashful? Shy? Nervous? Embarrassed? If so, send me two dollars and I will show you how to control others at a glance; how to make your face appear twenty years younger; how to use certain Oriental secrets and dozens of other vital topics."

I am none of these things, but I would like to know how to control others at a glance (especially my Latin teacher). So I clipped the coupon, beginning to feel more magnetic every minute.

In a week, I received an impressive red volume with magnetic rays all over the cover. I opened the book and hopefully began to read. Alas! the book was a mass of scientific drivel cunningly designed to befuddle the reader, and keep him from realizing what a fake it was.

I learned that every time one yawns, a quart of magnetism escapes, that it takes four months to recuperate from a cigarette. And as for a cocktail! Words fail me. Another common exit of magnetism is light literature of any kind, movies, and such unmagnetic foods as cucumbers and eggs. I never realized that a cucumber was so potent. They always impressed me as watery and tasteless.

And how is magnetism acquired? So far as I can make out, one must sit perfectly still for hours reading the dictionary or something equally uninteresting, then, laden with magnetism, one should arise with tensed eye (whatever that is) and with slow steady steps, bear down on one's quarry like a steam roller.

Did I find out how to control others at a glance? I certainly did, but never had the nerve to try it. Here is how it is done: I must look my victim squarely in the eye, say in a low, severe voice, "I am talking and you must listen," then, intensify my gaze and say, "You cannot escape me." My victim completely subdued, I was to say, "I am stronger than my enemies." Get thee behind me Satan. Imagine me trying that on Mr. Baker!

I think the book was right in saying that by following its instructions I could make myself the center of interest at every party. Interest is putting it mildly!

"I live with the constant threat of possession," Burroughs states in his 1985 introduction to Queer, *"and a constant need to escape from possession, from Control."* Even as a young child, Burroughs felt the threat of *"an outside malevolent presence ready to invade him,"* according to his biographer Ted Morgan, who points to a mysterious trauma involving the four-year-old Burroughs, his nurse, and her boyfriend. Burroughs has explained shooting his wife, Joan, in 1951 as a form of possession by an *"ugly spirit,"* against which he has struggled ever since.

William S. Burroughs

Fred Chappell, age 18, at Duke University.

FRED CHAPPELL

*F*red Chappell, who grew up amid the conservative pragmatism of an Appalachian mill town, has long been drawn to flights of imagination. Much of his oeuvre—which includes the novel *Dagon* (1968), *Moments of Light* (stories 1980), and *Midquest* (poetry 1981)—concerns the mysterious forces waiting to transport us to dreamlike places of rapture, torment, or enlightenment.

Born in 1936 in Canton, North Carolina, he was raised by his school-teacher parents on his grandparents' farm. "Having two sets of parents got kind of stifling after a while," he told one interviewer, and the town itself seemed an obstacle to the adolescent Chappell. His roots have become increasingly important to him, however, and he's been writing about them more and more, he says. His 1985 novel *I Am One of You Forever* brims with a surrealistically nostalgic affection.

Chappell read broadly as a child, devouring *A Midsummer Night's Dream* a half dozen times before age twelve. The play is still a favorite of his, he says, for its deft merger of realistic and supernatural elements, a salient feature of Chappell's own work, and one he experimented with in the teenage story below.

As its introduction in Duke University's literary magazine, *The Archive*, points out, Chappell's story "contrasts the daily high school routine familiar to many with That Other Landscape known only to a few—the beautiful sphere of fantasy."

Chappell first wrote this story as a junior in high school and worked on it further as a senior. When he arrived at Duke University, he submitted it to the student literary magazine, The Archive *("not immediately," he says, "took a while to work up the nerve"), where it was edited "slightly— nothing substantial" by the editor Reynolds Price, then a senior. It is the lightly edited version that appears here. In the '60s, Chappell completely rewrote the story and published it under the title "Band of Brothers."*

And with Ah! Bright Wings

(circa 1953, age 16–17)

*T*he boat was chained to a willow growing on the bank, but often they would pull and push it out to feel the drifting, denizen motion of it. The lady, whose husband owned the boat, lived across the river, and she continually watched them through parted blinds; she expected them to steal it. They sat smoking king size Chesterfields; occasionally one produced a pipe, would finger and mouth it, but not light it.

They were speaking of floating a raft down the Mississippi River. One of them, whose name was Kurt, wore a blue shirt with a streak of white threads across the shoulders of it. His eyes were brown, his face wide. Sometimes he looked at the other, sometimes eyefollowed snakefeeders, butterflies, soaring things, sometimes watched the slow water move over the rocks beneath its surface. The other, named James, watched Kurt most of the time, but often stared at sky, opposite bank, and the water.

Kurt talked slowly. His widest teeth met deliberately at the end of each word, and the thin lips were connected over the open space by strains of saliva; the spiderthread of it collected in one place and another, never parting, never immobile. James watched this, not with the vague disgust he usually associated with spit, but with a wonder somehow connected with nurses and their lipstick.

Kerry said, "I have a liferaft. It is one that Dick or Joe got from an old Army Surplus Store. I have it fixed up with waterproofing now. I'd like to take it to Wisconsin or Minnesota—where does the River start?—"

"Minnesota, I believe," answered James.

"Down, all the way down, to New Orleans at the mouth. To the Gulf of Mexico."

"Atch, himmel—you will drive me nuts if you mention New Orleans. Or, for that matter, any place at all besides here."

And James moved his pipehand around his left, slashing across the face of the roaring town to his back. The pipe returned to his teeth again. Then he disengaged it, and slapped his palms with its stem. Observing the stem, he noticed teethmarks on the edge of it, where he had bitten into it with greater force. He wore a redwine corduroy coat with large pockets on each side. There was a large hole in the left pocket, and occasionally he stuck his fingers through this hole, and watched them flex and bend. His hair was long, in contrast to Kurt's sanitarily closecropped head, and a long slice of hair was carried along the side of his head like a sparrowwing. His almost closeset eyes rippled wavelike under the chasms of his black brows. A scar slanted along the plane of his right cheek, raindropping apart in a small fold of flesh an inch and a half above his scarlet mouth. His chin was cleft in a semidimple, not receding, but definitely weak.

"I don't know how much you could load in this liferaft, but I guess you could get enough in to last two or three weeks anyway," said Kurt.

"If you could put a case of cigarets on, it would be much better than loading up all the valuable space with useless stuff like food and water for instance," said James.

"You could always tie up at a town if you needed anything. There are all kinds of towns along the river."

"Give me enough money and I'm off. I guess. I might have to work in the store this summer... Come to think of it, I know damn well I will. In fact, I probably won't even go to Mexico with Surrett."

◄ *"The kids are always grousing about the dull pokiness of their home town,"* explains the author. *"They speak incorrect German on purpose—as part of their inside jargon, their largest source of humor."*

◄ *"It might have been myself I was trying to describe,"* says Chappell, *"merely in order to give my character some physical presence."* In writing several stories during that period, he would occasionally rely on the mirror to provide physical detail. *"Sheer laziness,"* he calls the method, *"or self-centeredness, who knows?"*

"Ah, why not? I thought you boys were already gone."

"They told me I'd have to quit smoking—so I quit."

"Yeah: it looks like you've quit: a cigaret in your hand and a pipe in your pocket."

"Oh, this aint really smoking. It's just inhaling nicotine."

Then James rocked, shifting his weight from side to side, so that the water sucked loudly at the air streaming around the side of the boat. He thought of nothing. A bird cut across his vision, momentarily blotting out some of the sky and the tops of many trees. Kurt was talking also, but nothing registered in James' ear.

"We have an Arabian horse up at Gene's now..." Kurt began.

The pendulum weight of James arced the boat more into the edge of the water, and he noticed a thin pane of it trickling in over the top. He put his hand on the rails of the ship, saltwater spraying up into his eyes. He noted the seasalt odor and the sun odor, and felt the regular pull of weight on his left side where his sword was belted. Shipmast was holding sails of silk to the furnacing wind. He was not surprised to find a great black beard on his chin, and for a moment he rested his hand on his handsome facefabric. He knew there were fleas in the beard and he took it for granted. A man upon a higher deck was holloing across the sunlit space to him. This man was clad in many bright colors: red and green and yellowgold. What words were forced through those far fangs did not interest him, for he had to climb the rigging. And so he sprang upward, caught this rope and the next one and the next, hand over hand, arms snakewinding over and over, wrists constantly in friction. After a while he was tired, but he had climbed far enough that he looked over the blinding sea. Here and there were other gaudy silksails, pressed flat like smudges of color on sheening sheets of gold. A rimming shoreline ran against the horizon, and often the pencil structuring of temples broke the golden sky with their casual daggertips. He looked far beneath him at the deck. Many men, with windingtoy automatism, were going about sailoring, here winding ropes, and there holding mops to the deck, and looking at their white swords. He thought of his own sword strapped to his thigh, and slipped it from its scabbard. He touched the blunt edge of it with a quick tongue, tasting the metality; then he swerved it above his head severing all the supporting rigging except a single rope, which he cut also, almost as an afterthought. And then he fell, one foot entangled in the billowing rigging, hands flung grotesquely at angles with his body, his beard separated into two flapping streams, parting round his face, leaving his eyes clear to watch the mast shoot away and upward.

James murmured.

Kurt was silent; he looked up the river at a bridge over which a black car was passing. It was a Chevrolet, and he remembered that Gene almost wrecked one like it once. His eyes continued upward, and he observed the sky, clouded over by dark, immobile and apparently unmovable, clouds. Slices of sun shone around the dirty edges of them. His inner ears dictated the sound of a distant cowbell to his brain. He remembered churchbells, and then schoolbells, and glanced at his watch.

"We'd better go," Kurt said. "It's almost time for second period to start."

"I don't want to leave, but I guess I have to. What class did you lay out of, anyhow?"

"Hoot Ward's. He don't even check the roll. What do you have first?"

"I got study hall under Miss Millikan," replied James. "I always tell her I had to thumb up or something and she don't care. I don't stay in there half the time anyway. Always go to the library at the first of the period, and don't come back till it's over."

"It's a little bit early, but let's go up now. Might find Stafford and get him to run us over to the

> ← In his adult work Chappell has largely abandoned tacked-together words such as "windingtoy." The technique, he says, was inspired by Gerard Manley Hopkins. Chappell used it in several other stories written in his teens. "Later it seemed artificial."

> ← Equally impetuous and wild, the "real" Blackbeard appears in Chappell's story "Thatch Retaliates" (1980), a whimsical, if dark, tale set in the early 18th century.

Donut Shop. I could use a cup of coffee right about now."

"O.K. I could use some myself."

They stood up and the woman across the river was certain that they were going to steal her husband's row boat, and she peered even more closely at them. But they did not. They were stepping carefully onto the damp bank, grasping bushlimbs and treeroots with their thin paperwhite fingers so that they would not fall into the river.

James noted the limp coolness of the small stretch of undergrowth about them. Ribs of greenleaves swished across his face, and grass sometimes reached his knees, and then he was lying in greater woods by a small pool. His attire was his rowboat attire, but there was a girl with him. She was beautiful, but her nose had some irregularity. Honeybrown hair slid down her back, along the Greekcolumn curve of her neck, flipped itself into the female of her cheek. She was lying on her back listening to the poolinsects, feeling cloudsky press heavily upon her sight. James was playing with his pipe, not nervously, but because he liked the feel of it in his fingers. He had with him a volume of Hopkins and the knowledge that beyond this place was his home, where there were two more copies of this same book. He tore out each page and put it in a small pile beside him to burn as an offering to the Unknown God. Occasionally he read aloud to the girl. Then he stopped tearing and read a sonnet:

The title of this story is taken from the Gerard Manley Hopkins poem "God's Grandeur." The poem, like Chappell's story, affirms the presence of divine splendor in the world amid humanity's pedestrian routines. Revelation of God in nature remains a strong theme in Chappell's work. ➤

"The world is charged with the grandeur of God.
It will flame out like shining from shook foil;
It gathers to greatness like the ooze of oil
Crushed."

The shape beside the pool stirred slowly. James glanced reverently. He could not ascertain whether she was bored or puzzled or sleepy or pleased or tired or restless. He asked, somewhat fearfully, "Do

You like that?" She did not answer; she smiled at the sky, and he thought that she was dreaming of a lover with a harp or trumpet. And a taste of citrus came in his mouth because she answered that she thought it very pretty. He tore another page, reading from it:

"Glory be to God for dappled things,
For skies of couplecolour as a brinded cow;"

Slowly he closed the crippled book. He put a cigaret in his mouth and lit it, lit also the pages beside him, watched the sheets curl in agony like dawnstruck roseleaves, watched the smoke speed up the air. He looked at Athenavenus beside him and wanted. He threw the cigaretbutt into the pool, but it immediately offended his eye, and he had to net it out, darkening hand and sleeve with wet.

Chappell's mature writing is rich with references to mythology, history, and the Bible. In "Linnaeus Forgets" (1977), the narrative contains a brief visit by the goddess Flora accompanied by ◄ Apollo and Diana.

"I don't see Stafford's Mercury. He usually parks it over there," said Kurt.

"Maybe he didn't come to school today," said James.

"He might already be gone."

They were walking in shortshorn grass that belonged to the town's recreation park. A concrete swimming pool, surrounded by a fence, was on their right. It contained no water at that time, for it didn't open until May 28: this was April. Directly in front of them was an Armory made of brick, silent boxsquare, standing at attention like all military buildings. A small highway was on their left; northwest was the schoolhouse. Crossing the highway, they moved toward it.

They came to the side entrance of the school, where boys clustered at lazy moments to smoke cigarets and spit. Some were there now, but James and Kurt knew none of them.

"Has the second period bell rung yet?" asked Kerry.

"Na, activity aint even started yet," replied a boy.

"Your watch is wrong. It said 10:25 over there," said James.

"It aint even 10:00 yet," commented another boy.

So there was nothing to do, but smoke another

cigaret, and wait for the bell to ring. At that time, it was allowed that those who wished to might smoke at this entrance. Some of their friends would be out then. The boys gathered there were underclassmen, and they did not recognise them. They stood about, idly blowing grey peacock plumes of tobacco smoke into the morning. James tried to blow a smokering, but the breeze was too great.

Another boy came out. He was small and wore darkrimmed glasses. He had red hair which was differently shaded in the different seasons of the year. Now spring made his hair carrotorange. He had thick lips, large round nose, nearsighted eyes which peered through glasses like observers.

"Well well, if it isn't littul red Buddy Brickhouse. You red little ass, I just Ddoubledare you to ask me for a cigaret," said James.

"Give me a cigaret, Taylor," said Buddy, matteroffactly.

"Bwah, do you know what I do to people that always scrouge cigarets off of me? Say. Do you know? Say."

"Yeah, I know what you always do to people that always bum cigarets off of you. You give them a cigaret. So give me."

"Now you little, Buddy Grant. I might have given you a weed, but you got smart. You got too damn smart. So now you don't get none off of me."

"So . . . I get one off of Cassell."

"Grant, you snivelling idiot. . ." And Kurt began.

All the time, they were shaking Buddy, pummeling, beating him with their fists, but he was not hurt by it. He pulled his lips over and away from his teeth and pushed his brows together. This was their ritual.

"Where's Anderson?" asked James.

"He'll be down in a minute," replied Buddy.

They waited on Anderson. Buddy had a cigaret finally, and he was trying very hard to light it with a lighter. Finally he produced a match, and scraped it across his shoesole. Kurt was standing near a rusty barrel, gazing and spitting into it occasionally.

James leaned into the schoolhouse brickwall, and watched Buddy trying to light. The flame sprang up from the sulphur, and Mikrokosman ran along the green avenues in pursuit of the spider. Mikrokosman was strong as an ant, and now he was armed with the sharp point of a nettle. Green grass enclosed all sides, sharp blades overtowering him, jabbing at the sky. Eight legs hammered into the ground; the weight of Arachnid hurtled along the green avenues, flailing out the grassblades. He accelerated more and soon was directly behind the spider, but this was not enough. Fast and faster; sweat boiled from his pores. He turned off the path of the monster, and ran into the miniature forest around it. Now on the path again, ahead of the spider, he launched himself onto the leafstem of a low-growing weed. He pulled himself along the stem on his stomach, lying flat on the leaf. The spider came. He lay very still so that the many eyes would not glimpse him; grasped the nettlepoint more tightly. Now closer—he could discern certain small hairs on the speeding body. Knotting his muscles, he prepared to leap.

In Chappell's work, vast worlds can be found within such modest settings as the strange plant in "Linnaeus Forgets," or Uncle Gurton's infinite beard in I Am One ← of You Forever. *As a 15-year-old, James in* It Is Time, Lord (1963), *has the imagination to perceive "rivers with islands, flames, tongues, heads of dogs, men, and bears" in the grain of his bedroom's paneling.*

Anderson entered on the outside with the sound of the bell. The four boys went out against the fence to talk, for a crowd always gathered around the barrel. Anderson was extraordinarily ordinary looking. His mind was brilliant and whimsical, but undisciplined.

"Buddy Grant, according to the upstate reports, is a littul red brick outhouse," said Anderson.

"Anderson is sahn, according to Buddy Grant," said Buddy Grant.

← *In one of the dreams that attend his nightmarish de-evolution, Peter Leland in* Dagon *is cast as a "spider; no, a daddy longlegs.... His size was protean; grew monstrously; diminished."*

Kurt asked, "What did you have in English this morning, Anderson?"

"Same old crap," answered Anderson. "She got mad at me again."

Grant laughed.

"Y, what for?" asked Kurt.

"Well, I asked her if I could go to the library and

← *sahn: jargon for* son of a bitch

she said no, but I went anyhow."

"Ah," Kurt breathed.

"I was standing right by the door when I asked and I left before I heard her."

"She hollered as loud as she could at you to come back," reported Grant.

"Well, I was already out the door. I didn't hear her," Anderson rationalised.

"O yeah, yeah, O yeah," murmured Grant, sarcastically.

"Not that I'd have come back anyway, you understand. It's just the principle of the thing."

"It's just an excuse," said Kurt.

"If I could get out like that it would be allright," said James. "I can get out allright, but it's four points off my grade and go see the principal, to boot."

"She never does tell me I can leave," Anderson complained. "She just makes me sit in there and take it. If she told me I could shut up or get out as many times as she tells you, I'd leave; but no, I've always got to stay in there."

"If she would just teach us something. I feel like I'm wasting my time," said James. "You remember at the beginning of *Macbeth*? She spent at least half the period explaining that 'Foul is fair and fair is foul' business to us."

"That's stupid. You should be in our class. She only gave us about fifty pages to read for tomorrow. You must be in an awful dumb class."

"No," explained James. "She just likes to bore us."

"Somebody ought to bore her," declared Chapman.

Chapman had come up and was standing with them. He was of average height, with freckles on his back, and he walked with a slight limp. His eyebrows were far down over eyes which stared out like lamps in a dark cave. They reflected no light and showed no sign of intelligence. His adamsapple was monstrous large, and his face was peppered

Delivering himself of a → long, scholarly sermon on paganism, Peter Leland in Dagon *realizes that he has bored his congregation witless. "Do you know what hell is?" his wife chides him later. "It's edification without entertainment. Big mountains of boredom."*

with pimples like forkmarks on an unbaked piecrust. His mind was not an observer, but it coveted that status. He liked only too much to make impressions upon people.

"Whose has got a cigaret?" asked Chapman.

James gave him one without comment, for he did not like to listen to him talk. Chapman's speech was disconcerting because he used unusual words, textbook words, in sentences that had no connection with grammar. Sometimes his sentences broke into a vague, shifting rhythm. Often he gave long speeches of one minute, babbling without break, and these speeches seemed to contain no meaning. Occasionally a coherent thought forced its way off his tongue and stood alone, but usually the wordflow was a muddy stream: noise being caused by unseen, subsurface objects.

"Ah, a Breasterfeel. Glad to have be seeing it. Are you there, Calypso Bill?" This was Chapman.

"Mmm," Anderson mmmed.

"I wonder if we have anything new to play in band today," James wondered. He was not concerned with that, but he wished to change the subject, if there had been one.

"We'll find out in just a minute, because the bell is going to ring in just a minute," prophesied Grant.

"Brickhouse, you ought to be cured of being so smart," said Anderson.

The bell stung the air; the adherents deserted the rusty barrel and went into the building. The quartet left its post, flipping cigaret butts in four directions. Kurt had to go to biology, a class which he had failed long ago. The rest were going to music, to bandclass, to blow upon golden or ebony horns; James to play tympani.

The bandroom was an uproar, composed of pretty cleareyed girls and dulleyed boys. Mr. Mannle, the director, had, and would, not come for a time. Grant took his black clarinet from its rainwarped case and blew it once, very softly. He

◄ Chappell continues to be intrigued by the impenetrable. In "Moments of Light" (1979), for example, Doctor Burney claims—as a joke— to have received a message written in "Mars-man dialect." "Ur, gleet edd gromious Orban!" it begins.

had never learned to play it well; his interest in bandclass was confined to visions of card games in hotelrooms and bandbus. Anderson brought the spaghetti structure of his baritone from its bulky case and blew his breath through it, making no noise. He then went to his seat and flipped out scales, his fingers pressing the valves with the regularity of a watch secondhand. Up and down the C scale, F scale, B flat scale, the notes as beautiful as snowsilence. Chapman was in the corner, loudly blowing snatches of everything that flashed through his unwieldy mind: introduction to "Basin Street Blues," now the "promenade" from *Pictures at an Exhibition*, then the "Sultan" from *Scheherazade*, "Santa Claus is Coming to Town." James took his place in the corner parallel to the trombones, and lifted the cardboard protectors from the animal tympaniheads. He opened the drawer of a waist high cabinet, and searched through it for the cottontufted tympanisticks. Finding them, he bestowed a few idle whacks to the drums, then

The author was no musi- ➤
cal prodigy, he admits in
The Fred Chappell Reader
(1987). But one of his two
best friends when he was
growing up was an aspiring
composer. And music—
especially its spiritual proper-
ties—is important to
Chappell's adult work.

began trying a rhythm: the beat of *The Rites of Spring*, which he had tried vainly to get for a long time. He thought of trying to tune that singing thunder, but there was too much noise. He had to wait until class was started and all was quiet. He stood and listened to the soundstream flooding the air with its gregarious syrup. Reedhorns were shrieking like swine; higher brass, trumpets and cornets, laughing like tenor madmen; traps and snares began a staccatostutter; bass and tuba brought bursts of subterranean bellow from their depths. Under and about it all was the chatter, the unimportant important conversation, some of it as purely musical as the winding phrases of the saxaphones. Chapman switched to the fatetheme from *Carmen*, blatting like an auto horn.

Mr. Mannle entered, and the students sat; the noise did not lessen. He pointed to a title scrawled on the blackboard, a march, and many struggled to find it in their folders. James was disappointed.

Field marches do not have tympaniparts; he leaned against a shelf watching. The director tapped his stand with the orange pencil he used for a baton, and the cornets and trombones set out in fortissimo triplets for eight bars, flinging finally into the wooden melody of the fast strain. James found that it was five miles to the ground from his knee; twenty from his eyebrow. He was wearing nothing; cloudnude he stood, feeling the earth suffuse into his toes, feeling the light, darkblue sky wrap his neck, feeling the moist air weave into the curl of his thigh, his leghair. The sun shone into his planets of eyes, filling every crevice and chasm of his oncedark brain. Sunstream flooded his mind and spilled out upon his face, feminising the red lip, illuminating the scar. The folds of each ear gleamed into great curtains. There was not dark, not even in nostril or mouthroof, both now sun sodden. He felt the transfusion of light's blood: a slow first flush of it in the neck, a piercing and stabbing in the chest. His legs began to glow, and his chest became incandescent. No warmth, taste, no emotion, sensation accompanied. It was a blind light. A noumenal, unphenomenal, a knowable, but unsensable light. Watching the rays spear out from every pore of his skin, he ventured to step. His body corruscated with the movement. He stepped again, and again. He lifted his arm; he laughed, sunshine rivering out of his mouth. Behind him, the sky, now deprived of the support of his shoulder, sagged dangerously.

◄ Being a Gemini, an air sign, "nothing so pours through me as the blueness of the sky in a cold clear day," explains the narrator (also named James) of It Is Time, Lord. (Gemini is also the author's sign.)

The music continued for an hour. Marches and suites, excerpts, scales bounded energetically against the narrow walls of the room. Finally the bell rang, and time became 11:30 third period.

◄ As he embarks on his profound transformation, Peter Leland in Dagon watches his reflection in his grandparents' glass doors with similarly intense self-consciousness. "He dropped his pale hand to his side, and in the glass the movement coruscated."

Chapman and James gathered their books from the shelf by the door, and went upstairs to English. They sat in close desks and talked.

"What are you reporting on today?" asked James.

"*Tom Jones*," replied Chapman. "What are you?"

"*Madame Bovary*, I guess. How did you like the Jones boy?"

"Well, he really wasn't the Jones boy."

"That's right," James laughed.

The teacher entered the room: a woman with a sharp nose and thick glasses. She announced briefly that the reports would be oral, and called names to stand before the class. James sat and listened to a beautiful blondehaired girl tell of a hero who lived long ago; and a boy told of something else; and then his name was named.

He went to the front of his row, standing before two girls and two boys, and began his novel.

"The title is *Madame Bovary*, by Goostov Flobare."

There was laughter from one boy. He was amused by the name.

"This is a French novel..."

There was more laughter from the class.

"...about a woman who is a romantic, and her husband who is positively not. In fact, he is a very dead deadhead..."

Chappell characters are often rising and falling. In "Moments of Light," Haydn's spirit flies off on a quick cosmic tour as he looks through a telescope. In "Mrs. Franklin Ascends" (1980), Ben's wife believes she is approaching heaven. Even the cat Drummond, in "Notes Toward a Theory of Flight" (1987), has day-dreams about soaring: "So far as Drummond could see it was feathers and feathers alone which made the difference." ➤

He glanced over the faces to see if this was amusing, but saw only the sea stretching out for miles and leagues unending, blue and white, green, sea colored. The sun was very hot; it covered most of the sky. His father was behind him, uttering words of caution. He looked at his feet. They were wearing sandals. He looked for his arms, but he had none: there were, instead, great white wings, white as music, feathered as music. He lifted their lightness and rose from the earth a few inches. To fly, to fly. He jumped toward the sea, vaning out his wings to catch the bright air; was pulled softly up by the gods, like a paper on a string. Seasmell reached him, tracing gently through his nostrils like mosquitos. Flipping, dipping, flying, drifting, like a snowstorm over the face of the sea, he gazed into the sun. And pushed lightly toward it. Toward it, diagonaling up into the hot face of it, bowels twining and curling within him for the agonyectasy.

He did not know, but there was laughter splashing on his ears. Chapman, however, was not laughing, but wondering. He looked at James, standing beneath the pale yellow light, both arms outstretched, head hung to one side, eyes closed. The girls in front of James looked as if they were kneeling—huddled as they were in their desks.

James opened his eyes to tell of Madame Bovary, but could not speak for drowning.

Fred Chappell

Carolyn Penny at age 5, visiting her grandparents outside Raleigh, N.C.

CAROLYN CHUTE

*I*n 1985 Carolyn Chute (born Carolyn Penny), then a thirty-seven-year-old grandmother trying to scrape together a living in her native Maine, made a big entrance into the book world with her best-selling, highly praised first novel. *The Beans of Egypt, Maine* presents characters struggling to remain human in the face of dehumanizing poverty. Though the author has lived in poverty herself, the spirit of her writing is infused with an embracing humor that mitigates her characters' hard lot. Lee, who has been sharing his bed with his daughter, Earlene, while his spooky wife is institutionalized; Ruby, who goes on obscene hunting sprees; Beal, who has sired a pack of babies with his Auntie Roberta—the book shuns none of them.

Filled with playful, fresh imagery, Chute's writing is rambunctious and highly stylized. She is "quite possibly the only true original stylist this last ten or fifteen years has produced," wrote Madison Smartt Bell upon publication of Chute's second novel, *Letourneau's Used Auto Parts* (1988). (Chute credits Bell with having lent her the money to mail out her *Beans* manuscript.)

"We were not a literary family," says Chute of her childhood.

> There was a lot of *talk*, however. Lots of gossip and stories. Until we got a T.V. when I was 7 or 8. Then things quieted down. I really resented the T.V. Eventually in teenage years I spent more time in my room alone to get away from T.V. I didn't do homework in my room. I either pretended or wrote stories or listened to my radio. But not homework. School and I wasted each other's time. The only valuable time was spent alone or with my family when the T.V. was off.

After learning "the truth about meat," she invented the following story around the age of eight. Or at least some variation of it. As no printed copy from childhood exists, Chute has re-created it for *First Words*. And although it can't be considered as an authentic example of juvenilia, it is still a great pleasure to read.

Adventures out in
THE WORLD
BY CAROLYN ANNE PENNY
(circa 1955, age 8)

*O*nce upon a time and all the time...even this very minute...is a terrible terrible place where hogs have to go. Nancy always thought you got hotdogs and stuff from hogs that died of old age. Her parents and grandparents and uncle told her that hogs died of old age and then that's when they made them into food. That's not so bad. Hogs hardly know after they're dead. But then Nancy was in school and she always drew nice pictures. The teacher always said to Nancy's mother My my your daughter draws very nice pictures and all the kids copy her pictures because they can't think up any of their own. They are kids who do good arithmetic papers. Terrible in art. Nancy says ha ha. You think you are good at everything but too bad. Anyway Nancy was drawing a nice smiling hog one day with a blue sky and the sun had a smile too and

long rays. Green grass. A little house in the distance for you to live in. The hog was the best
ever. VERY pretty spots. Tail curled. Nice day.
Very big smile. This teacher was not so bad as the
one we had in first grade. She put _____ _____
behind the piano with trash from the waste basket
in her mouth which had paint on it...then around
her mouth and head all this masking tape. Then
Mrs. _____ said, okay all you kids line up. Time
for lunch. Next day _____ _____ was okay. But
it was weird after that. Made you not want to
move much of your muscles, just sit and think.
Anyway the teacher said Nancy drew a nice hog
but a boy in the next desk who drew something
whatever it was, started to laugh mean and say
hogs don't smile. Nancy said yes they do. He
said, no hogs don't smile because they are killed
for hotdogs and stuff and when they die they
scream and cry and try to get away and there is
nothing to smile about. He said Nancy would
have a better hog to show it screaming and crying. Nancy figured somebody was lying. Nancy
almost wished the teacher would put the boy
behind the piano. Nancy didn't want to ever talk
about hogs again or make pictures of hogs only in
secret. Nancy one day couldn't stand it any more.
She walked to the terrible place when farmers
brought hogs to scream and cry and be tortured.
Nancy went around back of the place and sure
enough, there they were waiting. Very many hogs
and some sick cows. Nancy could just about
stand it. She went over to the gate and kicked
that old thing right off its hinges and all the hogs
and sick cows, probably a million...they ALL
SMILED. Then they headed for the gate. They all
ran out of the gate in a giant stampede like you
see on TV out west only these were mostly hogs.
Meanwhile Nancy's first grade teacher was out
on the sidewalk prancing around like she
does...going to the store or something. Very tall
teacher. Very strong. The stampede first tram-

← *Chute has left the characters' names blank because
they used to change every
time she told the story.*

← *In* The Beans of Egypt,
Maine, *Uncle Loren, a hog
farmer, compares pigs favor-
ably to human beings.
"Folks are ratty messed-up
back-stabbin' sons-a-
whores.... Pigs was created
in the Lord's image."*

"Any bird, bug, or animal including the human animal can be self-serving, cool, and steely-hearted," Chute writes in her own epigraph to Letourneau's Used Auto Parts, *her fictional return to Bean country. "It is only the superhuman who can rise to Compassion."*

pled the terrible people who worked at the hot-dog factory. Then the stampede squished the teacher FOREVER. Then the stampede escaped the city and Nancy arrived out there too and said now what should we do? We have to escape, they said. The woods are nice. Very quiet. Nobody around. And adventures. The hogs and sick cows said okay. And off they went.

Carolyn Chute

Judith Ortiz at age 18. Noting the scratches on the photo, she says, "It looks like I have gray hair! I didn't then (do now)."

JUDITH ORTIZ COFER

"*I* grew up in two worlds, the tropical island and the cold city," writes Judith Ortiz Cofer in her memoir *Silent Dancing: A Partial Remembrance of a Puerto Rican Childhood* (1990). As a "navy brat" she divided her youth between Paterson, New Jersey, and—when her father was stationed in Europe for extended periods—Hormigueros, the pueblo in Puerto Rico where she was born in 1952. She says that the childhood imperative to belong was often frustrated by this shifting arrangement. But because of it, she learned about the power of language, and she resolved at an early age to build up "my arsenal of words." During long stretches of solitude, she became a voracious book reader.

Born to a mother only sixteen years old, she found additional nurturing in her forceful, benevolent grandmother. "To me she looked like a wise empress right out of the fairy tales I was addicted to reading," she writes. "Mamá" was a much beloved storyteller, whose voice strongly influenced the budding author. As a child, Judith Ortiz made up her own tales about the well-known folk hero María Sabida, "the smartest girl in all of Puerto Rico."

Later, the geographic and emotional disruptions imposed by her father's career provided a compelling literary subject. It continues to play a key role in her mature work—which includes the 1989 novel *The Line of the Sun* and *Terms of Survival* (poems, 1987)—and is clearly central to at least two of her early short stories, included here.

"The process of searching for my beginnings as a writer has been educational for me," says the author. "I had forgotten (or repressed) the laboriousness of the apprenticeship, so many false starts. Good thing I didn't know enough to be discouraged."

Visionary
(1971, age 19)

*C*ome in, he says, into my Barcelona eyes
where my pupils dance the Flamenco,
come in and meet my iris while
I play my teeth like castanets
for your pleasure,
but please do not, how do you say?
get carried away by the beat, my sweet
Señorita, for if you betray
my sensitivity,
I will blink you right out of my life,
and not a tear will I waste.

As Cofer relates in Silent Dancing, *her grandmother told cautionary tales about roving male lust that have resurfaced in the author's dreams and poetry. In "The Life of an Echo" (1988), the poet's persona meets Manuel and "the vagrant love of men." →*

Still Life
(1971, age 19)

Our wedding picture
Makes an interesting still life
You being the strong vegetable
Tall and grim
Destined for serious things
Like stew
And I'm definitely a fruit
Ripe and vulnerable
I think…
I am a peach.

Graduation
(1971, age 19)

*T*ime to punctuate the compound-complex
Four-year sentence,
Join the educated paragraph
In the essay of America.

Sea Brides
(1971, age 19)

*P*alm trees
Think only of oceans,
See how they lean
Towards the restless sea?
They remind me
Of the lonely brides
Of sailors
Waiting,
Always waiting.

*Judith Ortiz Cofer's father,
because of his navy career,
was often apart from his
family. What she calls the
"continuing conflict with the
absent father" appears
throughout her work.
"Father was...like the
wind," begins her poem
← "Fever" (1988).*

FROM

Untitled
CHAPTER 1
(1971, age 19)

*T*he afternoon President Kennedy got killed
she had been standing in a corner of the playground
of public school no. 11 it was a bitter cold day and

The author's 1992 short story "American History" similarly features a young Puerto Rican girl enduring the cold of the school playground and envying "the black girls who could jump rope so fast that their legs became a blur." Soon, a P.E. teacher delivers the news that Kennedy has been shot. After trying to write about this subject at age 19, says the author, "I guess I thought about it for a decade or so before bringing it to fruition."

the wind was making her cry hot tears which left streaks on her wind chafed skin. She had been watching the long legged black girls jumping rope in that complicated way they did. No matter how long and how hard she practiced at home, tying one end of the rope to the heater pipe and making her little brother swing the other end, she could never get as good as the black girls. She didn't care anyway, they'd never let her join in. The black kids didn't like Puertorican kids and the feeling was mutual. Almost every day there were fights in the playground. The P.R. kids had quick tempers and the "moyetos", the Spanish equivalent of nigger, knew all the right ways to make them lose their tempers.

On the day Kennedy was shot Miriam had stood apart from both groups near the fence gate, waiting for the dismissal bell to ring so that she would be the first one out. She didn't want any part in the fighting. And besides her father had the night shift that week and would expect her and Reynaldo her brother home in exactly 15 minutes, he had once timed how long it took to walk from their apt. to the school counting both lights red and if they stopped to play or talk he'd know it and start walking towards school. The sight of him, short, chunky, and always serious never failed to give her a jolt. It's not that she feared him exactly. He had never beat her or Rey, or even raised his voice to them. But he watched them and their mother constantly, perseveringly and worst of all silently. In all of her 11 years of life Miriam had never discovered the reason for his silent observation of them and until recently, since a couple of her classmates had begun to jeer her for being such a baby that she had to be walked home from school, she had never thought his behavior too peculiar. After all all P.R. fathers were strict with their children.

On that particular day of death, Miriam's perception of her life, her parents and the world around her began to change. When the sixth grade teacher, Mr. Kordas, blew his whistle for everyone to line up

Miriam felt something was wrong. His usually pleasant smiling Greek face was all twisted up in grief,
which Miriam at first mistook for anger, being an
emotion she had learned to recognize early in adults.
After lining up the kids more or less Mr. K. as
everyone called him called for silence.

"Children the President is dead" he said dramati-
cally. He waited hands on hips head downcast for reaction. Noone said anything. Accustomed as these pathetic
slum children were to shootings and death, someone's
father, uncle mother always getting shot or [....]

*◄ The author was unable to
find the rest of the manuscript.*

FROM

Untitled
(1971, age 19)

I had not danced with such abandon
since the year I left
My parents confused over their
endless cigarettes
regret smoldering in ceramic ashtrays.
No curfews and the Age of Aquarias
blasting from a record player
my father gave me for my
15th birthday. It was not
easy to walk out the door—
the rebel dragging the cause.
Two trips for the record albums
And they just watched silent on
their vinyl sofa.
I could leave them but not my music.
After the parties we sat numb
with exhausion, holding on to
each other and
calling it love. We lost ourselves
in the adoration of words
we [. . . .]

*These are notes for a
poem. The manuscript
◄ ends suddenly here.*

The Mango Tree

(1971, age 19)

*I*t crowned the hill behind Grandmother's house. Summer afternoons we'd follow her up, a tribe of grandchildren trailing behind her slow ascend over brambly bushes and through the child sized opening in the barbed wire fence big enough for a small woman and us. She'd spread her shawl under its umbrella of branches and embroider yet another pillowcase while we set up the swing at the edge of the hill taking turns flying out over the precipice.

"I remember that tree as a natural wonder," Cofer writes in Silent Dancing. *"It was large, with a trunk that took four or five children holding hands to reach across."* In its shade, her grandmother told mesmerizing stories. *"It was under that mango tree that I first began to feel the power of words."*

Untitled

(circa 1971–72, age 19–20)

*I*t is a grey December afternoon and as Mara steps up to her ankles in the melting slush she feels an icy chill creep through her numb feet to her bones. He is coming home today. After a tour of duty with the Navy. Six months away. And she doesn't know whether to be happy that her and Ely's confinement would soon come to a temporary end (there's a tour every year) or whether to fear the homecoming of the stranger her husband has become in the last two years.

She is making her way slowly to P.S. #13 her daughter's school. The snow plows have lined the street with a brown wall of snow and mud and it is almost eye level to Mara who is only five feet tall. In her madaras wool scarf which she has wrapped several times around her neck and her navy blue coat and rubber boots, she looks like a school child. The policewoman at the corner (a new one this week— they don't last too long in this neighborhood) eyes her suspiciously—playing hookey?

Mara jumps over a puddle and lands smack in the middle of another. She curses the day she was born in Spanish. Although she has been in the states on and off for the past nine years—and her English is passable—she prefers the Spanish for cursing—it has the force of vocabulary she needs for expressing her emotions. "Carajo!" she repeats as she pours the slush out of her galoshes—leaning on the Salvation Army wall. The policewoman has been watching in unfriendly amusement—"Dumb Spic." She turns her attention to the other side of the street where a small blond child on a bicycle is approaching.

Elisa is a small boned thin child with a mass of black hair framing her oval face. Her brown eyes are enormous and liquid, buried in her bulky imitation fur coat, she looks like a frightened squirrel. Like her mother Ely is thinking about Lucas' homecoming. Actually she has been brooding about it all day, acting even more shy and detached than usual; to the extent that her teacher, a severe thin woman who made it a point of asking the children personal questions in front of the class, had asked her if she was sick.

"No." Ely had tried to hide behind her spelling book.

"No—what?" Mrs. Delate had approached her desk menacingly.

She looked to the girl like a long legged bird about to swoop down on a little worm, for the sake of seeing it squirm between her talons.

"No, Ma'm" She managed to croak.

"Then what is it child? Troubles at home? You moving again? I swear some people don't care what harm they do their children's education with their irresponsible back and forth shuttling. Is that it, Elisa?"

"No, Ma'm. We are not moving. My father is coming today from Europe."

She hoped this answer would satisfy the nosey old bird. She was likely to go on for fifteen minutes about a kid's personal life.

"Well that's no reason to mope around all day, is it? Or is that the way people look happy where you come from?"

Luckily at that moment Joe Izzo popped some gum in the back of the room and the vulture was distracted by the smell of fresh blood.

And now, waiting for the blue bundle wearing boots to meet her at the corner Ely felt frozen to the ground. Only a few more hours of privacy left before the man invaded their apartment and their lives.

Mara reached her daughter's side and linked arms with her. They were almost the same height and looked truly like sisters. Mara had had Ely at the age of sixteen and child and mother had reared each other so that their knowledge and experience was almost equal. And only when *he* was around did the boundaries of their status as wife and daughter

In The Line of the Sun, *Marisol also notes the sisterly resemblance to her mother, Ramona: "She was what I would have looked like if I hadn't worn my hair in a tight braid, if I had allowed myself to sway when I walked, and if I had worn loud colors and had spoken only Spanish." Marisol wishes her "gypsy mother ... with her wild beauty" would dress more like Jackie Kennedy.* →

become visible and tangible again. It was as if he were the chemical that made the invisible ink of their differences show up.

Ely felt her arm warm against Mara's arm and looked up to see her mother looking at her oddly. "Something wrong, Querida?" she asked in a concerned tone, as they waited for the red light on the corner of Market street.

As if she didn't know thought the girl. "No, just tired, I guess. And I can't wait to have some hot chocolate when we get home."

"Good idea. Except it coffee for me." They hopped over a puddle still holding on to each other, and both landed in slush up to their ankles.

"Carajo, again and again, maldita sea la nieve y los Estados Unidos de America."

Ely couldn't help laughing at her mother's traditional Spanish curse on the weather and the adopted homeland.

Finally Mara gave up trying to get the sticky snow from inside her boots and joined in Ely's escalation of a snow bank blocking the road.

The policewoman noticed their awkward giggling climb and yelled, "Hey! you're jaywalking."

Too late, by then they had slipped down to the sidewalk and disappeared into a grocery store.

"Spics, don't know nothin' about rules. Otta ship em monkeys back to the jungle they come from." And she wobbled over to her corner, a red faced woman in her fiftys, overweight and morose. The children all called her the Ironlady for a slap on a lagging behind crossing her corner could send a sturdy child through the Salvation Army wall.

As Ely followed her mother into the deli she felt again the sense of resentment at the man, she only called father aloud, for even disrupting their simple meals with his demands for special items when they had to eat canned spaghetti when his checks were late. But not tonight. Tonight they would eat imported ham. Baked slowly and served just right by

In The Line of the Sun, *Guzmán in Puerto Rico fantasizes about snow; for him it symbolizes the north's exotic promise. His niece Marisol, who has lived much of her life in New Jersey, however, describes the cold realities of slush: As soon as the snow "touched the dirty pavement it turned ← into a muddy soup."*

← Marisol's father escapes "the brunt of racial prejudice only because of his fair skin and his textbook English." But Marisol and her mother "were a different matter altogether."

the subservient Mara, who other times would have to be reminded by Ely that the water for the instant soup had been boiling for five minutes.

It was hateful the way they both would have to change their habits to conform to his.

She took the bag from Mara and they both plunged into the cold day for one more block to their apartment on Straight Street.

Ely took a deep breath and asked the question she had been putting off for days.

"Mara, how long is Lucas going to stay this time?"

She had always called her parents by their first name and only he objected, so to his face she called him formally, Father. But her mother was her best friend.

They had reached the street door to their third floor railroad flat. On the bottom floor there was a liquor store owned by the Morowski brothers, Polish W.W.ii refugees who had done well in Paterson. They owned the apartment building as well as two liquor stores. They did not normally rent to Puerto Ricans but had made an exception for Lucas' family.

When they were in the darkened lobby Mara made the announcement that she had too postponed.

"Ely I have to talk to you about this. In your father's last letter he said that he was home to stay this time, my love. He has gotten a medical discharge. Let's get indoors. It's freezing." She hurried up the stairs. But Ely did not move for several minutes. When she finally found the strength to lift her foot to the first step she felt as if someone were pouring molten lava into her skull which was hardening at her feet and making her heavy and tired.

Already at their apartment door Mara called loudly for her to hurry.

Marisol also resents the → disruptive intrusion of her father's visits. "We would prepare for his homecomings as if for a visiting dignitary."

FROM

Untitled

(circa 1971–72, age 19–20)

What happens to a man who finds himself totally displaced, in circumstancial exile from his country, surrounded by people who do not understand (and often deride) his values, his behavior, who sees no escape from his situation, on whose efforts several other people depend? He goes slowly mad, that's what happens. Not all at once, not violently, not even perceptively, except in the very last stages. It (insanity) creeps into his system gradually, like a viral organism, making its way into his bloodstream, polluting him in invisible ways until one day it matures and begins to multiply, eating up the healthy cells around it, surreptitiously taking over the functions of the system and replacing the host organs with lookalike tumors and the whole time the body is getting used to the little deaths within it, it is growing accostomed to dying and that is when the bile surfaces and becomes manifest in the form of schizophrenia or psychosis or any other fancy monster modern medicine has invented. Every age has called it something different "possession" "demon" it is all the same though, it is the dissolution of a personality due to pressures, to pain, to torture (physical or psychological) which are too intense for him to bear. In nature there is always an exchange taking place, nothing is given for free—in the case of some people—my father for instance—he traded his soul for a living.

The fitful decade of the sixties had passed for me in the cushioned, insence-sweet womb of a convent school. The nuns, like the negatives of angels in their black habits, had managed to protect the purity of our

◄ *In* Silent Dancing, *Cofer also describes the "cultural schizophrenia" that was "undoing many others around me." Her work often focuses on how people deal with displacement.*

The year 1971 marked the first time that the author wrote on a regular basis ➤ and saved her writing. Hence the spate of juvenilia from this year.

political convictions, if not always as successful with our bodies; and now, in the second semester of my first year away at college, in the glorious year 1971, I was free. Free to excersise my constitutional right to sleep till noon on a Saturday morning, if I so desired. And I so desired. I stretched in my narrow twin bed and inspected my dormitory room with satisfaction. A poster of the soul group, The Fifth Dimension was taped on the ceiling facing me. Two black men and two beautiful black women wearing huge smiles and waving down to me from a multi-colored hot-air balloon. "The Age of Aquarious." Directly in front of the bed was a bookcase with a ecclectic collection of reading materials ranging from the portable Marquis de Sade to a leather bound Bible (going away present from Sister Lucia Beata, in whose church history class I had excelled, as a by-product of my insatiable curiosity about corrupt popes). After leaving St. Elizabeth Seaton's Academy for Girls, I engaged in a debauchery of uncensored reading beginning with John Updike's *Couples* (a black market item at the Academy), passing through *The Valley of the Dolls*, on a continuing journey that would finally lead me through avenues of little light. My true destination, I discovered after working myself out of the maze my starved imagination had led me to, was literature.

Recalling her school days in Silent Dancing, *Cofer writes: "The nuns kept a hawk-eye on the length of the girls' skirts, which had to come to below the knee at a time when the mini-skirt was becoming the micro-skirt out in the streets." ➤*

 I would be an English teacher. Though I applied myself to my courses, my first year at college was an exploration of myself. When I chose the small college in a medium sized Georgia city, I had done it for unacademic reasons: I wanted to get away from New Jersey; I wanted to get away from the kind but smothering presence of my Mother; and, I did not want my teachers to be nuns and priests. All these objectives had been met and more.

Perhaps a moment of self-consciousness caused this shift from first person to third. ➤

 Upon my desk now sat a 8 by 10 glossy of the main reason I was staying in bed so late this morning: Charles Beaumont. I had gone out with him every night for the last three months, and their relationship was getting better all the time. He was a business major in his junior year, handsome, athletic, and a Methodist. It was the last item that would be difficult to take home to Mother. I wasn't too worried though, love conquers all, right?

Just last night we had made love for the first time at his apartment off campus. It was in an old house that had been broken up haphazardly into groups of rooms to rent to students. Charles and his roommate occupied the section of the house that had once been the sitting rooms, so that the walls were panelled, the ceilings were high and the windows went from ceiling to floor. Our favorite room was the sun room which faced the garden, now overgrown. There was a skylight, and on clear nights Charles and I would lie back in the ancient setee, and he would teach me the constellations. "Those three in a row are Orion's belt." He traced the next formation on my back. "And the one that looks like an M is Cassiopae." The astrology lessons kept us busy for hours. Last night it had rained, not one star could be seen though the thick layer of clouds, and it threatened to continue all night.

"Let's do it from memory," Charles suggested. "I'll trace the constellation on your back. And you tell me what it's called, O.K.?"

Well, I was a bit hesitant at first. Though I felt secure in my talent for storing information, this was a much more complex version of the game than all my reading had prepared me for. But Charles was delineating Ursa Major on my thigh before I realized that I had been preparing for this exersice all along.

Our lovemaking was tender and exciting, the rain and the room with its musty smell, and the windows with the ivy creeping and the man holding me were not what I had dreamed about during my years at the Academy surrounded by black and white, I had dreamed of a golden man and a guilded bed, but this would do. I was in love. Good morning sunshine. It is the dawning of the age of Aquarious.

◄ *In* The Line of the Sun, *Mamá Cielo banishes her son Guzmán, the good-hearted sinner, for marrying Sarita, the insufferable moralizer. Still, this union, is presented as a near-magical example of love's conquering all—almost! There, as here, the author is winking at her readers.*

Deep in the lassitude of my liquid love of the night before, I was not prepared for the harsh sound of the buzzer in my room. In the antiquated set-up of the dorm it meant I had either a phone call or a visitor waiting for me downstairs. I threw my covers off. Maybe it's Charles! Slipped into my jeans and a sweater, on the floor from last night, and ran down the hall. At the top of the stairs stood Mrs. Carpenter, the house mother. Strange. She never comes upstairs.

"It's long distance, Rose," Mrs. Carpenter said, heaving a little, out of breath. "Says it's an emergency." Mrs. Carpenter huffed behind me down the stairs. The black phone receiver was lying on the reception window counter like a dead bird. "Better hurry, it's long distance, you know," Mrs. Carpenter pointed out to me, unnecessarily. The old woman hovered behind me as I greeted my Mother. Mother came right to the point as usual.

"It's your Father," she said. Her usually thin high voice sounded strange, husky, as if she had been crying.

"Father? Isn't he supposed to be on his way to California?" I asked. Father had returned from his final tour of duty with the Army. He had spent 15 months in Viet Nam as part of the advising team of technicians left to train the native forces. He was due to retire in two years and that time was to be spent on some easy P.R. assignment; traveling around the country recruiting or something. Had there been an accident?

"Is something wrong, Ma? Where is Father?"

"He's in St. Alban's Hospital, Rose." I knew it, an accident. Father was a helicopter flight instructor. A crash. The very thing Mother had spent her life worrying about had finally happened.

"How bad is he?" Gruesome pictures of explosions and charred bodies flashed through my head. Poor Mother, she must have been histerical when she was told. And me having a good time down here. Funny she seemed so reluctant to speak.

Maybe she was still in shock.

"When did it happen, Ma?"

"Rose, what are you talking about?"

Oh, no, I thought. She's worse than hysterical. She's incoherent.

I decided to be gentle with her. Make the questions simple.

"I am talking about Father's accident, Ma. When did it happen, and how serious is it?"

"Rose," she said in that strange husky voice, "Your Father has not been in an accident, however his condition is very serious. I need you home right away."

Cancer. A heart attack. Why didn't she just tell me?

"What's wrong with him, Ma!" I shouted into the receiver, making Mrs. Carpenter drop a paperweight or something behind me.

Silence.

"Mother, please." I was irritated now. How dare she play nerve games with me over the phone.

"Rose, it's not easy to explain. Your Father is very sick. He has had a serious breakdown. You have to come home." Her voice was breaking down into that sob that had been strangling her.

"Ma, Ma, what kind of breakdown? It can't be that bad. He's probably just tired."

She was crying now. She sounded so far away.

"They called me from the hospital last week. He had been there a month. I had no idea. He hadn't written but he called as usual. Seems there had been trouble on the recruiting tour. Your Father got in a fist fight with a young man."

"A fight? Are you sure?" Father was such a by the book man, I couldn't picture him in a brawl.

"I don't know the details, Rose, all I know is that they want to issue him a medical discharge."

"That's crazy, Ma, a medical discharge because he got in a fight? Did he get hurt that bad?"

"The doctor I talked to was a psychiatrist, Rose."

"A psychiatrist, what the hell for?" Mrs. Carpenter was practically at my elbow now, pre-

← The author's father did die in a car accident about five years after this was written. The incident described here (and mentioned vaguely in the previous piece) refers to the mental health problems he began to suffer around this time, says Cofer.

tending to be checking the message board.

"They say....they say...." Mother. I wanted to be there to hold her. How bad can it be? Just exhaustion or something.

"Take it easy, Ma. Take your time."

"Schistzophrenia."

"Schistzophrenia?" I thought I had heard wrong. That's a word out of a psych 101 textbook.

"Are those people crazy?" As soon as I said it I realized how stupid I sounded, but there had to be some mistake.

This excerpt represents half of the first chapter of an unfinished work. ➤

"He tried to...kill himself, Rose." And in a strangled voice, "Please, please come home." [....]

Judith Ortiz Cofer

Pat Conroy, standing between numbers 22 and 24, on the Beaufort High 1961–62 basketball team. ("It's hard to tell that Southern schools were segregated back then, isn't it?") Randy Randel stands last on the right.

PAT CONROY

*P*at Conroy, who was born in 1945 in Atlanta, moved on average about once a year throughout his "ruined and magnificent childhood." After growing up under the thumb of his Marine Corps father, Conroy would later write out some of the emotional turmoil he'd been storing. Whether the subject was the appalling educational conditions on a South Carolina island where he once taught (recalled in his 1972 autobiographical account *The Water Is Wide*) or family tyranny (explored in his novels *The Great Santini*, 1976, and *The Prince of Tides*, 1986), Conroy could tap great reserves of passion.

The many readers of his books can recognize a recurring personality in Conroy's work: the playful smart aleck, the iconoclast struggling against malevolent authority, the "bona fide cracker boy" who has stretched beyond his limited horizons. Perhaps most central to that personality, and the side represented below, is the spirited poet yearning for expression.

In a recent letter, Conroy describes his poem "To Randy Randel," written while the author was a high school student in Beaufort, South Carolina. (The other poem included below—on the same subject—was the author's first attempt at verse.)

> I found this poem by accident in 1989 when I was visiting my high school English teacher, Eugene Norris. Gene is one of those life-changing figures in my life whom I still keep up with and try to thank at least once a year for the unimaginable generosity they showed me as a child. We were going through his collection of Beaufort High School yearbooks and came across the poem to Randy Randel.

Randy and I had sat beside each other in Mr. Norris's English class and had become good friends after playing football, basketball and baseball together and sharing a teenage joy in teasing Mr. Norris. Randy's father, Morgan, was the superintendent of schools and Randy used to tell Gene: "Treat me kindly, Norris. Give me high marks, or I'll have your job."

Randy was a splendid athlete who could throw a football seventy yards, had a beautiful touch on a jump shot, and who everyone thought would one day pitch in the Major Leagues.

Conroy goes on to describe the first baseball game of Beaufort High School's 1962 season, in which his friend, after striking out five of the first seven batters he faced, mysteriously collapsed and died "and changed the lives of all of us on that field forever."

"I like it very much that my first urging toward art came at a time when a friend died and my heart was broken and I wanted to drop a note to the world. This poem means a great deal to me and lets me know what kind of boy I must have been. I wish I'd been a better poet then….no, I don't."

In Memoriam To a Dear and Cherished Friend
(1962, age 16)

Conroy presented this poem to the Randel family shortly after Randy's funeral. It now hangs in their house, and the Randels have kindly sent a copy of it for inclusion here.

*T*all and limber as a tree in the wind
Sinews growing, and muscles to tend
Why did the Lord so mighty and strong
Pick Randy out of this plentiful throng?
The Lord released a snow-white dove
Go, go get Randy, the Randy I love
Bring this child to my judgement seat

I want to caress this young athlete
Tell his mother and father to wait
For they will meet again at the golden gate.

*In Memoriam
To a Dear And Cherished Friend*

Tall and limber as a tree in the wind
Sinews growing, and muscles to tend
Why did the Lord so mighty and strong
Pick Randy out of this plentiful throng?
The Lord released a snow~white dove
Go, go get Randy, the Randy I love
Bring this child to my judgement seat
I want to caress this young athlete
Tell his mother and father to wait
For they will meet again at the golden gate.

Pat Conroy
March 15, 1962

In The Water Is Wide, *Conroy's account of his year spent teaching impoverished kids on a coastal island, Conroy recalls Randy Randel's death. "I watched Mr. Randel as he looked into his son's face and felt his son's heart and held his son's hand," Conroy writes in that book. "And in that instant was born the terrible awareness that life eventually broke every man...."*

To Randy Randel

(1962, age 16)

I have ceased to wonder at the rapid flight of day.
The slice of birds and winters shout
Are but an effort meant to render nature praise.
Myself I wish to think about
A hundred friends who walk a pathless street alone
In search of lost and youth-grieved dreams.
Once a boy, fluid-limbed and not quite fully grown
Gave love to life and life it seems
Surfeited with the honey tooth of perfect joy
Yet darkness lit another place
Far off among the hills. So shadow wrapt the boy
In death and pressed his guiltless face
Into the flawless pages of eternal rhyme,
A snow fleeced lamb of earth and God bound child
    of Time.

The author notes the influence of Thomas Wolfe.

Pat Conroy

Michael Crichton at age 20 (in front of window), listening to Marianne Moore at Harvard.

MICHAEL CRICHTON

*M*ichael Crichton was an early achiever. At sixteen he managed to publish in *The New York Times* a travel article about his family vacation. To help put himself through Harvard Medical School, he cranked out thrillers published under the pseudonym John Lange. He also wrote an award-winning mystery, *A Case of Need* (1968), under the name Jeffery Hudson. (Part of Charles I's court, Hudson was a famous dwarf; the use of his name was in winking reference to Crichton's own towering height.) Still in med school, Crichton became a best-selling author at twenty-six with *The Andromeda Strain* (1969), published under his own name. He's increased his fame with subsequent thrillers—including *The Terminal Man* (1972) and *Jurassic Park* (1990)—that, like *The Andromeda Strain*, are written in a quasi-documentary style rife with scientific references and hi-tech graphics. In addition to directing a few movies (among them *Westworld*, 1973; *Coma*, 1978), Crichton has also written several nonfiction works including *Five Patients* (1970) and *Electronic Life* (1983), which demystify medicine and computers, respectively—two of his great interests—for the general reader. His most recent best-seller, the novel *Rising Sun* (1992), decries the Japanese invasion of American business and industry.

Though he completed medical school, Crichton decided not to go into practice, because, among other reasons, he says, his fantasy life was too strong. In his essay "Quitting Medicine" (*Travels*, 1988), Crichton explains that he used to listen to patients' stories for material for his fiction writing. "I was not behaving like a doctor that *I* would want to consult. So I thought I ought to quit."

Born in Chicago in 1942, Crichton says he wanted to be a writer from early childhood. His father, a journalist, was an influence, with his impressive bedtime stories and an ability to illustrate them on the spot. Crichton recalls, in *Travels*, a third-grade assignment to write a puppet show, for which he created a "nine-page epic.... My father said he'd never read anything so cliché-ridden in his life (which probably was true)," writes Crichton. "This hurt me and confirmed a pattern of conflict between us that persisted for many years."

The author himself is critical of these early samples of his work. "As you will see from the selection," he notes, "I have been unflinching."

Johnny at 8:30
(circa 1957, age 14)

*T*he bad guys had him, Johnny had to admit,
Trapped in a winecellar, black as a pit,
Outside were the villains, forty or more,
And the only thing keeping them out was that door.

The heroine, too, was trapped in the dim,
John had to protect her, no matter what happened to him,
Now they were breaking the door down and with a rattle,
John drew his sword, and prepared for the battle.

And now the door was splintered,
And the multitude poured through,
But John promptly skewered them,
And flicked them all askew.

The much relieved heroine let out a long sigh,
The villains were dead, and with a wave of goodbye,
John jumped on his horse and into the sunset so red—
Turned off the television set and went up to bed.

In The Terminal Man, *Crichton has Dr. Ross hear gunshots coming from Harry Benson's hospital room, shots that we soon learn are coming from the TV. This mild manipulation of reader expectations is a more subtle variation on the joke Crichton is playing with here.* ➤

Untitled

(1960, age 17)

"Well?"

"Well what?"

"Well, what did you find out?"

"Nothing."

"Really?"

"Not a thing."

"No kidding. That's a tough break."

"Yeah."

"You mean, you went to talk to him, and he still didn't say anything?"

"Yeah."

"Well, didn't you pry a little and try to find out what's going on?"

"Of course. That was why I went."

"And he wouldn't talk."

"Not a single word. And I was over there for nearly an hour. I couldn't stay any longer and have him figure out what was coming off."

"Yeah, that's true....Have you talked to the girl?"

"What girl?"

"Julie or whatever her name is."

"Oh—yeah, I did. Or, at least I tried to."

"She have anything to say?"

"Nothing much."

A silence.

"Looks like you got problems, kid."

"Hell! I just wish I knew."

"Nobody else talked to you about it at all?"

"Nope."

"In other words, you don't really know if it's true or not."

"Yeah, I guess so."

"Maybe he doesn't know anything about it either. Maybe that's why he didn't mention it. Was he friendly?"

During his high school years, Crichton wrote a lot on the side. "...I suppose it was really a form of self-therapy. I had tremendous energy; I was getting something out, though in retrospect I can't clearly see what. I do remember that I had a great interest in trying to be spare. Minimalism rearing its youthful head."

"Yeah, he was friendly. I mean, as friendly as he ever is. You know, like always."

"Did he give you any funny looks or stuff like that?"

"I don't know. He's always giving me funny looks. Ever since I've known him he's been giving me funny looks. He just kind of stops whatever he is doing and looks at me like he was trying to figure a math problem written on my forehead. You know that funny stare he has."

"No, I never met him."

"Oh. I thought you had someplace. Lots of guys know him—more than you think."

"Yeah, I know quite a few guys that met him, but I never have."

"Well, he has this real funny stare. And he's never completely serious anyhow. You can never tell whether he's serious or whether he's just kidding around."

"You scared?"

"I don't know. Would you be?"

"You mean if I were you?"

"Yeah."

"Probably."

"And what would you do, if you were me."

"Hell, I don't know. I don't have any idea. I mean, I never thought about it."

Crichton no longer remembers what this story is about. "For a long time, the most common criticism of my writing by teachers was that it was too unclear—or too subtle. (For better or worse, that is no longer a criticism that is made!)"

FROM

Life Goes to a Party
(1961, age 18)

*T*he party was noisy, red, loud and laughing, and despite himself, Mark enjoyed it. He stood leaning against a wall, off in one corner, and he watched. It was a typical Joan Gilbert party, with lots of room and lots of people and lots of little bits of food and cookies and rather heavily spiked punch. In a way, it was like all the Gilbert parties he had been to during high school, and in a way it was not. Now, everybody there was a freshman in college, back for their first Christmas, so it was a big sophisticated reunion, with all the guys smoking brand new pipes and all the girls trying hard to show that they had, in their own way, been equally enlightened.

Of course, nobody was paying any attention to the fact that five days earlier, Jerry Barnhill, who had been in their graduating class in high school, had been on the plane that had crashed over Brooklyn, splattering metal and skin all over the apartment houses. After all, he was buried now, so what the hell.

Not that he, Mark Heggerman, leaning against the wall with a glass of champagne punch which he had further fortified by a quiet trip to the Gilberts' bar, was thinking about Jerry Barnhill. Jerry Barnhill was not particularly any friend of his. Not at all.

From across the room he saw Joan Gilbert, weaving through the little knots of guests, stopping momentarily to talk and laugh with one or another of them. She was wearing a red dress, and she looked good in red, and she wasn't bad looking anyway. Mark smiled; it was good to see her again.

She returned the smile. "Well," she said. "I didn't see you come in. You must have been late. Are you going to stay late?"

Mark bowed. "Your wish," he said gravely, but it didn't turn out so well because he spilled part of his drink when he bowed. The liquid hit the wood floor noisily.

"Say," Joan said, laughing. "How many have you had?"

Mark felt confused. "I'm sorry," he said. "Where can I get a cloth to clean it up?"

"You can't. It doesn't make any difference any-

In Rising Sun, *Peter Smith doggedly investigates the death of Cheryl Austin, who is described by the business leader hosting a huge party one floor below the murder scene as "a woman of no* ◄ *importance."*

way. Just put that drink down and dance with me."

He did, and was surprised that they could slip so easily back into the old groove again together. She curled her hand up behind his neck the way she always did, and dropped her head on his shoulder, and it was all just as if they had never stopped.

"I'm glad you're back, Mark."

"I am, too." He was very aware of her soft hand on his neck. Without a doubt, there were certain disadvantages to going to a men's college. "How was college?"

"All right," she said. "You?"

"Okay."

"Have you talked to any of the kids? Everybody's here."

"A few," Mark said. "It's funny. I thought everybody would come back changed, but nobody is, really. Their clothes are just different or their hair is longer or shorter, but they aren't changed."

"I know. What do you think about Jerry Barnhill?"

"It's too bad," Mark said, and that was about all that there was to say, so he didn't say anything more, and she didn't say anything either, and they just went along until finally somebody took off the record or something; anyway, the music stopped. Joan drifted off, and Mark began to wander around the room.

To one side, he found a small knot of boys busy remembering all the high school football games and baseball games and track meets they had been in. In their midst was Tom Radasch, a tall stocky boy who had been the best athlete in their class. He was speaking as Mark came up.

"And you remember that time when we played Manhasset the second time, away? It was all tied up with thirty seconds to go and we had that big old last second jumper to squeak it out?" He waited for all the nodding heads and laughs of remembrance. "That was the greatest play of all. I got the old apple from half court and I was

Crichton at age 17, receiving a basketball award.

really shook but I popped it up and snap! It hits the old nets for two as the buzzer sounds." He shook his head, laughing. "What a game. That Emerson almost blocked it, too. Remember Emerson? That blonde kid from Manhasset, played forward? He was on the track team, too. He high jumped. You remember. He did five-nine that time we had a meet in the rain. He was pretty good. But we still won the old meet. That was the day I cleared twenty two feet in the broad jump, and the Goddam pit was a sandy puddle. What a day." There were more laughs and more talking; Mark drifted off.

Liz came up to him, out of no place in particular. She slapped him in the stomach, and it was a pretty hard slap. Mark was glad he wasn't carrying his drink.

"Hi, Liz. How's Bennington?"

"Great," she said, her long blonde hair swirling as she moved her head. Liz always had had beautiful hair, and she had always been proud of it and kept it long. "Just great. How have you been?"

"Fine."

"Did I tell you I'm glad you didn't go to Williams? I am. The kids at Williams are creeps. But I mean creeps. But I met this kid at a mixer, who is quitting at the end of the term, and he's great. Really cool. You should meet him. You would like him. The only thing is, he lives in Vermont."

Well, Liz hasn't changed, Mark thought. "How is your skiing?"

"Fabulous. Only it should be better. I wanted to go to Stowe this week but my parents wanted me to stay home. Sometimes they give me a hard time. You know parents. But I skied a weekend before I even came home, and it was really good."

"I guess you heard about Jerry."

"Barnhill? Yes, sure. Doesn't it just make you sick, Mark? I mean the whole thing. About dying in a crash and all. It's sickening, any way you look at it. He was so young, he never had a chance to find out what life is all about."

Mark didn't say anything. He wondered if Liz knew how ridiculous she sounded.

"The whole thing just makes me sick all over. It wouldn't be so great to die when you're all old and everything, but it makes me sick to think of dying so soon. And you know what else? Nobody even thinks about him. Nobody at all. He's just dead, so what the hell. Nobody thinks or remembers him. It's just like he never was. Like what Hemingway said in—"

"Oh, come on, Liz."

"But it's true. Nobody went to the funeral."

"Really? I heard there were a lot of people there."

"Oh sure. But not kids. Lots of old people and friends of Mr. Barnhill and of the family. People like that. But not many kids."

"Well, maybe they weren't back for their vacations yet. I wasn't."

"They were back. They just didn't bother to come. I think it's pretty rotten, too. The kids in our

Lauren, Peter Smith's ➤ ex-wife in Rising Sun, *has much in common with Liz. She, too, "had the privileged person's deep belief that whatever she happened to think was probably true.... she could be impassioned in expounding her beliefs," which were easily subject to change.*

Crichton's high school year-book offers the following pro-file: "Big Mike," "journalist," "Honor Society," "Latin Scholar," "basketball star," "that different laugh!" and "a verbose intellectual."

class are so rotten, Mark. Look at them now. Do you think they are paying any attention to the fact that Jerry's dead?"

"Yes," Mark said, looking around. "I've heard a lot of people talking about it."

"Oh, sure, talking. Just like they'd talk if the Russians had sent a man to hell. It's just a topic of conversation. But are they paying any attention, really?"

Mark sighed. "What do you want out of them, Liz?"

She frowned. "A little respect, that's all. Just a little respect. Just for a while. Just to be decent about it."

Mark didn't say anything, and Liz took another sip of her drink. "By the way, did I tell you I'm entered in the Sugar Slalom. It's at Mount Mansfield. Last year I finished eleventh. But this year I should do much better."

Mark would have said something, but Liz quickly excused herself and slipped away, into the central tangle of dancers. He turned around, and there was the ubiquitous, smiling Fred Adams.

He liked Freddy; back in high school Freddy had been the president of the student council and Mark had been the vice-president. They had worked diligently together for a long and conscientious year as the political leaders of their fair school. And now here was Freddy, his hand stuck out, with his best and most winning smile on. He was wearing a ROTC uniform.

← According to his high school yearbook, Crichton was "G.O. Veep." He was also named class writer (male) and among those "most likely to succeed."

"Hi, Fred," Mark said, taking the hand. "Good to see you. How's school?"

"Good, very good. Couldn't be better." He gave Mark what Mark thought must be Fred's most firm, confident and cordial handshake. "And you?"

"Fine. I see you're in Rotsy."

"Yes, yes," Freddy said, running his hands over his sides, feeling the buttons.

"And I see you're wearing your Rotsy uniform."

"Listen, I *like* this uniform," Freddy said positively. "I think it's sharp. I don't see what's wrong with wearing this uniform. Just because nobody else does doesn't mean it's wrong or something. I think it's a sharp uniform. Why shouldn't I wear it?"

"No reason at all. Free country."

"That's what I say. And our armed services are doing a great service to our country, and it ought to be more grateful. Lots of places, this uniform is a contemptible thing, and it shouldn't be. I think it's cool." He fingered the brass, casually.

Mark nodded, and said nothing.

"Listen," Fred said. "There's been a lot of talk about setting up a scholarship fund in memory of Jerry Barnhill. His family wants to do it, and some people called me up and thought that it would be, you know, nice if our class sort of started it off, since we were in his class and everything. So I'm going to go around to all the parties and see all last year's seniors. Think it's a good idea?"

"Sure."

"Then why don't you start off the contributions? Don't give anything too much so it will look funny. Just—well, you know."

Mark took a dollar out of his wallet and gave it to Freddy. Freddy didn't say a word, but reached into his own wallet and conspicuously took out a five and put it in his hand with Mark's one. He smiled. "Well, I'm off. Wish me luck."

"Good luck."

Mark felt like another drink, and he headed off toward the bar. On the way, he met Mr. Gilbert. Mr. Gilbert was really a pretty good guy, as far as parents went, and he had always been good to Mark all the time he had been taking Joan out.

"Mark my boy! Good to see you again. How's school?"

"Fine. How've things been for you?"

"Very good, as a matter of fact. Can't complain. They working you pretty hard up there?"

"Yes, pretty hard."

"Well, we've all heard that you're doing very well.

The author addresses difficulties he had with his own parents in Travels. *In* Jurassic Park *one of Crichton's characters makes an interesting connection between parents and dinosaurs: "children liked dinosaurs because these giant creatures personified the uncontrollable force of looming authority.... Fascinating and frightening, like parents."* ➤

Say, isn't that thing about the Barnhill boy awful?"

"Yes, it's a real shame."

"I never knew the boy—Jerry, wasn't it?—except by sight. Did you know him?"

"A little."

"Nice boy? Seemed like a nice boy."

"Yes," Mark said. "He was a good guy."

"Well, sooner or later they're going to have to do something about these Goddam airlines, that's all." He shook his head and clicked his tongue. "Well, I'll talk to you later, Mark."

"Right," Mark said, but he was already gone. [....]

In his most recent fiction, Crichton continues to condemn characters who shirk any responsibility for the state of the world. In Rising Sun, *a senator's handler explains how older American voters don't want to hear about ← conservation and its implications for the future. "They think their kids don't care about them, and they're right. So they don't care about their kids. It's that simple."*

The Most Important Part of the Lab

(1961, age 18)

I ate quickly and headed for the lab right after lunch. It was a clear, windy March afternoon, but not very cold. As I came up Mt. Auburn street, I saw that Elsie's was crammed with wonks, all standing around with their elbows high, munching. They stared out at me through the dirty glass, beneath the neon sign. I walked by quickly.

As I passed Elsie's, I heard someone trip on the brick sidewalk behind me, and then I heard a groan. I looked back without breaking stride, and saw someone lying there, stretched out on the ground. It was a guy, lying half on the pavement, half in the street, and he wasn't moving. I waited for a moment to see if someone nearer the guy would stop and help him, but nobody did, so I went back, and bent over him. People walked by me on both sides, their coats flapping in the wind. They gave me funny looks as they passed, as if I had done something to the guy.

← "I think that this is a first-rate piece of writing," Crichton's writing instructor notes in the margins. "The second half—the part in the lab—is just beautifully done. Why don't you send this off to the Advocate? *It may just not be their 'style,' but that's their problem. Try it, anyway.... I wish I could have read it to the class.... Maybe you ought to change the title. Curtail it, I guess."*

The fellow's eyes were shut; his forehead rested on the edge of the curb, and the skin was split slightly. He was bleeding, but not much. As the people walked by, I caught snatches of conversation over my head.

"...doesn't have any idea how to run a seminar..."

"I don't know why she said it..."

The guy was young, an undergraduate. Carefully, I shook him by the shoulder. I felt a little foolish, squatting there in the early afternoon at the corner of Mt. Auburn and Holyoke, shaking some guy lying on the ground.

"Yes, but is it *valid?*"

"...never knew he drank until I saw him sober..."

People kept looking back at me, but nobody stopped. At knee level, I watched them all hurry by. Somebody kicked my bookbag, but didn't even turn around to see what it was.

The guy didn't move, so I shook him a little harder. I didn't really know what to do. Once, I had taken a first aid course, but I had forgotten it all. I wished somebody would stop, but nobody did. Finally, I grabbed the coat of a professor-type as he went by, and asked him to find a cop. I told him this fellow was hurt. The professor gave me a funny look, and said he would try to find a cop, but he kept right on going and never once looked back.

It was about then that the fellow on the ground opened his eyes. He seemed dazed, and tried to sit up. I helped him. Then the crowd began to gather, and almost immediately a whole group of people was standing around, talking and flapping in the wind. They completely enclosed the two of us, him sitting, and me squatting beside him. A car came past us, and I helped the guy move back, so he wouldn't get hit. I gave him my handkerchief for his cut, which was bleeding more now.

He looked at me. "I'm all right," he said.

"What happened? I heard something, and looked around, and there you were. You've been out for a bit."

"I'm okay now."

Hammond, Jurassic Park's *loathsome magnate, delivers this business tip: "Personally, I would never help mankind."* ➤

"Are you sure?"

"Sure." He began to get up, but I held him down.

"Just wait a minute. Don't rush." I used to faint when I got shots when I was a kid, so I knew he shouldn't get up too soon.

But the guy was looking up at the crowd, towering over us. He seemed embarrassed, and tried to straighten his tie. "I've got to get going."

"Why don't you go over to the Health Center?"

"No, really, I'm all right now."

"You probably need stitches," I said. "And you still look pretty pale. What happened? Did you just pass out?"

"Really, I'm fine. I feel fine now. I'll just go eat lunch." He stood up, and so did I. The crowd moved back, murmuring to itself. No one said anything to either of us. I wished again that a cop would come and make the guy go to the Health Center. People don't just pass out in front of Elsie's for no reason.

I looked up toward the Square, hoping to see a cop coming down. There was none around that I could see. When I looked back, the guy was gone. I looked at the crowd, at all the faces, and finally said to some girl with black hair and big eyes, "Where did he go?" She looked at me like I was nuts, to be talking to a total stranger like her. I turned to a man with white hair. "Did you see that fellow that was here a minute ago? Where did he go?" The man shook his head and shrugged.

I looked around once again, and broke out of the crowd. I went around the corner to look down Mt. Auburn Street. He was nowhere in sight. I went back to the crowd, which was still standing in the same spot, talking quietly. Apparently, everyone had forgotten why they had gathered there in the first place.

I remembered my lab, and rummaged around all the legs looking for my bookbag. Above me, the people watched with detached interest. Finally I found it; a girl with wrinkled stockings

Crichton loves a medical mystery. In The Andromeda Strain, *he clearly enjoys having the scientists puzzle over what exactly has wiped out* ← *an entire Arizona town.*

← *"This section is slightly more feeble than the rest," suggests Crichton's teacher, referring to the next two paragraphs. "From here on in, it's fine."*

and fat ankles was standing on it like it was her pedestal. I tugged at it, but she didn't notice. I asked her to please move, interrupting a conversation she was having with some balding section man. Annoyed, she wordlessly got down off my bookbag. I headed for the lab. I looked back once, and the crowd was still there.

I arrived for the lab two minutes late, and Mr. Hopkins, the lab man, had already begun his little pre-lab talk. When I came in, he gave me his best withering look—he has several grades of them—and I tried to look contrite.

"I was just telling the class, Mr. Gordon, that when you cut down midsection, you must be very careful not to puncture the diaphragm. And you must work quickly. If you are lucky, you may still see the lungs in operation." He turned back to the rest of the class. "If you are not in time, you can still inflate the lungs by cutting through the trachea, inserting an eyedropper, and blowing air into the lungs. After you have observed the lungs, cut the diaphragm and expose the heart." His voice droned on. I opened the lab book and stopped paying attention to him. I noticed vaguely that we were dissecting rats, but my mind was on the guy on Holyoke Street. He really bothered me, and I couldn't help wondering what had happened to him.

An angry dinosaur pursues Grant around a laboratory in Jurassic Park, *until the scientist saves himself by injecting the encroaching beast with a syringe of toxin.* ➤

Finally, Hopkins stopped talking. He began to inject drugs into the rats, bringing the injected rats around to members of the class. With a sickening smile, he gave me mine first. "I thought you'd like to get an early start," he said. "Just let it run around; it'll collapse in a minute." He paused. "But you will, of course, want to record the effects of the narcotic." I took the rat by its thick tail, and set it down on the desk in front of me. It scurried about for a while; when it began to get away, I would drag it back by the tail. Soon, it began to stagger, and then it sagged, and lay panting on the desk top. Behind me, I could hear Hopkins explaining to some girl that the effects were similar to alcohol in humans. My rat just lay there, spread-eagled on its stomach, panting.

Hopkins finished handing out the rats, and came back to me. "I don't want to belabor this, Mr. Gordon, but you've been late for the last three labs. I'm sure the rest of the class would appreciate your being on time, and avoiding interruptions. It's not that much to ask, you know."

I decided then to explain the whole thing to him. I didn't really care about Hopkins' opinion, only his grade. That was why I told him. Hopkins listened without a word, wearing that flat, pleasant look which was his interpretation of scientific objectivity mixed with humanism. "Well," he said finally, "you've had an interesting day, haven't you?" He looked down at the rat. "I believe you can begin dissection now."

The rat had completely passed; its eyes were shut and its mouth was open. I picked it up carefully, feeling its disturbing warmth, and dropped it into the pan on its back. I pinned its paws down, stretching the fur across its stomach.

People around me had already begun cutting. One fat Cliffie was going at it passionately; her fingers and scissors were all bloody, and, as she bent over the animal, her chubby nose was pleated in reaction to the smell. I adjusted my glasses, stalling, but finally, when I caught another of Hopkins' looks, I had to start. I snipped the rat open, slowly. With each cut, I could feel the texture of the skin and fur.

I cut through the fur, then the muscle, exposing the insides. They were all red, and I drained away some of the blood. I was too late to see the lungs going, so I cut through the diaphragm and looked at the heart. It was small, but still beating. I examined it, but couldn't tell much. It was just a small pulsing spot of red stuff, not very interesting at all. You would have thought a living heart, any heart, would be interesting, but this one wasn't.

As a medical student, Crichton often met health care professionals who were a bit short on humanism. Like the resident in Travels who would yank at patients in their beds, shouting "No, no, not like that, just stay ◄ the way I had you!"

◄ The premed track at Harvard was "nasty and competitive," writes Crichton in Travels. In his Chem 20 lab, for example, other students would give misinformation "in the hope that you would make a mistake or, even better, start a fire," recalls the author (who started more lab fires that year than anyone else). "I thought that a humane profession like medicine ought to encourage other values in its candidates."

By now, the smell of rat-insides had pervaded the whole lab. Hopkins was gleeful, hopping from desk to desk, glancing from rat to student and back to rat, making infinitely helpful suggestions but never doing any of the work himself. Occasionally, he would stop to address the class as a whole. "Class, class, listen up, please. Cut away each organ and examine it as you go. And be sure to get the whole of the small intestine. You'll need it for the next lab. Work quickly; you mustn't waste your time." He chuckled. "Or the rat's."

All around me, bored students were cutting up their rats, slicing out organs, sticking them under microscopes, drawing pictures. The only interested people seemed to be the ones that enjoyed it. "I wish we didn't have to do rats," someone said. "Frogs are much nicer. I did a frog once in high school and it didn't smell at all."

"It's because they're mammals," explained a Cliffie. It was the one with the braces. "Closer to man and all."

"Hey," shouted a boy in the back. "Mine's pregnant!"

Everyone looked up, and Hopkins scampered over. "Class, I want you all to look at this," he said. "We'll put one of the embryos under the dissecting scope, and be sure you note the embryonic form, and the structures that are developed." He put something under the microscope. "Why, you can even see their little hearts beating," he announced. "Quite remarkable. Be sure you take a look at this."

I worked steadily, fighting my disgust. I had never dissected much of anything before, and I disliked the whole business. Personally, I would rather learn it from books. It seemed a great waste to kill 30 rats for as many students, just so they could cut them open and take a quick look. After all, you couldn't learn much. Aside from the actual experience, there was very little of value.

At the end, I cut out the small intestine, smelling the stink from the colon. I dropped the

Ian Malcolm, the ➤ mathematician in Jurassic Park, *faults scientific discovery as an "aggressive, penetrative act.... Discovery is always a rape of the natural world. Always."*

All of Tim's reading indicated that dinosaurs had a poor sense of smell—yet ➤ this seems to be contradicted by the velociraptor that is stalking him in Jurassic Park. *"Anyway, what did books know? Here was the real thing," Tim concludes.*

intestine into a test tube of preservative and put the remains of the rat into the trashcan. With relief, I washed my hands. Then, remembering the embryos, I went to the scope and drew a quick sketch. It was nearly transparent, with a large eye, and a curled body, mostly head. The limbs were just forming, the fingers still webbed. It was an amazing thing to see, but I felt a little sick, and I wanted to get out.

As I prepared to leave, Hopkins clutched at me. "I hope you remembered to save the small intestine. It's very important."

"Right here," I said, displaying the test tube. He looked disappointed.

"Good lad," he said.

As I left, the one slob who lives in Adams and always makes a mess of things was washing his hands, which were covered with blood, bits of fur, and pieces of innard. I walked out of the lab, and only then remembered the guy on the street again.

I walked home the same way I had come, down Holyoke Street, past the faces in Elsie's. There was no indication that anything had happened there earlier in the day. It was time for dinner, but I didn't feel like eating, so I decided to take a walk along the river. I went to the other side; the sun was setting, and it was getting windier. It was actually a little unpleasant, and I did not meet anyone I knew. I was glad. The day had left me depressed, and annoyed with people in general, though I couldn't say exactly why. And that, in itself, was annoying.

Crichton's characters often express irritation or annoyance. Harry Benson in The Terminal Man *is visited by a vague, disturbing feeling as one of the electrodes implanted in his brain is tested. "I can't describe it. It's like sandpaper.* ← *Irritating."*

Michael Crichton

I think that this is a first-rate piece of writing. The second half — the front to the back is just beautifully done. Why isn't it your send this off to the Advocate? It may just not be their "style," but that's their problem. Try it, anyway. It's just beautifully compact. I could have read it to the class.

THE MOST IMPORTANT PART OF THE LAB

Maybe you ought to change the title. Curtail it, I guess.

I ate quickly and headed for lab right after lunch. It was a clear, windy March afternoon, but not very cold. As I came up Mt. Auburn street, I saw that Elsie's was crammed with wonks, all standing around with their elbows high, munching. They stared out at me through the dirty glass, beneath the neon sign . I walked by quickly.

As I passed Elsie's, I heard someone trip on the brick sidewalk behind me, and then I heard a groan. I looked back without breaking stride, and saw someone lying there, stretched out on the ground. It was a guy, lying half on the pavement, half in the street, and he wasn't moving. I waited for a moment to see if someone nearer the guy would stop and help him, but nobody did, so I went back, and bent over him. People walked by me on both sides, their coats flapping in the wind. They gave me funny looks as they passed, as if I had done something to the guy.

The fellow's eyes were shut; his forehead rested on the edge of the curb, and the skin was split slightly. He was bleeding, but not much. As the people walked by, I caught snatches of conversation over my head.

"...doesn't have any idea how to run a seminar..."

"I don't know why she said it..."

The guy was young, an undergraduate. Carefully, I shook him

Michael Crichton

Stephen Dixon at age 19, hitchhiking in Europe. "A gentleman always traveled in his sports jacket," says the author. "Met a lovely Danish woman and she took the photo.... She was wild; I was reserved but adventurous. I wish I had hair like that now."

STEPHEN DIXON

Stephen Dixon is one of the most prolific American short story writers, with more than four hundred published to date. "He's as entertaining and powerful a producer in that genre as anybody we have around," says John Barth, Dixon's colleague at the Johns Hopkins Writing Seminars. "I rank him among the best of our American contemporaries." Dixon earned some overdue recognition when his 1991 novel *Frog*, described by *The New York Times* as "a crazy quilt" of interrelated tales, became a PEN/Faulkner and National Book Award finalist. His many other books include the story collections *No Relief* (1976) and *Time to Go* (1984) and the novels *Too Late* (1978) and *Garbage* (1988).

While often humorous, Dixon's fiction has a nightmarish cast. His characters seek control over chaotic environments: sometimes New York City (where he was born in 1936), sometimes the treacherous terrain of the obsessive mind. Dixon knows what we're afraid of—being knifed or robbed or heartbroken—and he plays on our strongest insecurities about alienation and survival. Put more simply, Dixon says he likes to write about "the worst things that happen and the worst things I can imagine happening."

His typical protagonist is a bedraggled fellow, chronically worried, and—like the boy Richard in *Knock Knock*, which follows—trying to secure some modest foothold in life. Richard's concerns in the following excerpt are hardly the traumas to be found in Dixon's later work, but they are examined with an intensity that foreshadows the author's trademark obsessive style. And Dixon's literary voice—bold, quirky, and immediately recognizable in his adult work—already is beginning here to speak.

Stephen P. Dixon
29 West 75 st.
New York 23, N.Y.
EN 2-3311

-1-   *[handwritten: 10 give day bounces over, press, pen shut]*

The screen door bounced shut. Richard looked up from his lettuce, tomato and cucumber sandwich at the final tapping of the door and then at his mother who walked quickly through the kitchen into the living room. She would be back in no time, he thought. A few minutes later she returned, her arms draped with his father's socks, his sister's undershorts and ~~UNDERSHIRTS~~ *[handwritten: UNDERSKIRTS]* and two wrinkled pillowcases. She stopped before Richard, told him he wouldn't be allowed outside until he finished his sandwich and milk, and then complained to herself *[handwritten: ABOUT]* what a bother it was washing so many clothes every Wednesday. She kicked open the screen door and walked outside into the yard, the door banging twice behind her, as if giving her a little push.

It was four years after the year the war began; August, hot, sunny, occasionally breezy, sometimes humid, but the screen door slamming twice against the wood frame made all the seasonal aspects of that day plain enough to Richard. The small crash of door against a splintery wood frame—a sound Richard could not produce by either sucking in or gargling his spit, or forcing out his breath between *[handwritten: his]* ~~his~~ sealed lips—meant that it was summer, people in summer clothes are going in or coming out of the house, or maybe just banging or kicking the door for no reason at all; or best of all, the wind was rattling against the door after someone had left the hinge unlocked, or left a shoe between the door and the frame so as to get a little more air than what usually seeped through the screen. That second or third bounce of the door—which

FROM

Knock Knock
(circa 1956, age 19)

*T*he screen door bounced once, twice, then shut. Richard looked up from his lettuce, tomato and cucumber sandwich at the final tapping of the door and then at his mother who walked quickly through the kitchen into the living room. She would be back in no time, he thought. A few minutes later she returned, her arms draped with his father's socks, his sister's undershorts and undershirts and two wrinkled pillowcases. She stopped before Richard, told him he wouldn't be allowed outside until he finished his sandwich and milk, and then complained to herself about what a bother it was washing so many clothes every Wednesday. She kicked open the screen door and walked outside into the yard, the door banging twice behind her, as if giving her a little push.

It was four years after the year the war began; August, hot, sunny, occasionally breezy, sometimes humid, but the screen door slamming twice against the wood frame made all the seasonal aspects of that day plain enough to Richard. The small crash of door against a splintery wood frame—a sound Richard could not produce by either sucking in or gargling his spit, or forcing out his breath between his sealed lips—meant that it was summer, people in summer clothes are going in or coming out of the house, or maybe just banging or kicking the door for no reason at all; or best of all, the wind was rattling against the door after someone had left the hinge unlocked, or left a shoe between the door and the frame so as to get a little more air than what usually seeped through the screen. That second or third bounce of the door—which automatically swung shut by a faulty spring—sounded more like summer to Richard than anything

Dixon is known for deliberately winding, awkward sentences that bounce with neurotic rhythms and convey his characters' ◄ insistent thoughts.

else. The sound could have meant about everything that summer was; from cool morning swims, swimming trunks, and the chafing from those two; to midafternoon breezes, the inflated Wednesday washes, and his mother's shrill voice calling him in for lunch almost every noontime, and just a half hour ago.

He bit into the middle of the cucumber, spitting the seeds on his plate; they were indigestible and nobody could tell him otherwise. The rest of the cucumber was bitter, although still tasty, and he felt he was getting used to the vegetable, since he had never really tasted it before this summer. Actually, he had never wanted to taste a cucumber because he thought the seeds would get stuck in his small throat, which still had its tonsils, and he'd choke, cough, vomit, and eventually die, his face numb and blue. He used to eat pickles, seeds and all, until he heard they came from cucumbers. He had considered the pickle to be at most, only a strange vegetable, until his father explained the process to him. He remembered that he just shrugged his shoulders then, shook his head knowingly, said something like, "Yeah" or "Yes, Sir," and walked out of their city dining room not believing a word his father had told him, but leaving behind an unchewed pickle on his plate. He thought his father was smart, but what he said just couldn't be. Although both the pickle and cucumber were green, long, pimply; one was bitter and the other sour, and they smelled differently; and one he plucked out of a fat barrel, while the other his mother weighed and bought in a vegetable store; so they really couldn't be one and the same. But a few months later, after someone had repeated his father's story about the process of mixing cucumbers and dillseeds together in large vats, he changed his mind and right then and there swore off pickles forever because he found only a few soggy seeds to spit out.

The screen door slammed again. His mother stood before him, her hands filled with neatly folded dry colored clothes. Without looking up, he bit sheepishly into a large piece of crust pushed to one side of the

The constant threat of danger in daily life pervades Dixon's adult work. ➤

Even as young as eight, Dixon would argue with his father over various ethical and moral issues. "Part of me believed him because he was my father, but part of me fought against it." ➤

plate; and his mother walked away. A minute later, the half-filled glass of milk at his lips and his mother's sad reminder that European children his age would go without a night's sleep to get a cup of milk still ringing in his ears from the morning breakfast, his mother returned, her arms laden with crumpled damp sheets, and walked out of the kitchen to hang the linens on three strips of gray rope. The door slammed loudly; he looked up; it bounced again, softly. This time the slamming made Richard think of nothing else but finishing off the sandwich and milk before his mother came marching through the kitchen with another load of wash. He stared at the milk and wished he had a spoonful of Hershey syrup and a straw to help him down the glass in one easy spurt. He sipped at the milk-stained glass, leaving a small semicircular imprint of his lips on the smoky-white rim.

Richard, pausing to stretch the tight swimming trunks which clung to his crotch, took his hand out of his trunks to wave to Mrs. Silver and Mrs. Long, who also lived at Goldman's Bungalow Colony for the summer. The two ladies turned, said, Hello, Richard, simultaneously, and resumed their chattering as they walked down the main road that led to the colony's recreation hall, ice cream parlor, grocery store, synagogue, and lake, and which separated most of the colony's odd and even numbered bungalows. Richard resumed his scratching and pulling, before making a temporary adjustment. Then he ran down the road past the women, who barely noticed him, and stopped to kick a rock down a shortcut which also led to Goldman's Lake. He waved to the ladies, who perfunctorily raised their arms an inch or two, and then took the shortcut himself.

Richard was heading for a good, long swim, sunning on the raft so as to make his body browner than his sister's, and some more talk with his summer buddies on just about everything. Two days before their conversation had become very interesting. One of the boys asked a few of them who were sitting on the raft

In his mature work, ➤
*Dixon's dialogue is even
more stylized and, as it does
here, blends into the voice of
the surrounding prose. A
typical line (from* Garbage*):
"'I don't understand you
but do that you don't want
to talk about it, so okay.'"*

*Dixon would later take the
idea of a craving for milk to
ludicrously funny extremes.
In "Milk Is Very Good* ➤
*for You" (1976), Rick
Richardson's children clamor
for more and more of this liquid symbol of clean living,
continually interrupting his
own gluttonous sex orgy.*

Despite their arguments, ➤
*Dixon appreciated his
father's warmth, humor,
and severe work ethic—and
longed for his approval. "I
really wanted him to be
proud of me."*

what they thought was the most fun. One immediately said: Just this, sunning, sitting on the raft, or swimming, and another said: Dances, eating, I guess, and then consecutively and sometimes together, they mentioned: reading, comic books, Hardy Boys' adventures, bingo games every Tuesday night at the recreation hall, stealing warm bottles of soda from the grocery store and sneaking into the woods to open the caps with their bare teeth, or, riding into town for a movie, a good one. Richard had said that these were all good, especially swimming, and maybe one was better than the other, but he thought that sitting down with the folks and his younger sister, Harriet, and just eating all the food he wanted to and drinking all the milk if he wanted to, maybe that was the best.

—Best my eye, one boy said. Sitting at the dinner table with your folks ain't fun, the others chorused.

Richard thought they may be right, after all, they all thought the same thing. But that evening his father had told one of his rare, funny jokes. Richard laughed himself silly when his father started laughing and winking at Richard, indicating that he approved of his son's sense of humor. Soon his mother was laughing and Harriet, though she could hardly understand, nearly choked on a piece of meat she laughed so hard; all proving it was a good joke. Richard thought that his friends would really mock him if he showed up on the raft the following day with proof that eating with the family was definitely the most fun. Feeling they were indispensable for a good summer, he decided to keep his mouth shut. When they asked him the following day, he said: Sunning on the raft, sort of doing nothing exactly. That's the most fun.

They shook their heads agreeingly. One of the fellows said I told you so. Another boy challenged this fellow's right to take full credit.

—But yesterday I said it. You know I did.

—I know nothing. We all said it one time or another. Richard now also.

That evening, Richard had told his father how he

had to bow to his friends' wishes. His father said that Richard was only playing both ends of the candle, something like that. Richard didn't understand. His father explained: To light, to light both ends of a candle means that you can enjoy yourself at home and say that's the best and enjoy yourself with your friends and think that's the best. Sort of like a diplomat. He understood everything except what Diplomat meant. His father explained again: like lighting both ends of a candle.

Richard shook his head knowingly.

—It's all very simple when someone tells it to me very slowly, he had told his father then.

Richard ran through the thick brush, his towel over his shoulder and his polo shirt wrapped around his waist. On flat ground again, he made two leaps over a large rock and a long piece of wood, and landed in the sand. He threw off the towel and shirt and ran into the water, walked out as far as he could stand without swallowing some, and swam the rest of the way to the raft.

Later, after an hour of sun bathing which made his body feel extremely warm and at least another shade darker than when he first approached the beach, his friend, Hank, asked him, what he wanted to be when he gets much older, "today, that is." This gave them the right to change their minds tomorrow, even though they made their decision after much silence and deliberation.

With a broad grin, he lifted his chest a foot off the raft, took a deep breath, scratched his chin and with the most commanding voice he could muster up, said: Diplomat.

—That's nice, Hank said. A minute later, his head flat on the raft, his eyes closed and body still, he asked: What's a diplomat?

This was expected. It took Richard about five minutes to explain what a diplomat is, what he does, the exciting life, the things he got into and got out of, and that they sort of play both fields, his country's and the country he lives in then.

These dialogue dashes were inspired by the European books Dixon was reading at the time.

—Like lighting both ends of a candle sort of, Hank said.

"—Sort of." To himself, he admitted that Hank was much more suited to be a diplomat than he, the way he picked up the meaning.

—Well, I can't think of a better job than that, Hank said. But you got to be smart, that's for sure.

He nodded that that's what you had to be. Hank nodded also. Then both of them jumped in the water, swam back and forth to the children's swimming pen, tried to dunk each other's heads underwater, and, panting, climbed on the raft. Hank, lying on his back and directly facing the sun, soon fell asleep. Richard lay awake on his stomach toasting his pale back and peering through the raft's slats at the strange designs being made in the dark water.

Turning off the main road and up the path leading to his family's rented white bungalow, he heard a great deal of noise and saw his father waving his hands to someone on the porch. Richard ran to see what was the matter. Mr. Roth, Richard's father, was trying to quiet two excited neighbors, from bungalow 28, [and] stood at the foot of the stairs leading to the porch, which led into a small dining area. His father told him to be quiet before Richard could even open his mouth. He tugged at his father's arm to know why Lou, who was Mr. Goldman's son and a college editor who hung around Mr. Roth because he was a living example of an ex-newspaper man, was standing on the porch so strangely.

—Lou broke a hornet's nest for us and now they're flocking around him on the porch. If he doesn't make a move they'll go away.

He knew of no greater terror than hornets who had their nests burned or busted with a broom. He stood on the first step staring at Lou who was standing as straight as can be, a few hornets circling him. He waved at Lou. Lou's eyes, following the flight of the hornets, noticed Richard when a hornet flew towards his direction. His eyes blinked hello, and a slight smile quickly came and went, something Richard never expected.

—Stand still, dad says, he said.

Lou smiled again. This he couldn't believe. His mother and her friend, Mrs. Simpson, gaped panic stricken through the screen of the window overlooking the porch. He tried to signal them but they only looked at Lou. He jumped off the step when a hornet got too close and stood a few yards away from the stairs for more than fifteen minutes before the hornets hummed away. After it was over, his father had shook Lou's hands and said how he really had sweated out that one with him. Richard looked up at Lou and said: How you could of smiled I don't know. There were hornets all over.

—I know, I was there, remember, Lou said, combing his hair.

—I would have run.

—They would have caught you.

He looked at his small, undeveloped legs. They might have at that, although it would have been a good race. Had it been a long-distance race, tho, he would have killed them. He looked at Lou's longer, much stronger legs sticking out of his basketball shorts. But not you, he said.

—They'd increase their speed for me, kid, but they'd get me, believe it.

It was something he couldn't believe right away. A small kid like himself was something he could understand but the person the size of Lou, who had lots of breath and long, muscular legs, this was something else. Something with a motor maybe could outrun Lou, because he had seen him scoot around bases faster than anyone he had ever seen, and jump from one corner of the tennis court to the other corner in almost one leap. And, he thought, his own future looked pretty bad if Lou was right. He didn't like the idea of having to stand still, his hands at his sides, praying, sort of—that way—to get rid of a hornet or a bee. He would rather have had his intelligence in his legs.

◄ *Dixon still prefers passive characters confronted with active situations, as opposed to take-charge characters, whom he associates with "old-fashioned fiction.... We're more reactive than active," says Dixon, who likes to push his protagonists to their limits.*

Later, it was his job to sweep the broken hornet's nest into the ash can. He took the broom, Lou's weapon, and smashed it down repeatedly on the nest. It soon looked like hay. He aimed the broom at a couple of small shreds and, imagining it was one whole threatening nest and he was under attack, brought down the broom with all his force. He swept the pieces, some the size of filings, into the pan, and dumped it in the ash can.

The slamming of screen doors many times by many people almost always made his father's blood boil. With your aunt Louise, and Bertha and now your sister, Bessie, his father would yell at his mother, why, this place is just swamped with visitors. Then he heard his father say something that he had been saying every summer for the last four years: This is the last time I'm renting this place for your relatives, you know. His mother countered by rattling off names of his sisters, a brother and a few cronies who had spent many summer evenings with them. This happened at least twice every summer. Tonight, aunt Bessie showed up. She had called up that afternoon and said she just had to get away from the stifling city and she wondered if they'd mind if she stayed with them a few days.

—Like that, she talks, his father said, imitating Aunt Bessie. Then he did what he had always done when he was mad; he took out his pipe, hastily pressed a wad of tobacco in the bowl, and smoked up a storm.

If for no other reason at all, Richard enjoyed Aunt Bertha's occasional summer visits because she usually surprised him with a present. This time she at first surprised them all by showing up two hours earlier than they expected, tapping repeatedly on the screen door and rubbing her palm over the screen, like someone rubbing a stick over a washing board.

Aunt Bessie appar- → ently has merged with Aunt Bertha into one composite aunt.

—Hello, she yelled out. Everybody looked up; and his father, particularly irritated by the grating sound, shook his head with his hands frozen-clapped over his ears. Then they all kissed. Aunt Bertha, still smiling, looked at Richard and, snapping her fingers as if she had just remembered something very important, brought out from her traveling case a box of something solid wrapped in white paper and tied neatly with a pink ribbon.

—For you, Richard, she said, and then giving it to his mother, said: It's chocalate candy, and your mother's the best judge of that. She put her hands out, but he hesitated, so she approached him confidently and smacked his cheek with her large, wet lips.

—Now Bertha, his mother said. I don't know what you mean by saying I'm the best judge. I mean, you, too, Bertha. Aunt Bertha tried to say what she meant—but Mrs. Roth broke in and said, Oh, I know what you mean, you know, but that gift will be sorrowful temptation for the judge. In fact, I'd call it a bribe, but let it go at that.

Aunt Bertha laughed; laughed almost continuously after that and made a lot of noise and gestures doing it. Richard didn't laugh. He said, Thank you, after his father told him to say, Thank you, and wiped his cheek again after Aunt Bertha had planted another wet kiss on him and said, You're welcome, little nephew. Everybody laughed when he wiped his cheeks hard to make them dry and not smell of spit. He didn't like Aunt Bertha telling him what was in the box before he opened it nor depriving him of the gift [...] giving it to his mother who had already ended up with a pair of black gloves and who liked candy a great deal. His father got a tin of pipe tobacco and Harriet got a doll's dress, which was the easiest and fastest way to please them both, and make them forget temporarily about everything else.

Richard asked for the white wrapping paper and the fancy pink bow. The paper, which had Loft's Fine Chocalates written all over it, was folded conscientiously to the size of an index card and with the ribbon stuffed into his back pocket. Later, he would put the ribbon around the bedpost, allowing the bow to hang just a little, and fold a boat out of the paper, the one heavy sail flying the colors of Loft's Chocalates. Mrs. Roth broke into Richard's thoughts by offering one candy from the box, he having the first pick

*Abandonment, crime, →
illness, and death are rife
in Dixon's adult fiction.
"Pleasant events don't make
for good fiction," he says.
"The tougher, traumatic
things stick out, just like
they do in life."*

because they were really "all" his, then he should pass
the box around to the rest of them, saying all the time
that these were certainly the best candies made.

At the dinner table that evening, Aunt Bertha
talked a blue streak about disease, sickness, death and
dying. Many times during the meal Richard's stomach
seemed to curl up. He tried not to listen but she went
on, talking louder than anyone else who had ever sat
at their table, and he remembered that as long as he
could picture Aunt Bertha sitting at their table, she
had always talked about the same sad things, and
always in the same manner. His father made slurping
noises with his chicken soup which only made him
more irritable. At times he couldn't swallow. His
mother asked him what was bothering him but he
knew it would be impolite if he told her—his parents
had warned him about that before—so he said he was
resting a minute between spoonfuls.

—Just horrible, horrible, Aunt Bertha said.

—How young a man is he? His mother asked.

—Don't you know?

—It was a long time ago.

Aunt Bertha was talking about a man he had
never heard of; someone who was supposed to be
what Aunt Bertha called: A sceighty-eighth cousin of
his mother. She said he was suddenly stricken with
what is certainly a mortal disease.

—Has he seen another doctor? Mrs. Roth said.

—Doctors? Doctors? What are they going to do
for him, Aunt Bertha said. She tilted the soup plate,
and with her large spoon scooped up the remaining
drops and rice and strings of chicken. Soup's delicious, dear, she said.

—Just how mortal a disease is it? His mother asked.

—A few months, the most, I believe.

—Awful, awful, his mother said, very sadly.

—Out of nowhere; like that, Aunt Bertha said,
snapping her fingers. Just awful, awful, his mother
said again.

Richard said he couldn't finish the soup, and was
it all right?

His mother didn't answer, but only collected all the soup plates, his on top because it still was half-filled. She returned from the kitchen with Harriet behind her, the two of them carrying the vegetables, meat and two glasses of milk on large trays.

—Dig in, Bertha, Mrs. Roth said.

Bertha dug in. They all did, but Richard swallowed very little. The minute Aunt Bertha started all over again about death and dying he knew he probably won't be able to eat anything but didn't know how to explain skipping out of the main course.

—The nicest children you've ever seen. Really, Aunt Bertha said. I'm just surprised you haven't been in touch with them these past few years.

His mother tried to explain.

—One of the girls is a perfect beauty, Aunt Bertha went on. A beauty. Fourteen years old and with long legs like a dancer. She takes lessons and will be somebody.

Mrs. Roth smacked her lips appreciatively, bit into a hard roll, and drank a full glass of ice water without stopping. Richard tried to down his milk but finished less than half of it.

—I tell you she'll be something when she gets older.

—How are they financially, his father said.

—Not too good. Something like this comes on and where do you think the money goes. I ask you. A live-for-today and die-tomorrow type if you ever saw one.

Richard would have liked to have known what the last phrase meant. Live-for-today and die-tomorrow kind of fellow. He picked his head up to ask but everybody seemed to be deeply concerned with their roast chickens. When he looked up again, the same question on his lips, they had their forks in the salad, and mash potatoes and asparagus.

—Why aren't you eating, Richard? his mother said.

Richard lifted his fork and stuck it in the potatoes and then in the asparagus. This was usually enough time for his mother to stop thinking about his eating habits and worry about somebody elses.

← *"Every day is Labor Day," his father would say, and indeed Stephen Dixon began working at the age of 10. "I did what he did. I didn't want an allowance. I had this example of my father working forty hours a week...while going to dental school."*

—Harriet? she said. Harriet wiped her greasy fingers on her napkin and began tearing a slippery leg apart.

—Wonder what kind of insurance he has, his mother said. If it covers everything?

—No insurance covers everything, Aunt Bertha said.

"It's a rotten disease," his mother said. "I mean, you'd think they'd know more about it wouldn't you?"

"You'd be surprised how much they say they know and how much they really don't. Guess work, sometimes, really."

"Are you joking?" Mrs. Roth said.

"I'm telling you, Dearie," Aunt Bertha shot back.

"And there are many things they should know about too—lots of things, just as important—discoveries that should have been discovered long ago."

"You'd think so," Aunt Bertha said, while, with her finger she pushed an asparagus tip on a quarter-slice of soggy rye bread.

Then, for a minute, they passed between them such words as: pity, horrid, a damn shame, the horror of it all, and other handy descriptive references to the fate of medicine and their second cousin, before Mr. Roth pleaded with them to change the subject. Aunt Bertha and Mrs. Roth dug immediately into their chicken wing and drumstick respectively before them, tearing off first the skin and then the meat from the bones. [....]

This excerpt represents the first 14 manuscript pages from the novel. ➤

Stephen Dixon

Rita Dove at about age 10.

RITA DOVE

*M*any years before her book *Thomas and Beulah* won the 1987
Pulitzer Prize for poetry and before she was named—in May 1993—to be
the nation's poet laureate, Rita Dove was practicing her art by composing a
small verse about a rabbit. "I remember writing 'The Rabbit with the
Droopy Ear' during a free-choice period in school; it was near Easter, of
course," she recalls. "I was particularly proud of the twist at the end of the
poem, especially since I began writing with no idea whatsoever of how the
rabbit was going to solve his dilemma."

In her first published novel, *Through the Ivory Gate* (1992), Dove
explores childhood creativity. Focusing on a young woman's quest to fulfill
her artistic aspirations, *Through the Ivory Gate* is also about coming to terms
with youth's confusion and pain. Its protagonist, Virginia King, is a visiting
artist-in-the-schools, who is drawn into her students' lives as she strives to
inspire their imaginations through puppetry.

Dove, who was born in 1952 in Akron, Ohio, found her own imagination stimulated in grade school, as the excerpts below from the wonderfully convoluted *Chaos* demonstrate. Written when the author was ten, this
twenty-eight-chapter novel was Dove's solution to a vocabulary-building
classroom assignment. She explains further:

"*Chaos* was written over the period of one semester. Our fourth-grade
teacher allotted approximately twenty-five minutes each Monday afternoon for spelling: we were to acquaint ourselves with the new spelling list

and do the exercises in our text. I would quickly finish the exercises, then write the next chapter of my epic science-fiction saga. The only rules were: (1) each spelling word had to be used in the form presented, (2) the order of the list must be honored, and (3) no peeking at the next week's list. Needless to say, I had no idea what developments in plot or character were going to occur—language was the gondolier, and I was open to adventure."

The author has re-created ➤
this poem from memory.

The Rabbit with the Droopy Ear
(circa 1962, age 10)

Mr. Rabbit was big and brown,
But he always wore a frown.
He was sad, even though Spring was here,
Because he had one droopy ear.

They were the handsomest ears in town;
'Cept one went up, and one hung down.
And to think Easter was almost here!
Alas for the rabbit with the droopy ear.

The Rabbit went to wise old owl,
And told his tale 'twixt whine and howl.
The owl just leaned closer to hear
And said, "I know the cure for your droopy ear."

In Through the Ivory
Gate, *Virginia recalls the*
childhood desire to fit in.
She "knew that gaze well—
a child staring into the mir-
ror wondering if she were a
freak, gawking at her own
eyes staring back." ➤

The next day everyone gathered 'round to see
The incident at the old oak tree.
Mr. Rabbit hung upside down
From a branch on the tree, and gone was his frown.

Hip, hip hooray—let's toast him a cup,
For now both ears were hanging *up!*
All the animals raised a cheer:
Hooray for the rabbit with the two *straight* ears!

FROM

Chaos

(circa 1962, age 10)

Chapter II.

*T*he robots had to tackle and tickle the man to make him stumble. The man began to struggle, for he was to smuggle eggs out of the country. As he began to scramble, the eggs became scrambled. It was a horrible sight. The robot was very noble about it, and made it into an article in the Robital Daily. It took up a single column. The robot offered the man a half dollar for an advertisement for a buckle. This was used as an angle. The advertisement was in a triangular shape.

Chapter V.

"The total of 5 and 5 is ten," said the robot student. He was a major in the human brain. He thought, "I will betray myself," for he was a pilot on duty. The mission was beyond and beneath his belief. He smelled bacon, and the odor gave him a fever. Suddenly he felt evil, and could not digest his desire, crazy and severe as it was, to erase the word "unite" on his paper. But all this is past, and we passed on.

Chapter VII.

It was a gloomy and weary day. The rain was steady and dreary. The robot had a fancy that he heard a stingy but dainty lady, but it was too foggy to see the greedy maid. She was a hearty woman, and she promised to identify any envy in a person. But just then, the levy broke, washing several houses away. The lady said, "Now we can modify this neighborhood and the houses will occupy less space. Let's

◄ The author has selected eleven complete chapters for inclusion here. Chapter one, she says, does not contain any information useful to understanding those that follow.

The reader may confidently deduce that similar words in close proximity to one another came from the ◄ spelling lessons' lists.

In Through the Ivory Gate, teenage Virginia discovers the down side to a superior vocabulary when she scares off one potential boyfriend unfamiliar with the word exempt. "It sounds like a very useful word,'" he says, after her self-conscious explanation. "'Thank you for the lesson.'"

notify the architects and have them apply for the jobs." The robot thought his actions were justified. He said, "Isn't this weather nice?" She laughed and walked into the fog. Whether she heard him or not, no one knows.

Chapter VIII.

"The cat is in the pantry!" she cried. The robot answered, "Don't give him any mercy!" Then, on second thought, he added, "Sign a treaty with him and maybe you shall have the victory." He was playing with a battery, while saying, "Honesty is the best Policy." He had a salary to watch over the women, and he had a theory that if he made an inquiry as to what variety of oil he had, she would say "Petroleum." He hated petroleum. It was a mystery, since her amount of property got her in high society. The majority of her clan grabbed at opportunity and a dull personality. It's the quality, not the quantity; the ability, not the activity. As a principal once said, "It's the principle of the thing, not the outcome."

"How could someone mix up the animal deer *with the salutation* dear?" *wonders Virginia over a suitor's poorly spelled love note in* Through the Ivory Gate. *"Children memorized that rule in third grade."* ➤

Chapter IX.

The rocket ship named *Vanish* was receiving a second coat of varnish. A robot had to punish a boy who had gone to publish the news about the ship. The boy had to furnish enough guns to astonish the people. Another robot went to establish a launching pad, and accomplished it. When the rocket began to operate, the people began to debate as to whether a graduate should ride. One robot made an estimate and decided to cultivate a garden, investigate it to find the astronaut, and congratulate him. He began to organize a searching party, and realized he would have to civilize the members before they could recognize a man. When asked how to choose an astronaut, he said, "I did the choosing, and I chose a man who was the best to be chosen."

Chapter X.

It is legal to get a mental case and make him the

country's ideal. Seymour, the robot, thought it natural to create a Paris original and to be loyal to it. He was the local doctor, he gave all physical tests, and was practical about it. He made an electrical maid who was very dismal. She turned into a criminal and looked comical. The actual maid was official. There was a similar case to this, which is very peculiar. A very popular man saw a face familiar to his. He has been more particular than his twin since then.

Chapter XIV.

The lawyer made an action against the robot who took a portion of a pie, not to mention a position in the air force. The solution seemed to be to find the location of this robot so keen on aviation. The situation had a solid foundation and an operation had to be performed by a doctor of that occupation (aviation), to solve it. The doctor's imagination was great, and his idea of civilization was a sort of organization. He had a mansion and was on a mis-

Rita Dove at right (about age 10), with siblings Ray and Robin.

sion. He has a pension and hated religion. His opinion of fashion was "stupid!" He liked to write but wasn't a writer. When he puts his words in writing, wise ones are written.

Chapter XXIII.

The robot made a wreck out of the wreath when he began to wrestle with a sword. He bumped against a door knob, and knit his brows in concentration. He used his knowledge to judge whether he should go to the lodge that night. His mind was filled with doubt, and he realized he was in debt. But the robot was calm, and began to study his palm, from which a corn stalk had grown. He had salmon for supper and a cake prepared from scratch. Then, with a sign, he arose and began to design a type of freight train, used to carry foreign goods. As he read a newspaper column on the subject, he thought, "I plan to have planned this train by tomorrow, so I better start planning."

Chapter XXIV.

With a rope around his waist, Seymour the robot began to sow the ground on his farm. He wished for a soul, but kept tight reins on Knight, the old plow horse who was born on a pier while his mother waited for a ferry boat. He felt like he was dying, but of course he wasn't due for his annual oil checks. Seymour also wished for laws, and he worshipped a straw idol. The border of his farm and his sneaky neighbor, Malkolk, was a river with big mouth bass in it. Malkolk had found a vein of gold near the river, the color of an egg yolk. With the money he decided to marry a robot who was a bore. He was halfway up the aisle when a colonel rushed in with a council behind him. He said, "I will try to tell you, but I need many tries." What he had tried to say was that the gold was Seymour's, and he had been trying to stop the wedding.

Chapter XXVI.

A robot college student was to diagram the principles of democracy for a biography of a man interested in photographs. This was his project for his senior year. He also wrote a paragraph about an amphibian he had seen through a telescope. When he sent the beast a telegram written by a stenographer, the beast looked at it under a microscope and said there was a germ on it. The thermometer read 100°, and the beast, which was a dinosaur, began to look at a cloth catalogue. The college student also studied chemistry at an academy. His motto: "long after the dinosaur becomes a skeleton, someone will look over the horizon and wonder about a planet like ours. During this period, cameras inside a satellite will be busy, taking pictures of space. Remember, when one busies oneself, he appears busied, and usually means business."

Puppets, rather than robots, act out the imaginative impulses of Virginia's grade-schoolers in Through the Ivory Gate. *"Puppets don't have the limitations of human beings.... They are free from any real feeling. They are indestructible, even immortal...," says Virginia, explaining children's attraction to these surrogates. "Put a puppet into a child's hands and she knows all these things instinctively."*

Chapter XXVIII.

The human cowboy was singing a solo while riding a bucking bronco. He was an alto, but could sing soprano. He came to a deserted pueblo village and captured a burro. He radioed into the president, who vetoed the idea of issuing an embargo to the robots. When the cowboy yelled hello to a cliff, an echo came back. He looked up at the cliff and saw a robot eating a tomato sandwich and potato sticks. His motto was, "A buffalo can't kill a mosquito, but our cargo yesterday was late." A volcano in Honduras coughed, and the hobo in New Jersey found a domino. But the cowboy had given up banjo lessons in order to find his lasso. His success in finding this necessary equipment was a definite disappointment.

Rita Dove

Clyde Edgerton at age 15.

CLYDE EDGERTON

*L*ike the buzzard who narrates the first piece below, Clyde Edgerton
has enjoyed a bird's-eye view of his native North Carolina. An Air Force
pilot who served in Southeast Asia in 1970 and 1971, Edgerton flew his
own plane—a 1946 Piper PA-12 Super Cruiser—above the Tarheel State
until a recent accident grounded the craft.

Born in 1944 near Chapel Hill, where he lives today, the author of
Raney (1985), *Walking Across Egypt* (1987), *The Floatplane Notebooks*
(1988), *Killer Diller* (1991), and *In Memory of Junior* (1992) specializes in
warmly humorous chronicles of southern life, replete with home-fried
okra and homespun folk tunes. His characters are generally good-
hearted—some of them slightly wayward, or poignantly ingenuous—as
they concern themselves with, among other things, how to be good
Christians in their own highly varied circumstances. Occasionally they are
the objects of pointed satire, though more often Edgerton lets them off
easy with some good-natured ribbing, the kind he is practicing below on
his schoolmates and on himself.

The author sets up his juvenilia:

> When I was fifteen, a sophomore at Southern High in Durham,
> North Carolina, two friends and I got lost in the woods behind the
> school one day. My English teacher, Linda Hunt, asked me to write
> about the experience for the school newspaper, *The Southern Script*. I
> had never written for publication and I did not consider using my real
> name....

The following year, Mrs. Hunt asked me to write a piece on basketball practice for the school's literary magazine, *The Southern Drawl*. I
complied.

It is clear to me that the "new journalism" of the late '60s (Wolfe,
et al.) sprang from these two pieces.

Buzzard Gets Bird's-eye View of Three-Man Adventures

CHICK, CLYDE, BURTON LOSE THEMSELVES

IN TRUE WOODSMAN STYLE

(1960, age 15)

I'm a buzzard and not very used to writing for
newspapers, but what I'm going to write I figured
was good enough to write so I decided to write
about it. Well, anyway, while I was floating around
over your high school the other day, I noticed three
suspicious-looking characters venturing away from a
group of students on a field trip (it was one of Miss
Honeycutt's classes if I'm not mistaken). From what I
could hear I learned that the three boys were Chick,
Clyde, and Burton and were on a great adventure to
free a poor little crawfish from a cooped-in fishbowl.
They traveled down Cook Road for a way and then
down a bank by a bridge to a creek. With tearful
goodbyes from our three explorers the crawfish was
freed into cool, calm waters.

While standing there watching the crawfish
slowly swim away, Clyde said, "Boys, I think we'd

better hurry back. You know what Miss Honeycutt said!"

"We could take a short cut across the creek, and through the woods and come out right behind the school," Burton replied.

The one called Chick, who looked to be about three feet eight inches tall and weighed about seventy-five pounds said, "Second the motion."

Well, I didn't think they were ever going to find a place to cross the creek. But finally a rather narrow place came up, and after a heated argument over whether to wade, jump, swim, or build a boat and paddle across, they decided to jump. After the three jumped, it ended up Burton, being dry as a match, Chick the same, and Clyde as wet as a drowned rat. After a few laughs Burton started singing "Davy Crockett" and the boys started walking in the direction in which they thought the school would be. Well, folks, they walked and they walked and they walked, and then walked some more. After a while they stopped in a little opening and looked at each other real funny like.

Chick looked up at his comrades and said, "Boys, I think we're lost."

In unison Clyde and Burton replied, "Me too."

With an air of authority Chick calmly stated, "Now let's figure this thing out, boys."

So they commenced to figure things out. They decided to decide in which direction the sun set and at the same time imagine how they were sitting in sixth period, and then they could add things together and come to the conclusion of where the school was.

Chick said, "Now, let's see, where does the sun set?"

Instantly the three woodsmen pointed in three different directions. From my position I could see that Burton was pointing east; Clyde, South, and Chick declared that if the sun didn't set in the north he would eat every tree in sight.

After considerable mumblings, pointings, etc.,

Edgerton chooses an even less expected narrator for part of The Floatplane Notebooks: *a wisteria vine, which, like the buzzard, serves to observe human activity from a certain* ← *remove.*

At his English teacher's request, the author illustrated his own text.

they started off again, this time running, hoping to come out at any familiar place. In about five minutes they stopped again, out of breath. It was decided that somebody was going to have to climb a tree and see if he could see the school, and instantly four eyes were upon Chick.

A tall, sturdy tree was found. But there was one small problem—how to reach that first limb which was a pretty good way up the trunk. But after about fourteen tries the point of destination was reached.

In his wee, squeaky voice Chick said, "I (pause) think (pause) this limb's (pause) gonna break."

"Pull up, crazy," came an order from below.

About that time there was a loud crash and down came the limb, Chick and all. A footprint was planted on Clyde's shoulder and another directly above his left ear. With three thuds Chick hit the ground (he bounced three times) and got up with a groan. While all this was going on Burton was leaning against a tree holding his stomach with laughter.

After the Jungle Jims stalked through the wild for a while more, having no idea where they were, they came to a place where a road was being built through the woods. A spark of hope came and the boys began walking down the road, hoping to come out somewhere where there was a sign of civilization.

"Boys, if we come in all clean and tell 'em we got lost they won't believe us. I think we ought to walk through a little mud," said Clyde (his clothes were dry by this time).

"You first," said Burton.

But it was too late. Clyde had sneaked around behind him and given him a push into a nice mud puddle. Then the chase was on, Burton after Clyde. About the time Burton caught up with Clyde a mush, muddy, gushy place in the road was reached. All at the same time Clyde slipped, grabbed Burton, and started miring up in the mush. There was no refuge for Burton but Clyde's back, so upon it he went and Clyde was in mud well over his sock tops.

◄ *Still partial to the drama of a character out on a limb, Edgerton has Robert cling to a rotten ladder in* Walking Across Egypt *and Wesley hang from a sagging house gutter in* Killer Diller. *Like Chick here, they both fall— to great comic effect.*

After things settled down it was discovered that Clyde had lost a shoe in the mud. It was quite a sight to see him fishing in the muck for it, while Burton and Chick were sitting on a stump laughing heartily.

Many more steps were taken but soon the boys came up behind the school and I expect they felt about like Balboa when he saw the Pacific.

The last time I saw them they were entering one of the back doors of your building. I don't know what happened after that, and if you wish to know, I guess you'll have to ask one of the Three Musketeers.

—Buzzy

An Afternoon in the Gym

BY GYM MOUSE
(1960, age 16)

Ted Sears, the highly satirized college president in Killer Diller, *is continually seeking out his own reflection, even in the polished surface of his desk top. "If he tilts his head just right, he can see if his rooster tail is holding down."* ➤

To begin the typical day of practice, Steve Utley has the team to sit quietly around the dressing room while he reads his many love letters from all over the United States (especially Washington). Then while everyone is getting into his gym suit, we see Floyd Couch standing in front of the mirror flexing his muscles and admiring the handsome young fellow he sees before him.

Being fully dressed, everyone heads for the gym. John Wheeler rushes through the gym doors, trips over a floor mop, falls onto a ping pong table, and gets things started off with a bang.

Next the terrible task of mopping the gym floor now stands before the players. Floyd Couch and Crawford Williams volunteer. These two young men will not turn down the call of duty. So striking in there like brothers, they fight through the dust and have the floor spick and span in three minutes flat.

Now everyone must do at least fifteen or twenty push-ups. And we see the president of the student body, good 'ole honest-faced Eddie Tice (who is captain of the team, and should set an example) sneak over into a corner and do exactly three and one half push-ups.

Well, after push-ups comes the task of jumping rope. Tyree McGhee and John Whitley have a considerable amount of trouble getting the rope over the top of their heads. Perhaps some day ropes long enough for them will be found.

A few more exercises are performed and then a commotion is heard at the door and in rushes Dan Hill and Danny Walker, about an hour late. They were sure that the Varsity practiced last, so they had gone shopping. Wonder what for?

Now is the time for lay-ups and Tyree McGhee gets his ear hung in the net. Woolard Lumley and Crafton Mitchell rush in with the first aid kit. During the rescue job, these two swell managers, armed with scissors, manage to give Ty a nice haircut and cut off three-fourths of his left ear (swell managers?).

After lay-ups the team goes through a few plays during which Lawson Baker springs his little finger and lays out of practice for the next two weeks. You know, it hurts when he runs.

To complete practice, the team usually runs from twenty to thirty laps (John Wheeler never runs over twelve) and then heads for the showers.

Everyone realizes, I'm sure, that there are certain trouble makers on every team. And there is true evidence of this after practice. The well behaved boys such as Garwood House, John Wheeler, Dan Hill, Clyde Edgerton, and Danny Walker have a very hard time enduring the misbehaving and unruly frolicking of Eddie Tice, Crawford Williams, Mike Knowles and a few other naughty ones. These

The adult Edgerton continues to get laughs out of sports-and-cartilage mishaps. Raney's kid brother ends up with a miscast "fish hook ◀ hung in his nose."

inconsiderate boys always manage to leave the locker room in complete turmoil, while the well-behaved boys I spoke of before reserve all of the blame and have to clean up the mess.

Thus endeth another day of practice.

Everyone retires to Hill's Brown Bomber, Crawford's Grey Ghost, Edgerton's Blue Bullet, or Mitchell's Green Dragon and heads for home leaving John Whitley lingering behind saying, "See 'ya tomorrow, coach."

"He's one of the least of → these my brethren," says Wesley, inserting a bit of biblical phrasing into a casual conversation. The misfit protagonist of Killer Diller is preoccupied with the Bible. Like other Edgerton characters, he reads it often, refers to it, and argues its meanings.

Clyde Edgerton

Stanley Elkin at age 18.

STANLEY ELKIN

*B*orn in the Bronx (in 1930) but raised in Chicago, Stanley Elkin earned three degrees from the University of Illinois where, as a freshman, he penned the following essay "Malice in Wonderland." Forty years after this complaint about the vacuity of Hollywood, Elkin developed the same theme for *Harper's* magazine, which had dispatched him to cover the 1988 Academy Awards. Elkin's curmudgeonly zeal for the subject had grown in the intervening years, and he came home with a vibrantly witty portrait of vanity, hype, kitsch, and glitz—some of the same irritants that had stuck in his teenage craw.

A long-time film buff who once claimed to be able to name "every movie house where I saw any movie," Elkin jumped at the chance to write a Hollywood screenplay when he was solicited in the mid-1960s. The result, *The Six-Year-Old Man*, a farce about a young boy in a man's body, anticipated the charming gimmick of the Tom Hanks hit *Big* but has yet to be produced. This inequity is perhaps due to the script's considerably darker vision, one akin to the tragicomic world of Elkin's novels, which include *George Mills* (1982), *The Magic Kingdom* (1985), and, *The MacGuffin*, (1991).

In his adult work, Elkin strives to replace sentimentality with—to borrow a phrase from Max Apple's review of *The Magic Kingdom*—"an honest look at the grotesque possibilities we all carry around." This demand for honesty and freshness forms the heart of "Malice in Wonderland."

Malice in Wonderland

RHETORIC 102, THEME 3

(1949, age 18)

In his screenplay The Six-Year-Old Man, *Elkin challenged Hollywood expectations by killing off the protagonist's parents. Elkin's Hollywood contact did not find this funny or appropriate. So, writes the author, "I merely crippled them for life in the revision...."* ➤

*T*here is a game they play in Hollywood. In two dozen leather bound offices, two dozen leather bound movie people sit around long tables poised and ready. They are waiting a signal from their secretaries. At the appointed hour, each of these cinemaniacs will begin to work himself into a Hollywood frenzy (which is not to be confused with an Omaha frenzy or a Cedar Rapids frenzy) to see which of them can come up with a movie that is the exact prototype of the movie they made last week, or last month, or last year. There are rules in the game; the movie potentates must be very careful not to let the public suspect that this is where they came in. Triteness, ridiculous situations, juvenile appeal, and virgin stupidity are par for the course. To achieve a note of ultra-realism, they often send out for the studio-guides to write the script.

Upon occasion, a producer or director will forget where he is and he will make a picture like *The Lost Weekend* or *The Snake Pit*. If he ever repeats his carelessness and creates something worthwhile, he is given an "Oscar," and then, nobody will ever speak to him again.

The above might seem to be a travesty on the motion picture industry, but I seriously believe that something close to the things I have described actually happens in Celluloid City. Elsewise, why should the motion pictures remain on such a consistently low level? Is the American public so stultified that it cannot recognize first-rate entertainment? Or is it resigned to the fact that there "ain't no such animal" as a good motion picture? If it is the latter, why should it be? The

American public demands, and gets, the best automobiles, the best radios, the best fountain pens, and the best pop-up toasters. In fact, there is a superlative before the name of almost every American product. Why should we lag behind the rest of the world in our films?

I think that there are several factors that determine the paucity of quality in our movies. One of the most important of these factors, I believe, is based upon the reports the studios receive from some of their exhibitors. These reports remain constant in that they are always from the same people and that they always claim movies which are designed to appeal to a more intelligent audience do not have much of a tendency to make money. The "noble experiments" of the movies are box-office mis-fits, and Hollywood is just a little bit cautious of duplicating pictures that will not "pull." If it is ever to attain excellence in its productions, Hollywood will have to pay less attention to statistics and give more attention to intelligent criticisms of their films. They will probably find that they can make just as much money with a good picture as they can with a bad picture.

Wonderland must do something about its own unadulterated poor taste if it is ever to make pictures for people of an adult mental age. It concentrates on magnificent backgrounds for its pictures and completely ignores what the protagonists are saying. Many movies impress me as though the actors and actresses were making the whole thing up as they went along. Hollywood will spend one million dollars to construct an exact duplicate of the Taj Mahal so that Tyrone Power can say, "I'm warm for you, baby," to some sexy Indian princess. When they concentrate on dialogue with the same diligence they expend in reproducing the minor details of an eighteenth-century drawing room, we will have good pictures.

When those pillars of Hollywood "longevity," Bob Hope and Lucille Ball, launched into their vapid banter as part of the Academy Awards show, Elkin—so he describes in his Harper's *essay—felt a wave of anger. "From my resentment pool, deep as some sea trench, rises a* ◄ *personal bile."*

No subject is taboo in ➤ Elkin's fiction: sex, disease, diseased sex, an unflattering portrayal of God, flatulence. . . . His writings, according to the The New York Times Magazine, "mischievously violate nearly every canon of good taste and literary decorum."

If we are to list filmdom's major faults, we must mention this iniquity. Some things you must never say to a movie producer are: Insanity, Sex, Mercy-killings, Jews, Irish Catholics, Adultery, Alcoholism, Negroes, and Bastards. Those are only a few; the list of controversial themes which are verboten in the land of Technicolor and the double feature is as long as the list of Hopalong Cassidy pictures. For every *Lost Weekend* and *Gentlemen's Agreement*, there are hundreds of *Blondie Goes Home to Mother*. For every character delineation that is to any degree worthwhile, there are hundreds of *Portraits of Lassie*. Hollywood has to learn to stand up and fight and not hide in the corner every time the Legion of Decency puts on a long face.

Hesitancy to make good pictures for fear that they will not pull at the box-offices, extravagance of production, negligence in script, and the phobia against anything controversial are the three cardinal sins that hold Hollywood back and keep good movies from our screens.

Until they learn to straighten out these difficulties, the picture boys of California are going to go on producing "B" (for bad) pictures. But no matter what they do, I'll keep on going to the movies. I'm just like everyone else. I like popcorn!

Stanley Elkin

George Garrett at about age 10.

GEORGE GARRETT

After reading George Garrett's story "Escapes," written when he was fourteen, it is fascinating to read "Noise of Strangers," the novella that caps his retrospective collection *An Evening Performance* (1985). Both tales feature a prisoner's confrontation with a pillar of the community, and both reflect the author's continuing interest in piercing the facade of respectability. Even the fourteen-year-old Garrett seems aware of his doctor character's hypocrisy. And, as often occurs in his adult work, according to R. H. W. Dillard, Garrett's sympathies go out to life's losers, in this case the hapless prisoner Willie. We can already trace Garrett's abiding interests in human folly, twists of fate, and, as Dillard would put it, the "Christian fallen world," in which "sins deadly or merely degrading do not just afflict human beings but are of their very nature...."

Garrett was born in 1929 in Orlando, Florida, to a lawyer and musician. For most of his adult life, he has taught at various universities and has influenced a distinguished roster of younger writers, including Madison Smartt Bell and Kelly Cherry. Of his more than twenty books of fiction, poetry, drama, and biography, he is best known for his historical novel *Death of the Fox* (1971). And yet he is also the author of the wildly unconventional novel *Poison Pen* (1986), an uninhibited send-up of contemporary culture.

He has provided the following introduction for *First Words*:

> I have been writing things all my life, beginning even before I could read or write for myself, when my patient father, in the evening after work and when we weren't all listening to the radio or something,

took down my earliest stories in dictation. None of these things, I hope, survives. But some things, a little later on, did and do survive. Enough has survived, it seems, to teach me some humility. As if yet another lesson were needed.

The first of these, the earliest thing I could locate, is the text of a little homemade booklet, "Our River Trips," written on assignment for myself and the rest of the fifth grade at Mt. Kemble School in Bernardsville, New Jersey. I was a child of the public schools of Orlando, Florida, and, more specifically, at that time, of Delaney Street Grammar School. Which is also where (never mind how and why) Mary Lee Settle had her elementary school education. Anyhow ... in the spring of 1940 my parents sent me off on a wonderful train, The Silver Meteor, to visit my aunt, Helen Garrett, who ran a small "progressive" school in New Jersey. Helen Garrett, as it happens, was a writer herself, and a very good one. Of children's books. She loved Nature. It would have been her idea for us, her fifth grade class, to follow a river from its source to the ocean and while doing so to notice as much as we could in between. I seem to have noticed a lot of birds and plants and trees, among other things. Not so surprising. We got up every morning at 4:30 or 5:00 A.M. to go birdwatching. I learned and knew more about those things then than ever before or after.

I had forgotten all about this little booklet until now. Some part of me remembered, however, because some thirty years later, in the novel *Death of the Fox*, I wrote an imaginary account (Ralegh was picturing it) of the Thames from its beginning at seven clear cold bubbling springs near Cheltenham to the sea where: "Waves shrug ermine shoulders. Shrieking gulls claim possession of blustering air."

"Escapes" came three or fours years later and was a blatant attempt to write something that might be publishable (though by whom and for what I hadn't the slightest idea). I was ready to be a writer. Whatever that was. I knew that a short story was supposed to have plenty of plot. So I tried to make one up. The results speak for themselves.

Our River Trips

THE LIFE HISTORY OF A RIVER
(1940, age 10)

Foreward

*T*he 5th grade of Mt. Kemble School decided to follow a very, very, very small stream just outside our school we found it joined Mine Brook, Mine Brook joined the Raritan, the Raritan was joined by several others rivers and finally the Raritan reached the sea coast. We saw how from a small stream the Raritan grew to be large and the center of cities and industrial life. Our adventures and the many things we saw are described in this book.

Chapter I

The stream began a little way east of the school and it came from under ground. It is supposed to be very fine drinking water. The ground around it was very marshy and soggy. We noticed a little water-cress. The stream was joined by several small streams near there. [....]

The author and editor have organized this abridged version of the original ◄ account.

Then the stream entered a pond, which had goldfish in it. It then headed south, under the highway, and into a pasture. The stream grew wider and had a very rocky bottom. Then it entered Mine Brook and became a small stream.

Chapter II
The Stream

[...] We noticed lots of interesting things along the way such as, a red-eyed viroe's nest, a buzzard, strange insects nest, a mean old man, cat tails, and shale. [....]

In Death of the Fox, *Garrett returns to the image of the river path—in this case the Thames as it wends through the crowded landscape of British history and culture. Garrett contrasts the relatively timeless river's "indifference" to a familiar Garrett interest: "the wonders and follies of man's making."*

Chapter VI

[...] The stream continued, became deeper, wider, and slower. After crawling under electrified barbedwire we noticed several spring beauties and after walking about 50 yards we heard a Phoebe. [....]

Chapter VII

We began our journey this time by returning to the spot where we began our journey and measuring it. We then drove on [....]

Twice we got out of the car and took observations. The first time we saw a large mansion in the distance and two negroes—close—apparently fishing. [....]

Chapter X

We drove along a road with hills on the east and the valley of Raritan on the west. In the distance in the west we could see the Cushyitunk mountains. We were looking for tributaries and types of industry. We stopped at every small stream that was named. [....]

Chapter XII

This time we were going to take a boat trip. We drove over to New Brunswick and to a boat yard. The boat was docked on the old Delaware-Raritan canal. We found our boat and loaded our lunch into the cabin. [....]

On this journey we saw many things such as the new Edison bridge, a U S arsenal, copper works, Staten Island, ships grave yard, tankers, factories and many other things. We ate lunch on board and we had a wonderful time.

Now we had seen how from a small brook the river had grown very large and had emptied into the sea.

*George Garrett
at about age 14.*

Escapes
(circa 1944, age 14)

Willie was restless in his cell all day. All day long it had rained. The grim walls a scant three hundred yards away looked more grim and foreboding to him than they had ever seemed before. In the gaurd towers around the walls lights gleamed through the steady downpour. This was just the day that Willie had

When Ike Toombs, in "Noise of Strangers," is faced with the possibility of a life sentence, he has a fuller idea of what he's giving up than does Willie or his 14-year-old creator. "All the women he has ever known, in fact and in the rich harem of the imagination, are dancing before his eyes...." →

Even at age 14, Garrett seems to have established what will be an enduring suspicion of the trappings of status. This mistrust finds its darkly humorous expression, for example, in some of the letters to celebrities included in his novel Poison Pen. *"We are deeply impressed," writes Garrett—through several layers of alias—to Cristina DeLorean, "... by your good looks and good health and good luck and all your material possessions." →*

dreamed of and planned for during eight long years in that cell. At night he had lain on his hard cot watching the ceiling and thinking. Eight years is a long time in a jail. At first Willie thought he could go the stretch, but in six weeks he knew that he would never make it. The awful brutal monotony of it wore on his nerves. He never knew how much color meant to him. He came to loathe the ever present prison grey. He longed to see the green of a tree or the multi colors of dresses on the streetcar. Sounds. He was almost crazy for the sounds of the city. He would have given his right leg gladly to hear a little jazz music. He said so. He longed for his wife. He never thought he'd want any woman that badly, but he wanted one now. At first the letters had been more or less frequent, but in the last few years he had heard nothing. Every night he had lain in bed looking at the ceiling and plotting. Now the time was here. Everything he had striven for in years was to reach a climax that night in one great effort. Casually he wondered if he would make it.

Nine miles away, Dr. Frank Leads came home from work. He drove his shining new Buick up the gravel-paved drive to his house. He looked at the luscious green of his carefully planned landscaping. His big Colonial house looked wonderful after a day in the operating room, despite its whiteness. He had everything that a really successful surgeon should have—a nice conventional wife, three nice children, a nice home, and a nice lucrative practice. He wondered about the cars in front of the house; then he remembered the party. Looking into the rear view mirror, he ran a comb through his greying hair. Seconds later he turned the polished brass doorknob and entered the house.

"Why here's the Doctor now."

"Come in! Come in! We've been waiting for you doctor."

"Have an Old Fashioned, Darling."

"We've just been discussing the new Anti-Strike Bill. Now do you think..."

Willie walked boldly across the great yard toward the steam and boiler house. He did not have to make an effort to seem nonchalant; for he had been going over to the boiler room every night at seven for the past three years to turn a knob that let the steam out of a large pipe to the outside. This was a little precaution to keep the great boilers from blowing up as they had done some years back. Willie, the trusty, clicked on the light in the boiler room. He felt the heat of the room begin to dry the rain from his clothes. He moved quickly; everything had been planned so minutely. He had to work fast. At the wall he removed a section of pipe which he had loosened carefully for the past month. That great pipe was big enough in diameter for a man to wriggle through, if the man was thin enough. For two years, Willie had been one of the only prisoners who could not clean his plate every meal. Quickly Willie slipped out of his prison clothes. He rubbed his naked body with a mixture of soap, hair oil, and pork fat until his thin frame gleamed with grease. Without delay he slid down the dark pipe. Down and out he wriggled; then the unforseen happened.

Dr. Leads had just finished his fifth cocktail and was busy making polite love to that charming young Mrs. Harrison when he was called to the phone. He returned with a frown.

"What's the trouble, Frank?"

"Some damn idiot tried to break out of the state Pennitentury on a night like this and didn't quite make it. They need me out there in side of ten minutes; so guess I'll have to go."

Dr. Leads roared out there in less than the required time. With the speedometer touching eighty all the way he tore down the slick highway. With no loss of time he was ushered to the boiler room. A crowd of gaurds and anxious people were gathered around the wall where Willie had made his attempted escape. Down the pipe thirty feet, Willie was sweating and praying. Some farsighted prison official had forseen the possibility of an escape through the pipe. A wire mesh trap had been made thirty feet down the pipe at a spot where the pipe made a slight curve.

Garrett narrator Jack Towne employs a similarly ironic tone to discuss romantic peccadillos in the 1978 story "A Record as Long as Your Arm," which begins: "Ray, old buddy, one of the things I'll never be able to forget is the look on your face when you strolled into your bedroom and discovered me there ◄ with your wife."

"I can only say a couple of things about this effort," recalls the author. *"One is that I was listening to 78rpm jazz records all the time and saving and spending all my money to get them. There's that much truth to it. And there is, disguised, a deeper memory. In the old Spanish fortress of San Marcos in St. Augustine they used to show the dungeon with a tiny slit window through which some captive Seminoles, including the warrior Osceola, somehow managed to slither and escape. They did it by starving themselves and greasing their bodies. Like Willie. Whose luck wasn't as good as theirs."*

Willie was caught in that trap, and he knew that in a matter of minutes they were going to have to turn on the steam to keep the boilers from exploding. They had heard his frantic calls for help, but, try as they did, they could not free him from the wire trap. He was hopelessly tangled by his right leg in the mesh.

Willie was surprized to see a slim naked man with a scalpel in his teeth slither toward him.

"Look son, I'm going to amputate your right leg at the knee and get you out of here before they turn on that steam. I've got a little chloroform on this rag; so sniff it."

The last thing that Willie heard before he passed out was Dr. Leads whistling an old jazz favorite "Blue Turning Grey Over You" as he started cleanly cutting at the right knee joint.

ESCAPES

Willie was restless in his cell all day. All day long it had rained. The grim walls a scant three hundred yards away looked more grim and foreboding to him than they had ever seemed before. In the gaurd towers around the walls lights gleamed through the steady downpour. This was just the day that Willie had dreamed of and planned for during eight long years in that cell. At night he had lain on his hard cot watching the ceiling and thinking. .ght years is a long time in a jail. At first Willie thought he could go the stretch, but in six weeks he knew that he would never make it. The awful brutal monotony of it wore on his nerves. He never knew how much color meant to him. He came to loathe the ever present prison grey. He longed to see the green of a tree or the multi colors of dresses on the streetcar. Sounds. He was almost crazy for the sounds of the city. He would have given his right leg gladly to hear a little jazz music. He said so. He longed

George Garrett

Ellen Gilchrist at about age 15.

ELLEN GILCHRIST

"As you can see," Gilchrist notes about her juvenilia, "I was obsessed with death—a good beginning for a writer."

Gilchrist was alerted to the mysteries of death from an early age: The sacred Indian burial mounds on her grandparents' plantation; the children's small tombstones at the local cemetery; the deaths of her maternal grandfather and her cousin's husband—these all made strong impressions on her, as she would recall in her journals *Falling Through Space* (1987).

"I was mad at God," she writes in that book, evoking her childhood reaction to death. "I hated him. I sat up in a magnolia tree ... and dared him to make me fall."

Gilchrist, who didn't publish her first book until she was forty-four (*The Land Surveyor's Daughter*, poems, 1979), finds the two teenage poems about death printed below "funny" and "textbook predictable." Sometimes disturbing, sometimes blithe or mystical, her adult work is driven by an intense philosophical curiosity. Often, as in such stories as "Suicides" and "The Man Who Kicked Cancer's Ass," it returns in fresh, riveting ways to the subjects of death and near death. Gilchrist's fiction is also recognizable by (to use Jonathan Yardley's phrase) its "spoiled, willful yet captivating" southern female protagonists. They appear and reappear across her various books, which include the story collections *In the Land of Dreamy Dreams* (1981) and *Light Can Be Both Wave and Particle* (1989) and the novels *The Anna Papers* (1988) and *Net of Jewels* (1992).

Born in 1935 in Mississippi bayou country, Gilchrist spent her early years at Hopedale, her grandparents' small cotton plantation, and her school years in the Midwest. She elaborates in a recent letter:

> My father was an engineer in the Corps of Engineers. Later he was a struggling road contractor. We were never poor and we never thought of ourselves as rich. I was raised by deeply religious people, half Episcopalian and half Presbyterian, who believed in work and love and Girl Scouts and Boy Scouts and knowing how to use a compass and how to swim the Australian crawl and being polite and not hurting people's feelings and telling the truth whether you wanted to or not. I was unbelievably rich in the things that mattered and I have always been aware of that. "Devotion is knowing how rich we are," the Buddhists say and they are right.

Regret
(1951, age 16)

I think I should not mind to die
If only I could see
How the world could go on
Unceasingly
Without me

Life has treated me kindly
And I should not mind to go
If only it would make a difference
It won't tho'
I know

To think that I existed here
For a number of years
And my departing only cause
A few tears
(And cheers)

Dudley, the fictional older brother in a series of Gilchrist stories, makes fun of his sister when she buries an assortment of her things in "The Time Capsule" (1989). "'She thinks someone's going to be interested in her after she's dead.'"

Almost Seventeen
(1951, age 16)

Why am I who could not wait
To grow up
Suddenly hesitant
Why do I fear to blow out
The candles
On the chocolate cake
Seventeen of them this time.
A little matter—blowing out candles
I wish there were only seven
And I could blow them all out
With one breath————

Since this tame discussion of mortality, Gilchrist has invented some bold and startling images of death. In her short story "Rich" (1978), for example, a distraught father shoots his difficult young daughter. And the girl's "disordered brain flung its roses forth."

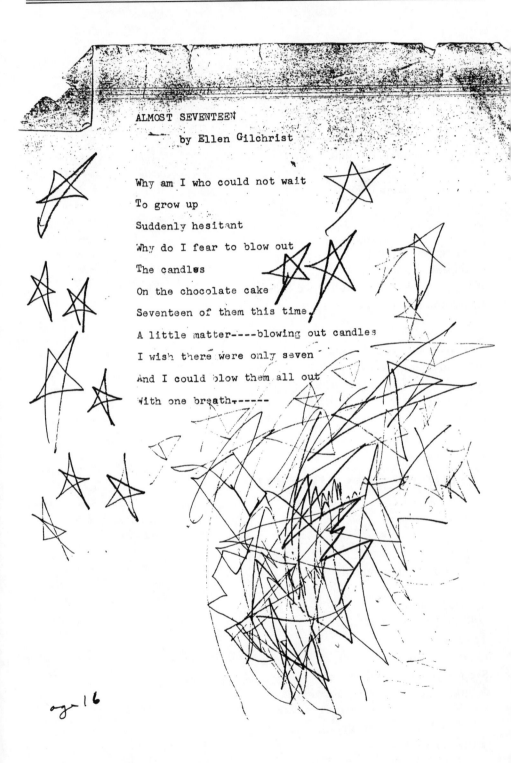

ALMOST SEVENTEEN

by Ellen Gilchrist

Why am I who could not wait
To grow up
Suddenly hesitant
Why do I fear to blow out
The candles
On the chocolate cake
Seventeen of them this time
A little matter----blowing out candles
I wish there were only seven
And I could blow them all out
With one breath------

age 16

"It's pretty amazing," says the author, "how much my smile hasn't changed from when I was 15 until Jerry Bauer took the adult photo several years ago. Strange wonder of us."

Gail Godwin at age 14 or 15.

GAIL GODWIN

*A*fter her parents separated, when she was two, Gail Godwin lived with her grandmother and mother, who supported the three of them in part by writing pulp romance stories. In her autobiographical essay "Becoming a Writer" (1979), Godwin says that her father was absent from her life for so long that she didn't recognize him when he showed up at her high school graduation. Three years later he committed suicide.

Best known for her novels, including *A Mother and Two Daughters* (1982) and *Father Melancholy's Daughter* (1991), Godwin is especially attuned to the tides and turbulence of families. In prose fluent in the languages of emotion, psychology, and spirituality, her works often describe her characters' efforts to understand and rise above childhood pain—especially when it involves a missing parent.

Born in Birmingham, Alabama, in 1937, Godwin grew up in North Carolina. She wanted to be a writer from the age of five and began composing short stories four years later.

"The Choice," written when Godwin was fourteen, predicts elements of her 1985 novel *The Finishing School*, in which a fourteen-year-old girl searches for the path that will make her most alive. And *A Southern Family* (1987) refers on numerous occasions to the Catholic school that so shaped the novel's protagonists, albeit in ways more various and subtle than Godwin's juvenile short story "The Accomplice" would suggest.

Looking back at her file of juvenilia, Godwin observes in a 1987 essay: "What is interesting is that, though the writing has improved, the old themes haven't changed very much." Society's pressure on the individual, life choices, ambition and thwarted ambition are among the key issues that have followed Godwin through the years.

"Each of these childhood concerns," writes Jane Hill in her 1992 critical study of the author, "finds its way into almost every story and novel Godwin has written as an adult."

In a 1982 essay Godwin writes: "At the age of nine, of twelve, I took it for granted I could enter the mind of any character I wanted to." Years later, after a period of self-consciousness, the author had to "re-learn" this lesson.

The Autobiography of a Tin Cup
(1949, age 12)

*O*h me, what a life! How embarrassing it is to sit on a washstand morning, noon and night and hold toothbrushes! Rather lonely, too, when none of them will associate with me. That is, all except Mortimer, the only Angle toothbrush on the place. He keeps me in contact with the rest of the camp since he is carried every morning from the washstand to Cabin 7 until six p.m. when he returns with Colmer Colgate and Archibald Amurol. They sleep in me all night.

It seems that my mother originated in a tin cup factory some years ago. Oh! but she was a beauty. Her arms, long and graceful, were always on her hips. That shows signs of character, you know. She was a bright silver color and had "patent no. 350" inscribed on her back. All the tin cups used to clog up the machines they were in to attract my mother's attention. One of those naughty cups was my father. The Podunk Tin Works was my home (after the death of my parents) with lots of other little cups and pans. That is before Gertrude. Let me tell you about Gertrude.

Godwin's adult work, especially in recent years, is guided by her fascination with and gift for empathy; she plays with it here by choosing a most unlikely point of view. Margaret in Father Melancholy's Daughter *is so inclined to consider the other person's side that her teenage friend Harriet chides: "If you ask me, Margaret, you overdo the empathy thing. It's not healthy."*

One day a fat little girl (that's Gertrude) ran into the factory and into old Mr. Black's office. He is the manager of our little home and also an old "bag." Anyway, he came walking out of that office laughing!

It was like Vesuvius erupting orangeade. He picked me up by the handle and dropped me in a bag which was slung over Gertrude's arm to be carried home and next day to camp. All the way I stayed in that disgusting bag and let my head bump against the top from time to time, in hopes of getting out.

After that first year of camp, I retired to a farm where I was used to feed the pigs, catch lightening bugs, and hold chewing gum (sometimes tobacco). The next year I returned to the same camp with a different owner. It was that year that I had my accident which left me armless. Some "ornery critter", (I learned that on the farm) who was paying no attention whatsoever to where he was going, stepped on me.

At the moment, I'm patiently sitting on the washstand with toothbrushes hanging over my sides, waiting for someone to rescue me before I get rheumatism or gout, or something of the like. If you're a camper (which you most likely are) look for a worn-out old cup. No handle, no bottom, no paint. Remove those toothbrushes and take me to a place I can call home. You won't be sorry. I'm a mighty useful little cup!

Clare, the writer character in A Southern Family, *recalls a story she wrote in childhood about a "dog on holiday, from the dog's point of view." Godwin herself wrote such a story as a girl.*

Gail Godwin at age 13.

The Accomplice

(1951, age 14)

Nancy had feared Mother Blanche ever since that awful fall day when Mother and Daddy had deposited her at St. Catherine's. The huge nun had glared down on Nancy with unwavering intensity and Nancy had felt that her whole appearance was dreadfully offensive and hastened to bend down and tug at a knee sock and pat the heavy pigtails in order to correct some of the offensiveness.

Mother Blanche had icy eyes which were the shape and color of granite slabs. Her body was obscured beneath the heavy black folds of her garments, and only her terrible red face could be seen peering through the frame of the stiff white bonnet.

Also in A Southern ➤ *Family, Thalia remembers sending her daughter to Catholic high school: "'It cost more, but I'm sure glad we did it.... There was this nun there that sure did straighten her out.'"*

"We shall see that Nancy gets the proper discipline and training while she is at St. Catherine's," she boomed to Nancy's parents. "And of course all our students from the first grade up are required to learn French and to speak it during all recitations. We are, as you probably know, a French order."

Nancy noticed that Mother Blanche had not fawned or fumbled with her fingers as Miss Rippy the first grade teacher at P.S. 88 had always done in the presence of parents.

And ever since that first day Nancy had been haunted by the possibility that she might sink further into disfavor with Mother Blanche.

When she heard the familiar thudding walk on the dormitory halls late at night, when she saw the nun thundering across the wooden-floored assembly room to call roll before morning prayers, when she looked out the window and spied her crunching angrily through the helpless autumn leaves on the way back from the chapel, Nancy always went over the whole day in her mind and tried to think if she had done anything wrong. Every time Mother

Blanche came in Nancy's direction, she was sure that she had done something that she shouldn't have.

Some of the other second-graders had whispered to Nancy that Mother Blanche had two extra eyes in the back of her head and that even when she appeared to have her back to you she was really just watching you out of those other eyes which were hidden cleverly behind the crisp black veil. "That way, she can catch you doing things better," they informed their terrified new classmate.

And then Nancy had been caught talking to Barbara Van Amm, the girl in front of her, as the class marched in from recess. She had been telling Barbara about how the other school had been last year and how the teachers were just ordinary people who wore dresses and skirts and things. Nancy knew you weren't supposed to talk in line, but she had not been talking very loud. Nobody could have possibly heard her. But Mother Blanche of the four eyes and the supersensitive hearing had heard. She suddenly halted at the head of the line. She turned and snatched her silver whistle which hung from a chain around her neck; she blew the whistle, and then faced Nancy with a face made redder by the effort of blowing the whistle.

"You there! You were talking in line," she announced dolefully.

The whole line seemed to shrink back. Only Nancy was left to face the large black opponent. She looked desperately down at her dusty red loafers and had the absurd thought that the dust would not come off and she would have to get another pair of shoes.

"No recess for you tomorrow, Lady Chatterbox. You will sit in the summerhouse and write your French verbs." And the huge nun swung around and resumed her striding leadership at the head of the silent line. The children marched stiffly and obediently into the classroom, some turning furtively to give Nancy a curious look, and the crisis was over. But not the fear which now mushroomed into gigantic proportions within Nancy's heart.

Trudy Callahan tried to explain all about nuns to

◄ *After* Ralph, A Southern Family'*s patriarch, tells an off-color joke about a nun, Julia finds the laughter to be forced. "Julia and every one of Lily's children had gone to St. Clothilde's..., and images of real nuns, particular nuns, were rising reproachfully in each of their memories...."*

St. Clothilde's was "the place in town to go" in A Southern Family, *regardless of the child's religious affiliation.* ➤

In her October 8, 1982, diary entry about visiting her old convent school, Godwin is flooded with a sense of feeling "thirteen again." It is a sentiment she will draw on in A Southern Family *when Clare, on a visit home, feels as though she has never left. "It was as if, after all, the core of her had never escaped, never traveled ... or written and published books; this part of her remained forever stuck in the nightmare of adolescence...."*

In A Southern Family, *Mother von Blücher "was famous for her ill temper. 'Boy, she really hates us!' the little girls would exclaim, fascinated by her perpetual wrath."* ➤

Nancy: "You non-catholics have a hard time understanding the sisters because your churches don't have any. But don't feel bad. A lot of the kids that come here to board don't know any more than you do. They're 'prodahstunt' like you. St. Catherine's has lots of 'prodahstunts' because their parents realize that it's a very good school."

Nancy said yes she knew that, because Mamma had SAID they would make her a lady at St. Catherine's, or else...

"Well, anyway, as I was telling you—about the nuns," Trudy continued instructively, "they give up their lives to Jesus and never get married and shave off all their hair and devote their lives to praying and teaching us."

"But why?" Nancy wanted to know. "Does Jesus ask them to do it?" Nancy knew all about Jesus. The nuns loved to talk about him. The whole upstairs parlor, where the nuns sat and talked and saw visiting parents was filled with pictures and statues of him. And he was all over the chapel. Especially in front of the altar where old Father Murphy spoke in Latin before breakfast. Jesus was up there too, only this time he was almost naked and he was stretched out on that cross. Nancy could never understand how he could look so calm with all those nails stuck in him.

"No, silly," said Trudy in a patronizing tone. "But they KNOW he wants them to become nuns. Because they have grace and they love him very much."

"Do you think Mother Blanche loves him? How could she love anybody? She screams at everybody."

"Oh, yes. She loves him." Trudy was sure. "She's always going to chapel to visit him. Remember how many times we see her going from the window?"

Nancy said she remembered.

"And you should see when she prays. I watched her once, you know, at vespers when we kneel right behind her, and do you know I looked at the side of her face and it was so peaceful and it wasn't hardly red."

Nancy concluded that Mother Blanche must really love Jesus if he had this effect on her. She was sure now that Mother Blanche would never roar at Jesus.

She decided to investigate and find out more about him. Wouldn't it be wonderful to be someone who did not worry about getting on the wrong side of Mother Blanche!

At table that evening, she asked Mother Mouquet about him. The old nun seemed very pleased and wiped the tiny grease smudges out of the wrinkled corners of her mouth with her napkin and settled back in her chair and told Nancy about him.

"He is the Lord," she began slowly in her broken accent. Nancy had to bend towards Mother Mouquet to understand her.

"He was sent here to take away all the bad things that people on earth had done. He was crucified for our sins."

"Why does he make people respect him so?" Nancy wanted to know.

"Oh!" The old nun's eyes brightened, then narrowed. "Because he punishes those who do not respect his laws." She patted Nancy's arm. "It is always a good idea to stay on the right side of the Lord, my little one."

"But what kind of laws did he make?" Nancy demanded eagerly. She had broken enough laws at St. Catherine's already. She hoped there would not be too many more.

"Love him, love your neighbor, that is enough for you to remember. Just think before you do anything: 'whatever I do to my neighbor, I do to him.' If I hurt my neighbor, I am also hurting him."

"That's one of the rules?"

"That *is* the rule. Woe unto the person who does not treat his neighbor as he would treat Jesus himself." She shook her bony finger at Nancy and Nancy shuddered.

Nancy had lain wide-eyed for what seemed an hour before "lights out" that night. Finally, just before sleep threatened to close in, she figured something out that she had not known before. It concerned Mother Blanche. Mother Blanche was not obeying the law. If she went around shouting and frightening people and not loving them like she did, then she was doing the exact same things to Jesus. Mother Mouquet had been very clear about this law.

She groped around under her pillow until she found the plastic cross that all the boarders got when they came to St. Catherine's. You kept it under your pillow and Jesus was with you all night to guard you from unpleasant things.

There was a moon tonight and some of its thin light seeped into the dark room where Nancy and two other boarders slept. She held the cross in the small square of moonlight on her bedspread. There was just enough light to see the figure. She felt the carved outline with her fingers and wished that she could pull out some of those awful nails.

It was then she decided to make the pact. "Don't worry, Jesus. It's going to be all right. We'll give her one more chance."

She put the cross back under her pillow and fell asleep.

*   *   *   *

Mother Blanche simmered down remarkably the next day. Nancy was not sure if it were just a coincidence or whether Jesus had warned her. But she had not fussed at anyone for loitering in assembly that morning; she had not punished Barbara Van Amm for coloring the pictures of *le cheval* and *la salle á manger* in her book before she knew how to pronounce them. And at recess when Nancy sat penitently in the summer house listening to the playing sounds of the other second graders on the playground below and writing in her best Palmer method handwriting "je suis, vous êtes, il est, elle est..." Mother Blanche had strode regally up from the playground and said, "Nancy, you accepted your punishment admirably." Nancy could smell the starchy black habit and the faint odor of soap which always clung to Mother Blanche's body. She almost hoped that Mother Blanche would get through the day.

But doom struck in the form of the boarders' Friday night movie. Every Friday night, all the boarders from grades one through eight would assemble in the small auditorium for a movie. The movies were old ones, because Nancy had seen some of them with her parents before she came to St. Catherine's. The man who showed them worked in the projection room of one of the theaters in the city. He was a Catholic, Trudy told her, and offered Friday nights up to God for good works.

The movie was about an old general who had come home from the war. It was in black and white and, although some of the seventh and eighth graders laughed once in awhile, Nancy thought it was very boring. She shifted restlessly in her folding chair which squeaked loudly every time she moved. She bit her fingernails. She looked around at all the other boarders and at the nuns. Some of the younger boarders had dropped their heads and closed their eyes. Others lolled listlessly in the uncomfortable seats. Some of the nuns watched the movie as if they were mildly interested. Old Mother Mouquet was sitting on the back row saying her rosary with her eyes closed. Nancy felt close to the wrinkled old nun who had explained everything last night. Neither of them thought the movie was any good at all.

It was finally over. The lights went on and all the boarders had to file past Mr. O'Keefe who was rewinding the movie and say: "Thank you, Mr. O'Keefe." Nancy's eyes felt gritty and the new light made her squint. There had only been one part of the movie she had liked. That was when the old general ran madly up the winding stairs and yelled to the top of his lungs: "CHARGE!" Several of the sleepy boarders had looked up and laughed. Nancy had thought it was extremely funny. Even Mother Blanche had chuckled. Nancy had heard her all the way across the darkened room.

As the boarders mounted the stairs to their rooms for the night, some of them started talking about how funny the general was, running up the stairs and yelling like that.

← Gretchen, the searching young writer in Godwin's 1972 story "Some Side Effects of Time Travel," recalls falling in love at age 12 with Mother Maloney, a 39-year-old convent school nun. During the Friday evening movies they would sit together, "and when the lights went out they held hands in one of the deep pockets of Mother Maloney's habit."

"Even Mother Blanche laughed," said Trudy to Nancy.

"I dare somebody to rush up these stairs like he did and yell "Charge" challenged one of the older boarders with a malicious gleam in her eyes.

Barbara Van Amm, who never did anything outstanding, pretended to yell. "Charge!" she whispered, brandishing an imaginary sword as the general had done with his.

And then Nancy saw her moment to forever become Mother Blanche's friend. No longer would she have to be scared of the wrathful nun. Nancy would re-enact the general's scene and make Mother Blanche laugh again.

The red face appeared on the landing below Nancy. This was it. Pushing past the boarders in front of her, she raged fiercely up the last flight of stairs. She raised her sword.

"CHARGE!" She screamed magnificently.

The silence was deafening. Nobody laughed. Nancy's echo encored her scene. Mother Blanche turned white and then slowly the red reappeared, deepening in color this time. Fire blazed in the colorless eyes.

She swept back her sash, picked up her long black skirts and made her frightful ascension up the steps until she reached Nancy's level and towered over her.

"It seems," she began, pronouncing each word meticulously, "That some people around here have a flair for creating disturbances. If you are so fond of the summerhouse, Nancy we shall see about letting you sit there every day. But in order to impress it upon you that we do not shout out to the top of our lungs at this hour of the night—"

Several of the nuns who had not gone to the movies stuck their heads out of doors up and down the hall at the top of the steps. They had taken their veils off, and all that remained on their mysterious heads was a stiff, white covering. Nancy thought of white mice peeking out of their holes.

"In order to impress it upon you that you have

Julia, in A Southern ➤ Family, *once wrote sassy "jump-rope chants" at convent school, "until Mother von Blücher had overheard one and she'd almost been expelled. (Skinny Vinnie got the minnie, it had gone. Raged and screamed and cried. / She flushed and flashed / Then trickled and pickled / Until she got so mad she died.)"*

created a disturbance," continued the terrible one, "No movie will be shown at all next Friday night. This is your fault, and the girls will obviously not be pleased with you for it."

She closed her mouth as abruptly as a snapping turtle. Her eyes were cold and dangerous like a pond frozen over with thin ice. "March to your rooms." That was all.

The boarders grumbled under their breaths as they resumed their climb. A few of the seventh and eighth graders passed Nancy and muttered rude things without looking at her. One of them was the boarder who had suggested the whole thing in the first place. Trudy said sadly, "Aw, Nancy. What didja do *that* for?"

Nancy undressed quickly while her two roommates went into the bathroom with their toothbrushes to talk about her. When they came out, she was already balled up under the blanket, clutching the cross with both hands. They knelt by the side of the bed and executed a rapid "Hailmery." Then the lights went out, and Nancy heard the familiar "clomp, clomp" of the heavy heels grow closer to the door, then pass, and recede into the farthest corner of the hall where— as Nancy knew—*she* slept.

"That's the last time she will ever walk down this hall," Nancy said, stroking the cross. "We certainly did give her a fair chance." She placed the object against her cheek. It was cool and comforting.

She was running, running because she had to get there before it was light. She ran up to the altar, pushing past a silent Father Murphy who was deep in prayer and did not notice her. She stood on tiptoe and pulled with all her strength until, one by one, the nails fell on the floor. And then she took him by the hand, and covered him with the bathrobe she had brought him because it was chilly in the early mornings before it got light. Together, they stole out of the chapel past Father Murphy who still did not look up but acted as if he were in some sort of a

In the title story of Godwin's 1976 collection Dream Children, Mrs. McNair *also achieves devoutly wished nocturnal communions—with her* ◄ *dead child.*

trance. Across the hard ground where most of the leaves had been pulverized into dirt by now, and up the stairs and back down the hall, only this time further. And then they opened the door and stood before her—a monstrous mound of blanket with only a little white head covering sticking out from the end. He raised his hand and made magic motions in the air like Father Murphy sometimes did. And it was over. She was finished. As they ran back to the chapel, it was getting light and Nancy wondered how she would look when they found her huge, still form in the morning. They were running, running and then he started pulling her, pulling and jerking her until her whole body jolted and lunged.

She looked through the clumps of sleep-grit clustered in the corners of her eyes. She was being shaken by the shoulders by a figure whose hulking shadow obliterated the window, shutting out all of the morning sunlight, except for a thin line of light which haloed the black head.

"Nancy!" boomed Mother Blanche. "You have overslept and missed morning prayers."

Godwin's fiction pays much attention to dreams. In Father Melancholy's Daughter, *Margaret is abruptly awakened from one by her father, the Rector of St. Cuthbert's. He tells her that in the night vandals had sawed down the church's street-corner crucifix.* ➤

The Choice
(circa 1951, age 14–15)

The township of Clove, ➤ *N.Y. in* The Finishing School, *is a similarly insulated place, where teenage Justin is trying to discover her own specialness.*

*T*he placid little village of Sunny Bay was for the first time in a state of uproar. During these last few days everybody had been scrambling about in a mad rush to go nowhere. Lately there was an air of importance in this humble habitat. The whole thing could be traced back to the day Lucille LaRose had decided she was bored with being called the "Torrid Lover with the Velvet Lips", tired of the city lights and night clubs, and just plain sick of hundreds of adoring beaus and boxes of a dozen red roses. It was then Lovely Lucile had decided to grace her home town of Sunny Bay as a sort of game.

Mayor McCraw had been wired, (incidentally it was the first telegram he had ever received in his life) and pictures of Lucile were immediately tacked up on every billboard and telephone pole within ten miles of Sunny Bay. The villagers were attacked with house-cleaning-itus and the modest little cottages brightened up with enthusiasm. Their windows were washed so clean they outdid the scrubbed flawless complexion of a child. Sunny Bay awaited the one and only thing they could boast about.

Most eager of all the villagers was Sally McCraw, the mayor's daughter. The fourteen year old brown eyed dreamer had been faithfully saving her allowance for three weeks so she could pay the admission necessary to feast one's eyes on Lovely Lucile.

Now on the long awaited day Sally counted her nickels and dimes. By sacrificing love magazines and skipping Neptune Bars, her favorite food, she had somehow managed to scrape up enough to give her seventy-five cents which seemed like chicken feed after all her efforts. Anyway she had just enough.

Miss La Rose was to appear at Town Hall since Sunny Bay did not own a theater. The appearance was scheduled for ten o'clock. However, Sally McCraw was going to take no chances and set out an hour early so she would be sure to get a seat.

The morning felt warm and comfortable and the rays gave Sally a feeling of being half in a dream. She took the Old Harbor Road and lingered as she came to the Bay. The water sparkled so that she blinked once or twice and the shimmering ripples wiggled and flashed like the lights in a big city night........ Madame McCraw leaning on the arm of a luscious Latin American with a moustache stepped from her red sedan. The crowds roared as she nodded and lifted her dainty hand in acknowledgement of the praise and yells. She held the graceful folds of a net dress in her other hand......... Sally walked fast yet she was somewhat astonished when she found herself in front of Mr.

Nora, the writer character in Godwin's "Notes for a Story" (1976), recalls writing "The Magic Lipstick" as a child. In this tale, a glamorous older woman transforms a young girl's miserable time at the dance by sharing her lipstick. ➤

In The Finishing School, *14-year-old Justin is "enchanted" by artistic Ursula DeVane. In an effort to connect with her idol, Justin buys a bottle of the same body lotion she noticed in the woman's house, and, while rubbing it on herself, pretends to become her mentor. In "Some Side Effects of Time Travel," Gretchen performs a similar body-lotion ritual in honor of her idol, Mother Maloney.* ➤

Stringer's hardware store. It was only a matter of a few blocks now. She wondered if she were too early.

A sign in the local drugstore caught her eye and her heart did a handspring. The sign said, "Be Lucile Lovely with ENCHANTMENT Facial Soap." Underneath was a very flattering picture of Lucile La Rose herself rubbing up a lather of ENCHANT-MENT on her delicate face.

Now Sally was somewhat upset. She had saved faithfully to see Lucile La Rose and dreamed about it many times. She would get to shake the star's hand and might be lucky enough to receive a 10 X 12 autographed picture of Lucile suitable for framing.

Yet suddenly she lost some of her enthusiasm. She gazed at the soap ad and then at her own reflection in the plate glass window. She could either see the star or buy the soap. If she bought the soap she would not have enough money left to get into Town Hall.

The clock in Tom's Jewelry Store told Sally she had better hustle. The soap ad in the window beckoned her. Villagers swarmed into Town Hall two blocks away. Pretty soon the crowd would roar applause and Lucile La Rose would step out of her automobile.

Sally wanted to be able to tell her grandchildren she had shaken hands with the most glamorous star of her day. Yet would it be worth it to spend the rest of her life remembering she had actually touched the star? She liked the thought of Latin American Lovers and red sedans. If she bought the soap she could be as lovely as Lucile. Would it be better to dream or do?

The mayor's daughter disappeared into the local drug store. Some distance away a distinguished car horn blared forth. The crowd broke out with a roar.

So Nice of You to Come

(1955, age 18)

*T*he whole day had a gray flavor, even though the sun was shining and it was April. She ate her lunch in haste, thinking about the unpleasant afternoon that faced her. It was not that she was petrified of dentists anymore—as she had always been as a child. It was just not the kind of thing one looked forward to—an afternoon at the dentist's. She dressed in more appropriate clothes than her usual campus attire, shed her beat-up loafers for trim suede heels and brushed her teeth with care, taking extra pains with dental floss and allowing herself a few extra squirts of mouthwash.

Dr. Hutchinson always remarked about how well she kept her teeth and it flattered her—always a compliment about her "pretty eyes," a pleasant inquiry if she were engaged yet. She acknowledged the fact that she would not dress quite so carefully even if the college did require it, had Dr. Hutchinson not been so flattering—and so unmarried.

He had moved his office from the third floor of the Professional Building to the second floor, and now he had a whole corner of the building to himself. She noticed that he had bought a new set of modern furniture. As she had arrived ten minutes too early, she removed her gloves and picked up a magazine which she had no intention of reading. A receptionist appeared from behind a cloudy glass partition and told her she could go in. Last June he had not had a receptionist.

He looked up, friendly and impersonal, washed his hands and seated her. Greetings were exchanged. "Is this right?" he asked, adjusting the back of the chair.

"Fine," she answered. She wiped her lipstick off

while he took instruments out of drawers, arranged them neatly on the table in front of her, adjusted lights, hummed to himself. He was a small, slender man who looked more like a starved lawyer than the prosperous young dentist she knew he must be. His eyes were dark and sad and brown and always a little bloodshot. They made her wonder where he had been the night before. His hair was straight and black and receding at the temples. He smelled antiseptic, but she did not mind.

"What seems to be bothering you honey?"

"Nothing in particular, Dr. Hutchinson, but it's been almost a year since I last checked with you."

"I see. Well, keep your fingers crossed, honey."

He clanked his instrument against her teeth, holding her hand gently against his stiff white smock. The instrument paused... clanked again, this time with a hollow sound.

"One little thing, darling. Not bad. It won't hurt." He busied himself with preparations.

"I faint with novicane." She said.

He returned anxiously to her chair and laid a hand on her arm. "It would be much better this way," he coaxed softly, "Otherwise it will take much longer. Please trust me."

She closed her eyes tightly. He held her top lip firmly and there was a sharp, nagging sting. "There. That's not bad, is it, honey? All you really feel is a little bit of pressure you're not used to."

Her lip began to swell. She was surprised when she looked sideways at the mirror and did not see a huge bulge on her face. Surely, she thought she could have reached out and touched it. It was uncomfortable.

Almost as if he sensed her discomfort, he pressed his palms on the sides of her head and talked to her. He told her that she was safe with him, that he had never lost a patient yet, about how important it was to have a dentist you could trust. "Sometimes you approach a new man and you don't know whether he will be rough or gentle. In this office, you need never be afraid." The phone rang and the receptionist came in and asked him if he could take it. He excused himself and went on the other side of the glass partition. She heard him talking to someone in monosyllables, as if he were taking directions, or receiving signals over a two-way radio.

Then he came back and smiled broadly and pinched her on the cheek. She did not feel it. He began to drill.

At her slightest wince, he would stop the drill instantly and cradle her head against his chest.

"Water, honey?" And then he would drill some more, alternating between a heavy drill that shook her head and roared in her ears and a light drill which whined and buzzed like a mosquito ready to strike.

"I'm petting you," he told her as he lay aside the drill.

"Is it over?"

"Yes, honey." And he gave a mock sigh and with one final flourish he squirted water in her mouth and sent the receptionist to mix the filling.

"Glad it's over?" he asked sweetly.

"Yes, but you're painless," she replied smiling as she slipped her arm around his waist. It was good to have a dentist that was so warm and understanding.

"It's been almost a year," he went on, "And you are prettier and don't look one bit older."

"No, you," she returned, flattered as she had wanted to be. "You are the one. Why don't you get married, Dr. Hutchinson? You're old enough. Or are you saving your money so you can give her everything when you meet her?"

"Oh, saving it till the right time comes, I guess." He blushed. "You have a nice mouth. So fine and clean. A dentist could fall in love with your mouth." He was bending down, his eyes fixed intently on her face. She thought at first he was looking at her teeth. But then he kissed her. On her nose, her temples, her cheek, and then he touched her lips with his mouth. She responded while thoughts swam in her head. What was this? Kissing your own dentist? His breath was clean

In Father Melancholy's Daughter, *Margaret develops a crush on Adrian Bonner, a psychoanalyst-clergyman more than a dozen years her senior. Like Dr. Hutchinson, he is, in his own way, unattainable. "I wondered if he was married," muses Margaret upon meeting Adrian, one of several parent-figure love objects that* ← *populate Godwin's fiction.*

and sweet. She laughed inwardly at the irony.

"That was the sweetest one I've had in a year." His hands were trembling.

"Most of your patients must be men, then." She struggled to get just the right casual tone of amusement.

"No," he said, "Believe it or not, most of them are women."

"Oh, really?" She felt vaguely piqued.

The receptionist came back into the room holding a tiny metal container of liquid silver. He finished the tooth.

"Don't you think it would be a good idea to take some X-rays and see if there are any more little cavities?" he asked her.

She said yes, by all means. She wanted to come back again.

After the plates had been developed, he brought them in to her and they searched for dark spots like two little children searching for buried treasure. "There is one tiny one, just beginning, honey. I guess to be on the safe side we should take care of it, don't you?"

"Yes."

"Would Friday at eleven be all right?"

"Oh, dear, I have class."

"Then, how about here?" He had taken her outside to a desk and his finger pointed to eight fifteen on the appointment book.

"But, that's so early!" She protested. "I didn't know you even got here that early."

"Shhh. I'll do it for you." His eyes were warm, promising.

"Let me get your coat." He slipped it around her and for one second her body brushed his. When she went out into the waiting room, there were more people—three women and a man. She resented the time he would give all four of them that morning.

*   *   *   *

From Monday to Friday was an incredible length

of time. Of course he was interested in her. Or was
he? Maybe he treated all his patients this way. Why
was he not married? He had the gentleness, the
appeal, the money.

   She would sit on the front campus, her skirts
spread wide over her ankles, and talk about trivial
things with the other girls. Once she imagined that
he would drive up into the campus and get out of his
car and come toward her and she would excuse herself from the silly girls and go over to meet him. She
wanted to tell someone about this new adventure,
but she knew that most people wouldn't approve or
would think it terribly silly of *her*. So she kept quiet
and wondered. In class she once wrote his name
lightly on her lecture pad, then stared in horror at
what she had written and erased it furtively. At
night, she lay in bed, her legs stretched out on top of
the covers because it was warm. And she would feel
the night breeze stroll up her calves and she pretended it was his hand.

   Friday morning, she was up with the sun. Wasn't
this crazy? Getting up at 6:00 for a dentist appointment—and not in dread, but in anticipation so wan-
ton it was almost vulgar. She took a long and
leisurely shower, rubbing the soap vigorously into
her skin, hoping the fragrance would last for three
hours. She chose her clothes carefully, as she would
for an interview or a very special date.

   The skies were threatening, but it would have
seemed too real had the sun been shining. Things
like this always happened to her on overcast days.

   She was too early again. She stopped by the elevator and ran a comb through her hair which had
been slightly dampened and blown by the muggy air.
It fell to her shoulders, loose and careless.

   When she opened the door, she saw his figure
through the glass. He immediately came out to greet
her upon hearing the door open and close. The
receptionist was not there. His hands smelled of
soap and he was looking at her expectantly.

   "Good morning, sweetie. Come in."

*In "Notes for a Story,"
Nora remembers that the
stories she wrote in childhood "usually featured a
solitary person, a
◄ Romantic Outcast."*

She removed her gloves and hated her fingers for shaking.

"Oh, it's too early in the morning for this," she protested gaily. He laughed.

"When you leave this office, you'll be the most wide awake little girl in the world."

"Are you threatening me?"

"No angel, have a seat."

She sat down and he gave her some tissue. She rubbed at her lips and then threw the pink-smudged wad into the wastebasket.

"Bulls eye!" He shouted. "You get half-prices for that." He was standing over her. "You're beautiful. I've thought about you several times this week." He bent down and she closed her eyes and gave him the response she had wanted to give him for four fantasy-filled days. His breath was still clean and sweet, although this morning it was tinged with tobacco. His kiss was a kind of preface to better things. She put her arms under his and clasped her fingers over the center of his back. He made a little sound and pulled her close. She knew this should stop. She pulled away.

"Dr. Hutchinson, I have to go back to school soon."

"I'll see that you get back." His voice was husky.

"I think we ought to start drilling. Please."

"Oh, you can come back. I want you to."

"No, no, no. I can't enjoy this for thinking about the drilling that has to come."

"Oh," he chuckled, "You're putting me off."

"I wouldn't ever do that."

"You're beautiful. You're lips are so full. Where did you get those nice full lips?"

"I, uh————mmmmph."

"Oh, angel."

"Drill me."

"All right, all right." He became completely professional, opening the right drawers, making the right selections. She hated his impersonal manner, because she felt she had lost his attention as a woman and become a mere client.

"We're going to deaden it a little," he announced. "In about the same spot we did yesterday."

"Oh."

"Please trust me. It won't hurt."

He was rubbing her gum. He paused and put her tense arm around his waist. Then the needle pierced her skin. When it came out, he kissed her lightly. He started drilling. If she flinched, he would stop and kiss her.

"Oh, I can only feel you on one side." She joked.

"I'm doing a part time job then, aren't I, angel?"

"Don't do that," she snapped.

"Why not?" He was the rebuffed little boy. "I was just feeling your shoulders."

"If I had wanted you to, I wouldn't have bothered to wear a dress."

He went into a fit of laughter. "Oh, angel! You have a sense of humor, too!"

Then it was over. There were no more fillings. No more check-ups and no more appointments. The air was tense for her.

"Come back in six months, don't forget, honey," he was professionally cheerful.

"Dr. Hutchinson, you are a wonderful dentist," she said.

"And you are a beautiful girl."

"Just keep on making your patients feel secure, giving them what they need—"

"Give them what they need?" It was a question. He drew her to him and kissed her long and hard. She knew then that he wanted her. He had led her toward another room she had never seen.

"This is the recovery room," he told her. There was a neat single bed, made in hospital fashion, only with a Bates bedspread. There was a bare table. There was a chair.

She looked into his eyes. They were almost unfriendly in spite of their fire. They were asking her a question, and suddenly she didn't want to answer now that she was pressed.

"Oh, no!" She shook her head violently. "Oh, no!"

"The young woman in the South ... is taught covertly ... how to 'handle' a man (as one might 'handle' a temperamental stallion) in order to get maximum benefits, but 'without threatening his masculinity,'" Godwin wrote in a 1975 essay "The Southern Belle." Godwin heroines, however, often bump up against such constricting ◄ *codes of behavior.*

In her late teens, recalls Godwin, she "wasted" many pages in her diary "cataloguing the boys who fell into, or eluded, my snare" ("A Diarist on ◄ *Diarists," 1988).*

His manners immediately eclipsed the previous gestures. He was all the competent, sympathetic friend.

"Honey," he chided, "Do you really think I'd be so crude?"

"I don't know." She felt ashamed now for even thinking he had anything in mind.

"Don't you trust me?" He stroked her arm paternally.

"Yes." She answered, as if hypnotized by his tenderness.

He led her to the bed. "Sit down. I want to tell you something." She sat stiffly. He cradled her statue-like form in his arms.

"Angel, I'm—I'm one of those old married men," he began. The bottom dropped out of her stomach. Damn it. She would not let him think that she cared.

"You just kind of got under my skin," he went on. "And I think you felt the same."

"Oh, you're just natural. I mean a married man is still a man," she said casually. "I mean, after all—"

There was a silence.

"Have you any children," she asked disinterestedly.

"Yes. Two girls."

"Oh, I see. That's too bad. You would have made a wonderful bachelor." Another weak attempt at lightness. "I can just see you tearing down the road to Florida in a Jaguar."

"Oh, can you?" He looked flattered. Then, defensively. "We go to Virginia Beach. I drive a station wagon."

And then he kissed her again. She was tense. It was the last time.

He drew away. "You are going to make some man very happy," he said. "You are beautiful and human." His face clouded. "But never, never take your husband for granted. It will be a temptation but don't."

He called her a cab and held her hands in his before she stepped into the waiting room.

In Godwin's 1972 short story "My Lover, His Summer Vacation," a mistress pines for her married lover. She counts the days till he returns, visualizing—with the aid of AAA maps —his family's progress on their trip to the beach. →

"Goodbye, and good luck." He said.

"Goodbye," she said, and closed the door behind her. She wondered if her lipstick, or what was left of it, was in the wrong place. Then she remembered she didn't have any on and stopped and remedied this.

The elevator came and as she let it carry her down one floor, she felt absolutely nothing.

"I think it's going to rain today," said the operator to a prim nurse who was sticking bobby pins into her starched cap.

The next morning she woke up with an ache on the side of her face and when she got up and looked in the mirror she saw a swollen jaw. She had had too much novicane the day before.

Gail Godwin at age 19 or 20.

A Short Story by Gail Godwin

SO NICE
  OF
YOU
   TO COME

The whole day had a gray flavor, even though the sun was
shining and it was April. She ate her lunch in haste, thinking
about the unpleasant afternoon that faced her. It was not that
she was petrified of dentists anymore - as she had always been
as a child. It was just not the kind of thing one looked forward
to - an afternoon at the dentist's. She dressed in more appropriate clothes than her usual campus attire, shed her beat-up
loafers for trim suede heels and brushed her teeth with care,
taking extra pains with dental floss and allowing herself a few
extra squirts of mouthwash.

Dr. Hutchinson always remarked about how well she kept her
teeth and it flattered her - always a compliment about her "pretty
eyes," a pleasant inquiry if she were engaged yet. She acknowledged the fact that she would not dress quite so carefully even
if the college did require it, had Dr. Hutchinson not been so
flattering - and so unmarried.

He had moved his office from the third floor of the Professional
Building to the second floor, and now he had a whole corner of the
building to himself. She noticed that he had bought a new set of
modern furniture. As she had arrived ten minutes too early, she
removed her gloves and picked up a magazine which she had no intention
of reading. A receptionist appeared from behind a cloudy glass
partition and told her she could go in. Last June he had not had
a receptionist.

Gail Godwin

"Allan Gurganus at age 18, in Navy work clothes, Boston Naval Shipyard, writing fiction."

ALLAN GURGANUS

Allan Gurganus made his literary debut in 1974, creating the first gay protagonist to appear in a *New Yorker* short story. The work had been submitted, without Gurganus's knowledge, by his mentor and admirer John Cheever. Fifteen years later Gurganus made an even bigger entrance with the publication of his first book, the acclaimed, best-selling novel *Oldest Living Confederate Widow Tells All*. It's a huge book, big-mouthed and big-hearted. Gloria Naylor, in her judge's report for the Book of the Month Club, wrote, according to *New York* magazine, that "she felt as deeply for Gurganus's Confederate citizens as she did for their slaves."

In "Garden Sermon" (1989), an essay about his novel's origins, Gurganus tells how, in 1968, soon after being forced into the military, he made the ironic and upsetting discovery that his ancestors had been slave owners. That realization directed Gurganus to an engrossing and ever-widening theme: the moral consequences of one person's subservience to another.

"Garden Sermon" also traces the author's voice to its beginnings. In the essay, Gurganus characterizes himself this way: "I start as a stupidly well-brought up young man, a young whitie, of middle class privilege, of country club dances, in North Carolina...." In reading the excerpt from "Just the Idea of Being in Georgia" that follows, we join with this young man—eighteen years after his birth in Rocky Mount, N.C., in 1947 and shortly before he will discover his own, disturbing southern legacy.

Gurganus introduces his story:

I'm grateful this anthology made me face a dusty manilla folder, one stowed in closeted shame for years, one bound by rubber bands already dried to death when Lyndon Johnson led us, a binder marked, even by me, even then when so very young: "Early."

Just as our fingerprints remain constant from infancy to senility—so persists our adoration of what we each consider the most sating and ideal sentence. There from the start, our peculiar metronomic underlying prose rhythm, our cranky sense of humor, our visual gluttony, our moral preoccupations. I study this, the opening of a slightly mechanical very early short story. It seems markedly influenced by the painterly young Updike and by Flannery O'Connor, that builder of gorgeous ethical bear-traps her characters must step into being themselves gorgeous and ethical bear-traps. I see I am already preoccupied by questions of racial justice. I am interested in the mysteriously predetermined characters of obdurate children. I'm tracing the distance between dreamed Edens and actual family auto vacations. Decades later, these obsessions transmigrate across reams of paper, over changes of address and saddening hair loss; these preoccupations span a life lived despite one's better judgment: they each survive, reincarnated in my novel, *Oldest Living Confederate Widow Tells All*. And in *White People*, my book of novellas and stories.

This fragment of an "Early" tale strikes me—a long time teacher of writing—as heartening for some reasons, hopeless for others. The narrative's attempt to create complacent trust-funded foils seems heavy-handed and very very young. But this fragment is heartening in its love of detail, its crude willingness to begin inside a dream (something I'd never do now), and mainly in its punch-drunk love of language. And yet, on the basis of this sliver alone, I might not predict a life of daily writing for this ethically certain and therefore quite satirical young man. What struck Mr. "Early" as sophisticated strikes me now as endearingly naive.

Here's a writing exercise for you: Go find your birth certificate; study your own baby fingerprints. Look, they're no bigger than punctuation! Now, ink your grizzled adult hand; press it down beside that helpless little chimp pawprint. Recognize yourself, already formed there on the baby page, helplessly and already so … so damn … you. Then weep.

Or sigh, rejoicing. Alternate the shaking of your head side to side with rueful grateful laughter. Your case has been on file since Time's efficient Hall of Records got constructed eons back: your subject matter was decided then. And the writing that you're doing now, is it being saved in a binder marked "Middle" or one marked "Late"?

Tell me I can yet progress. Don't call me A Major Novelist; let me be an inkling. Say I have, at least, a chance someday to get it right.

Curve your left palm against my right cheek and lie to me: Tell me, "Baby? It's still Early. Baby? You're still Early."

Luther's Dream

Luther Smythe dreamed he and his family were sitting, quite naked, on a very white beach. How peaceful and ridiculous our life is here, he thought, smiling at his ~~beautiful~~ wife, Millie. Her eyes flirted over the green husk of ~~the~~ coconut she seemed to be drinking from. Earlier, the children had been kicking sand at one another and wading at the edge of the azure water but they had now settled down nearby. Dennis, their son, sat smoothing sand over a second green coconut. His blonde hair sunbleached blonder shone oddly in the tropical light. Some slight distance from them, facing inland, their daughter, Cora, sat, stripped of everything but her perpetual expression, pouting even here in paradise. Her chest, so recently like her brother's, was changed, Luther saw. Her faint nipples seemed to be pouting, too. Millie saw Luther watching Cora. She dropped her coconut on the sand and crawled over to her husband on all fours, her own breasts framed, pendulous between her stiff, moving arms. Sand flew as she scrambled toward him. Luther noticed abruptly that only he was clothed, wearing the paint-splattered khakis he used for working in their little garden back in Cambridge. Millie crawled up, knelt beside him and whispered into his ear, over the sound of the surf which he'd not noticed until now, "Cora bores me, Luther. She _is_ our daughter, certainly, but can children be bores? I think Cora's one."

FROM

Just the Idea of Being in Georgia
(1965, age 18)

Luther's Dream

*L*uther Smythe dreamed he and his family were sitting, quite naked, on a very white beach. How peaceful and ridiculous our life is here, he thought, smiling at his wife, Millie. Her eyes flirted over the green husk of coconut she seemed to be drinking from. Earlier, the children had been kicking sand at one another and wading at the edge of the azure water but they had now settled down nearby. Dennis, their son, sat smoothing sand over a second green coconut. His blonde hair sunbleached blonder shone oddly in the tropical light. Some slight distance from them, facing inland, their daughter, Cora, sat, stripped of everything but her perpetual expression, pouting even here in paradise. Her chest, so recently like her brother's, was changed, Luther saw. Her faint nipples seemed to be pouting, too. Millie saw Luther watching Cora. She dropped her coconut on the sand and crawled over to her husband on all fours, her own breasts framed, pendulous between her stiff, moving arms. Sand flew as she scrambled toward him. Luther noticed abruptly that only he was clothed, wearing the paint-splattered khakis he used for working in their little garden back in Cambridge. Millie crawled up, knelt beside him and whispered into his ear, over the sound of the surf which he'd not noticed until now, "Cora bores me, Luther. She is our daughter, certainly, but can children be bores? I think Cora's one."

II

Luther woke with the conviction that they should all go to the tropics, the sooner the better. Four weeks later, at sixty miles an hour, they were returning from a compromised fulfillment of his dream, two weeks camping in Florida.

A long dent in the radiator grill gave the snoutish front of the Citroen the look of a squint or grimace. Two years earlier, the left rear door snapped open while turning a corner. It refused afterwards to shut and had since been tied closed with the cord of a broken Venetian blind. Headed due north on US 301, Luther Smythe drove the Citroen wagon he'd bought new eleven years ago with money his parents gave him when he finally got his Master's from Harvard. An aluminum canoe, longer than the car, was overturned on top of it, held there by a network of twine and ropes. The car wore it like a helmet with numerous chinstraps. Millie's red bandanna, so recently her halter, had been tied to the back end of the boat and now swam straight out behind it. Provisions packed under the overturned canoe had been wrapped in a clear plastic tarpaulin. Most of this covering was unfastened after two hundred miles of wind, and it now whipped and billowed up out of the canoe, smothering, then releasing the red bandanna. The tarpaulin fanned out feet behind the car like some theatrical equivalent of water.

Inside the car was quieter. After a last Florida breakfast, all slept but Luther who sat, contentedly, hands around the wheel, feeling in control of more somehow than just the car. Autonomous, he thought; I feel distinctly autonomous. The white shirt he wore was half-buttoned and some tanned ribs showed. The khaki pants were splattered with yellow housepaint and flecks of red clay from a ceramics class he'd taken. The road came in to him through smudged tortoiseshell glasses, mended at the nosebridge with a grimy loop of adhesive tape.

Just across the state line, Luther felt a sudden

← *Obsessed with finding his old Civil War battle sites, Captain Willie Marsden loads his pregnant wife (later known as Oldest Living Confederate Widow) and eight small children into the Model T for a three-week road trip that, like Luther's trek, examines some North-South scars.*

Confederate soldier Willie → Marsden, newly home from the Civil War, pities his mother, injured in the burning of the family mansion—but even more, perhaps, he pities her former, vain, indulged self.

Young, white Lucy → Marsden ponders uncomfortably the segregation of "Baby Africa," the shack ghetto on the outskirts of turn-of-the-century Falls, North Carolina.

pleasurable contempt for all the sleeping residents of Georgia, and then, an equally irrational pity for them. The night before, he'd explained to the children while they roasted marshmallows how, until Northern people like their father had come down to demonstrate how wrong it was, there had been public bathrooms marked "White Ladies", and others marked "Colored Women". Over their speared marshmallows, the children had eyed him suspiciously. It pleased him that they could not conceive of this sort of cruelty.

He now scanned the landscape for what he'd always imagined as the essential meanness of Georgia, a quality so real to him he'd assumed the vegetation would reflect it by being, as he pictured the residents, all scrubby and gnarled. Maybe I've misimagined a few details, Luther conceded as he eyed suspiciously the passing farmland; the foliage *may* be lush, but the meanness is not gone. This early on a Sunday morning, it is still stretched out somewhere, snoring.

For a moment, a delicate fear like stagefright came over him, and he wished the others were awake to help him watch for whatever it was he was expecting, but he dismissed this, finally, as ridiculous and let himself be soothed by the sound of his automobile moving himself and his sleepers straight through and out of Georgia. Having just spent seventy dollars in preventive repairs to the aging car, Luther felt the Citroen now repaying all his trust in it.

Savoring the lack of traffic, he felt exempt from all the usual daytime irritations. The children had slept, then woke and bickered inventively for an hour, and now, after breakfast, they had fallen back to sleep again. The car moved through thin strands of mist still stretched across the highway at this hour and, gazing through the dampness these left on the windshield, Luther felt refreshed, a new man ready to forget what had annoyed him on the trip down: the dashboard ashtray full of Millie's cigarette butts, missing their usual lipstick stains since vacation began, the silver casing and dangling wires of a

A budding painter at age 12, Gurganus sold one work to a local art-history professor who encouraged his creativity and inquired after the boy's ideas. "I had been thinking for twelve years and nobody had ever asked," he told New York *magazine.*

stereo casette tape player that had been yanked, semi-professionally, out of the car in the guarded parking lot of Bonwit Teller in Boston which apologized but would not assume responsibility. Nor did he see the few remaining tape cartridges, left behind as if in judgement on the Smythe's musical taste: a Segovia one, for instance, just to the left of his sleeping wife's red polished toenails. Luther, rather, drove on, as fast as the car would go with the gas depressed as far as his blue deck shoe could press it.

Haiku had been his hobby since undergraduate days. And now slightly exceeding the Georgia speed limit as a matter of principle, the bow of his overturned canoe forming a cozy eave, a widow's peak over the landscape, with his small, planned family, so recently well-fed, simplified by sleep all around him, Luther fiddled happily with words, stress, syllables, all bent on praising aspects of an almost overripe papaya he had enjoyed at breakfast. Occasionally, he muttered a line aloud to himself, sometimes slowly repeating it a different way. "The juice's route down chin...The spilled pink juice lives now in the napkin...briefly tinting a man's mouth...tinting pink briefly." Fifteen minutes passed quietly like this, one twenty fourth of Georgia.

War and Peace slipped off his wife's lap and fell face down onto the sandy floor, trapping an orange peel. Luther looked over at Millie. She stirred slightly, reached up, still asleep, and using her index finger, scratched, with delightful accuracy, the very tip of her sunburned nose. Her arm fell back to her lap. The soundness of her sleep had always seemed to him, at better moments, her attempt to compensate for his insomnia. He silently admired her, head back, brown neck taut. He looked quickly to the uneventful highway and back at Millie and back and forth. She was as tanned now as when he met her at a party in Bermuda fifteen years ago. She had been seated, in her white dress, on a white rattan lawn chair and he'd assumed she was French until, finally introduced, she lifted her hand to him and spoke forth in the very voice of Radcliffe College, a glib, opinionated girl,

◄ In Gurganus's story "Adult Art" (1988), a school superintendent (and former art history major) similarly harbors, beneath his quiet outer life, an erotically charged aesthetic sensibility. With haikulike brevity, he captures the beauty of his current object of desire this way: "A vein in his neck beats like a clock, only liquid."

interested, she said that night, in "everything and nothing". Over the miles, her skirt had inched its way up her brown thighs, slightly glossed, as if polished. One of her sandaled feet was twisted at a poignant angle, resting on its side, and her opened legs, crammed voluptuously into the space under the dashboard, pleased him to look down at.

Captain Marsden also ➤ indulges in pleasurable, proprietary visions of his young bride, picturing her at home in bed every half hour. He suggests that they synchronize their day so that he can accurately imagine her at certain moments, say, touching herself.

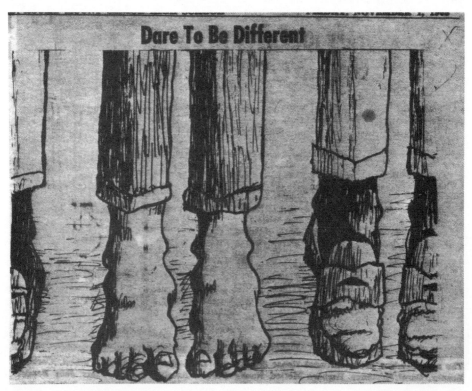

Gurganus drew this cartoon for his high school newspaper. "At 17, I was in love with how unlike others I was," he writes in his essay "Garden Sermon."

Allan Gurganus, "more or less grown."

Mark Helprin in 1968.

MARK HELPRIN

A cache of Mark Helprin's juvenilia, kept by his father in the family safe, was stolen about twenty years ago along with the rest of the safe's contents. The burglars must have been too much in a hurry to examine their plunder, says the author, otherwise they surely would have left his childhood writings behind. Their illicit, and no doubt unappreciated, gain is certainly our loss.

Helprin, who was born in 1947 in New York City, decided to become a writer when he was seventeen. As he remembers, he was recovering from a motorcycle accident in Paris when one evening, after experiencing a crippling headache, he perceived an unusual clarity of mind. In the middle of the night, he tried his hand at a description of the Hagia Sophia—Istanbul's famous cathedral-mosque, which he had never seen in person. Upon rereading his words the following morning, he was impressed with how much they seemed like the words of a real writer. Four years later, Helprin's short stories began to appear in *The New Yorker*, and he published his first collection, *A Dove of the East*, in 1975. His subsequent works include *Ellis Island* (stories, 1981) and *Winter's Tale* (a novel, 1983). In 1991 he published his third novel, *A Soldier of the Great War*. The great war, he told *The New York Times Magazine*, is "in a sense, life," a point he also considers in the following story, "Lightning North of Paris." Written, as he recalls, right around his twentieth birthday, "Lightning North of Paris" first appeared in *A Dove of the East*, yet it lands within not only the letter but also the spirit of this anthology; the story exudes innocence, due to the abandon with which the budding author seems to revel in Hemingway's Paris.

When asked by the *Times Magazine* if Hemingway was one of his influences, Helprin (who says that he found the question immaterial) could not resist this droll response:

> My answer to that is this: The novel that he wrote is good and the novel that I wrote is good and the two novels are good and if you read one novel you know that they're good because the heart of the first novel is good and the heart of the second novel is good and a man knows that a good novel is good when he reads it and it doesn't matter that another man has written it and it will always be that way.

Lightning North of Paris
(circa 1967, age 19–20)

*I*t was approaching five o'clock on a cool afternoon in late October. Harry Spence sat on a stone railing in front of the Jeu de Paume, and as he waited for Shannon he looked through a maze of autumn trees stirred by a wind promising of winter and challenging in its direct cold northernness, a wind which lighted fires. Shannon was extremely tall and graceful. This, her face, and her dancer's body were a continual proclamation that she be taken dead seriously. In fact, anyone not always alert with her would find himself left behind as if in the slipstream of a fast train which had just passed. She stared other women down like a man; they often hated her. In a café she had the same effect as music or a fireplace, quickly becoming the center. Men were drawn to her because they did not immediately fall in love. Her power put them off until they got close enough and then went mad, leaving lovely wives and waiting for Shannon on the street, where if she passed they became speechless as she crossed in leotards and a long skirt, a soft silk scarf trailing.

When Harry took up with Shannon he knew she would leave, but he was privileged to be with her for a time because he would not scare. He was always on guard, convincing her that he too was arbitrary and painfully free, as independent as a cloud sailing across frontiers. It was an act he put on successfully, but it was exhausting. Only a young man could have kept it up. He thought that if her demands had been made on a man older than twenty-five he would have died; frequency of intercourse was only a small part of the monumental task. That year was like a Channel swim. He wondered how he had done it, and how Shannon could always remain Shannon. They all moved like figures inside a furnace, which at the time was appropriate, and constructive, for they sat during the night at small desks and penned words or music, or played instruments, or painted, not knowing who was really good and who would fall back to the small towns of New York and Ohio never to be heard from again, perhaps to be unknown interpreters of those who had remained.

Harry Spence had not come to Paris because it was Paris, although once there he realized that even in imitation long after the originals (none of whom had really been first) the city was still a blaze and a dream. He had been granted a restricted fellowship stipulating that he live in a section of Paris dear to the benefactor and considered by him to be magical in its effect on musical composition. When flying into the city that September, he wished he were a writer of words rather than music. The prospect was stunning, spread white into the bordering fields. Masculine ministries enclosed luxurious gardens of mathematical green—from the air this appeared to be the hallmark of the city. He had had the feeling that he was returning to the vortex of civilization, having indeed been there before, that the inhabitants were possessed of a strange combination of clarity and feeling and were at that moment lighting fires over secret magnetic zones which crisscrossed the earth,

In Winter's Tale, *Helprin imagines the magic of New York City. The bridges and streets, says Praeger, " 'I believe that they're alive ← unto themselves....' "*

making artists, and converged at Paris in the center of wheat and wine-filled French prairies sobered and chilled by blasts from the North.

Wherever children gather at a forge or fire, its red heat giving them warmth in darkness, they learn quickly principles of art. This is what Harry had thought when very young as he sat by a fire with his father and uncle and grandfather in the middle of autumn fields which they knew would see frost by morning. The grandfather had passed through Paris on his way to the front; the father and uncle had crossed the Seine riding on the same tank. They had ached from their hearts to see Paris in peace, to live and work there. They had carried cartridges through Saint-Germain-des-Prés and been continually on edge and nervous, for they then were sent to bosky woods near the German border to fight and kill. After his father returned, his life had calmed. He never yearned for the war, but he knew it had made him. There was plenty of thunder in the following peace, haystack-leveling winds to test him, obstacles to his dreams, but none of his later adversity had defined and shaped him as had the war. He wished with all his might that he would not communicate this to his son, that the boy, born after the fighting, would find other means to know himself and would not repeat the horror for the sake of becoming a man. He wished for his son peaceful storms and not the waxen white light of artillery duels. He prayed for this. And Harry *was* different, soft, a baby beyond his time, unknowing of combat and the continual deathly backdrop of war, an almost effeminate university-bred tortoise-shell-glassed composer of music. His father and uncle, the survivors of that session by the fire, rejoiced that he would be thrust into the heart of Paris in a piping time of peace, peace, said the uncle a veteran of four years of solid war, peace, God bless it.

He set up in a small apartment overlooking the Champ de Mars and on the first day of autumn when the returning population was in full frenzy, in a cop-per-colored bar where he stopped early in the morn-

"Whatever you do, don't join the army," Alessandro's father implores him in A Soldier of the Great War. *"Is that clear?"* →

ing to drink chocolate and eat pieces of buttered bread which he paid for as he took them one by one off a round plate, as the streets were washed down and men in blue coats streamed in and out, he looked across the room to a bank of sunny windows where the white dusty light was coming in on Shannon and made her look like an Irishwoman in a Sargent portrait.

Because she was so beautiful in her enlightened posture and expression, and because an intelligence radiated from her, he became very daring and approached the table, cup of chocolate in hand, a beautiful leather briefcase under one arm. He said *"Sprechen Sie Deutsch?"* at which she smiled and then laughed, because if they had been two Texas longhorns standing there in the corner of the café it could not have been more obvious that both were Americans; the fact was like water pouring over a dam. They went out and walked away hours. His daring began to extend itself for a year's tenure. He fell in love with her, having the peculiar feeling which new kisses can bring, an overwhelming sense of being alive in the face of the present. The world became an energetic frame. It was almost like being the leading man in an opera. Within a week she had moved two wicker trunks into his apartment. She did ballet exercises in the middle of the floor while they talked. She could not have told him that the first night when they walked up the Champs Élysées and basked in the lights and September fountains, a red-bearded Rumanian architect sat staring at her former bed and cursed himself in Hungarian, French, and English, and eventually threw a glass full of Scotch flat up against the wall.

And then she disappeared each morning and came back only after dark, having danced every day down to exhaustion. Harry was writing music, at which he was becoming masterful, in which he was beginning to be able to do anything he wanted. By terrifying bouts of sustained work he was forcing the creation of a great bed of experience, so that in the strong frame and healthy body of his twenties could be found an old man who had lived since the turn of the century, and whose wisdom at the craft astounded and amazed even competitors and the nearly deaf. He could write pieces as deep and blue as a fjord, echoing and quiet, and he could write as red as he pleased, American jazz born of a rich heartland and the death of the wilderness. And strangely, the better he got, the better he got, with no chance of slipping. This stood even Shannon in awe. Once he had said, I can do anything, absolutely anything. I am almost a master, and she had looked mean and tough and said, You can do *nothing*, leaving the room in a fit of envy which meant he could have her for at least another six months until their powers evened out again and she was able to glide and swirl naturally and gracefully beyond the ecstatic points to which his labor had taken him. But he was going farther, and they both knew it.

Winter passed. They had an enormous electricity bill, for the lights burned late at night, with Harry bearing down on his blinding white music pads and then touching the piano as if he were stroking a horse. Shannon danced and danced, slept from exhaustion, and danced again, becoming like Harry one of the ones who did not return in quiet and sadness to the starting point with a series of exquisite memories and some first editions. She danced at the National Theater. His pieces were really performed. Sometimes he conducted, in a light gray and blue tweed suit and his tortoise-shell glasses, and when he turned at the close and faced an approving audience, their feet stamping, the timbers of the hall shaking as if the earth had quaked, it threw him off balance for weeks during which he stuffed himself with good food and could write only music which was so squeaky it sounded like rusty wheels in the high Gare du Nord, music which if played for the pigeons would have made them rise in intolerance and bend in a sheet of white and gray across the plane of Paris sky.

And he ran in the afternoon amid the blue which met buildings softly under the clouds, panting, pushing his glasses back on his face as they tried to fall to the ground. Eventually he built up a routine of going

---

"If you really want to ➤ enjoy life, you must work quietly and humbly to realize your delusions of grandeur," advises Alessandro, as an old man, in A Soldier of the Great War. When the boy Nicolò replies that he doesn't have such delusions, Alessandro counters: "Start to have them."

Helprin's visual images of music remain a trademark of his fiction. In "The Schreuderspitze" (1977), Wallich, listening to Beethoven on the radio during a lightning storm, "could hear cracks and flashes in the music as he saw them delineated across darkness. They looked and sounded like the bent riverine limbs of dead trees...." ➤

all the way out to Neuilly and back, and as he got stronger it wrote Shannon in for another few months, for she could love only strength and could not face weakness. But it was so hard, to run and write, to eat like a beast and then starve, to make love until the dawn and then be fit only for the morgue, to be moved so by the music that it was like an electrocution, complete surrender and exhaustion.

That summer they went to Greece. The winter's rain seemed as far away as medieval European cities, and yet it was in one of these cities that Harry wrote in thundering clear classical style. He took the opportunity to take down good Greek music, and to write barrelhouse rolls to limericks they made up. These became extremely popular at a restaurant in Nea Epidavros called "Yellow House of Nonsensical Pleasure" where the foreigners gathered in the evenings. Of several dozen Swedes, Englishmen, French, Greeks, Americans, and Italians, three had birthdays on the same day, two (including Harry) had perfect pitch, all knew the fountain at Aix-en-Provence (or said they did), and everyone except the women except one was in love with Shannon—as if drawn into the maelstrom; the bright challenge took them up in its hands like moths.

Harry and Shannon slept on the roof; a phonograph played them to sleep. As they watched the stars they became separate. Harry knew she was in love with the doctor, an Oklahoman who had been broken in Vietnam and then come back stronger. He was both larger and wiser than Harry, although he could not compose music, and he called Harry "Spence." Next to him Harry felt like a young midget, and because he was not fresh or new at Shannon's game he lost early on in the subtle war of deferences at the Yellow House of Nonsensical Pleasure. Harry retired to the piano and played his barrelhouse rolls, and then stopped going there altogether, and then Shannon did not come up to the roof.

He cursed himself for not having the wisdom war brings. His father had told him of lying awake in an

As they embark on their 70-kilometer hike, old Alessandro presents to young Nicolò this code for living: "You must give everything you have. You must love unto exhaustion, work unto exhaustion, and ← *walk unto exhaustion."*

← *Alessandro subscribes to this same idea when he speaks about having been "broken the way one sometimes can be broken" and yet becoming "stronger than before."*

open meadow with an automatic rifle across his lap, waiting for the enemy while the sky was filled with artillery flashes and the white lightning of battle, a terror which numbed the little patrol in the field, something Harry might never know. It was one of the major reasons Harry loved his father, his sense early on that the man knew terror and bloodshed, and was grateful and loving just to be alive. They, the men in his family who had started out as merchants and professors and been made into warriors, knew something he could not. But they envied him for his cradle of peace. There was no way to compete with the Oklahoman, with the bronzed face and tranquil eyes which had seen men die in war. Harry was at a loss but determined to push with the same energy which had led them to survive, toward a depth in peace *they* could never know. He too was a fighter of sorts. To take in the whole great compass of the world—this was his task. The expanse of it could kill, and he had to dodge as best he could the potent backlash of music's ecstasy. He left for Paris precipitously, almost without thinking or looking back, and when he arrived he forwarded Shannon her wicker trunks, wondering what she would do with twenty-five pairs of dancing shoes in a wild rocky spine of the Peloponnesus. She had written that if she returned she would meet him at the Jeu de Paume at five o'clock on October 27, the day after her ticket expired.

It was already five-thirty. He could smell roasting chestnuts. He was in his light gray and blue suit, and he carried the leather briefcase under his arm. It was filled with musical manuscripts he had written since his return from Greece. He was steady, slept soundly, spoke softly, and smiled more. He was older, and felt like his father, enjoying little things. His desk looked more chestnut-colored, and the bright lights of autumn were sharper than they had ever been. He knew now who was good, and he knew he was good. Massive clouds made the dark come early. Cold lightnings could be seen far north of Paris. High in the air birds rode thermals, tiny white flecks against the gray clouds. He loved the cool air, and looked up and

> *This theme of adversity breeding a simple appreciation of life is vividly represented in "The Schreuderspitze," the story of a photographer seeking to still his grief by exposing himself to the dangers of winter mountain climbing in the Alps: "Like soldiers who come from training toughened and healthy, he had about him the air of a small child."*

down the paths, but they were emptying and the leaves just rustled on the floor of the Tuileries as if they were a German forest. That night he would sit under his lamp and pen the blinding white sheets; every day he felt himself rising a little higher, quietly, powerfully. He jumped off the railing and walked toward the Champs Élysées. He was due at dinner with a friend whose sister was to be there. He was in the Ministry of Finance and she was a model who had appeared on the covers of *Match*, *Jours de France*, and *Elle*. One evening Harry had been at a restaurant alone and had stared at her picture, feeling himself fall into a trance somehow allied to the sweet darkness outside. My God, he said, as his heart opened to her image. The serenity was numbing. He found himself walking with quick step as a winter wind came down the Champs Élysées.

He passed a tall girl with a beret. That bittersweet frame and the cold rushing air, the leaves like percussion, made him shudder. His friend's sister had deep blue eyes and on the cover of *Elle* she had been wearing a blue velvet gown. He knew he would be loving her soon, in the quiet of autumn, smooth, silent, and blue.

Alessandro as a young man of 20 places great value on his fountain pen, which he ◄ uses to write everything. "It was the most precious of all the instruments he possessed, including his penis, though, admittedly, the pen was replaceable."

Nine-year-old Alessandro is smitten by the sight of a young member of a royal entourage. With similar mingling of hope and presumption, he decides that later he "would ascend not to his room but to the room of the blonde girl in the velvet dress.... They would spend the entire night alone in the dark, pressed together, motionless. This would mix their hearts forever.... He decided that her ◄ name was Patrizia."

Mark Helprin

"The author of 'The Boy's Tennis,' age 10—contemplating that masterpiece with a little too much complacency, three years after its creation," said John Hersey.

JOHN HERSEY

*I*n 1946 John Hersey published *Hiroshima*, the profound and enduring journalistic narrative of six survivors caught in that city's atomic explosion and the aftermath. In other notable Hersey works, the author similarly focuses on victims caught in dire circumstances. His 1950 novel *The Wall* depicts the oppression of Polish Jews inside the Warsaw ghetto. In *The Algiers Motel Incident* (1968), Hersey investigates white racism and the deaths of three young black men during Detroit's summer of 1967. Other deeply afflicted characters can be found in his novels *A Single Pebble* (1956), *White Lotus* (1965), and *The Call* (1985).

Though he was a self-described agnostic, the fact that Hersey was drawn to attend to the suffering of others may be traceable to his roots as a missionary's son. Born in Tientsin, China, in 1914, Hersey lived there his first eleven years, during which time he saw, on the periphery of his own sheltered existence, images of the poverty and distress his parents were trying to alleviate.

Even in Hersey's juvenile piece included here—a capering, boyish adventure—the protagonists witness other characters' misfortunes and attempt to provide relief.

"The Boy's Tennis," written by Hersey at age seven, is a fun companion piece to his 1988 short story "God's Typhoon." Like the juvenile piece, the adult story, a haunting remembrance, is about two young Western boys living in China and their reaction to a freak accident. Considered in this light, "The Boy's Tennis" becomes a significant relic, an actual embodiment of the youthful perspective Hersey later evokes.

Three years before his death on March 24, 1993, the author discussed his juvenilia in a letter to *First Words*:

> Enclosed herewith is a photocopy of the original ms. of an ill-told tale of mine, "The Boy's Tennis"— a title which seems to have nothing to do with the story that follows. I wrote this in China in the summer of 1921, when I was seven. I can date it accurately because it appears in a scrapbook of my activities kept by my mother, on the page before an issue of *The Hersey News*, dated September 9th, 1921. I had started writing the family newspaper earlier that year on my father's L.C. Smith typewriter, which also produced this story. (I was apparently already, at that age, groping—if it can even be called that—for my lifelong metiers in fiction and journalism.) Besides reporting such news as that the Hersey family had recently returned to Tientsin from the North China summer resort of Peitaiho, the paper carried ads—e.g., one offering my two older brothers as laborers at low wages; one that reads "For free distribution: SMILES, furnished in quanities by JOHN HERSEY"; and another advertising Ivory Soap, with the legend: "IVORYS HERE ITS BETTER THAN BEER."
>
> I've concluded that the title of this story must have derived from a notion that as the action begins, Bob and Johnny are walking home after playing tennis at the Peitaiho courts near the so-called "American Beach" and near Rocky Point, on which the first of the two villains fetches up. "Tobad," as Bob so poignantly puts it at the end of the story, that the author forgot to tell the reader this.

THE BOY'S TENNIS
Chapter 1.
THE NARROW ESCAPE

Bob and Johnny were going home the long way from school.
They long way was along the beach a mile and another mile
up the hill.. They were going along the beach when they saw
the bully, Bert Brown swiming. He had with him some other
boy. They then realized that Albert was , as usual bullying
the two boy's little friend- Billy Harrison. The moment the
bully saw the boys he swam for all he was worth(That was not
very fast)but poor little Bill could not swim at all. " Come
back here yoy big bully!" Yelled Bob. "If you dont we'll make
you"put in Johnny. The bully stoll refused to and as he swam
along not looking ahead but at the boys he swam crookedly
and he soon found himself on the sharp rocks of thebay near
the boys. but what about Bill. He was now under water and The
boys swam for their friend's life. THey soon reached him and
tugged him to the shore. They thought he was dead, but they
went to the hospital on their way home and left him there. they
said that were coming there that after noon to see about it.
They were now going to the Harrison house to tell them about
Billy 's misfortune.on the way they had to pass the paint shop
where many cans of paint were stored. Across the read was the
hospital.

A boy was walking along the sidewalk . He was playing
with matches. A girl of about seventeen came along the street
on a bicycle. The boy carelessly threw the match into the stree
but it landed on the skirt of thr riding girl. She looked
aroung at her burning. An auto came at about the rate of 30
miles an hour. the driver was looking at something else when
all of a sudden he ran into the poor girl. The girl was thrown
in the display window of the shop

Chapter II
"DO THE RESCUE!!!"

The paints in the window were now on fire. The boys
were not idle. They immediatly to the door ran and broke in
the show window. Bob ran for the girl and Johnny went toward
a little hand fire-extinguisher and did his best at putting-
the fire aroung the girl out he managed to get most of it

out. Then there was Bob.He carried the fainted and limp
girl out of the shop and laid her on the ready boxes on
the sidewalk which had been put there by the alreadybig
crowd. Just then the kindest nurse came along.."Why"she
said,"That is Betty Jenkins. She just got out of the infirmery today. she went for a bicycle ride, didn't she?
She is seventeen and came on bussiness and sudtenly fell
sick," "Yes she was riding a bike." saib Bob. "Tobad."

The Boy's Tennis
(1921, age 7)

Chapter 1.
THE NARROW ESCAPE

*B*ob and Johnny were going home the long way from school. The long way was along the beach a mile and another mile up the hill. They were going along the beach when they saw the bully, Bert Brown swiming. He had with him some other boy. They then realized that Albert was, as usual bullying the two boy's little friend—Billy Harrison. The moment the bully saw the boys he swam for all he was worth (That was not very fast) but poor little Bill could not swim at all. "Come back here you big bully!" Yelled Bob. "If you don't we'll make you" put in Johnny. The bully still refused to and as he swam along not looking ahead but at the boys he swam crookedly and he soon found himself on the sharp rocks of the bay near the boys. But what about Bill. He was now under water. The boys swam for their friend's life. They soon reached him and tugged him to the shore. They thought he was dead, but they went to the hospital on their way home and left him there. They said that [they] were coming there that after noon to see about it. They were now going to the Harrison house to tell them about Billy's misfortune. On the way they had to pass the paint shop where many cans of paint were stored. Across the road was the hospital.

A boy was walking along the sidewalk. He was playing with matches. A girl of about seventeen came along the street on a bicycle. The boy carelessly threw the match into the street but it

Hersey further realizes the dramatic potential of a friend's water rescue in his novel A Single Pebble, *in which Old Big, a Chinese junk owner, recklessly launches his sampan into the turbulent Yangtze in pursuit of his drowning comrade, Old Pebble.* →

landed on the skirt of the riding girl. She looked around at her burning. An auto came at about the rate of 30 miles an hour. The driver was looking at something else when all of a sudden he ran into the poor girl. The girl was thrown in the display window of the shop.

Chapter II
"TO THE RESCUE!!!"

The paints in the window were now on fire. The boys were not idle. They immediatly to the door ran and broke in the show window. Bob ran for the girl and Johnny went toward a little hand fire-extinguisher and did his best at putting the fire around the girl out [and] he managed to get most of it out. Then there was Bob. He carried the fainted and limp girl out of the shop and laid her on the ready boxes on the sidewalk which had been put there by the alreadybig crowd. Just then the kindest nurse came along. "Why," she said, "That is Betty Jenkins. She just got out of the infirmery today. She went for a bicycle ride, didn't she? She is seventeen and came on bussiness and suddenly fell sick." "Yes she was riding a bike." said Bob. "Tobad."

Dr. Wyman, the proud missionary in "God's Typhoon," is not so fortunate as Betty. He is eviscerated by a flying piece of sheet metal, a freak accident that leaves its mark on the story's two young
◄ protagonists.

"The same person, still smug, approximately three quarters of a century later," Hersey added.

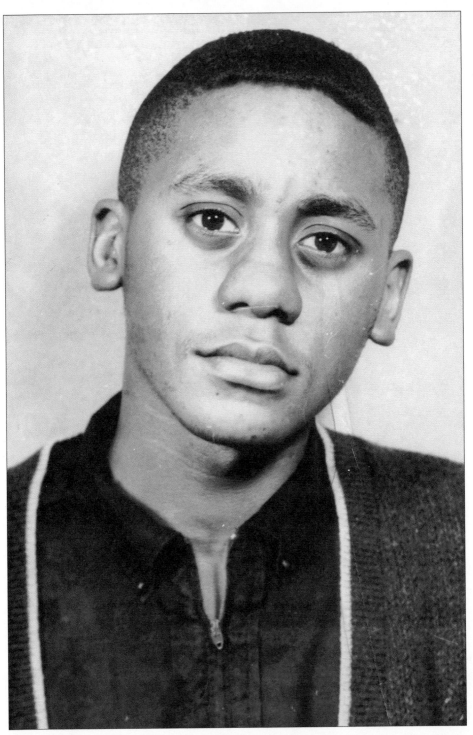

Charles Johnson took this self-portrait to fulfill a high school photography assignment. "What's odd about this photo to me," he says, "is that in it I'm 17, which is the age my son Malik is now (he's a much better looking kid than I was, thanks to his mother's genes)."

CHARLES JOHNSON

*C*harles Johnson gained wide recognition when he won the 1990 National Book Award for his novel *Middle Passage*. Johnson's fourth book of fiction, *Middle Passage* is about a newly freed bondman, who, in order to escape some debts and a romantic commitment, stows aboard an Africa-bound slave ship, on which he undergoes a voyage of self-discovery. The novel is suffused with philosophy (the subject of the author's graduate studies), politics (an interest since high school), and religion (Johnson describes himself as an "on-again-off-again Buddhist")—all the while spinning its sea story. And in this multifaceted way it explores a key Johnson theme: the Self's journeys across racial, class, cultural, and other boundaries—a theme with which the author was already experimenting in his late teens. Of the four pieces of prose that follow, the first three were composed for a high school creative writing class and appeared in a school publication; the fourth is a letter to the editor of his college newspaper.

"I never saw myself as a writer," says Johnson of his youth. In high school writing was a sideline while he devoted himself to his true passion, cartooning. He drew a comic strip, "Wonder Wildkit," coproduced bimonthly with a classmate; and contributed illustrations, as well, to the high school paper.

Born in Evanston, Illinois, in 1948, Johnson, an only child, describes himself as having been a "serious kid ... very introspective" and pensive about "the world around me. Why it was the way it was. I don't think it's easy to be a black kid growing up in the fifties and be frivolous."

He credits his mother with fueling his intellectual and artistic curiosity (she often brought home discarded books from the Northwestern University sorority where she worked). His father, a city employee, exerted a more businesslike influence and once signed Johnson up for a surprise summer job: "Doing what?" asked Johnson, just home from college for summer break. "You're a garbage man," his father announced. "He taught me how to work," says the author.

Man Beneath Rags
(1965, age 17)

Rutherford Calhoun, the wayward freedman in Middle Passage, *recognizes his kinship with the Allmuseri slaves below deck and other fellow sufferers aboard the* Republic. →

*E*vening was growing colder as the white-collar workers scurried home to warm fires and after-dinner pipes. A large pair of eyes, half closed by cataracts, watched them with uncomprehending envy. Calloused hands rubbed vigorously together to fight the chilling night air, as a bent back leaned against a locked doorway. A doorway that is always locked.

Another human shuck in tattered cloth joined him on his doorstep throne. Exchanging names was unnecessary. Two pair of eyes, tired and bored, watched humanity passing. Exhausted minds recalled better days, happier moments, dead ambitions. Thick tongues licked long, drooping lips as a half-empty flask sprang from the remains of a once-proud jacket, and into a hand that welcomed the friendship which the decanter offered. The bottle was passed without a word. They were silent strangers, and in some way also brothers, united in defeat and misery.

A dark figure with a dangling nightstick rounded the corner, and trod silently towards them. Automatically they rose and separated, leaving behind a thousand silent companions. They didn't run. They were still men.

50 Cards 50

(1966, age 17)

Richard stared in awe at the glistening Christmas tree before him. Little silver angels and stars gleamed from each branch as the huge pine illuminated the entire room. There were no presents under the tree, but Richard was, nevertheless, the happiest boy in Harlem.

As he sat arranging a nativity scene, the apartment doorbell chimed, and his mother admitted a portly mulatto woman bearing ribboned packages. Richard ignored them; like most eight-year-old boys, his thoughts were on Santa Claus, the rotund deity who would deliver gifts to children throughout the world. Richard was wondering how Santa would enter their apartment since it lacked a chimney. They certainly couldn't leave the door open—not in *their* neighborhood.

Johnson drew this accompanying illustration for his high school paper.

The cheerful "goodbye" and "Merry Christmas" of the mulatto woman aroused Richard from his fantasies. He noticed a tempting package on the sofa

"Why can't I imagine a white Santa Claus?" asks the adult author. In this story, Johnson laments the "racial polarization" that has suddenly been imposed on a boy who "wasn't thinking about race."

across the room. His mother must have bought it from the woman who had just left. After reassuring himself that his mother had returned to her kitchen chores, Richard stole across the room, and gave vent to childish curiosity by unwrapping the box. His nervous fingers lifted the lid and a chocolate Santa Claus grinned foolishly at him, as his sleigh drew him across the narrow width of cardboard. There were fifty such cards in the box, and Richard stared dumbly at them for long minutes.

These were not the jolly men with rosy cheeks and button noses that he had seen on street corners, jangling bells and seeking charity. They were not like the red-suited Santas he had seen inside the shiny pages of the magazines his mother brought home. For some reason, the ebony Santa was meant for him, alone. For some peculiar reason which he could not grasp, he was not supposed to visualize a Santa Claus with bright cheeks and a merry, red nose. Richard suddenly realized that the room was strangely dark, and he no longer cared how Santa entered their apartment.

Even though he thought his son's ambition to become a cartoonist impractical, Johnson's father funded two years of correspondence art classes. Johnson went on to publish more than a thousand drawings, including these samples of a high school comic strip [opposite], as well as the Santa and King drawings.

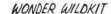

Rendezvous

(1966, age 18)

*D*ense smoke curled slowly above the still cylinders of exploding gasses, each a dull, ashen gray, pock-marked with meteors. Both had crashed violently mere yards from one another and hurled their frail occupants, swathed in space-age shrouds, to safety on the yielding, white pumice of the soundless world, the mute moon.

Commander Jarius Langford Dillin, USAF pulls himself slowly, agonizingly toward the remnants of the USSR's finest and most elaborate instrument for piercing the bleak cosmos. He stops at the still figure spread-eagled before him, helplessly drowning in its cumbersome flight helmet and pressure-resistance suit—a woman. The woman, her Ukranian features beaming in undisguised joy, clutches the Commander to her as the two clumsily embrace through their bulky flight uniforms. Their two smashed vehicles finally explode in two silent, blinding blazes of white flame and then vanish moments later from the absence of oxygen.

The two figures, mocking human anatomy in their monstrous uniforms, cast their eyes earthward to await the rescue ships they know will eventually come. The Commander, his eyes now on the woman, quietly whispers into the radio-communicator lodged in his gleaming helmet, "Natasha, I love you, but we simply can't go on meeting like this."

Johnson's comic technique has since grown more subtle. Still, the author can't resist the occasional one-liner: The doctor in "Popper's Disease" (Johnson's 1982 story involving a space vessel crash), upon discovering a space alien who resembles a "huge boiled crayfish," confesses an urge to spread the other character with tartar sauce. ➜

Individuality, not collectivity, is vehicle for attaining equality

(1968, age 20)

To the Daily Egyptian:

Much ado about race is made with justification these days, and virtually everyone agrees that the desirable end of all civil rights endeavors should be universal equality. The means for attaining this goal is undoubtedly where our conflict arises. Sprouting up everywhere are a myriad of self-appointed groups, black and white, who assume their union of forces will somehow alleviate the current race crisis.

If equality and eventual brotherhood are the goals in sight, the vehicle for attaining this goal must lie within the individual, not in collective forces. The individual must undergo the grueling chore of recognizing himself as a unique entity and define his own goals, strengths and weaknesses.

Having done so, he will be in a position to appreciate and respect others who have done the same, and perhaps be eager to help those who still struggle with their existence.

The progress of race relations must take place in the enlightenment of the individuals that compose our society, not in the groups who sacrifice the individual for a collective intelligence.

In Being and Race: Black Writing since 1970, *his 1988 book of literary criticism and philosophy, Johnson takes issue with certain racially based arts movements for deemphasiz-◄ ing the individual.*

Johnson's novel-in-progress, Dreamer, *takes a fresh look at Martin Luther King to try to answer the question: "How do you become a saint?" He published this editorial cartoon in his college newspaper in 1968.*

Charles Johnson

Stephen King at age 9, with Queenie.

STEPHEN KING

"*K*ids are bent," writes Stephen King in *Danse Macabre* (1981), his survey of contemporary horror. They still have the imagination to "think around corners." This faculty fades, he adds, with the coming of adult-hood—except perhaps in fantasy-horror writers (such as King), whose job "is to make you, for a little while, a child again."

Readers often presume a deep-rooted deviance on the part of the fantasy-horror practitioner, inspiring such questions, King writes, as, "Was your mother scared by a two-headed dog while you were *in utero?*" As a four-year-old, King might have seen a playmate killed by a train (King's mother told him years later that he had come home in shock). Upon hearing King recount this story at a mystery-writers' convention, one psychiatrist-novelist asserted that King had been writing about the childhood event ever since.

King dismisses the train incident as a motive for his career. He does, however, point to this crystalizing moment: his discovery, at about age twelve, of a cache of fantasy-horror paperbacks in his aunt's attic. These works by H. P. Lovecraft and others were left behind by King's father, who abandoned the family when King was two years old. The father had tried his hand at horror stories but never published any and lacked, according to King's mother, a "stick-to-it ... nature."

King himself possesses this nature in abundance. He has published (under both his own name and the pen name Richard Bachman) more than thirty books of fiction, including the novels *Carrie* (1974), *The Shining* (1977), *The Stand* (1978), *Cujo* (1981), *It* (1986), and *Misery* (1987).

Born in Portland, Maine, in 1947, King has lived in the state most of his life. A quiet child, he wrote the following story at age nine for his Aunt Gert, described in a recent letter to his agent as his "first patron. She was amused by my story-writing hobby and used to pay me a quarter a story. Naturally I inundated her!"

"By the way," the letter adds, "one thing about the enclosed should make you feel that entropy doesn't *always* apply; you'll note that at least my spelling has gotten better."

Given that King and others have made the connection between fairy tales and horror stories, it seems fitting that the following early King effort is indeed in a Grimm mode. Like his hero, "Jhonathan ... the cobblers son," King has gone on to seek out his share of evils and been rewarded with far more than 5,000 crowns.

Jhonathan and the Witchs

(circa 1956, age 9)

King, who also grew up → in a household of modest means, is still partial to child protagonists, especially underdogs, like Carrie and like the kids who make up the Losers' Club in It.

*O*nce upon a time there was a boy named Jhonathan. He was smart, handsome, and very brave. But, Jhonathan was a cobblers son.

One day his father said, "Jhonathan, you must go and seek your fourtune. You are old enough."

Jhonathan, being a smart boy knew he better ask the King for work.

So, he set out.

On the way, he met a rabbit who was a fariy in disguise. The scared thing was being pursued by hunters and jumped into Jhonathans arms. When the hunters came up Jhonathan pointed excitedly and shouted, "That way, that way!"

After the hunters had gone, the rabbit turned into a fairy and said, "You have helped me. I will give you three wishes. What are they?"

But Jhonathan could not think of anything, so the fairy agreed to give them to him when he needed them.

So, Jhonathan kept walking until he made the kingdom without incedent.

So he went to the king and asked for work.

But, as luck would have it, the king was in a very bad mood that day. So he vented his mood on Jhonathan.

"Yes, there is something you can do. On yonder Mountain there are three witches. If you can kill them, I will give you 5,000 crowns. If you cannot do it I will have your head! You have 20 days." With this he dismissed Jhonathan.

Now what am I to do? thought Jhonathan. Well I shall try.

Then he remembered the three wishes granted him and set out for the mountain.

In the author's short story "Word Processor of the Gods" (1983), an unappreciated husband finds he can control reality with his newfangled computer. The story is a high-tech twist on the ◄ archetypal wish tale.

*   *   *   *

Now Jhonathan was at the mountain and was just going to wish for a knife to kill the witch, when he heard a voice in his ear, "The first witch cannot be peirced.

The second witch cannot be periced or smothered.

The third cannot be periced, smothered and is invisable.

With this knolege Jhonathen looked about and saw noone. Then he remembered the fairy, and smiled.

He then went in search of the first witch.

At last he found her. She was in a cave near the foot of the mountain, and was a mean looking hag.

He remembered the fairy words, and before the witch could do anything but give him an ugly look, he wished she should be smothered. And Lo! It was done.

Now he went higher in search of the second witch. There was a second cave higher up. There he found the second witch. He was about to wish her smothered when he remembered she could not be smothered. And then before the witch could do

Carrie, the title character ➤
in King's first published
novel, similarly has merely
to wish for something to
happen and it does, through
telekinesis. In that fairy tale
gone awry, however, Carrie
also plays one of several
witchlike parts.

anything but give him an ugly look, he had wished her crushed. And Lo! It was done.

Now he had onley to kill the third witch and he would have the 5,000 crowns. But on the way up, he was plauged with thoughts of how?

Then he hit upon a wonderful plan.

Then, he saw the last cave. He waited outsid the entrance until he heard the witches footsteps. He then picked up a couple of big rocks and wished.

He then wished the witch a normal woman and Lo! She became visable and then Jhonathen struck her dead with the rocks he had.

Jhonathan collected his 5,000 crowns and he and his father lived happily ever after.

Stephen King

JHONATHAN AND the Withs
By Stephen King

Once upon a time there was a boy named Jhonathan.
He was smart, handsome, and very brave. But, Jhon-
athan was a COBBLERS SON.
One day his father said, "Jhonathan, you must go and seek
your fourtune. You are old enough."
Jhonathan, being a smart boy knew he better ask the King
for work.
So, he set out.
On the way, he met a Rabbit who was a fairy in disguise.
The scared thing was being pursued by hunters and jumped
into Jhonathans arms. When the hunters came up Jhonathan
pointed excitedly and shouted, "That way, that way!"
After the hunters had gone, the Rabbit turned into
a fairy and said, "You have helped me. I will give you
three wishes. What are they?"
But Jhonathan could not think of anything, so the fairy
agreed to give them to him when he needed them.
So, Jhonathan kept walking untill he made the kingdom without that
incedent.
So he went to the King and asked for work.
But, as luck would have it, the King was in a very
bad mood that day. So he vented his mood on Jhonathan.

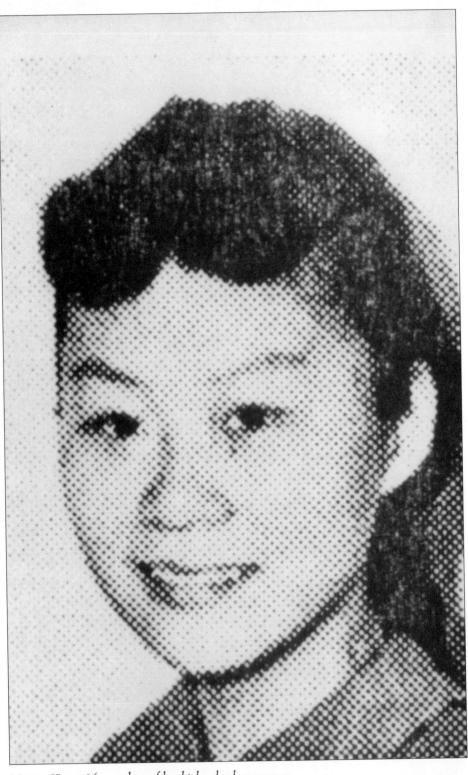

Maxine Hong, 16, as editor of her high school newspaper.

Maxine Hong Kingston

"When I first began to write," says Maxine Hong Kingston, "I thought of writing as an act of cowardice," a chance to vent feelings without confrontation. And so, not surprisingly, her journal entry below about the night of the disastrous dance, written when she was fourteen, reads like a private complaint. By the time she became editor of her high school newspaper, however, she had worked up enough courage to take some of her concerns public. Today her mature work is respected for, among other things, its conviction and bravery.

She established herself as a writer in 1976 with her memoir *The Woman Warrior*. In it she recalls a Chinese-American girlhood haunted by racism, sexism, the past, and her uncertainty about the boundaries between fact and myth. After a companion work of creative nonfiction, *China Men* (1980), she published her first novel, *Tripmaster Monkey*, in 1989. Like the younger self Maxine Hong Kingston describes in *The Woman Warrior*, protagonist Wittman Ah Sing is a rebel, a social critic sustained by a vision of justice, willing and able to deliver a blazing editorial when necessary.

Born in Stockton, California, in 1940, Maxine Hong was shy as a small child. In middle childhood, a "mysterious illness" kept her bedridden for more than a year, and she went through a phase, which she describes humorously in *The Woman Warrior*, when she worried about her habit of conversing with imaginary beings. By the book's end, however, she has come into her own, finding in high school validation for her future career.

"I may be ugly and clumsy," she tells her parents, trying to assert herself during a teenage outburst, "but. . . . I'm so smart, if they say write ten pages, I can write fifteen."

Just days after Maxine Hong Kingston contributed the following samples of her juvenilia, the rest of her childhood writings—as well as her manuscript in progress and her entire home—were consumed in the October 1991 fires that ravaged the Oakland Hills.

Journal entry, July 7
(1955, age 14)

*M*y Louisville Slugger bats arrived. They're not *really* bats. They're a pen and pencil set with holders like bats. Only cost me $.50 (cents). Writes nice, doesn't it? Ted William's and Ralph Kiner's autographs are on them.

This is my new notebook—since the other is filled.

I hope this helps rush in the spirit of summer.

There are 66 days of vacation left.

I bought a thick note-book about three times the size of this. I'm going to write stories in it. (I don't like to type them.

This note-book is supposed to have a picture of the Cisco Kid on it; a picture of Jane Wyman on the other.

Journal entry, July 15
(1955, age 14)

Went to club, Theta Pi, dance—Rhythm & Blues. Had miserable time—First dance of mine. Of course we had to work because we were giving the dance—People just leave their manners at home when they come to dances it seems. They come & show off—and act up—even people that I *used* to think were at least O.K. — People, trying to sneak in for free—People rude, noisy, boastrous, gossipy—.

◄ Wittman Ah Sing, the poet protagonist of Tripmaster Monkey, *is often confronted with behavior he finds offensive. "Normal humanity," he remarks early in the book, "mean and wrong."*

Its pitiful—after we worked *so* putting up decorations and everything in the ladies room & all — they tore them down — laughed — Its mean — absolutely so! Priscilla heard someone make remarks about my pigtails—If a person can't say a thing to another's face—they're cowards to say them behind their backs. No, I don't expect people to be perfect but at least they could try. At least we took in $9.08—about $5 profit.— Hope we never give another dance again—never, never, never, never!!!!!!!

Corrinne had her tonsils out yesterday. I gave her lots of presents—paper dolls, put together animals—about nine presents in all—for her to open on different days but she is impatient & opened them all at once.

◄ Corrinne is the author's sister.

Today I went to the movies with Priscilla & Bonnie at the Esquire. We had to wait in line in the lobby for seats—there were so many people! We saw Tex Barker in "Bitter Ridge"—a western & Donald O'Conner in "Frances Joins the Navy." Both good and entertaining.

M.H.

July '54 —

1955

July 15
Went to club, Theta Pi, dance
Rhythm & Blues. Had miserable
time. First dance of
mine. Of course we
had to work because we were
giving the dance. People
just leave their manners
at home when they come
to dances it seems. They
come & show off
and act up even
people that I used to
think were at least
O.K. People, trying
to sneak in for free.
People rude, noisy,
boistrous, pushy

Letter
(1956, age 15)

219 E. Hazelton
Stockton, Calif.
June 24, 1956

*D*ear Lily:
 That's right, we haven't seen each other for a long time. And things have really changed since the old Lafayette days. The gang is all split up now, almost. Some of the kids have moved like you have and some of the others I hardly see any more. But then the ones that I do see are just as nice as they always have been. Like Priscilla, remember? And of course, there are a lot of kids that we go around with that never did go to Lafayette. Wish you could meet them. Wonderful people. Edison is really wonderful and I'm sure I like it as much as you do Tech. I took geometry too, but I don't like it half as well as algebra although I did get a pretty good grade.

The specific grade ("an 'A'") ← *is modestly slashed out.*

 I'm not going any place this summer, either; but I don't particularly mind. I sure nuff hope you get that baby sitting job. Be sure to tell me if you do.
 I don't think it was the fourth of July that we last saw you. It was once when we were coming home from school, I think. Felomina Juanitas was there too, remember? Here's my picture. Have I changed any? I can't tell because I see myself in the mirror everyday. I haven't seen any of the girls yet. But I'll pry some photos off of them for you as soon as possible.
 Give my regards to Betty. Does she still remember me?
 Thanks a million for your letter. Please write again and tell me all about yourself.

 Always
 Maxine

219 E. Hazelton
Stockton, Calif.
June 24, 1956

Dear Lily:

That's right, we haven't seen each other for a long time.
and things have really changed since the old Lafayette days.
The gang is all split up now, almost. Some of the kids have
moved like you have and the others/ some of the others I
    hardly see any more! But then the ones that we do
I do see are just as nice as they always have been. Like
Priscilla, remember? Some And of course, there are a
lot of kids that we go around with that never did go to
Lafayette. Wish you could meet them. Wonderful people.
Edison is really wonderful and I'm sure I like it as much
as you do Tech. I took geometry too, but I don't like
it half as well as algebra although I did get an /A//
a pretty good grade.
I'm not going anyplace this summer, either; but I don't
    particularly mind. I sure nuff hope you get that
baby sitting job. Be/ Be sure to tell me if you do.
    I don't think it was the fourth of July that we last
saw you. It was once when we were coming come from school,
I think. Felomina Juanitas was there too, remember?
Here's my picture. But I haven't seen any of the girls yet.
But I'll try to try some photos of them for you.
Have I changed any? I myself can't tell because I see myself
in the mirror everyday. I haven't seen any of the girls
yet. But I'll try some photos off of them for you as soon
as possib.e
Give my regards to Betty. Does she still remember me?
Thanks a million for your letter. Plese write again
and tell me all about yourslef.

    Always
        Maxine

Collections

(1956, age 15–16)

Friends and relatives through
the years have urged Wittman
Ah Sing (in Tripmaster
Monkey) not to wear green,
because, he is finally told,
"We look yellow in that color."
It had to do with racial skin.
And, of course, from that time
on, he knew what color he had
to wear—green. . . ." ➤

a. stuffed animals

b. art prints

c. pattern ads

d. articles on authors

e. [or *l*] green clothing

m. perfumes, esp. French

In My Opinion

HIGH SCHOOL NEWSPAPER COLUMN

(1957, age 16)

Women can out-think, out-talk and out-smart men, and those are proved facts.

Didn't Joan of Arc, Maid of Orleans, send the British forces flying before her inspired army until Charles was crowned king at Rheims? Wasn't it Elizabeth Cady Stanton's, Lucretia Mott's and Susan B. Anthony's burning orations for women's suffrage, which fired the forges of male-partisaned government to cast the die for a nineteenth amendment to the Constitution? And wasn't it Cleopatra who led Caesar to war, Ptolemy to oblivion, and Anthony to a lifetime of servitude?

Then why, pray tell, are men endowed with certain inalienable rights which we women are denied? Why are they bestowed with the privilege of having a second lunch period for luncheon meetings, while we girls slave on in class? Why can they have a Key Club for "outstanding" boys, while we have nothing?

There are girls with leadership qualities and a creditable amount of brains, too, you know. We deserve something. After all, girls can do anything boys can — and better, too. [. . . .]

The double standard applied to girls seems especially rigid among the older, Chinese-born men that Maxine Hong Kingston describes in The Woman Warrior. *In one scene, her great-uncle makes his preference for grandsons quite clear. Pointing to the six girls consuming food at the dinner table, he calls each ◄ of them a maggot.*

* * * *

Four Negro churches were dynamited recently in Alabama. A Virginia newspaper asked the Supreme Court to reverse its integration decision since there was such an "amount of evidence before it of the enormous opposition in the South."

Why, Thomas Jefferson must have turned over in his grave. As a Virginian, he, too, had written about men's rights; but he said that "all men are created equal." A Negro's a man; so's a Caucasian, and a Mongolian, too. That makes us all equal. Who can deny that "quantities equal to the same quantity are equal?" It's proof — geometric proof — and no Southern rebel can tell me different.

In My Opinion
by Maxine Hong

Women can out-think, out-talk and out-smart men, and those are proved facts.

Didn't Joan of Arc, Maid of Orleans, send the British forces flying before her inspired army until Charles was crowned king at Rheims? Wasn't it Elizabeth Cady Stanton's, Lucretia Mott's, and Susan B. Anthony's burning orations for women's suffrage, which fired the forges of male-partisaned government to cast the die for a n i n e teenth a-mendment to the C o n s t i tution? And wasn't it Cleopatra who led Caesar to war, Ptolemy to oblivion, and Anthony to a lifetime of servitude?

Maxine Hong

Then why, pray tell, are men endowed with certain inalienable rights which we women are denied? Why are they bestowed with the privilege of having a second lunch period for luncheon meetings, while we girls slave on in class? Why can they have a Key Club for "outstanding" boys, while we have nothing?

There are girls with leadership qualities and a creditable amount of brains, too, you know. We deserve something. After all, girls can do anything boys can — and better, too.

* * *

I've got it figured out at last why there was such an outbreak of resorting to fisticuffs near the fifty wing and in the . . . er . . . establishments (shall we say?) across the street just before Christmas vacation. It was Peterson Hall! Why, they have a ball up there at Christmas time. There's gifts from everybody — the San Joaquin County Farm Bureau, Salvation Army, Junior Red Cross, Civitan Club, First Christian Church, North Stockton Kiwanis, Manteca Cub Scout Pack 35, Rho Mu Sorority, and the 521st Engineer Company. Those comic books had me disillusioned. Crime does too pay.

* * *

Four Negro churches were dynamited recently in Alabama. A Virginia newspaper asked the Supreme Court to reverse its integration decision since there was such an "amount of evidence before it of the enormous opposition in the South."

Why, Thomas Jefferson must have turned over in his grave. As a Virginian, he, too, had written about men's rights; but he said that "all men are created equal." A Negro's a man; so's a Caucasian, and a Mongolian, too. That makes us all equal. Who can deny that "quantities equal to the same quantity are equal?" It's proof—geometric proof—and no Southern rebel can tell me different.

MH

Maxine Hong's winning silk-screen print. "The elf's name is Wit (like my character Wittman)," says the author.

Journal entry
(1957, age 16–17)

I just won two honor award ribbons for my printing and silk screening at the San Joaquin County California Industrial Education Association Festival. They were both won under Norman's name however. (Mr. Britt's idea) because girls just don't enter industrial art shop festivals.

"I minded that the emigrant villagers shook their heads at my sister and me. 'One girl—and another girl,' they said," writes Maxine Hong Kingston in The Woman Warrior. "The good part about my brothers being born was that people stopped saying, 'All girls'...." (Norman Hong is the author's brother.)

Journal entry

(1957, age 16–17)

Now for the unhappier part of life—and boy(!) it's really tear-jerking. My grades are hitting bottom—not rock bottom either—slimy, pulling, quick-sandy bottom. Miss Trachiotis is giving objective instead of essay tests now and I hate those!!

Doug Kim is trying to get MY column for himself come next year! We had a good old argument about it the other day. I told him the feature page was MY page and he wasn't going to write MY column as long as *I* was here and as long as I'M editor of MY feature page. He told me he *was* as long as it was HIS newspaper and HE was the editor-in-chief. That's what he thinks—CAUSE NOBODY IS GOING TO WRITE "IN MY OPINION" AS LONG AS I AM A MEMBER OF EDISON SENIOR HIGH SCHOOL. Then we started arguing about writing editorials. He told me he was going to write *all* of the editorials!! I told him he wasn't as long as editorials were on the second page. We—or I, at least— decided if he had an idea, he'd write it. If I had an idea, I'd write! Professional rivalry is bringing rivals to a state of dueling now.

Then there's the matter of E[——] E[——] R[——]. She got caught smoking! She's been expelled!!! At first it was just probation—but now she's expelled!! She can't receive a single solitary award at the assembly— and she's earned a lot from her music—believe me!! I don't care what Mrs. Rovetta might say—but to me smoking is not immoral. There's nothing wrong with it. Why, even Father smokes! This punishment was too severe! I don't know why she's taking it out so hard on E[——] E[——].

Still drawn to the theme of unfair punishment, Maxine Hong Kingston considers a far more serious case in The Woman Warrior. *In that work, she examines the cautionary tale her mother once revealed about an aunt in China whose extramarital pregnancy incited fellow villagers to ransack the family home. Disgraced and spurned, the aunt threw herself and her baby down a well. The author is haunted by the cruelty of her aunt's death and subsequent banishment from official family memory.* →

Maxine Hong Kingston

W. P. Kinsella in 1952.

W. P. KINSELLA

Bill Kinsella has written a lot of fiction about Native Americans and baseball players—sometimes simultaneously—though he himself is neither. His baseball stories and novels imbue the sport with transcendental significance ("Baseball is as close to the circle of perfection as white men are allowed to approach," asserts Drifting Away, in Kinsella's 1986 novel *The Iowa Baseball Confederacy*). Kinsella's magical approach to the game gained tremendous recognition when his 1982 novel *Shoeless Joe*—about an Iowa farmer's obsession with building a ball field so that the spirits of the shamed 1919 Chicago White Sox can play again—formed the basis of the hit movie *Field of Dreams*.

Kinsella was born in 1935 in Alberta, Canada. An only child, he spent his early years on an isolated homestead where his parents took pains to read aloud to him. Having to create most of his own entertainment "certainly contributed to my being a storyteller," he says.

The early pieces that follow were written, Kinsella recalls, in the summer of 1953. The futuristic device of "These Changing Times" portends Kinsella's adult preoccupation with manipulating time (the 2,614-inning ball game in *The Iowa Baseball Confederacy*, for example). And the emotionally candid, colloquially rendered narration of "The Custom" serves as throat clearing for one of Kinsella's most effective voices, that of his Native American protagonist Silas Ermineskin, whose forthright point of view oversees nearly one hundred interrelated short stories.

Although Kinsella's juvenilia below do not greatly anticipate the celebrated humor of *The Alligator Report* (1985), *The Further Adventures of Slugger*

McBatt (1988), or many of his more than thirteen other books of fiction, they do indicate his satirical eye toward bureaucracy and his sympathy for the frustrated romantic.

In a letter to *First Words*, Kinsella says this about his early writing: "As with all my work there are little bits of autobiography, anecdotes, etc. When I was working for the Alberta Government right out of high school there was a girl who worked in the steno pool who had the most marvelous dimples I've ever encountered."

When Kinsella finally asked her out,

> she said she was expecting an engagement ring for Christmas. I wasn't heartbroken, but I put myself in the position of one of the Land Inspectors, who spent most of the year out in the wilderness and had very little contact with civilization except for the Christmas break. I didn't feel the story worked so I never revised it to a point where I could send it out. But I kept it because I knew someday someone would want something I wrote when I was very young.

The Custom
(circa 1953, age 18)

Sittin' alone in the dark in a hotel room aint the best way for a fellow to spend Christmas Eve, but then I got lots to think about. Most of the fellows from the crew, have gone out with their girlfriends, or out visiting somewhere. Tim and Alex said they was goin' out to get drunk, and wanted me to come along, but I said no, 'cause liquor messes a guy's thoughts all up. First thing I'd do would be to start talking about this afternoon, and what I think about that, aint for guys like them to hear about. All they'd do is laugh if I told them, they don't think about girls the same way I do.

Every guy has a time in his life when he'd like to live forever, when he wishes that time would just stop dead and let him go right on living that particular moment. Every guy has at least one—mine came this afternoon, when I kissed Irene.

How long had it been that I'd dreamed of kissing her? Six months only, it seemed more like years. Time passes pretty slow for a lonely guy, when you're real young it's not so bad, the time goes faster, or seems to, but when a fellow gets to be twenty-nine like me and still lonely, the time passes pretty slow.

Working on Forest Surveys aint the most exciting job, or the best paying as far as that goes. But it's good for a guy like me who likes the outdoors. I've been with them eight years now, I'm top man on our crew, about as high as I can go with the education I have. But like I say I work out in the wilderness most of the year, except for a week in the summer, and a week at Christmas when I come into town to the office to work on our annual report.

Last summer was when I met Irene. All the figures and reports I'd made out had to be typed and the boss said that Irene was to do this work for me. Well I guess I fell in love with her right off, she was just about the prettiest girl I'd ever seen. I thought an awful lot about asking her out before I finally did. Takes a lot of courage for a fellow like me to ask a girl out, most folks wouldn't know what it's like to be scared that way. It took more real courage for me to ask her than it did the time up north when I got cornered by that mother bear and had to fight my way out with my hunting knife. But that's what comes on the spur of the moment, if I'd thought about fighting the bear ahead of time I'd have been scared. Well I thought plenty about taking Irene out and I was plenty scared to ask. But she was awful pretty, and always so nice to me, that I thought it would be alright. Yet when I was with her I just got like a scared kid and kinda lost my tongue. I felt like I was in the way all big an' clumsy, you know the feeling.

← In The Iowa Baseball Confederacy, *whenever Matthew Clarke recounts the story of the first time he embraced his wife-to-be, he tells his son: "If you're lucky, in a lifetime you get one moment in which you'd like to live forever. . . . frozen in time. . . ."*

← Editing his own work, the young writer crossed out an additional recollection of courage: "the time I got jumped when I was on sentry duty in the army, and had to fight with my bare hands for my life."

One day at lunch hour we were talking, anyway I was trying my best to make conversation. Every time she smiled I just kinda melted inside, you know how it is all like bubbles swimming up through you.

She smiled and I just stood there feeling all silly inside. She had the cutest dimples when she smiled. I opened my mouth though I don't much remember speaking. "Irene would you be doing anything Saturday night," I managed.

She stopped smiling then, and just kinda' looked at me for a real long time, or it seemed like a long time to me.

"I don't know," she finally said. "I was supposed to go to a party."

"W-W-Well then how about Friday, are you doing anything Friday?"

"I don't know, Bill, I—well—I'm supposed to be going steady. I guess you didn't know."

"No, no I didn't," I said, and I just stood there not knowing what else to say. I'd gone and spoiled everything now. She'd think I was a funny kind of guy, just standing there like that. Irene didn't look happy at all, she must have seen the hurt in my eyes 'cause she gave a half smile and said:

"Bill, I was hoping that you wouldn't ask me out like you did, yet in a way I was hoping you would, even though I couldn't go with you. Maybe some other time, we'll see, o.k.?"

"You're not engaged are you?"

"No Bill, I'm not." She smiled real nice at me again.

That was all that was said, some of the other folks came into the room then, I don't know what I would have done if they hadn't, I never knew how to end a scene like that.

I guess I just don't understand much about this goin' steady business. When I was younger we went around, a bunch of us, together, nobody had any special date. But times have changed it seems, don't know what I'd do with things the way they are now, I never could find much to talk about, and sometimes even used to get left out of the group I went with all the time.

The author still likes to →
name the occasional character
after himself: Ray Kinsella, in
Shoeless Joe, *for example.*

Well that was the way the week ended, Irene was real nice to me, and I tried to be nice too, but it just seemed that there wasn't anything for me to say to her. I always felt all kinda foolish when we talked, and I used to blush, even through my suntan. The boys used to kid me alot about that.

I went back out of town for the rest of the summer and fall. I looked up Irene's address in the office records before I left, but I didn't have the courage to write to her, wouldn't have known what to say, and besides I don't spell so good sometimes. I thought about her an awful lot and really looked forward to that week in the office at Christmas. I was afraid, though, that Irene wouldn't be working there any more.

Christmas finally came, and I found Irene still there. But from there on I didn't know what to do. She was friendly toward me but I was afraid to ask her out for fear of embarrassing us both again. The time just flew by until today the day before Christmas.

There was always an office party the day before Christmas. We had one every year that I had been there, it was kind of a custom. It wasn't really a party, just that everybody sat around and visited, not doing much work. This year was no different until one of the fellows brought in some mistletoe. Some of the girls came in from the other office, and the fellows all started fooling around with the mistletoe holding it over the girls' heads and kissing them. I just sat by myself, I've always been shy about things like that.

Then Irene came into the office. Alex noticed her, he was carrying the mistletoe. He held it over her head and kissed her, then he looked over at me. "Hey Bill, here's your chance," he called, still holding the mistletoe over Irene's head. I walked across to them, trying to act natural, but I was blushing worse than ever before, and I felt like everybody in the world was watching me. Irene just smiled at me, so I bent down and kissed her. Then I didn't care that the fellows were watching I wanted to pull Irene into my arms and hold her real tight, and kiss her again and again. I wanted those few seconds to

"Bill" here heads a line of lovelorn male characters that wends through Kinsella's work, including Gideon Clarke and his father, Matthew, before him in The Iowa Baseball Confederacy.

last forever. Her lips were soft and warm and she smelled all fresh and sweet of soap and perfume.

Alex winked at me and then went on his way around the room. Irene and I talked for a few minutes, but I couldn't bring myself to ask her to go out with me. I didn't even ask if she was still going steady. Some of the fellows said that Irene is going to get an engagement ring for Christmas, but I don't want to know for sure until next week.

That's about all there is to tell. We came back to the hotel after work, and all the fellows have gone out. All but me 'cause I got lots to think about.

Anyway I'll be back in the office for the week after Christmas. I'm going to ask her to go out with me again, I don't think she'd mind. I'd really like to ask her out for New Years, but then I wouldn't even know how to go about it, she'd want to go to some nice place an' well I don't dance good like most fellows. Lord I hope I can find the words to ask her again, but when I see her I just kinda get all tied up inside. Maybe she's still goin' steady like before, and wouldn't want me to ask her. If I only knew how she felt.

Well even if I don't ask her this time, I'll be in for a week in the summer, and then there's always Christmas. If I kiss her again things might be different—Heck a guy that's thirty aint too old to get married.

Many of Kinsella's most successful narrators, such as the recurring Silas Ermineskin, are, like "Bill," deeply ingenuous. Silas, for example, in "Weasels and Ermines" (1981) will tell his readers quite openly that his girlfriend, Sadie One-wound, is not really pretty, but when they make love, "she is more beautiful than Connie Bigcharles or any other girl I know."

Bill Kinsella   (1)   1600 words

The Custom

        Sittin' alone in the dark in a hotel room aint the best way
for a fellow to spend Christmas Eve,but then I got lots to think
about. Most of the fellows from the crew,have gone out with their
girl-friends,or out visiting somewhere. Tim and Alex said they was
goin' out to get drunk,and wanted me to come along,but I said no,
'cause liquor messes a guy's thoughts all up. First thing I'd do
would be to start talking about this afternoon,and what ~~happened~~ I think about that,
aint for the guys like them to hear about. All they'd do is laugh if
I told them,they don't think about girls the same way I do.

        Every ~~xxxxhxxx~~ guy has a time in his life when he'd like to
live forever,when he wishes that time would just stop dead and
let him go right on living that particular moment. Every guy has
at least one--mine came this afternoon,when I kissed Irene.

The Custom

        How long had it been that I'd dreamed of kissing her? Six
months only,it seemed more like years. Time passes pretty slow for
a lonely guy,~~whenxhexgets~~ when you're real young it's not so bad,the
time goes faster,or seems to,but ~~whenxxxx~~ when a fellow gets to be
twenty-nine like me and still lonely, the time passes pretty.slow.

        Working on Forest Surveys aint the most exciting job,or the
best paying as far as that goes. But it's good for a guy like me
who likes the outdoors. I've been with them eight years now ~~ever since~~
~~I got out of the army,~~I'm top man on our crew,about as high as I
can go with the education I have. But like I say I work out x
in the wilderness most of the year,except for a week in the summer,
and a week at Christmas when I come into town to the office to work
on our annual report.

        Last summer was when I met Irene. All the figures and reports
I'D made out had to be typed and the boss said that Irene was to do
this work for me. Well I guess I fell in love with her right off,

Kinsella published this story in an employee magazine (when he was a clerk with the Alberta government) under a pseudonym, because, he recalls, it seemed like the fashionable thing to do at the time. The pen name—Felicien Belzil—was pieced together, he believes, from names encountered on the job, and he used it for a couple of stories.

These Changing Times

(circa 1953, age 18)

Axgard tramped through the marble corridors of the House of Nations, crimson robes billowing behind made his massive body look even larger than it really was. The echo of his footsteps thundered and crashed through the empty halls. Axgard enjoyed thunder. It reminded him of war.

He entered Phillipets' office without knocking, brushed passed the Commander's small, dog-faced orderly and through the open door of Phillipets' private conference room. The heavy carpets silenced his heels; he stopped and bringing himself silently to attention, saluted, and waited for the Commander to speak.

"Well, Axgard, what do you find so important that you can crash into my private office without being announced. Perhaps I should remind you that you're only an assistant to the board and not until you become one of my three board members like Soloway or Banks can you enter without my permission!"

"What I want to tell you, sir—it's about Banks. I've made a very important discovery—he's a Perfidian."

Axgard smiled, a broad ugly smile, showing large, crooked, yellow teeth.

Phillipets let the words enter his mind slowly; he weighed them, turned and examined each one before speaking.

"That's a serious charge, Axgard, have you any way of proving it?"

Axgard smiled again, and produced a tiny roll of film.

"It's all there, sir, a whole sight and sound recording of a Perfidian meeting in Bank's cellar.

Can you think of a less likely place for a Perfidian meeting than in the home of a Director of Nations, but I found them, I've suspected Banks for a long time."

Phillipets' thin face was white now, almost as white as his Commander's silks, he pulled his skeleton-like form to its full height, and wavering in the air like a marble pillar, advanced towards Axgard.

"I don't think you realize just how clever you are Axgard, tell me why you didn't take your ingot gun and cremate the lot of them."

The big man shifted his robes uneasily, unwilling to answer the truth yet afraid to lie. He settled for the truth.

"Well sir, I thought if I brought the film to you and told the story you might see fit to give me Banks' place on the Board."

"You'll get along alright, Axgard, you do think once in a while, but you still haven't seen the point. What would the masses think if it was suddenly revealed that one of the chosen Board was a Perfidian? Even if he had been destroyed on the spot, think what it would have done for their cause. Now, Banks will simply resign his position because of illness. We'll keep him carefully guarded in his home for a few months and then do away with him. You've earned yourself a place on the Board, Axgard—even if you don't entirely understand why."

Banal bureaucrats and petty tyrants are a favorite target of the mature Kinsella—especially when they clash with his likable, ← underdog protagonists.

The big man's nervousness was gone now, he paced quietly about Phillipets' office, adjusting his robes and tunic, and smiling his crooked smile on unseen admirers. Phillipets interrupted his reveries by asking:

"Why did Banks do a ridiculous thing like that? He's always been one of our top men, and he was second only to Soloway for my job."

"It's about two years ago I think, sir. You remember when Soloway got his Spaceman's Honor Bar for breaking up that Perfidian meeting and killing all twelve that were there. That was

"Young people tend to be interested in sci-fi and fantasy because they have no life experience," Kinsella observes. "Then, as you get life experience, you switch back to more realistic things; later on, when you've written realistic things, I think ➤ you tend to go more toward the fantastical again in middle age."

Kinsella has some satirical ➤ fun with mass culture in his 1987 short story "Reports Concerning the Death of the Seattle Albatross Are Somewhat Exaggerated." Its space aliens' first glimpse of Earth is a television image of 50,000 baseball fans apparently worshipping the San Diego Chicken.

what ranked him ahead of Banks. The next day I remarked that I would have given anything to have been there when Soloway killed the Perfidians, and Banks hit me. I believe it was right then that he joined with them, after all we haven't killed more than a half dozen Perfidians in the last two years."

"Can you imagine it though, Axgard, here it is nearly 3000 A.D. and a clear thinking man like Banks still believes in the Perfidian way of life."

"I believe he only felt sorry for them at first, sir, but they're awfully persuasive if you start to listen to them. I guess that Banks just has a weak spot somewhere."

"Still it's hard to think of Banks as a Perfidian," Phillipets said. "Their system has been outdated nearly a thousand years. Can you imagine any clear thinking educated person believing in freedom for the masses, and of all things the principles of that ancient politics—democracy?"

W. P. Kinsella

Ursula Kroeber in 1935.

URSULA K. LE GUIN

"*I* went up to the trunk in the attic, a yellow footlocker actually, and explored," reports Ursula K. Le Guin in a letter to *First Words*. Unfortunately, she could not find her story, written around age nine and already predicting her attraction to fantasy, about a man tormented by evil elves. ("People think he is mad, but the evil elves finally slither in through the keyhole, and get him," she once recalled in an essay.) Nor could she locate her first science fiction effort from about two years later ("It involved time travel and the origin of life on Earth, and was very breezy in style"), which brought the author her first rejection slip.

She did find two poems, however, written during her first semester at college. Readers will recognize the author's self-described romantic streak, which in her mature work she blends with complex insights into social issues in such well-known novels as *The Left Hand of Darkness* (1969), *The Dispossessed: An Ambiguous Utopia* (1974), and her Earthsea series. Although much of Le Guin's adult writing is labeled science fiction, she "has purposely avoided most technical details," remarks one literary critic, "in order to concentrate on human problems and relationships."

Marriage, which the author once described as the "central, constant theme" of her work, forms the heart of her teenage poem "Song." Freedom from social roles and other such limits, another recurring Le Guin theme, predominates in her poem "December 31, 1947."

Born in Berkeley, California, in 1929, Ursula Kroeber as a child read myths and fairy tales (and "everything I could get my hands on, which was limitless") and inherited her anthropologist father's taste for fantasy literature.

Her earliest creative writing efforts were poems, which she began to commit to paper at age five, she says, once her brother Ted, "who was ashamed to discover that he had an illiterate sister," had taught her to write. While still four, however, the young author had to dictate the first of the following poems to its subject: her mother, Theodora Kracaw Kroeber.

To Krakie

BY URSULA KROEBER
(1934, age 4)

*B*ears like honey,
I do too.
I like you, honey,
I sure do.

Song
(1947, age 17)

*N*o swallow follows summer
So far as I would thee:
O love, my heart goes to thee
Like a river to the sea.

All my soul is turned to dust
Or to salt sea foam:
Return, return, return to me,
My love, my heart, my home!

December 31st, 1947

(1947, age 18)

*I*n this year nineteen-forty-seven
I have built myself to heaven
And as well
Have slung myself to hell.
In the year born tomorrow
I want no loss of sorrow,
Joy, love, madness, hate, desire, right, and evil:
God only keep me from the level,
The blind, the bland, the kingdom of the Devil!

In The Dispossessed: An Ambiguous Utopia, *the planet Urras—a world of extremes—is endorsed by the Ambassador from Terra. "I know it's full of evils," she concedes, "full of human injustice, greed, folly, waste. But it is also full of good, of beauty, vitality, achievement. It is what a world should be! It is alive. . . ." Whereas her own people back home have been forced, for survival's sake, into "absolute regimentation."*

Ursula K. Le Guin

Madeleine L'Engle, 12, at Chamonix with skis and stuffed animals.

MADELEINE L'ENGLE

"*I* am still every age that I have been," Madeleine L'Engle writes in her 1972 memoir *A Circle of Quiet*. "Because I was once a child, I am always a child. Because I was once a searching adolescent, given to moods and ecstasies, these are still part of me, and always will be."

Born in 1918 in New York City to a pianist and a foreign correspondent, Madeleine L'Engle grew up with an "overshy" nature. Her shyness was perhaps exacerbated by a demoralizing stint at a New York private school where she was made to feel clumsy and stupid. Creative writing became an early emotional outlet. In *A Circle of Quiet,* she describes some of the resulting juvenilia: a "sequel to the *Odyssey*, with Telemachus as the hero," and a now-lost novel about triplet boys who combine their various skills (academic, athletic, and social) and try to pass themselves off as one, very accomplished and well-rounded boy.

The search for wholeness appears, not only in the story "Six Good People," below, but also in her most famous work, the Newbery Medal–winning classic *A Wrinkle in Time* (1962), about three special children and their cosmic battle against insidious conformity.

The author of more than thirty books, including *The Irrational Season* (autobiography, 1977) and the novels *A Swiftly Tilting Planet* (1978) and *A Severed Wasp* (1982), L'Engle explores the spiritual quest of the individual and the salvation of love. An openness and warmth characterize her writings for adults as well as youngsters.

A Boy's Dream

(1929, age 11)

L'Engle's fanciful imagination once prompted a high school chemistry incident, confessed in her 1983 Library of Congress address: "One day while I was happily pretending to myself that I was Madame Curie, I blew up the lab."

At night I go to bed and dream
I travel to strange lands afar;
Last night I visited a land,
The country where the Romans are.

I talked to a Roman Poet,
The whole world knows of his fame.
I start to read some of his poems,
They tell me Virgil is his name.

I run into Julius Cæsar,
(In the middle of the night)
And Mark Antony and others,
Dressed in armour gleaming bright.

I didn't tell my dream to Father,
For I knew that he would laugh,
The only one that listened to me
Was a new-born baby calf.

Space

(1932, age 14)

My blood runs cold when I think about the sky—
Think that it never ends—
Think that it just keeps on being sky,
And stars,
And space.
But if it did have an end—
What would be beyond that?

Madeleine L'Engle at age 14, with Sputstzi.

Eternity

(1932, age 14)

In her memoir A Circle of
Quiet, L'Engle fondly discusses a Greek word for time,
kairos, which, unlike chronos,
is not measurable. "Kairos
can sometimes enter, pene-
trate, break through chronos:
the child at play, the painter at
his easel, Serkin playing the
Appassionata, are in kairos."

I wake up in the middle of the night
And hear the steady ticking of the clock.
Two, five, ten, seconds go by,
Never to come again.
Fifty seconds, a minute is gone . . .
More minutes come and go . . .
But minutes will keep coming throughout eternity;
Why should I worry because they go so fast?

Whimsey

(1932, age 14)

L'Engle combines the ele-
ments of space, time, and
whimsy in tessering, the
method of timespace travel
favored by the characters of
A Wrinkle in Time. Boy
genius Charles Wallace tries
to explain the concept to his
older sister, Meg: "The fifth
dimension's a tesseract. You
add that to the other four
dimensions and you can
travel through space without
having to go the long way
around."

I'd like
To fly
Up to the
Moon,
To sit on a
Moonbeam,
And slide back to
Earth.

The Wind

(1932, age 14)

*T*he wind is a slave driver,
Lashing the trees in fury,
Beating them, caning them, felling them,
Driving the cold whip of rain relentlessly through
     them;
Roaring angrily through the chimney,
Gnashing fierce teeth in the eaves.

The wind is a child,
Dancing in the grass,
Playing, leaping, gayly running through the
     flowers, the grass, the leaves, the trees.

The wind is a mourner,
Moving wearily through the damp snow,
Pausing by the trees, but ruffling not a leaf,
Wailing softly, softly.
The wind is a young mother
Resting soft, cool hands on the flowers,
Slipping gentle fingers through the leaves of the
     trees,
Roving happily over the hill top,
And gently playing with the clouds.

The wind is a wild beast in pain
Roaring down the mountain,
Screaming through the key hole,
Biting its teeth in the dust,
Tearing up the strong trees.

The wind is a dancing master
Teaching the young trees to dance.

*In her depiction of Mrs
Which, one of* A Wrinkle
in Time's *extraterrestrials,
L'Engle similarly combines
the corporeal with the
insubstantial. Here's Mrs
Which's first entrance:
"There was a faint gust of
wind, the leaves shivered in
it, the patterns of moon-
light shifted . . . 'I ddo nott
thinkk I willl matterrialize
commpletely.'"*

Madeleine L'Engle, about age 15, at a friend's house.

Six Good People

(1933, age 15)

*T*hey had never seen each other, or even heard of each other, yet they were from the same city, and were destined to enter heaven on the same day and hour. Now they were standing together, waiting for the pearly gates to open unto them.

Mrs. Lancaster was a fine old lady with white hair carefully dressed and beautiful clothes. Her eyes were bright and piercing, her nose aristocratic. Her mouth was stern and humorous and imperious.

Michael Carstairs had been on the earth only six years. His tan hair was ruffled all over his head, and his large wistful eyes were gazing wonderingly around him. Occasionally he would glance down at his thin little leg encased in a heavy brace, and a great hope would spring into his face.

Mrs. Amanda Griggs waited shyly, twisting her gnarled hands through her black and white checked apron, or pushing back a wisp of iron-gray hair. Her wrinkled face was full of confident expectancy, and her old eyes shone with child-like faith.

Young David Mallinson stood dreamily, occasionally running his long slender hands with the spatulate fingertips through his wild brown hair, or playing a fragment of a great composition as though he sensed shining ivory keys under them.

Grenfell Dredge sketched rapidly on a small pad with quiet precision, moving his fingers over his neat mustache, his scholar's mind succeeding in absolute concentration.

Little Nan [. . .] held an old rag doll in her arm and sang to it softly, thinking with all her energetic young brain. She watched the others, and after a while went and stood by Michael, but said nothing.

And so these six good people were admitted together into heaven. The great pearly gates drew apart in a burst of joyful music, and they stepped in, the proud Mrs. Lancaster leading.

She found herself in a great ball room hung with magnificent crystal chandeliers. The music was coming from an orchestra at the far end. She stopped in front of a mirror, and saw herself young again, arrayed in the gorgeous silks and satins of her youth, her young head poised proudly, her dainty feet tapping the floor in time with the music. In a moment she was waltzing away on the arms of a young gallant. After a time there was a stir of excitement. Murmurs of "the great LaFayette!" went around. And suddenly she saw him standing before her, asking her to dance. It was the greatest honor any young girl could have. Her eyes shone as she graciously gave him her arm. "Oh, heaven!" she murmured to herself.

Closely following Mrs. Lancaster through the gates was young Michael Carstairs. As he entered another boy came up to him, grinned pleasantly and said "Hullo! You're the new one, aren't you? We've been expectin' you. You're just in time for the race. Come on. You're going to run, of course, aren't you? We all do." Michael looked down at his leg. It was sturdy and strong. Eagerly he followed the other boy, and in a few moments he was running down a long level course, easily keeping up with the rest. In a while he found only two boys ahead of him, the freckled lad who had met him, and a long thin one with red hair. He breathed hard and drew level with the thin boy—then with the freckled one—then he was in the lead—and had broken the tape. Great cheers were shouted, and the freckled one and several others bore him off on their shoulders. He sat upright, looking as though it didn't matter. "This is heaven," he thought.

Amanda Griggs edged humbly in, and suddenly she found herself in a great city with golden streets and voices singing in beauty. She looked at herself,

*Due to a childhood →
illness, L'Engle's legs were
of uneven length, making
her an outcast in school gym
class, she writes in* A Circle
of Quiet. *"I remember quite
clearly coming home in the
afternoon . . . and thinking, calmly and bitterly, 'I
am the cripple, the unpopu-
lar girl,' . . . and writing a
story for myself where the
heroine was the kind of girl
I would have liked to be."*

and she was clad in a long white robe, and great wings were folded behind her. She raised her hand, no longer gnarled, and felt tentatively above her head. Yes, there was the halo. A great joy ran through her, and though she had never seen a harp before, she sat down before one and with the air of one greatly practised drew her fingers across the strings, and sweet music came forth. "Heaven at last!" she sighed.

David Mallinson followed the quavering Mrs. Griggs. As he stepped through the gates a great clapping arose, and he found himself in a great auditorium facing a vast audience, and bowing, once, twice, thrice. Then, slowly he raised his baton, and the music came softly from the orchestra, rising, rising, into magnificent beauty. The audience sat spellbound; no one moved. David was inspired with tremendous genius, and the music was so wonderful that it filled him with awe. "It is heavenly," he thought.

Grenfell Dredge put his pad into his pocket, followed the others, and stepped through the gates into a great observatory. A magnificent telescope occupied most of the space, and as he walked over to it he thrilled with indescribable awe—for this was the telescope that he had always dreamed of, the one that would show him far more than man had as yet been allowed to see. As he put his eye to it he murmured, "Ah heaven. Perfect knowledge!"

Nan entered last, into a most beautiful garden full of thousands of flowers, or were they flowers? Why no, of course not, they were fairies. A beautiful one fluttered up to her and in a voice that sounded like the tones one would imagine blue Canterbury bells would make swinging in the breeze told Nan that the fairy queen desired her presence. Nan eagerly followed her to a flower of perfect whiteness on a long slender green stalk. The fairy queen sat regally in its cup, dressed in a gown of rose petals. "Oh, beautiful heaven!" whispered Nan.

And so, these six good people together entered the gates of heaven.

The bond between faith and music, and the similar solace that they provide, is central to A Severed Wasp. *In describing a child's piano playing, L'Engle writes: "The gentle melody was an affirmation.* ◄ *Was prayer."*

Madeleine L'Engle

Jill McCorkle at age 7.

JILL MCCORKLE

In 1984 Jill McCorkle made a double debut with the publication of two well-received novels, *The Cheer Leader* and *July 7th*, when she was just twenty-five. Her fiction explores the complexities of marriage, divorce and remarriage, daughterly bonds and aggravations, furniture refinishing, therapy, therapeutic shopping, cats, family lore, and family skeletons. A North Carolina native, born in Lumberton in 1958, McCorkle lovingly portrays the shifting scene of her home state and the New South. Her canvas is the daily life she has observed there, and her medium is storytelling that gently enfolds both the comic and melancholy. In addition to two later novels—*Tending to Virginia* (1987) and *Ferris Beach* (1990)—she published her first short story collection, *Crash Diet,* in 1992. She had been working toward it since age seven.

"I wrote my first story, 'The Night Santa Failed to Come,' when I was in the second grade," she recalls.

> From then on, writing was a favorite activity, particularly if I could peddle the finished product to my parents. My profit lasted only as long as it took me to mount my bicycle and ride to what we called "the little store" and then disappeared in a little brown paper sack of Mary Janes and Bazooka gum.
>
> The summer after second grade my father brought home a huge wooden crate; it had originally housed a knitting machine delivered to a local textile mill. It was *supposed* to be a storage shed, but he had no sooner cut and hinged a door before I moved in: pallet, tea set, dress-

up clothes, my own fishing gear (another favorite activity), bricks for a faux fireplace, and bedding for my cat. He gave in. His tools remained crammed in a small storage room. My mother sewed curtains for the *new* playhouse. This became my writing place, and over the next four years much of my time was spent there. The house was sometimes opened to others as sort of a neighborhood playhouse (Rumpelstiltskin was a popular production). But for the most part it remained a private place for me and one of my biggest sources of inspiration: a huge black and white tom cat named Shon-Ton (the result of my misunderstanding the pronunciation of a French cat's name on a television program). People didn't "fix" their cats in those days and so Shon-Ton was usually sporting a few minor head wounds. The recuperating cat proved to be a wonderful audience for a long time.

My motivation when writing these stories was to get a laugh or a tear. I *had* to have a response. "The Twins" was written on this wonderful cool and rainy afternoon when I was experiencing what I'd now call an enjoyable cleansing kind of melancholia, but then knew only as wanting to cry and needing to *force* it. Being a great fan of Eugene Field at age seven and eight, I had learned that a child's death can guarantee total sadness, and I followed from there.

Jill McCorkle at age 8, holding her muse Shon-Ton. The author's writing place stands in the background.

The Night Santa Failed to Come

BY JILL COLLINS MCCORKLE
(1965, age 7)

← *Collins is McCorkle's mother's maiden name. Family names still hold significance for the author, who humorously presents two-time-divorcée Cindy, in* Tending to Virginia, *as Cindy Sinclair Snipes Sinclair Biggers Sinclair.*

Santa looked very sad and said to his wife, Rudolph is no where in sight. What can I do? I don't know, said his wife that is a problem. I just can't go tomorrow night then. It was a real foggy night. Santa told the deers and elves that they could not go. Then a little elf, named Doppy, said, "why can't we have a search party." "O-K," said Santa. But they could not find him. Then Christmas night at 7:00 no Rudolph. 12:00 no Rudolph. It was the night after Christmas no Rudolph at all. Then Rudolph ran in and said, "Santa, I heard you before Christmas eve say I can't go." "Oh Rudolph I could not go because I did not have you." "Well Santa its O-K. Look" in ran all the children from different lands—Texas, Lumberton, the Northpole and every where. "Rudolph where are your shoes?" "I lost them. May I have some for Christmas?" "Yes you can, Rudolph." Come on boys and girls get your toys and candy. Then they went home and said thank you. Then Rudolph told them about it. After that Rudolph was always on time and one time he came in July. He saw some cotten plants and thought it was snow but if he did come to early sometimes He was always there on Christmas night all so.

← *Jeffrey, the preschooler in "Sleeping Beauty, Revised" (1992), casually mixes a variety of fairy tales when he plays, showing that McCorkle is still in touch with the ways children improvise.*

My Funny Dreams
(1965, age 7)

*O*ne night when I went to bed I dreamed a funny thing. I went down to my grandmas and there was a white horse. He was a little wild. But I got on him and then I wanted him. But I woke up. I had another dream one night now listen to this one. I had a big slinkey I opened it up and there right in front of me was a H-O-R-S-E and I closed the slinkey and the horse was gone. But I always wake up in no time. But I think I am always dreaming about some kind of horse. Some made out of slinkeys and some wild. But I had rather dream horses then any thing else.

SLINKEY or not.

Dreams

(1965, age 7)

*D*reams take you far away over beams of light at night over a rain bow far away till you find the pot of gold you'v looked for all day at play. Dreams are funny don't you think some of a bunny licking honey. But you always wake up when it just got good of some thing like robin hood.

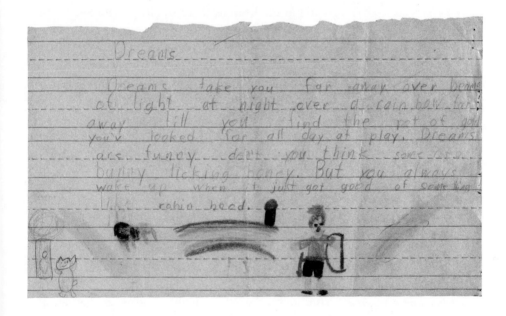

The Twins
(1966, age 8)

Reacting to the loss of her husband, Sandra drops too much weight in the story "Crash Diet" (1987). She checks into the hospital, where "they just put me in a bed and gave me some dinner in my vein. . . ." →

*T*here once were a set of twins that were happy all day long. Whenever the other was gone, the other was right along. Then one day the little boy got an evil sickness and died. The little girl she cried, when she had lost her twin. She wouldn't eat. She wouldn't play until she was frail and thin. Then early one morn she was put out of misery and pain. And in the heavens there she lived with her brother once again.

In the morn there was a note by her bed that said, "Take & keep" and under it there was a butterfly that was dead. There was a flower from the springtime and a tear that she had shed.

Shon-Ton
(1966, age 8)

In Tending to Virginia, Emily chides Lena for having fed cats "'better than people.'" Lena counters: "'Because they're better than most people.'"

Virginia wants to believe she's special because her high school art teacher, Mrs. Abbott, called her "little Monet." "'That woman's so full of shit,'" says Virginia's cousin Cindy. "'She called me her little Charles Schultz.'"

I know a cat whose name is Shon-Ton. His fur is Black and White. He's always having lots of fun and going off at night. And when he gets the chance—straight into the house he will prance. Don't ask me why I watch this cat or how I have the time. I'll tell you right this minute because that cat is mine.

Jill McCorkle

Norman Mailer at about age 10, dressed for a costume party.

NORMAN MAILER

Norman Mailer, who was once, as he has reluctantly described himself, a "nice Jewish boy from Brooklyn," has grown into America's perhaps most prominent literary celebrity. He has attracted attention since early childhood, when, according to his mother, as quoted in the Peter Manso biography, the family treated him "'like he was a little god.'"

According to the same account, Mailer's IQ, clocked at 165, was announced by the principal at Mailer's eighth-grade graduation. When his father sometimes complained about the mess in Norman's room, his mother would counter presciently: "Leave him alone. He's going to be a great man."

"Before I was seventeen I had formed the desire to be a major writer," Mailer recalls in *Advertisements for Myself* (1959). At Harvard he began a long stream of apprentice fiction, much of it in the style of Hemingway.

In 1948 at the age of twenty-five, he achieved instant fame with his war novel *The Naked and the Dead*. Soon labeled an *enfant terrible*, Mailer was launched on a roller coaster career, the high points of which have included his account of the 1967 March on the Pentagon, *Armies of the Night* (1968), and his "true life novel" about Gary Gilmore, *The Executioner's Song* (1979)—both Pulitzer prize–winners; his Egyptian novel, *Ancient Evenings* (1983); and, in 1991, *Harlot's Ghost*, the first half of his "mega-novel" about the CIA.

The childhood piece that follows is precocious in its prose and is an early foray in Mailer's ongoing exploration of masculine terrain but doesn't quite anticipate his roles as literary philosopher and cultural provocateur.

Born in 1923, Mailer displayed irrepressible energy as a young child. It was necessary to keep him occupied, according to the testimony of one cousin, who recalls a summer when Mailer's mother "bought him a pad and gave him a pencil and said, 'Here, write something.'"

Even as a child, the author operated on a grand scale. The full version of *The Martian Invasion*—most of which, alas, is discouragingly buried in family storage—reaches 35,000 words.

The Martian Invasion
(1933, age 10)

Recalling the inspirations ➤ for "The Martian Invasion," Mailer told Vanity Fair: *"I'd been listening to Buck Rogers on radio all winter. So that summer I wrote about my hero, Bob Porter. And there was a Dr. Huer—the origin of Hugh Montague in* Harlot's Ghost.*"*

Wanted for court martial and murder and hated by both sides, Captain Bob Porter and Private Ben Stein played their lone hand.

Chapter XI. A Mystery

The captives were placed in a prison for several days in which they were brutally treated by their captors.

Bob had a hard time restraining his temper. It was lucky for him he didn't as they might have killed him.

In Advertisements for ➤ Myself, *Mailer explains his pride over some of his adult fights: "I was a physical coward as a child."*

The next day they were chained onto the wall in the back part of a rocket boat. Bob knew in a hazy way that they were going towards the south in which there were the best places in the city. Among them was a huge castle that was crumbling to pieces.

Bob gave a sigh of relief that they were alone. The sigh turned into a groan as a pointed piece of iron fell onto Bob's arm. Bob saw that the edge was very sharp. Putting his teeth on it he started sawing at the chains. For a half hour he sawed at it before it broke.

Bob dropped the chains and took the piece of iron out of his sore and bleeding mouth. In an instant he was free. He then loosened the others bonds.

The captives then ranged on the front door. Bob then hit the metal door with a chain. The jailors came running over and opening the door rushed in. The Martians hadn't a chance. As each one came in he was knocked over the head until not one was left. The captives then ran through the open door locking it behind them.

They then rushed up on the pilots who met the same fate—all except one who jumping out swam towards shore.

In an instant the alarm was given and a dozen boats rushed over to easily capture the boat.

Two hours later they were again bound and guarded in a new rocket ship as the old one was demolished. They were rushed out and were herded into a small passage that led into a huge round ball building that had no windows.

They were ushered into a room where they were blindfolded and taken through so many corridors and rooms that they hadn't an inkling at the end of where they had went. Finally they were made to descend eighty steps. Bob counted them. They were then bound on their hands and arms. The guard then took a rope rolling it over them, then he fastened them to the floor with ropes.

The captives waited half an hour before they heard a thing, but when they did they wished they hadn't. A fearful laugh sounded all through the room. Then a part of the ceiling slowly began to move towards the floor. On it was a big Martian who with a big stick kept hitting it on his chair making an eerie sound.

Then to the surprise of all he said, "Welcome friends to our country." Bob gasped in amazement and the thought ran through his mind how did he know English.

The Martian reading his thoughts laughed and said, "My friend wants to know how I speak english." Bob noticed that he was purple with laughter.

Harlot's Ghost narrator *Harry Hubbard fears and reveres his mentor Hugh Montague, a.k.a. Harlot. "He had not only been my boss, but my master in the only spiritual art that American men and boys respect—machismo."*

Mailer's mother was so doting that, the author wrote in a 1991 magazine article, "If I had gone to the top of a tower in Texas and shot down seventeen people with a rifle, my mother would have said, 'Whatever did they do to make Norman so upset?'"

Mailer returns for some more French mischief by having DJ, the scatological narrator of Why Are We ➤ in Vietnam? *blurt out: "Oo la la, Françoise, your trou de merde is inoubliable for it is like the Camembert my mozzaire used to make when we were young, Boonkie."*

"They were going to beat him up, because they had not been as smart as he. It was not fair," thinks Al Groot, the teen hero of Mailer's story "The Greatest Thing in the World," written when he ➤ was 18. It won first prize in Story *magazine's 1941 college contest, giving Mailer vital encouragement.*

Bob had noticed that the man talked with a French accent. Bob had a smattering of French so he said, "Parlez vous Francaise." The Marsian answered, "Oui, oui, mons—you dog," he shouted, "the idea."

Bob lay back choking his laughter back. The Martian sputtered in rage and threw his scepter at him. Bob dodged it and it fell on the ground after hitting the wall.

Then he continued, "You shall die a nice death, a very nice death." The Martian again became purple. He then said, "Suffocation is nice isn't it. A slow long drawn out death, ho, ho, ho, ho, ho." And again the monster laughed.

Bob felt an eerie chilling of his veins and his heart seemed dead. How he wished he was loose and had an electric pistol.

The Martian calmly continued, "Do not try to escape as you would never get away. You will be fed but don't be happy, you haven't a chance. As for you, you silly dumbbell who thinks he is smarter than I, you shall not get anything to eat and the jailors will do so much that you will be sorry. Remember all of you that death comes five days from now." Saying these words he left the chamber letting the captives ponder over their fate.

Norman Mailer

Bobbie Ann Mason in 1960.

BOBBIE ANN MASON

Spence and Lila, the title characters in Bobbie Ann Mason's 1988 novel, seem genetically linked to the grandparents in her short story "The Afternoon Before the Morning," written almost thirty years earlier when Mason was twenty. Like Spence and Lila, and like the older generation in Mason's 1985 novel *In Country*, the grandparents of "The Afternoon Before the Morning" are stoic Kentucky country folk. They are bound to the rural life-style that has sustained them, and they are grappling with the impersonal modern age as it sweeps over everything—especially the minds of their beloved children.

Spence and Lila's "know-it-all" daughters have a lot in common with the somewhat smug granddaughter in the short story that follows, and their youthful restlessness also can be found in Sam, *In Country*'s seventeen-year-old female protagonist. Even though Mason, at age twenty, tells her early story from the point of view of the college student Linda, she displays some empathy for both generations.

Raised on a dairy farm in western Kentucky (Mason was born in Mayfield in 1940), she attended the state university in Lexington, where she wrote "Afternoon . . ." Her first published story, it appeared in the school's literary magazine. Mason pursued her education through a Ph.D. at the University of Connecticut, and ten years later, in 1982, she published her first book of fiction, the acclaimed *Shiloh and Other Stories*. The work includes several pieces that, like "Afternoon . . . ," are about young women revisiting their country roots.

The Afternoon Before the Morning

(circa 1960, age 20)

*I*t was time to go back and Linda had to see her grandparents the afternoon before she left. Summer was almost over and Linda knew that before long the sun would move further and higher into the open sky. She looked at the sun as she turned into the gravel driveway. It shone dully on the bent metal flag of the dirty whitewashed mailbox at the side of the road. The nameplate had worn off a long time ago and the flag dangled loosely. Around the curve a thick green bush brushed the car and two speckled hens cackled as they fluttered from their dirt havens under the cool foliage.

The car pulled up in back of the house and Linda saw her grandmother appear on the top step. She had been waiting, Linda thought. She could see her grandfather just inside the door.

She pressed down the metal handle of the car door, swung from behind the wheel, and touched her feet to the red, crunchy gravel. She walked toward the steps.

Both her grandparents had not grown old too fast, and they were not even young. They were straight, not overfat, not thin, and were bent only slightly.

"Come in, come in," said her grandfather with a calm jubilance, a complacent look of surprise which he alone had mastered.

Linda explained that she had very little time and hoped not to disappoint them by leaving soon.

"How have you been?" she asked.

"We've been rather poorly," her grandmother said, smiling in that half-apologetic humility of old age that seemed to seek appreciation.

In contrast to Linda, northern transplant Nancy Culpepper, featured in the Mason short story by the same name (1981), is eager to visit her parents and grandmother as she searches for her own sense of family and heritage. ➤

Linda entered the flapping door into the foggy screened-in back porch where the cistern stood. They used to drink the cold water straight from the bucket in the summertime, Linda remembered.

Entering this house, she met the rush of familiarity that one feels after a long absence from an old place. Again she saw the house with its old-fashioned warmth mingled with the cool unpleasantness of near poverty, the careful arrangement of makeshift things. Suddenly the memories were all there: the neat dirt of cracked flowerpots, the warm radiance of the old gas range, the quiet click of the cabinet door, the hard pad of worn, tired shoes against linoleum, the drop-leaf table painted and repainted a hard, thick enamel, the grandfather clock striking distantly. They were written realities in the faces before her, and Linda knew them far back even into time not her own.

In this house were imprisoned the thousands of details, both intangible and hard, that wove the small close fabric of the lives of her grandparents. Most of what they were came from this house and the soil around and from the less-than-houses of their forebears close before them. Their life history seemed only a half-life, but it overflowed with an earthy richness.

As she stepped inside this door she fancied she heard gospel music on the radio, which was not turned on. It blared loud when they listened to it.

The old floors bounded with footfalls as they went through the narrow hall separating two large front rooms. They sat in the living room, neat and separate, which joined the hall by a tall white-framed door. Linoleum covered the brown painted boards of the floor. The linoleum was clear and polished and the boards made ridges in it.

"When are ye leavin'?" her grandfather asked. They were all settled in a half-circle in the stiff chairs.

"In the morning," Linda said.

"Now, I just don't see what good's gonna come of this," her grandmother began in a thick tone of elderly wisdom.

*After visiting his wife in the hospital, Spence (*Spence + Lila*) looks around their farm and concludes that it offers everything of importance in life, though most people, including his children, look for their fulfillment elsewhere. "Everyone always wants a way out of something like this, but what he has here is the main thing there is— just the way things grow* ← *and die. . . ."*

*Sam's grandmother Mamaw (*In Country*) likes it "when children want to stay where* ← *they was brought up."*

Linda knew that she did not see. She had known that she would say that.

"Don't worry about it," she said stiffly.

Her grandmother sat in the big chair exhaustedly. Her brown cotton stockings, torn and ragged, were held by garters rolled just below her knees. The jagged holes revealed smooth, hair-worn skin covering large blue clots of blood vessels. Her bonnet was hand made of some material that had been left over from a dress Linda remembered her grandmother wearing years ago.

Linda asked what they had been doing since she had last seen them.

"The same old thing. It's a hard, hard life, sure as you're born," her grandfather sighed. "Went to bed last night at 8 o'clock but I couldn't go to sleep for a long time."

He clasped his hands together, scraping a thick fingernail over the cuticle of his thumb. His hands were brown and streaked and the skin was drawn tightly across the bones. The flesh of her grandmother's hands sagged in loose wrinkles. Linda looked at her own hands. Already she could see faint designs on her skin. She stretched her little finger and thumb so that the embryonic wrinkles would disappear.

"Doesn't the clock keep you awake?" Linda ventured. She could hear it ticking even in the living room.

"Oh, we couldn't sleep if we didn't hear the clock strike every hour."

"How can you sleep in the heat?"

"We're just used to it, I guess," her grandmother smiled. "We *have* to be," she added. She knew what was good and what was bad and the right way to live.

Spence and Lila's →
younger daughter Cat
admits to her sick mother
that she "didn't do the
right things the right way."

"It was pretty hot last night," Linda said. "That's probably why you couldn't get to sleep."

"I don't sleep too much any more," her grandfather said. "Gittin' too old, I guess." He laughed in his own way, heaving his round shoulders.

Someday he would sleep. Someday they both would. As a child Linda had prayed fervently that her grandparents would not die, but she had thought little about them lately. Now she wondered. She saw the phone call coming to school and she saw herself going home. The big creaky house would be full of flowers and old people and she would have to comfort the family and she would cry and then she would go back to school. Now she was mature, she thought.

"Do you get enough to eat?" her grandmother was saying then.

"I eat when I'm hungry," Linda laughed.

"You ought to eat regular," her grandfather said. "Then you won't ever have trouble with your stomach."

Linda told them about the dining hall where she ate. She told them the time she ate and the kind of food served. She said that it was a cafeteria and everyone waited in a line and got their food on a tray.

"Don't have to wash no dishes, then," the old man said, wondering.

Linda laughed again. "I guess not. We're paying for it. They can wash their own dishes."

She explained that she got breakfast and dinner on a meal ticket.

"Don't they feed you no supper?" her grandfather asked.

"That's what I meant—breakfast and supper. No lunch."

"Now, I always thought they was supposed to furnish what you eat," her grandmother said.

"I don't have much time to eat anyway," Linda said. "I have to study too much."

Linda's grandmother moved slowly with the rocking chair. Its motion seemed like a heartbeat. It seemed to sustain her. She turned her head and smiled that curious smile that dismissed what she did not understand.

"I have to study all the time," Linda repeated.

"What are you gonna be?" her grandfather asked.

"Nothing," Linda laughed. "I guess I'll just keep on going to school all my life."

"La' me," the old woman declared. "You'll get something wrong with your mind if you put that much learnin' into it."

← *Spence can't keep himself from imagining his wife's funeral. In a "documentary" fashion that is less painful to contemplate, the scene unfolds: "the flowers, perfunctory conversations with the kinfolks."*

Lila can't keep up with the barrage of new information that her children have learned after leaving the farm. "Nancy makes her feel dumb, with that bossy way she's always had of bringing home new ideas—cholesterol, ← *women's rights."*

"You'd better be thinkin' about making a living," her grandfather said. "You got to think about these kids at home. What'll ye do when your little brother gets old enough to go to college? Who's gonna send him?"

"That will be years yet."

"You ought to be a teacher," her grandmother said. "They make good money."

"No, teachers make about as little as anybody. It might not be so bad though . . . wouldn't have to work long hours."

"You'd better decide on somethin' to take up."

"I don't worry about it," Linda said.

"Well, you *ought* to worry about it."

"I can always find a job, so why worry about money? Why not worry about something more important?"

"What's more important? You've got to live, ha'en't ye?" Linda's grandfather's mild voice was not mild any longer.

"That's what I mean! Live!" Linda said desperately. Then she said, "I can always support myself, so that doesn't concern me. I've got other things to worry about." Then she stopped. They could never know what things.

Like Linda, Nancy with → her restless, rebellious nature used to pain her elders. Spence and Lila called her "Nancy, Nancy, quite contrary."

"You'll never learn, you'll never learn. I tried to tell ye," her grandfather said, shaking his old, knowing head. He laughed a superior, yet down-to-earth laugh.

"Oh, yes, you will," her grandmother said. "What're you gonna do if they send you home? What'll you do if you're out of a job and nowhere to go, nobody to take care of ye? What'll you do then?"

She closed her lips tightly and almost smiled because she knew what was right.

In Mason's story "The Rookers" (1982), college freshman Judy comes home for a weekend of studying and confounds her parents by describing photons. Their discovery, she relates eagerly, quoting "Bob," her teacher, "explodes all the old ideas about physics." →

The pair sat silent with that inherent and knowing smirk that condemned without words what they knew to be wrong but which they could not fight because they could not admit its existence. They could only destroy it by burying it. They sat and lived in that mixture of superiority and skepticism toward the modern mindless age, infiltrated with a devil-spattering of Wrong Ideas. They lived in a strange quiet tolerance of the outside, dismissing it with the calm and steady pursuit of what was Good and True. They traveled rapidly along a narrow path and never moved at all.

They had always had to worry about making a living. Now, because they had saved, they had money, but they did not use it. Food, clothing, and shelter were still the only problems of life, and a simple but complex religion gave this life its meaning. But life was not this struggle for survival, it was existence plus just a little bit more.

Then her grandfather asked, "Have you been to church any up there?"

"A couple of times," Linda answered slowly. "I have to study so much, I don't get time to do anything."

Linda had been to the church close to home that morning. She had seen the familiar preacher—a new one she had not seen before—bring the familiar message to the unchanged congregation in the same surroundings that had clawed at her soul since she could remember. The church was a live and stagnant thing. There its people lived and died. The pain of existence was softened there. There they believed they had found what they could not find anywhere else.

The church! It had held them in their places, pinned them to the pews, directed them along its path with a dim light they could not live without. At home again she saw the church in a new vision: it was a circular motion of life, a cycle measured by birth and death.

It was a poor man's church. The people that went there were old people and young children not yet gone astray. They had been baptized on that altar and their coffins would someday, soon, adorn the same altar. The old ones could never get away from the church. They had not tried. They would have perished.

She did not want to grow old with them. She felt if she escaped its circle she would escape from age. She would escape from the looming thing that told her she would die and that punctuated her life with Sunday Schools. She was a tangent to this circle, bursting off in a permanent youth.

← *Both Lila (from* Spence + Lila*) and Grandma Smith (from* In Country*) express their distress that churchgoing has fallen out of favor with the younger generation.*

Now in the living room of her grandfather's great house, church-like in itself, each extreme, wise in its own way, sat in silent combat.

Linda heard the grandfather clock striking in the bedroom. She could leave soon.

Sam, the alienated ➤
teenage girl in In
Country, *feels driven to*
leave her rural roots behind
and wake up in a strange
place. "*She wants to live*
anywhere but Hopewell."

And then, from the new hardness of the living room adjoining the soft heat of the kitchen, the three went to the front porch. The long porch, surrounded by the outside, descended by hard concrete steps onto the wide green mat of grass. It was the mid-afternoon and early evening respite, the quiet relief from the busy heat of a noontime kitchen or an after-supper relaxation in the midst of fresh country quietness.

The porch swing moved slightly in a lazy, indifferent response to the wind. Linda had swung in it when she was a child, her small thighs bouncing on the brown thin slats in the bottom of the swing. The chains had ground noisily, but now they were rusty.

The blue-green ceiling had never been repainted that she could remember. The dim yellow light bulb in the center was covered with last year's mangled spider webs.

A new green Ford passed on the road a hundred yards in front.

"Who's that, I wonder?" said Linda's grandmother. "Was that Jim that passed this morning?"

With her apron caught up in her right hand on her hip she squinted from her glasses at the dusty road.

"He went to the court house," Linda said. "It probably was."

From the porch the sweetness of the lilacs and the powdered choking taste of the gardenias had not changed in the years. The plants were thicker now, Linda noticed.

Even outside Linda could hear the clock ticking. She told her grandparents that she would write to them. Then her grandfather took a folded bill from his pocket and placed it in her hand.

"There's some of that 'unimportant' stuff," her grandmother said with her weak, humble look. It was a hurt look.

"Buy you something to eat with it," Linda's grand-father said.

Her grandmother smiled again in that visual tone that could not reconcile the newness of what was happening with what had been. In a broken voice she told Linda to "be good."

There was nothing for a moment. Linda saw the fullness of intensity in them that could never emerge. She stopped on the steps. She saw their faces looking for something they could not find any more. They looked down at the world, trying to see where it went. They could not accept the replace-ment. And now she was leaving.

She looked into their old sunken eyes, blue and faded, and the eyes moved away from her. Linda looked down at the ridge of cracked concrete that met the black and crumbling soil at the end of the steps. Beyond them, the mailbox, with no nameplate. Those who did not know did not need to know, she thought. Then she was backing out of the twisted driveway and they were waving from the side lawn.

◄ Such suppressed inten-sity is emblematic of the minimalist style with which Mason has been identified. Even in this early story, which spells out many of Linda's observations and feelings, Mason is already experimenting with such minimalist techniques as understatement, to imply the unspoken emotion.

Bobbie Ann Mason

Susan Minot at age 16. "On the dramatic side," the author says of this picture, "and amusingly ridiculous."

SUSAN MINOT

*S*usan Minot calls the juvenilia she's contributed to *First Words* examples of her "teenage despair," which "prefigure themes I can't shake off me." To judge from her 1986 novel *Monkeys* and her 1989 story collection *Lust*, these motifs include alienation, loss, and the dilemma of caring too much in an often uncaring world.

Sophie, whose point of view dominates much of *Monkeys*, is an elegant spokesperson for some of these issues. As a metaphor for her anxiety and malaise, Sophie reflects on one of the Madeline stories that her mother used to read to her, in which a young schoolchild is discovered missing from her dormitory in the middle of the night. "'Something is not right!'" recalls Sophie from the story. "One of the little girls is gone."

Born in Massachusetts in 1956, Minot grew up in a large Catholic family, which she would later draw on for the vibrant Vincent family in *Monkeys*. And, like the children in *Monkeys*, the Minot children lost their mother in a car accident. Susan Minot was twenty-one at the time of her mother's death.

According to a profile in *New York* magazine, her childhood "revolved around private school, television, and her six brothers and sisters." She and her sisters made up plays with good and evil roles for all seven siblings. Later, at Concord Academy prep school, she would dress in black and write prose-poetry until the early morning hours. In a concession to prep school life, she would play lacrosse, according to *New York*, "but smoke cigarettes at halftime."

The pieces that follow were written at Concord Academy.

Untitled
(1973, age 16)

i could lean without words
but they seem to be demanded
cramming in songs
before the time is done
these people chatter and rock
practicing the beat
they dance wildly near the fire
enhanced by the flickering
while outside the light
the forest the dark
the quieting the sleep
the snarls and still
it is accepted
so i will try

folds and wrinkles
of time and drapes
opening for the summer lunch
drawing for the snowy fire
i have seen little of it all
yet i sense some presence
swaying in the future
that holds shiny city streets
that bears heather fields and stones
that contains wide beaches
with seashell tide-tails in the sand

In Monkeys, *Sophie recalls her mother asking her to promise not to commit suicide, at least until age 18. "'I think you'll outgrow it by then,'" the mother explains. And yet, Sophie reports, "the dissatisfaction persisted."* ➤

they have told me
that the life will one day be good
that i won't plead with death
any longer
so i continue to move
between the streets
heavy with the mud

on my boots
my eyes alive with the rain
past the dripping ledges
through the thick air
then finally washing myself
in a rusty bathroom
leaning for a towel
i have had much of this
these little tunes
those mighty dreams beneath

it is not the same kind of melody
as the impressionistic paintings sing
hanging on those walls
it does not admire like the raincoat
beige and rain-speckled
resting on that arm
drying in the slow-clicking halls
it is none of this

so then i am frantic at
the thought of what to do
how to pour it all
down my throat and
absorb all the minerals
getting rid of the waste
and if i don't
my skin will crumble
and autumn will rule
my bones that must wither
like her brown leaves
nothing better
i suppose
nothing worse
i hope

*In Monkeys, Sophie's
teenage malaise moves her to
such pronouncements as:
"On top of everything else
◄ there was spring to bear."*

i will lean out some more
staring with the shrill song
in my head
high and jerking in spasms
stressing the point

*In "The Swan in the →
Garden," Evelyn's uncom-
mitted lover admonishes
her: "Care a little less."
Like other women in
Minot's collection* Lust,
*Evelyn retreats into a less
vital emotional state.*

till i frown and
twitch away
angry at my involvement
i was not light enough
not distant enough to breeze unhurt
through that foolish dance
i became too concerned
they tried to warn me
and help me but
i felt it all
dreaming in black
the words the pain
dusk to dawn to dusk to dust

i can sometimes see the horizon
flat at the ocean line
the sun setting across from it
up and over the sky's bowl
setting on the curving land
behind the hill
even so
the color reaches the water
brushing the surface
mixing bright-dull-bright
the hills dark
the ocean pink
the horizon always grey
i know because i face it
away from the dying sun
i lean
speechless
wanting to know real color
they tell me it is beautiful
the sound the sight
it is hot on my back
i will wait
though i cannot understand
the singing
those words

i am leaning
curved with cold face
now burning at my back
i have known it before
they have seen my shivering
and my sweat
i was not strong enough
they lied to me
just as i lied to them about my dreams
bending bending
the straight no-color
they call me again
i am afraid i will snap this time
i will splinter
i want no bandages
i cannot take their softness
my god i see it
broken and apart
i dissolve
leaving no trace
i am afraid i will leave no trace

In the story "Lust" (1984), the narrator describes how, typically, after sex she has ceased to exist in her seducer's eyes. She says of herself: "You seem to have ◄ disappeared."

Untitled
(circa 1973, age 16)

*t*hese early evenings are easy to remember. it was a hazy day all day and now the sun comes out just to fall. the ocean down the hill out this window is alive the gulls cry and evening sailors are moving slowly from the harbor. the rooms on the west side of the house are dazzled with the slanting light bright on the floors the mosquitos only seen. i know this light this hushed cry screaming gold quiet. across the driveway the green trees the sun behind them through them on leaves still as stillness. the cars quiet in the shade. my little sister's supper is being made at this dusky hour we will eat later when the crickets come out. she's waiting in her high chair the western light in the kitchen across the table. the ocean sounds out my shaded window the piano playing down in the hall the open doors the cats lying on the marble floor cool and hard. here behind the house the lilacs are dead brown and crisp the sun across the lawn. the 5:30 train goes by way down by the marsh i hear it blowing by all the weeds with its speed and quiet again. the motoring boats hardly heard clear across the water my brothers watching cartoons in the dark room waiting for dinner.

i know this light. i believe its slanting. the pollin caught in the air swimming in the sun the full trees *i have gone somewhere* the green yellow *have i lost myself* the table is being set the silverware touching the table. the light softer. my sister picks mint from the garden and goes back in through the dining room *i want to know where* the radishes aren't ripe. when they're big enough we will crush ice and put them in a bowl for before-dinner *that's all i want* we used to build houses we used to swim all summer long tennis sometime *what is this thing where have i gone* the boats going downwind their spinakers round with some wind. i hear a dog barking *what has happened* our dog ran away a few times and finally never came back *are you thinking of me do you know what you've done* the flowers in the sun screaming *come find me* the sun slanting screaming streaming across *if i think of you i will remember and i will cry* i used to have a garden with pansies and stones around it. i wanted a bigger garden but my father wouldn't let me until i had taken care of the little one *bring me back* i weeded it all day one day and then forgot after so it overgrew. the leaves crying the flowers are red and spiney flowers. not delicate but faded the motoring boats the yellow sky *bring me back* the quiet crying and i go away from this window and downstairs. the dinner in the kitchen is ready screaming and bright on the light slanting table.

The mother in Monkeys is killed when her car is struck by a train. Afterward, Sherman, one of the Vincent children, → is regularly haunted when he hears the train passing by "down at the marsh" near his family's house.

In Minot's story → "Sparks" (1987), a young woman on the verge of another nervous breakdown pines for Duer, who left her to attend law school in California. As in this piece, the narrator shifts between two sets of consciousness.

Untitled
(circa 1973, age 16)

*P*erhaps i will pick lint off rich men's
velvet jackets and quietly lean with open ears
toward the living room. it wouldn't matter
if i heard those voices anyway.
it wouldn't make a difference. for i would just wait
with my hair smooth my skin soft . . .
no i will not pick lint.
but what kind of life will i be leading then . . .
(i will fall away)
what kind of cracked plaster and fat rat life
will i be leading . . .
i will push trays of bread onto old bakery shelves . . .
shuffling from counter to oven in dirty hot air.
i'll be selling and scrounging.
i will give people their change.
i will bear no offspring.
i will not be thin (from eating too much starch:
i will be fat).
i will resent humanity.
i will slice bread—i will not pick lint.
i will paste magazine pictures on my wall.
i will drink coffee everyday at nine o'clock and
then i'll sit by that fountain where people throw
in pennies and wish. i don't throw any in—
i cannot afford to wish.
i will wind my clock.
i will put a potted flower on my windowsill and
lean out there and wait for someone to come take
a picture.
i will lose contact with all in my past.
i will dwell on my past always.
and i will take the loaves that are stale and turn
them into crumbs—sprinkling them in a dusty corner.
so that while i'm falling asleep i can feel something
present in my life: the rats their grey fur always
sticky with dust scurrying fat like me nibbling in
    the corner.

Susan Minot

*After scattering their
mother's ashes, the children
in* Monkeys *return to the
house, "no one with the
slightest idea . . . of where
← to go next."*

Gloria Naylor at age 18.

GLORIA NAYLOR

Gloria Naylor, who had always been a quiet child, grew painfully shy during puberty, she told an interviewer; she was able to express herself best in a diary given to her by her mother. "I began to associate the written word with the unspoken emotion," said Naylor, who made no distinctions between that diary and her fiction today: "For me it's all one continuum."

Naylor's *The Women of Brewster Place* won the 1983 American Book Award for best first novel. It weaves the stories of seven black women who converge on a decayed urban neighborhood, the hard lives that have led them there, and the grace they muster in spite of their circumstances. Her 1988 novel *Mama Day* also emphasizes the power of women as embodied not only in many of the characters but also in the impending hurricane (it "could only be the workings of Woman") that threatens to destroy their home—a magical, southern coastal island called Willow Springs.

Naylor's writing often pays tribute to the natural world. Though she was born in 1950 in New York City, her parents had arrived there recently from rural Mississippi, and Naylor's childhood home was filled with southern speech, food, and reminiscences. The setting of *Mama Day* alternates between New York and Willow Springs, where the title character, a venerated matriarch, practices her healing arts with the aid of barks, roots, and the wisdom of experience. Attuned to the terrain, the seasons, and her fellow islanders, Mama Day knows "every tree that falls and those that are about to sprout."

The following poem, which Naylor published in her high school literary magazine, is an early ode to nature.

Naylor's adult writing continues to celebrate the riches of nature, as in this description of Theresa's attraction to Lorraine from The Women of Brewster Place: *"Smoked honey. That's what Lorraine had reminded her of. . . . Dry autumn days in Georgia woods, thick bloated smoke under a beehive, and the first glimpse of amber honey just faintly darkened about the edges by the burning twigs."*

Hidden Wealth?

(1967, age 17)

Each year as the solars change
And bring the seasons into crown,
There comes a revelry of wealth
For which the heavens sound.

Gold is found on every tree
And rubies on the ground.
The wind—a cool smooth silk,
None finer can be found.

Jade is walked on in abundance
Jewels are picked from every field
Laughter is found semi-precious
Can treasures be more real?

The midnights are deep ebony
The stars pure diamond dust
The moon rich polished ivory
From other than a tusk.

The world then joyously beholds
Its wealth beyond compare.
So why do men search endlessly
For something that is there?

Gloria Naylor

Joyce Carol Oates at age 20.

JOYCE CAROL OATES

"My childhood seems to have been plowed under, gone subterranean as a dream," writes Joyce Carol Oates about the small New York farm, now gone, where she grew up. In a loving essay about her parents, Oates recalls the family fruit orchard, chickens pecking in the dirt, and the thrill of flying, very young, with her father in a two-seat airplane.

Other accounts describe a grim cast to her childhood, due in part to the depressed, backward nature of the region outside Lockport, New York (where she was born in 1938). "A great deal frightened me," she once told an interviewer without elaborating.

In elementary school, during the late 1940s and early fifties, she attended a single-room schoolhouse, where one teacher was responsible for eight grades. Nonetheless, by her early teens Oates was reading Faulkner, Dostoevsky, Thoreau, and many other literary giants. She was also an eager writer, who sent out her first novel at age fifteen. About a drug addict who finds rehabilitation in a black stallion, the manuscript was rejected as too depressing for young readers. She practiced, during high school, "by writing novel after novel and always throwing them out when I completed them." A scholarship recipient at the University of Syracuse, "she was the most brilliant student we've ever had here," said Professor Donald A. Dike in 1972. He recalled that Oates wrote mostly short stories, "but about once a term she'd drop a 400-page novel on my desk and I'd read that, too. She had some conscience problems about her writing in those days; she was afraid it was 'not nice' and might offend her parents, and I tried to reassure her."

Oates continues to be one of our most prolific authors, having published more than sixty volumes of fiction, poetry, drama, and essays. The novels *Them* (1969), *Wonderland* (1971), and *Bellefleur* (1980) are among the best known of her works, as well as several often-anthologized short stories.

She writes, in part, about the "harsh and unsentimental world" that shaped her parents' lives, a world that includes the Great Depression and abandonment (her father's father had once run off, and her mother had been put up for adoption as an infant after *her* father was killed in a tavern brawl). Oates's characters often lack a complete sense of self, harbor a cautious yearning, remember or repress a strained or hurtful family life, and cope with unpredictable surges of violence.

In her teenage story that follows (first published in her high school magazine), Oates experiments with elements that resurface in her adult work: the unappreciated child, the frightening parent, the pull and push of "home," the fragility of family bonds, and the power of memory to strengthen or diminish those bonds. Though Oates's work is concerned with a range of social issues, the emotional core is often familial: "A father, a mother, a few beloved people—" she told interviewer Joe David Bellamy in 1972, "that is the extent of the universe, emotionally."

A Long Way Home

BY JOYCE OATES
(1956, age 17)

The importance and peculiarity of memory is a frequent motif in Oates's work. "Memory is a transcendental function," she writes in a 1989 essay, our link to "'soul' or 'spirit.'" For this reason "the exercise of memory at certain times in our lives is almost too powerful to be borne." →

I can still remember the day Albie came home from the war. I can still remember how happy everybody was and how nice things were at our house while we were waiting for him. You might think that I was too young at the time to remember anything that happened so long ago, but when something very important happens it is often more difficult to forget than to remember.

When I got up, I could tell right away that the day was something special. Downstairs everything was clean and shiny and had a fresh, out-of-doors sort of smell, and there were flowers on the table—red, dark red, real dark red roses that Mom had picked from out along the fence. Some new yellow curtains, that she had been making for a long time, were up in the kitchen, and I could smell the warm, sweet smell of pie baking. The minute I went into the kitchen and saw Mom I remembered why everything was so different and so nice—today was the day Albie was coming home.

"Good morning, Jack!" my mother said. She was smiling and looked very happy.

"'Morning," I said.

"And did you have a good night's sleep?"

She had never before asked me this question, and I did not know exactly how to answer it. I said: "Okay, I guess," but I don't think she was listening. She was doing something else, and saying:

"Do you know where your father is?"

"No."

"He's gone down to the station."

"Huh?"

"The railroad station," she said. She took out a pie and put it on the window sill, holding it carefully with potholders so she would not burn her hands.

"The railroad station is where the trains come in, Jack."

"Oh, like in the movie we saw last week!"

"Yes, Jack, yes, you're right!" She looked very happy and even smiled at me instead of scolding me for being stupid as she sometimes did. "You're absolutely right! Oh, Jack, isn't it just wonderful?"

"You mean Albie coming home?"

"Why, of course! What else could I mean?" She went to the window and looked out at the road. "You don't know how afraid I've been, all these months. Thinking—just thinking, and not being able to do anything—sitting home here and just thinking

← It is not uncommon for Oates to write from the point of view of male characters. She is as sympathetic with any of them as with her female characters, according to her response to one interviewer. "In many respects," she said, "I am closest in temperament to certain of my male characters."

and worrying about him . . . so far away. But now he's here! He's why, he's within the state already, and he's coming this way. He's coming home."

"Will we go fishing again?" I asked.

"Not today."

"I want to go fishing today."

"No, no, you can't! Today is something special; your brother is coming home," she said. She was not looking at me. "You have to be dressed nicely and be very nice to him and make things as nice here as possible, so he will realize how valuable his home is. Out on the battlefield, away from his parents and his home, a boy might begin to forget . . . but not Albie."

"Maybe we can go fishing tomorrow."

"His letters were so short, and some of them didn't come for so long," she went on slowly. "And sometimes . . . Well, they must have been lost in the mails; the mails here are so bad, and of course across the ocean the mail service is absolutely terrible . . . everybody knows that."

"Wait till he sees how I painted the boat," I said.

"He'll love it here. Everything is fixed up for him. I've made a pie and we're having chicken for supper and everything is just going to be wonderful. Compared to what he's been through . . . he'll love it here."

"When will he be here?"

"What, Jack? What did you say?"

"When will he get here?"

"In about an hour." She turned and looked at me with a smile, but it faded from her face when she saw me. "Jack! I told you last night to put on your new shirt and trousers this morning!"

"But I'm going fishing afterward, and you always tell me to wear my jeans . . ."

"Can't you understand? Can't you understand that today is something special?" she asked. She was getting angry, and I did not want to be hit. "Your brother is coming home. Albie is coming home. Can't you understand that—don't you have any feelings at all?"

"I'm sorry," I said again.

One by one, family members leave or die and are replaced and soon forgotten in Oates's dystopian short story "Family" (1989). As they huddle together against their toxic world, the family members also struggle with their own failing memories — memory being, the story suggests, the necessary fixative of love.

". . . Daddy . . . hit me. I don't . . . know why. I . . . don't know if I was bad." So 11-year-old Kathleen Hennessy, in The Rise of Life on Earth *(1991), haltingly testifies to her bewilderment and lack of control, conditions often familiar to Oates's fictional children.*

"Oh, you're not really. You're not; you know it, you just deliberately forgot about it," she said. "You do anything to make me angry, when you know what headaches it gives me."

"I'm sorry," I said. "I'll put the other things on." I went out of the kitchen and back upstairs and changed my clothes, and this time I did not come back down again.

I sat by my window and looked out, and it was a beautiful day. There were birds in the tree outside the window, and they all seemed very happy, and everything was perfect. It was a good day for fishing, and I could not understand why Albie would not want to go. He always loved fishing, and I should have thought it would be the first thing he would want to do. It would be for me.

I looked at Albie's bed. Mom had made a new bedspread for it, a pretty blue one that was a lot prettier than my grey one. Albie ought to like it, she said, because it was so gay and pretty and he would want things to be gay and pretty after the war and everything. I did not know what she meant by everything, but when I asked her she just said that she did not know herself, and so I forgot about it. Up on the wall was the football letter Albie had got in high school. He had been wonderful; Mom told me he had been captain of the football team and in every activity at school and one of the most popular boys. She only wished that I would be like him, but she said that it did not look as though I would. It was funny, but I did not remember any of these things about Albie. I did not remember him in football games although I know I went to many of them. I did not remember him as sitting around home and being so nice and polite and helping with all the work as Mom told me he was, and as Mom told me I ought to try to be. I remembered Albie only as an almost faceless, pleasant boy who went fishing with me and even

Many of Oates's characters learn to withdraw adeptly from upsetting situations. Joy, for example, in "The Seasons" (1983), when asked if her abortion was painless, immediately responds that ← she can't remember.

← In Oates's story "Where Are You Going, Where Have You Been?" (1966), Connie's older sister June gets all their mother's praise. "June did this, June did that . . . and Connie couldn't do a thing, her mind was all filled with trashy daydreams."

let me row sometimes. I remembered that he smiled a lot when we were outside and that he was very nice, while my friend Bill's big brother would always chase us and never was nice to us at all. I remembered how we would talk late into the night about things, about Christmas and Halloween and school and how he would take care of any of the big boys who acted tough with me when I went to school on the first day. I remembered sled riding in winter and running out on the ice on the creek, and I remembered fishing again, and being taught how to pitch although I was really too young to be able to throw hard.

Her own bus ride to → school was filled with rough, bullying kids, recalled Oates in a 1980 profile. "It was exhausting. A continual daily scramble for existence."

I remembered Albie sitting with the big boys in the back of the bus; I remembered being proud and glad that he was as good as any of them and that he even talked to me once in a while when we were on the school bus. I remembered the day he went away with the suitcases and how everybody had gone along with him to the "station" and I had been left home with my sister, Ann, and how they had all come home very sad and were mad at me for any little thing I did. I remembered all these things although I did not even have to try, and although I did not even know that I knew them. They all came back just like that, and it made me glad to know that Albie was coming home after so long.

Later on I saw the car come into the driveway, and I went downstairs. My mother had run outside and had even let the screen door slam, so I did the same thing. I felt terribly happy and I looked to see if everyone else felt the same way so I would not be scolded or anything, and they all looked happy too and so I did not have to worry. My sister Ann and my mother and my aunt Alma were all out by the car. They were very happy, putting their arms around Albie's neck and kissing him and saying how glad they were that he was back, and how wonderful it was to see him again. Dad, too, was

very happy although he stood back and let my
mother and aunt and sister talk as much as they
wanted. I went up to the car to get a look at him;
it had been so long since I had seen him last. Now
that I got closer I felt almost sad, because I did not
know what I could say to him, and I suddenly had
the idea that maybe he was grown up now and like
my father and mother.

"Where's Jack? Hey, where's Jack? Oh, there he
is—! Hi, Jack," Albie said.

"Hi," I said.

"You don't look very happy," Albie said. He was
smiling in a funny way, and I could see that he was
not the same. It made me feel all the sadder, because
I had never thought that when Albie went away that
he would not come back Albie again.

"I wanted to go fishing with you," I said.

"Jack!" my mother said. She was surprised
and angry.

Albie looked over toward the creek. "I've been
thinking about fishing," he said. "I've been thinking
about it a lot."

"I go almost every day," I said.

"Who do you go with?"

"Oh, Bill, now."

"Do you catch much?"

"No."

He looked around at the tear-stained faces of my
mother and sister and aunt. "We'll go sometime,
you and I," he said. "You don't know how I've been
thinking about it."

"About fish?" I asked. "About the twenty-incher
you got that time?"

"No, not about fish," he said. "Just about the creek
and how we would go rowing on it, trolling at night."

"But we never caught much then."

"Oh, you two!'" Mom said suddenly, dabbing
at her eyes with a handkerchief. "Talking about
fishing, and at a time like this! Oh, Albie, you
don't know how wonderful it is to see you again—!

"I was always, and continue to be, an essentially mischievous child," Oates said in 1978. "This is one of my best-kept secrets."

But I must get a grip on myself, I must calm down. As you can see, Albie, since you went away, I'm not . . . I'm not very—*well*."

My aunt Alma put her hand on Mom's arm and said: "Now you just come inside. We'll all go inside and talk about things, and then it will be about time for lunch. Wouldn't you like that? Now, of course, you would.—You've gotten thinner, Albie, I do declare! We'll have to put some more of that fat back on you, won't we? My, how thin your face is!"

Albie brought his things into the house and put them upstairs in his room, and when he came down again we all sat in the living room and talked. My mother had very much to tell him, although I cannot remember any of it now. My father told him something about a job waiting for him, a good job and a place in the union, too, and how they were always looking for good men. My aunt told him some things about the family, about old Uncle Pete who had died last winter and how he had suffered at the end, and about Martha, who had had that terrible three hour operation, and about her own troubles that she was having with her heart—or she thought it was her heart. My sister Ann told him about some girl named Cindy that he apparently had known, because he was interested for a while. My sister said something about the girl coming over for dinner that night, but then Albie had stopped smiling. He did not look well.

"I saw Cindy the other day in town," Mom said. She was still dabbing at her eyes although she did not seem to be crying any longer. "Just the other day, in front of the bakery. Of course she knows all about your coming home, probably even knew about it before I did; I wouldn't doubt it any—! And we were both so excited; we were both so happy—! Why, even now I can hardly believe that—"

"It's all fixed up with this man, this Morgan, I was telling you about," Dad said. "You'll start in sort of low, of course, but pretty high compared to what you'd get in any other job. Like I said, they're looking for bright young men these days. Got to have bright young men to keep industry going. Union looking for 'em too. You're in, solid, and let me tell you that being my son might have just a little bit to do with it." He laughed and offered Albie a cigarette, which he took and lit for himself. "Yessir, just a little bit to do with it! You don't know how good it makes a man feel to be able to help his son out."

"Do you suppose you and Cindy will be getting married now?" my mother asked. "Such a lovely, wonderful child that girl is! Of course, both of you are young, so terribly young, but it would be so nice . . . She thinks the world of you, Albie, just like we all do!"

"And about transportation, son. There won't be any fooling around with buses or anything. You'll get a ride with some guys I know who go right by the plant—Al Robinson and Steve Martin. You know them, don't you? Sure you do, you used to go and watch me bowl and they were on my team. Well, you'll get a ride with them and there won't be any fooling around with buses—late half the time and so far to walk to anyway. Things are all planned. It'll be just like it would have been if you'd never even left."

"Cindy's coming over tonight. Did Ann tell you? Oh, Albie, I've made the most wonderful dinner for us—I can't wait till you taste it! It's so wonderful to have you back again, to see you . . . You know, you haven't changed a bit, not a single tiny bit! You're still my Albie, my little Albie . . . oh, thank God you're here with us and safe!"

Albie looked away from her and kept on smoking the cigarette. I did not remember that he smoked, but somehow it did not surprise me. He wasn't Albie. He wasn't the boy I remembered, the boy with whom I had gone fishing and fought and talked and gotten into trouble. He was somebody else. I

"You hypnotize yourself into loving your life because it's what you are doing and because it's life," complains Kim in Oates's story "House Hunting" (1987). Albie seems similarly disinclined to be mesmerized by the routine existence his ← *parents propose.*

did not know this somebody else, and I did not dis-like this somebody else, but I wanted to like him very much and I felt very sorry for him. I just kept staring and did not say a thing.

Albie looked at me and said:

"Maybe you're thinking you won't be wanting to share a room with me."

"No," I said. "I don't mind."

"Of course he doesn't," my mother said sharply. "He certainly doesn't—"

"Did you miss me, Jack?" he asked.

I did not know what to say. "Yes," I said after a moment. "I missed you at first because it was so lonely at night, and I didn't have anyone to go out on the creek with."

"And then—?"

"I sort of forgot after a while."

"That's good, Jack."

"Why, you terrible little brat!" my mother said. "Did you hear him, Harry? Did you hear what that boy said—to his own brother?"

"I'm sorry if it's wrong," I said. I was becoming afraid. I thought she might hit me. "I'm sorry, I really am!"

"Don't pay any attention to him," my father said. He was angry. "Go outside, Jack. Go outside and play with Bill. Go fishing—go on."

"Change your clothes first," my mother said.

When I had gone as far as the doorway, I heard Albie say:

"I'm going to go with him."

"But, Albie, we have so much to talk about . . ."

"I know he didn't mean what he said; he's so lit-tle. Think when you were his age!"

"I want to go out with him," Albie said. He had not finished his cigarette but he put it out in an ash tray.

"Albie," my mother said. She began to cry again. "Don't you want to talk to us? Don't you want to tell us everything that you did?"

"No," he said.

She wiped her eyes. "Albie, dear! Don't you see how everything is fixed up for you? Don't you see how pretty everything is?"

"Nothing's pretty," he said.

My mother got up. "Look at these curtains, Albie! Just look at them! Why, I worked for hours and hours to get them done in time for your homecoming, just for *you*. Don't you think they're beautiful? Would you like some in your room, maybe? I could make them if you wanted—"

"I don't want any in my room," he said.

My mother went to the table. "Look at the beautiful roses I picked! They're growing out along the fence yet, the same kind you used to pick me when you were Jack's age . . . Aren't they beautiful, Albie? Don't you think they're beautiful?"

"They're red," he said. He looked sick. "I hate red."

"Albie, is something wrong with you?" my mother asked. She went to him and tried to put her arms around his neck, but he would have none of it. "What's wrong? Can't you tell me? Don't you see how we've fixed everything up for you? Can't you smell the pie and the flowers, and everything—all for you?"

He would not answer, and she went on, trying to smile as though she thought herself silly: "Albie, you just can't imagine all the days and nights I've worried about you . . . all the things I knitted to send to you, and all the letters I wrote . . . Can't you say thank you? Can't you tell me you were glad to get them?" She could not smile any longer and said in a fast, shaking, almost hysterical voice: "The scarf! The one with your initials on it, in your favorite color blue! Didn't it keep you warm out there? Why didn't you ever say thank you for it? Can't you say thank you now?"

He turned away and did not answer.

She took hold of his arm. "I don't understand what's wrong with you."

He kept looking out the window. He said nothing, and I felt sorry for him because I knew he had nothing to say, in the same way that I no longer had

In "House Hunting," a matronly real estate agent tries to coax Joel Collier into the purchase of a home. But Joel, traumatized by the loss of his baby, is as alienated from her as postwar Albie is ← from his family.

anything to say to him.

"Albie, you act as though you don't love us! You act as though you—don't even know us anymore!"

She clutched at his arm, grabbing the dull khaki cloth. "Can't you say anything? What's wrong? — You're tired; that's what it is; you're tired and hungry and — Just go along now and change your clothes, and after you've eaten everything will be all right, everything will be just the way it was before—"

"But it won't!" Albie said. He pulled his arm away from her slowly, almost reluctantly. "You don't understand," he said, as though he himself did not understand either. "It won't be the same."

They looked at each other. My mother said: "What . . . won't be the same?"

"I don't know," said Albie. He was trying not to hurt her, but it was a difficult thing to do. "It's something you . . . can't understand."

"Albie—what—where are you going?"

"I don't know yet," he said, "but I have to leave."

"You can't, you just came home!"

"I have to leave," he said. "I can't stay here. I'm sorry, but I can't stay here." He felt bad about this, but he knew it had to be done, and he was trying not to hurt her. He was really trying his best not to hurt her.

They stared at him in silence. He left the living room and went upstairs, and when he came down again he was carrying his suitcases. He went right on outside again, not looking toward us, and they hurried out after him.

I went back up to my room. It was all mine now, but I realized that it had been all mine for a long time. I sat for a while on the other bed and felt the pretty blue bedspread and even got it a little dirty from my shoes. After a while I got up and took down the big football letter. It had been getting dusty on the wall and I knew that, underneath my shirts in the drawer, it would be much easier to forget about.

In Marya: A Life *(1986), the title character devotes herself to trying to escape her stifling roots, only to conclude that "she did belong here, as much as she belonged anywhere."* →

Home also presents problems for the teenage narrator of Oates's 1969 story "How I Contemplated the World from the Detroit House of Correction → *and Began My Life Over Again." She is emotionally disconnected from her parents' comfortable, but oblivious, suburban lives and flees into a nightmarish skid row adventure. Even after she returns, the reconciliation she forges with her surroundings is an uneasy one. ". . . I love everything here . . . ," she concludes, somewhat hysterically. "I am home."*

Joyce Carol Oates

Tillie Lerner in Omaha, 1927.

TILLIE OLSEN

*T*he major themes of Tillie Olsen's work—the "shaping power and inequality of circumstance," to use her phrase, and life's pressures against the creative spirit—were inspired by her working-class childhood and reinforced by early political awareness and activism. Born in either 1912 or 1913 in Nebraska to Russian immigrants, Tillie Lerner helped care for and support her five siblings. Though an omnivorous reader, she did not always excel in school according to her teachers' terms and left after the eleventh grade.

She then took factory jobs and tried from very early on to organize labor. After she published several pieces in the *New Republic* and the *Partisan Review*, the demands of raising a family largely postponed her writing aspirations. About twenty years later, however, the four stories collected in her first book, *Tell Me a Riddle* (1961), solidly established her literary reputation.

In 1978 Olsen published *Silences*, her nonfiction examination of how the writing life can be undermined—particularly for women—by social and personal circumstances. Reviewing the book, Margaret Atwood described the reverence that Tillie Olsen has inspired among women writers in the United States as being "not only for the quality of her artistic performance but, as at a gruelling obstacle race, for the near-miracle of her survival."

Yonnondio, the novel that Olsen started when she was nineteen and finally published in 1974—after piecing together a manuscript lost for years—chronicles the distressed existence of an impoverished family during the depression. The story included here, "Not You I Weep For," most likely was written only a year or so before she began *Yonnondio* and presages some of *Yonnondio*'s earnestness and passion.

At Fourteen Years

(1926–27, age 14)

I

Yetta is the author's →
younger sister Vicki, who
began reading at age 2½.
As Olsen recalls, the poem
cautions Yetta about the
sometime inadequacy of
words to convey what one
longs and needs to say.

A-B-C-D. Mumble 'em again, Yetta,
nice, meaningless sounds. They call it the alphabet.

Long ago my eyes were heedless too,
and I chanted A-B-C-D. No one told me
(and I shant tell you), but you're building you cages,
you're forging you chains. You ought to stop it.

Some day you too will stand
in a spring world articulate with buds,
and break your heart because you cant say
the right A-B-C-D.

II

I wish I had long hair now, to take down and braid.
I wish my bed were a cloud, my covers breasts of
     swans.
I wish I were tall as the sky and could walk on all the
     stars,
or small as an ant and could walk in a forest of
     Grass.

I wish the stars were real jewels,
kept in the velvet jewel box of night,
the green glitter of Taurus for an earring,
with the smolder of Antares. And the dim misty fire
     of the Pleiades in my hair.
I wish I could swing the Big Dipper round, fill it
     with night,
and drink the incredible nectar.

I . . . I wish they would stop chopping that fish
    downstairs,
It makes a noise like a tortured heart.
And if the wind didnt blow from the packinghouse, I
    could be happier.

← In Yonnondio, *the
stench of the nearby packing
house is a haunting
reminder to the Holbrook
family of their inescapable
poverty.*

I . . . I wish the world man made werent so ugly,
or natures world so beautiful. Then I might be happy
    sometime.

III

She Sits by the Window, Mocking the Earth
      O earth,
      stitched thru with snow,
      be not so proud.

      The snow
      that covers you
      will also be my shroud.

IV

Lullaby for Feverish Yetta.

Cool silver pours
into black night;
pearl rivers run
into jade seas;
white candles burn
to still blue flames;
and sleep sings
slow dark melodies,
and quiet sleep,
      and hushed sleep
shall sing you
dark slow melodies.

NOT YOU I WEEP FOR.

No, little Fuzzie, you shall not pass in silence. Perhaps the clot of bitterness, of sorrow over my heart would have softened, passed away unspoken, but this morning, hanging out the clothes, I saw how the shrill blades of new grass pushed up like spears through the frail white bodies of the last year's grass. And some horror thickened in me. I saw again the line in the paper, unnoticed, brief, "Nena Asarch, twenty, pneumonia," and staring at the grass my fist clenched, while over, over, I muttered in myself, "No, you shall not utterly vanish. I shall fling my passionate cry against time for you, lift my voice and call and call................"

But O little Fuzzie, it is hard; hard to stumble back, turning up painfully every dead leaf, putting up my hands to tear down the spider webs, to cleave through to the thing as it was then, when you and I were sixteen, to unmesh the tangles of pain. All I have now is the picture of you, huddled in the corner of the cavernous school hallway, weeping and weeping, and a remembrance of the things that were so dear to me....your quivering aliveness, the trick you had with words, your restlessness and rebellion, the way your mind groped, and the cancer, inarticulateness in your heart, eating up your desperate hope of writing. All I have to start with. And the sorrow I felt when I learned you had died; as if my own youth had died again.

Not You I Weep For

(circa 1931, age 18–19)

← *Tillie Olsen wrote another version of this story, using a third-person point of view. "When little Nena Asarch, at the age of twenty, died from pneumonia, there was little mourning," it begins.*

No, little Fuzzie, you shall not pass in silence. Perhaps the clot of bitterness, of sorrow over my heart would have softened, passed away unspoken, but this morning, hanging out the clothes, I saw how the shrill blades of new grass pushed up like spears through the frail white bodies of the last year's grass. And some horror thickened in me. I saw again the line in the paper, unnoticed, brief, "Nena Asarch, twenty, pneumonia," and staring at the grass my fist clenched, while over, over, I muttered in myself, "No, you shall not utterly vanish. I shall fling my passionate cry against time for you, lift my voice and call and call . . . ."

But O little Fuzzie, it is hard; hard to stumble back, turning up painfully every dead leaf, putting up my hands to tear down the spider webs, to cleave through to the thing as it was then, when you and I were sixteen, to unmesh the tangles of pain. All I have now is the picture of you, huddled in the corner of the cavernous school hallway, weeping and weeping, and a remembrance of the things that were so dear to me. . . .your quivering aliveness, the trick you had with words, your restlessness and rebellion, the way your mind groped, and the cancer, inarticulateness in your heart, eating up your desperate hope of writing. All I have to start with. And the sorrow I felt when I learned you had died; as if my own youth had died again.

But how little there is to tell of you; only that you were young, bewildered; only that you suffered, knew poverty and despair. And the dust is so thick over the years, it is hard to blow off; there is so much I cannot remember. Even the beginning, the first picture is smoky, as I first saw you, walking down the dim upper hallway of the school, your hair

"The rending, the vomiting of the volcano of adolescence had begun," writes Olsen of Nena in the other version of this story. Ruth (the narrator here) is described as a "quick, vivid, witty girl, very sure of herself," and plays a small role in that draft. It is she, however, who gently confers Nena's nickname (with a spelling variation): "'Your name isn't Nena any more. It's Fuzzy. . . . Because of your spread of hair. It makes a perfect circle—a sort of inflated halo. . . . Oh, don't be mad, I love it, I envy it, really.'"

enormous around your head, a great crinkly spread of it, standing almost straight up. And at my side, vinegary Jo is saying in that hard bright voice of hers, "Lookit, new freak. If her name isn't Fuzzie, it sure oughta be." And you drop your books, embarrassed, helpless, as if you hear, while your eyes, always undecided whether to laugh or cry, tremble on the verge of tears . . . .

You remember the studyhall, dear Fuzzie, where you and I first knew each other? The dusty smell of the air, the sound of the clock, hard, insistent, the weary pain behind our shoulder blades from stooping over, the blur before the eyes? It was the tomb of all our young restlessness, sifting the fiery streams of us over with the dust of far removed knowledge. Here it was you sat opposite me, trying to study, closing the books in despair, opening them again, drawing your long rail-road tracks of lines up, down, diagonal, over the desks, and lessons, and books; and where one day, noting my rebellious writhings, you passed me a note "How to be Happy though Imprisoned In a Study Hall." First abortive attempt at friendship that failed, because conversations were such obvious pain to you that fearing the falter in your voice, the pleading look that so quickly changed to shame, I stopped attempting them. There was one day I heard the shocking sound in the stillness of the study, of your pencil flung down, and turning saw you bury your head in your arms. The ridiculous tumble of your quantity of hair gave you the look of a sawdust doll, convulsively flung into a corner. It was a long while before you looked up again, your eyes shining with tears, and some emotion so intangible, I could not guess it. Though I tried to catch your eyes your look went beyond me, beyond the dingy desks and the bowed heads, beyond the window, to the glistening sky, the sombre clouds, the trees dripping with rain. And slowly, slowly, an unutterable radiance gathered over your pale face. For some reason, I too, was shaken. I too turned away, and buried my head in the safe darkness of my arms.

When the bell rang, I saw that your hastily closed notebook had on it the uneven ragged lines of verse. I stopped you in the hall and asked what the matter was.

"Nothing, guess I'm tired."

"Nothing?"

"No," the burst was violent, "only I hate it here. I hate school; they're trying to put my mind in a corset. I hate sitting inside when it's such glorious weather outside, rain and wind. I hate my lessons, I try but I can't get them right. Nobody knows I'm alive, except to laugh at, and I lost my after-school job again."

I was afraid you would cry; but you didn't. Instead you suddenly began to laugh, and cheerfully ended up,

"I'm just ooftigay, that's all. Don't mind me."

But I did. "Nena, come walking with me Sunday, and we'll talk. I'll meet you."

In Yonnondio, Olsen attacks the rigid hierarchy of school, particularly in its mistreatment of poor children: "stratified as dummies . . . condemned as unfit for the worlds of learning, art, ◄ imagination, invention."

◄ ooftigay: pig Latin for goofy

*   *   *   *

The sky that Autumn day was a brocade of copper and blue; the air sweet with mellow death. Beneath our feet as we walked the fallen leaves made a tiny crunching sound, like hidden laughter. And miraculously the strain, the tenseness was gone from your face, the stammering fear which had held you in silence, was vanished.

"Look . . . the tree. Isn't it ludicrous . . . all that shrubbery, the gaudy colors . . . like a short fat lady muchly overdressed. See, see (triumphantly) that twig is trembling, just trembling in outraged dignity.

"I don't feel like me at all. I wish I'd get introduced. And it's not because I've never climbed a hill before, neither. It's just because. . . . oh because.

"No, don't get ready to go on. I feel just on the edge of something, some discovery, some answer lying here. Everything, the river and woods spread out below makes me feel the whole world could lie like that, so clear, so definite, so . . . so explained.

"Look what I found in the wood I gathered . . . a caterpillar, half out of its cocoon, dead. Don't laugh.

Let's cremate it; poor little thing, crawling and struggling, groping for freedom, and now to die, never having flown. Let's put it in the fire, and make little flying sparks of it at least."

Later: "You know, I'm ashamed. I don't know why I say things like that about the caterpillar, and the tree . . . it's a sort of disease. I've read of people who can say things like that, and I'm always trying to feel I'm them, to feel I see the world through their eyes. Through sort of Katherine Mansfield eyes. But while I say them it seems false, false, and I never carry it off. No, don't look up at me. I couldn't bear it. Let's finish getting wood."

In the dusk the moving of your voice, not like a voice at all, but like a disembodied sound: "See how the eastern sky is a gray sea, infinite and sad, and the sunset in the west gives the trees the look of charred, crumbling wood. This dimness of dusk over everything makes me afraid, I don't know of what, afraid of death I suppose before I've lived. I feel so lost in spite of the day behind us. . . . . Let's make the fire . . quick.

"I tell you, there's something coiled in the heart of the fire, you can hear it hissing, like a snake." Sure enough, when I looked closer, little scarlet tongues sputtered at me. Behind, the darkness brooded, tall and dark. I felt frightened, till you handed me the porkchop.

"Listen kiddie, I'll never forget this—that it happened." You shivered in the savage nightwind, crouched to the embers, "To me. My saying what I couldn't even say to myself. It's you," stamping out the last ashes, "did it. The world . . . from the hill. Allright, we'll go," and groping down the path, you hummed a queer ghost of a tune, so absurd, we were shaken with laughter.

*   *   *   *

But the next day in study, you were as if the walk had never been; stricken, embarrassed, in the old way. Conversation was again impossible. But just before the bell rang you hastily gave me a bulky note. And after that, every occasion, every conversation flowered into a bulky note. From those notes, from the few times we were together, from the watching of your sensitive face, I grew to know and wonder at your enormous fecundity of reaction.

Everything touched you too deeply. It was as if you had never known them before, never been exposed to a decent hardening. Too often tears were in your eyes, too often wild joy and unbearable radiance. Taken-for-granted-things were to you new and compelling. And yet, in a strange way, none of this emotion was definitely yours. You seemed to feel them with the uneasy undercurrent that it was thus you should feel them; every emotion was barbed with this self-distrust.

The echo of what you read was always in your conversation, in your notes. Repetition of phrases, emotion, not yours. Yet this must have been only a way you had to say what was troubling you, and which you dared not express. In those first notes there was nothing of your utter friendlessness, the horror school was to you, the horror your home. This knowledge I stumbled upon slowly.

Slowly——shabbiness of dress, inability for conversation with my friends, an over devotion for me. Signs I did not see till the day I came to see you. Your frightened stammer over the phone, which I disregarded, "No, no, someone's sick. And I'm busy. Please don't come."

Through the crisscross of the car window, the neat bungalows of our neighborhood seemed to elongate, bloat, drain color as we passed from block to block. By the time I got to the street you lived in, the houses were all gaunt, ancient dwellings, placarded with "room for rent," "housekeeping rooms," "for sale" signs. Their original colorings had been tempered the drab hue of drouth eaten earth. Yours was like the rest, mournful, bleary colored; dirty children squabbling in the yard; broken steps; patches of stiffened weed alternating with old shoes, tin cans, brooms. The steps caved as I walked on them.

"Hey Neen, somebuddy's here for you," one of the boys obligingly called. "She's fixing up the house," he explained. "Hey Neen, NEEN."

You must have run to the door, for the sound of your footsteps came quick, uneven, like the beat of an overwrought heart. Stricken, talking the way you had when emotion was too much for you, (as if your throat was parched), you led me to your room. I had a blurred impression of frowsy wallpaper, unmatched furniture, dinginess, more children, sharp kitchen smells, creaking stairs, and then. . . . your room.

Your room. Forgive me Fuzzie, that I laughed then and hurt you; forgive me, for remembering now the shoe box you so proudly called your room, I weep. Your room . . . a rickety army cot trying desperately to cover its nakedness with a skimpy blanket, a scarred kitchen table, a sawed off chair, a packing box to hold your clothes. Your room...the efforts to make it beautiful. . . . pictures torn from books tacked on the wall, brass vases, scrubbed and rescrubbed to gleam in the dinginess, a round fish bowl, laden with freshly watered earth, pencils flowering out of a drinking glass, fruit boxes, stacked on each other for bookshelves . . . your room.

In Yonnondio, Anna tries to turn her family's "battered" house into someplace livable with those few pathetic touches at her disposal: "her banner of defiance—up the first day—the clean cheesecloth curtains, yellowing, browning."

And the pride with which you showed it to me. "Look, isn't it lovely the way the candle tallow drips down over that bottle...you should see the dim beauty it gives my room when it's lit. . . . . I feel so unforgivably rich when I look at all my pencils...that's Katie Mansfield up there, doesn't she have a beautiful battered face?. . . . . Smell this, it's my earth; don't laugh at my keeping it . . . I water it and it always has the odor of Spring in it . . . and here, what I've written you of my view, my wonderful view" . . . (a glint of river, a smear of lines low on the horizon, a Rhinish looking brewery) "down there the foothills; all the shades of color still left in the trees; oh, it was gorgeous a month ago. See over there, that's an abandoned brewery; sometimes the moon rises behind it. At night you see the reflection of lights in the water, and the headlights of the trains as they go over the hills. All the street lights, like stars fallen into the water. . . . you can't imagine how lovely. . . . "

Downstairs, your mother began cursing one of the children. Raucous, the words marched up the stairs, "dirty little brat; I oughta skin ya alive . . ." At the sound your radiant words faltered, leapt up again, sank into desperate silence; the luminous glow from your face vanished. The glamour which you had cast over your room vanished too, and I saw clearly, as for the first time, the askew blind, the rickety cot and scarred table, the unpainted rough boxes . . . I saw that a spider web hung in the corner, and that a faint garlic smell was over everything. For some ghastly reason I began to laugh.

Your face grayed. Through my eyes, you too saw it all as it really was. The gallant effort to hide the ugliness, to make it enchanting, was lost for yourself, forever. Some sound strangled in your throat.

"I've taken enough crap offa you today, Neen," came up the stairs. "Thought you was going to put papers on the kitchen floor; now Eddie's tracked it up so it looks like a privy. You come right down and mop up again."

"Aw leave her alone; she's got company," someone interjected and unceremoniously entered the room a moment later. "Well, I see what you were all bothered about, got here," the stubby girl volunteered. . . . "say, whassamatter, tonguetied?"

"My sister, Kate," Fuzzie awkwardly introduced.

"'Sabout time, the kid was having girl friends. Honest, I never seen such a droop. She needs somebody to perk her up and go places with."

I tried to murmur something. "Can it" I was interrupted, "I'm in a hurry, gotta get in my monkey suit and beat it, I'm hashing. Wanted to say hello. Somebodies gotta represent the family."

I kept my eyes on the door through which she vanished. I dared not look at you. After what seemed an interminable silence, I heard a low . . . "Let's go for a walk."

I tried to put my hand in yours, going down the stairs, but I touched only the walls. With a strange feeling of shame, as if I were responsible, I tried not to see anything as I went out. But too obviously, the poverty intruded. Over the woodstove, diapers were hanging, and their smell layered over everything. I was hardly conscious that we had left it behind, that we were walking up the dingy street under dingier heavens, until before us was a face like yours but strong, concrete. Somehow we walked on and after a while you explained, "My brother. Ed. Smell the packing house." Then dully, "I didn't want you to come, why did you?"

Your voice went on. Before my eyes, gigantic, heart draining, a picture of your life arose. Incidents recounted in the same dull voice . . . uncolored by emotion, by self-pity. Dog meat, begged from the butcher, trimmed and diced for soup to feed a hungry family; childhood nights lying awake, listening to quarreling parents, the heart pierced, wrung; fear clutching, fear of something unnameable, some terrible fate; and always poverty, cold over the house like a sea, threatening to engulf any moment; the shame of having to haggle for every penny. Seven children that should never have been more than casual acquaintances, forced into the closest intimacy. Blows, cuffs, sneers, teasings. Your clothes, you said, were given you by the officiously kind dean, and every titter at school, every look, became the derision of the original owner. I saw you on the grade school playground, shifting from one foot to another, enviously watching the play and laughter of other children.

I saw your father, your mother, your family, what life had done to them. For the first time, I felt the horror of existence. "And life becomes like dirty dishwater," you went on, "a drab succession of days, slaving to keep food in your belly. A merry-go-round . . . endless . . . round and round . . . eating, working, sleeping ... the head, a clotted whirl, nothing felt, nothing thought, nothing lived."

There trembled before me your fears that life would become for you what their's had. "There's a

In the story "Tell Me a Riddle" (1960), Eva recalls the hard times raising a family: "the soups of meat bones begged 'for the dog' one winter."

Reflecting on her family's many years of hardship, the narrator in Olsen's "I Stand Here Ironing" (1956) is melancholy but not without hope about her teenage daughter's future: "So all that is in her will not bloom—but in how many does it? There is still enough left to live by."

sonnet somewhere," your voice gained color, momentum, "that marches round and round my head:

> "I am less man this hour than I was yesterday,
> More than I shall be soon. The slow years whittle
> With tireless knives, body and brain away."

← Fuzzie is referring to Ted Olson's "Words to Be Graven on Sandstone."

"I'm haunted by them constantly . . . the tireless knives. Every day more lost, more broken, more torn away, less left to resist to live with; nothing learned; only lost, I'm so afraid, I want to live while I'm alive. . . . ."

We had come to the top of a long hill. Listening to you, I could see far below, the wind trouble the surface of the river, the patterns of smoke rising from a locomotive, the clouds shift through the skeleton cornfields.

You spoke of your longings for life . . . for this something indefinable, vast, intangible, glimpsed in brief moments. Of your love for books . . . but the barrier between them and you thin as glass, impenetrable as steel.

"To be young. They say, they envy us. I say, pity us instead, pity us that we are alive, not yet corpses for the world they ask us to survive in. Pity us, that we dream of what might be. They laugh at us, call us ignorant, rash. But it is we alone who are the wise ones. We alone who know too well what life should be. We, not yet tarnished and wearied, not yet whittled away. If you tell them, they laugh: 'I talked like that once too, you'll learn.' And they say it without tears. Think of it, without tears or shame they say, you'll learn; you'll change like us; you'll be degraded too, and become corpsy. You won't care about changing things.

"I don't know where I got this gigantic, oppressive desire to be. It only hurts more because I know that I have so little to live with. Already too much is crushed. I've no means of attaining that other kind

"Mazie. Live, don't → exist," urges Old Man Caldwell, in Yonnondio. *"Learn from your mother, who has had everything to grind out life and yet has kept life."*

of life . . . For me life can only be a matter of earning enough to keep existing, and only that. But these dreams, this hope. . . . it is worse than death."

"Fuzzie," I cried, helpless, unable to formulate more than [your] name. "Fuzzie." I too, was stricken; I too it crushed. And I didn't want to feel this, that was so alien to me. When you turned and looked at me, your face was bright like armor and I put my arms around you, hiding from that look.

*   *   *   *

After that your notes changed. And it was all notes now because you worked after school and weekends as a waitress, and we seldom saw each other. What you wrote now was more personal, more desperate. The old posing and borrowing of externalities were gone. Shadowy, the picture of you arose. Night after night, bending over your table, breaking yourself to write. A huge magnet, demanding, drawing you, and you with nothing to give. And the desire to write became more feverish than ever. Cancerlike it spread.

But the results of that racked striving were never shown. Too well, you realized its shabbiness. And before the things which you read and loved, which seemed so gigantic, your own efforts dwindled.

Even the joy in what you read was marred by this too-keen realization of its wonder. A sick sense of deprivation, of hopelessness would seep through you, and often you would cry in bitterness. "What happiness to be able to write like that, what incredible happiness." But the ironic joke was that you over-rated. Over everything you read you cast the radiance of your passionately individual interpretation. You would read to me, with eyes shining, some mediocre bit of verse or prose that in the fire of your reading became illumined with your own richness and intensity, and so filled and deepened to a work of art.

Amiel, Mansfield, Barbellion through their journals, Schreiner and Hearn, in their letters; you had

devoured every accent, every inflection of their personalities. You had a way of casually bringing one of
these writers into the conversation as if they were
mutual friends, even as if they were present.

And words—you used them in your own way.
The cliches that stirred in us only faint emotions,
were to you real and terrible. "The ashes of the sunset," you would say. "But it's been in ashes for the
last hundred years," I'd remonstrate, "you're seeing
it with the eyes of the past." "But it *is* like ashes, just
look," you'd answer, and it would be no use arguing.

And your hunger for knowledge . . . once,
standing in the library, your bitterness—"all those
volumes, tantalizing me, all their wisdom waiting to
be breathed into and made alive by my reading. And
I can't. There isn't time."

*← Eva, in "Tell Me a
Riddle," recalls from girlhood the desperate desire
to learn: ". . . knowledge
was holy. . . ."*

It was strange to me then, that this passion for
knowledge, this love for books failed to show itself
in school. Instead you were stupid. The lessons,
though pored over for hours, at nite after your
work, were only an aching jumble in your head; all
the knowledge seemed dusty and alien, a meaningless droning of dates and mummies. The weariness
of your body, the acid lurking sense of isolation,
made answering a question a torture so that invari-
ably you blundered and gave the wrong reply.

No, there was no way for your hunger for
knowledge to blossom there. Day after day, like a
shadow, you shrank in your classrooms, the dusty
chalkladen air thickening over your head, muffling
the vital noises of the outdoors. Day after day, like a
shabbily clothed shadow with a nimbus of sun-hair,
you glided thru the halls, unspoken to, unnoticed, in
the sea of laughter and entwined arms, and shouted
hellos. Significant that in school we seldom spoke,
that our only contact was letters. O little Fuzzie,
unimaginable, the sensitive torture of being a shadowy wraith, in this, your only world, for you had no
other, no outside life, except with me.

Your failure to become a recognized part of this
world must have eaten deeper than I guessed. This,

the torment at home, the backbreaking hours of
work, the ancient sadness and premonitions of youth
that come so directly, with no layer of experience to
dull; the quick primary emotions, not yet dulled by
association, crumbled your gayety into oblivion.
There was no more whimsy in your notes; you saw
me less and less; you were often absent from school.

*   *   *   *

Once, frightened by a two weeks absence, I
decided to come and see you. The world of autumn
had vanished into spring; the mournful house was the
same, but hard and unnatural against the blisters of
peeling paint, that left behind it in its peeling,
grotesque figures and grimacing mouths, the new
green lifted itself. The children, seeming scarcely to
have moved, were still squabbling in the corner of
the yard, the old shoes and cans still lay like spindrift
on the beach of last year's leaves; and in some inex-
plicable manner, as I stood there, all this became
inextricably bound up with you, became in some
way, you. As I stood waiting, I kept expecting to hear
footsteps, quick, uneven, like the beat of an overwrought heart, hurrying to the door, but there was
no sound, only after awhile the slow plod of someone's heavy feet.

The door opened. Looking up, I saw in the doorway a horrible caricature of you. The great halo of
hair was matted and decayed; the big pale eyes,
bleared with red, lay sunken down a terrace of
shrivelled flesh and the lips, gone sallow, opened to
say: "O you come to see Nena? Well, she's upstairs
in her room. She hasn't been feeling so good."

The dimness after the bright sun hurt my eyes,
but I saw you easily, writhing with a long, hacking
cough, on the cot. There was no word of greeting.
The disorder, around you who so loved order,
scalded my heart. Clothes were crumpled everywhere, mingled with dirty cups, medicine bottles,
decaying food. The window was clamped shut, and

from its bowl, your much loved earth gave forth a hard and rancid smell.

Unbelievably thin, your voice ribboned to me, "Lift . . . the window . . . . please." It was asked between paroxysms. The wind came tumbling into the room, spilling odors of spring earth, river damp, and lilacs, blowing the sourness into corners, making a strange twitching on your face.

"Now . . . you can help me . . . there, by the window." I slipped my coat about you and helped you into the chair. Your body was light, fragile. I smoothed out the bed, not knowing what to say. You sat very quietly, hunched into the coat, tracing with long fingers, slowly, abstractly, the dust of the table. The wind, tumbling in in quick gusts, stirred your hair as if it were alive; but silently you stared out the window, beyond the housetops, beyond the river, beyond the foothills, far, far beyond.

"You can't dream how I've yearned to be sitting here," you said at last. "Though it's torture. All those long days, lying there. . . ."

"What was the matter, Fuzzie? Why didn't you let me know?"

"Pleurisy. My fault. I went walking all night in the rain."

"That was dumb."

You did not seem to have heard. "All those long days, attaining the open window seemed an impossible dream."

"Were. . . you in much pain?"

"Pain?" The word seemed to root in you. "I supped and slept with it. All day pain's hand in mine, with all else fled. And the window, closed, shutting it in about me."

"I'm sorry, dear Fuzzie, I wish I . . . . ."

"Four walls, shutting in the pain. Through a splinter of window, a few branches in bud; and the pageant of clouds across the sky. Great full-bellied clouds they were. And now it's Spring again, think of it, Spring. Everywhere fullness of bearing, everywhere budding, only not in me."

← *Olsen contracted pleurisy twice as a teenager, she says.*

In Olsen's other draft, Ruth is more direct about her inability to handle Fuzzy's neediness and asks forgiveness for "'not being as inti-
← *mate as I could have been. . . . Goodbye, dear, dear Fuzzy,'" she says before going to New York and departing the story as well, early in the manuscript.*

"Dear Fuzzie," I begged, "don't excite yourself. It'll hurt you. You're not well."

"No, not well." You laughed. "There's a disease in me. Listen," you opened a drawer and flung out a dozen notebooks, "see these? They're my diaries, the manifestation of this disease, Here," you opened a tiny yellowed one, "the first symptom, four years ago:

> 'I shall write stories when I grow up, and not work in a factory. I shall write stories to make Eddie sorry. In this book, I shall write the things for my stories.'

"Four years, and now" you fumbled for another notebook, "this:

> 'Outside the great hush and weaving of rain. How lovely for her to come tonight and lend her jewels to the naked trees.'

Impatiently, you flipped the pages.

> 'Why doesn't she go to bed, why does she still sit here, writing meaningless words and staring into the night,'

("why indeed," you asked. The tone was vicious.)

> 'What is she afraid will happen if she turns out the light and gives herself to the dark? And why this shivering anticipation as she turns the page; does she think perhaps on this page she will write poetry? As if,'

the book tumbled into a corner. "As if." Your face was white. "I loathe myself for writing these things. For hoarding the words I say, the emotions, hoping they may translate into writing. I loathe these diaries; they sprawl there on the table like tombstones. And yet I persist in keeping them, incoherent records of an inarticulate life, year after year.

And it's no use, I can't say what I want . . . never, never . . . and is there anything really of me in these, really of my life? . ."

I put my hand over your mouth, "Please Fuzzie, please, be quiet, you'll hurt yourself. You mustn't talk like this; you're not strong."

You put your hand over mine to tear it away. But another fit of coughing shook you. The angry hand slackened—let go, lay supplicatingly on my shoulder. "I'm sorry," shyly, "perhaps, it's just that I've been bottled up so long. . . . ."

"Yes, I know. Here look at the book I brought you; it's an illustrated Fairy Tales, Wilde's. Just rest and breathe."

I began to pick up the clothes, to hang them up. The room was very quiet. Through the window I could see steam rising from the roof tops and the damp earth; the far foothills were covered with a thin wash of green, the near trees resplendent with furry little buds. New odors kept flooding the room, which seemed somehow to have expanded, to have taken in the outdoors. After a while you said, "It's so beautiful outside. I wish I were out walking in it."

"You will be. I'll come again soon, and we'll go for a long hike, down by the river."

A spasm quivered over your face. "It was down by the river, I went that night. There was such a misty rain. When I lifted my face in it, I could imagine I were crying."

"What made you go?"

"I don't know. The mocking weather. Restlessness." Afraid I was starting you off again, I went ahead straightening up, quickly talking about people, about books. And in a few moments, like the first Fuzzie I had known, you were posing a question: which would be more preferable to ride . . . a comet or the wind? and arguing both sides.

I came to your diary in the corner, where you had thrown it. And in a sudden impulse (not knowing, not dreaming) asked, "Fuzzie, show me something you've written."

In Yonnondio, Mazie walks a long way to borrow something to read from Old Man Caldwell. Sick and dying, he gives her a few books as a present—including those "fairy tales, Wilde's"—which her father promptly sells for ◄ fifty cents.

Out, now, the fatal question, irrevocable. Long distant now, blurred by the rain of years between, the hot shame still scalds me remembering how your fragile voice, complying, faltered out the awkward prosy verse. Sharp as a winter landscape the disordered room appears before me, the words plod back into my memory. . . . .

"Spring is a hard time to be young in
For us, who were taken out of the world as it
    might be,
Into a world we have not made.
You, the old ones, have had the years to
    teach you how to look on buds
To see but withered leaves as they will be in
    autumn.
But we who feel the buds tense swelling
How can we bear burdens of Spring never to
    turn Summer
Burdens of ancient wisdom telling what
    Spring could be?"

(It was here you suddenly caught fire with the emotion you had tried to express. Here that the hot shame ballooned out my heart to bursting. It was horrible, horrible, so poor, so crude.)

"Spring is a hard time to be young in . . . .
We cannot break into a myriad buds,
We cannot flush into an ecstasy of green,
There are no birds to fling into the sky,
Spring asks these from us, stands imperious,
    asking
For what we cannot give."

(From downstairs a great singing began spiralling up, a male bass, lusty and deep. It shattered your fragile voice, but thinly, tenaciously, you went on.)

"Already in our veins we know your world of
    winter
It creeps into us like frost into seeds lain in
    Autumn.

The sap that rises in us you gave no limbs to
  flow into,
The sun that warmed us turns to ice, the
  rain to hail.
You gave no seed for our quick soil to green.
Our birds die young, or strangled in the
  throat,
There is no air to send them in, but yours,
And that is poisoned."

(In my heart, I cried to you, cliche, cliche, maudlin, stop Fuzzie, but you went on trembling shamelessly now with emotion. And the singing downstairs, unbearably vital, seemed giving you the lie).

← Parts of "Not You I Weep For" read like a dialogue between the young Olsen's zealous, exclamatory impulses and her objective, critical responses.

"Spring does not care. She asks and asks. Our
  blood must listen.
She stabs us unarmed young with pricking
  spear buds,
With bayonets of shining rain. We have
  nowhere to hide.
Come snow, come years, and blow the dust
  into our eyes.
With monotone of days pierce out our ear
  drums,
Make us unknowing children like the old,
  Hide us from spring."

Done, done at last. I kept my burning eyes to the ground, grateful for the stillness, grateful for the singing that welled up triumphantly. But betrayed by my silence, exalted, you began to talk in that naked, personal way of yours.

"It was so hard writing that, hamering it out. I wanted so desperately to express the pity of us in this world."

I began to say, "Please be quiet, Fuzzie, please don't," but you went on: "I can't overcome the fear I have of what life does to people. It isn't happiness I cry for; it's only to feel emotion, any deep emotion that lets me know I'm alive. I've seen how that dies . . . my father, my mother . . . I've told you . . . almost everyone; it's horrible, walking the streets and seeing the faces; incapable of feeling, the well dried up."

"Who," I managed to say, "was singing?"

"My brother, Ed."

"He doesn't seem . . . . dried up."

"He's got some nourishment, something I've been cut off from. Something—but oh tell me it isn't hopeless; tell me I'll write. Everything has its articulateness, its flowering; even the century plant, once in a hundred years. And it seems only I never will. Never, never. Look at me, tell me it will happen, tell me I'll write."

I made a guttural sound. Too clearly I had seen the hopelessness of your writing, the truth of your despair. I had to escape . . . my heart seemed bursting; I could almost feel the crack of the thin flesh. Abruptly I said, "Fuzzie, I've got to go. Here, I'll help you back to bed. Don't mind. I'll see you soon."

The lightness of your body seemed an unbearably heavy burden. I grabbed my coat and ran down the stairs, bumping into your brother, who standing in stocky blue overalls was still singing; out the door, past the children I fled pursued by the sound of your cough, by the absurd song your brother was singing "tho-the-foe-is-up-today-he'll-be-down-tomorrow," pursued by the vision I had seen of you, hopeless, doomed. Left to become only another of those faded, ineffectual women that people the schools and offices, quivering to illness before any art, living everything "vicariously, vicariously." But hush—not even that was possible for you—I had forgotten your own words "for me . . . life can be only a matter of earning enough . . . to keep existing." Everything reeled. The world, enormous and terrible, the dark reeking places you would search out, I saw them crashing down upon you and I ran, ran down the street to the car, to home, to security.

After that, inevitably, our friendship dwindled. Whenever I was with you the sensation of suffocation, of reeling, overcame me. I began to evade you. Your letters grew madder, more feverish. Fear haunted them. I never answered. Gradually, you stopped sending them; gradually I managed to forget you. Somewhere I heard you had left school; somewhere else that you were working.

"Light she grew, like a bird," writes Olsen in a moving description of Eva's death in "Tell Me a Riddle." →

Olsen's other version of this story relates Nena's fate beyond high school. After losing contact with Ruth, Nena finds work in a tie factory (as Olsen once did), but she is singled out to lose her job during a strike. Hungry for romance, she takes her first lover. "She had read enough to lose any moral resistance. . . ." At this point the manuscript becomes fragmented. An abortion is mentioned, and the lover disappears from the picture. →

*   *   *   *

Months later, walking down the long corridors one night with the galleys of the school paper under my arm, strangely you were there too, huddled in the shadows behind a plaster statue, weeping and weeping. How you got there, or why you wept, I did not ask. I only know I put my arms around you, and I wept too. Once, though I may have dreamed it, with face distorted you cried, ". . all I have not had," and your gesture was wide and universal. But it may have been a dream, as perhaps all of it was, though I still taste the tears on my mouth, still feel the salt bite into my cheek. Like that I remember you forever, little Fuzzie, weeping in the empty hall under the menacing shadows, with somewhere the sad sifting sound of a cleaning brush being pushed over the stairs, "All . . . all I have not had."

I never saw you again. Once, before I went to New York, I tried, (I did try Fuzzie to find you again, I did) but when I knocked at the door (the paint long ago peeled, the porch steps long since caved in) no-one answered, and next door they told me, "Didn't you know? They moved, almost a year ago. Other people lived there since. The girl? which girl, oh the second—I think she was working for a while at Wilsons, but she got sick. No, they leave me no address, no." Thank you, I said, but the wind, whipping up the leaves and shadows, flung me down the street before it, and when I tried to turn and shout "Goodbye" to you, to somebody, the howling of the night and the cold rose about me gigantic. (No one could have heard anyway)

Three years ago. Now, grotesquely in the wrapping paper of a package from home, your name. "Deaths," almost at the end, "Nena Asarch . . . 20 . . . pneumonia." Nothing else. As if there were anything else to be said. Nothing—only that you were young and bewildered, only that you

◄ "Squeaks," the humor column Olsen contributed to her high school newspaper, won a national prize.

◄ "When she was a girl . . . O when she was a girl . . . The life she had dreamed and the life that had come to be . . ." thinks Anna, in Yonnondio, *articulating the disappointment and regret that often beset Olsen's characters.*

In the third-person version, Nena goes for a walk in the graveyard near her family's house and in the rain and wind begins to run in uncontrollable "ecstasy," shouting, "'I'm alive . . . alive.'" Soon she falls ill, experiences delirium then a brief creative breakthrough in her writing before she dies. "The room was fumigated immediately after the funeral, for the boy younger than Nena was anxious to have a room for his own." Nena's diaries are burned, unless they have sufficient blank pages to warrant fumigation and keeping.

knew poverty and despair. The line was enough. (But so obscure, so insignificant). Did it matter? the lightness of your body as I lifted you back to bed that day, the unutterable radiance gathering on your face in study hall, our birds dying young, or strangled in the throat? True, there was a gesture, lost in shadows, but wide and universal, and words "All . . . all I have not had."

Why am I crying now, tears raining down, tears, that rain of the heart after the congested swollen storm, tears blurring the brief words "Dead, Nena Asarch, 20, pneumonia."

No, not you, little Fuzzie, not you I weep for. For myself, for all our vanished youths— vanished without purpose or answer, vanished before we were ever young. Less—less than a blade of grass withering.

Tillie Olsen

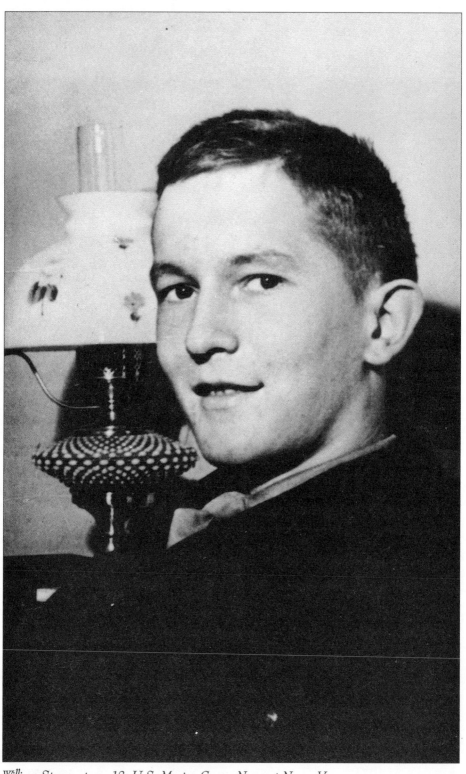

William Styron at age 18, U.S. Marine Corps, Newport News, Va.

WILLIAM STYRON

William Styron was first exposed to books when, as a small child, he served as his mother's courier to and from the local lending library. Bedridden with illness for much of her life, she died when Styron was thirteen; the loss would affect, the author says, his own depressive illness, as well as, at least one scholar notes, the dark vision explored in Styron's fiction.

Styron himself had almost died the year before when the small boat he was sailing capsized and sank into the James River of his native Tidewater, Virginia. This region, where Styron was born in 1925, figures prominently in such novels as *Lie Down in Darkness* (1951) and *The Confessions of Nat Turner* (1967). The near-drowning episode is fictionalized in his 1959 novel *Set This House on Fire*. With this incident, the narrator recalls, "there had been taken away from me that child's notion that I would live forever."

War and its losses would also influence Styron's literary vision, as demonstrated most strikingly in his 1979 novel *Sophie's Choice*. But during his high school years, Styron was eager to "taste the glory of military life," he writes in his collection of nonfiction *This Quiet Dust* (1982). Owing to a "strain of suicidal bravado," he left Davidson College (where he had written the following piece) in spring of 1943 to join the Marine Corps at the age of seventeen.

Styron's adult feelings about the military have certainly been more ambivalent. While he does not dismiss it as an institution, he has written sometimes-scathing critiques of the service when he sees it demeaned by the shortcomings and abuses of egotists, fools, and hypocrites. Writing as a patriotic teenager in the following satire, which takes the form of some clever literary parodies, Styron mocks the hypocrisy he sees in his college administration's efforts to keep him *out* of the service. He explains:

It has to do with the chaos on many college campuses during World War II. Students were being implored by many college administrations to remain in school (if the students were male) and get as much ("get all you can") education as possible before going into the service. However, students were getting drafted right and left anyway. In addition, at Davidson, the Army Air Corps had established a student training program, which caused an incredible amount of congestion as the original Davidson students found themselves being crowded out by the A.A.C. enlistees. This inevitably led to the suspicion (conviction, really) that the college was trying to have it both ways financially— getting money both from the students and Uncle Sam.

Get All You Can

A PARODY IN VERSE

BY BILL STYRON

(1943, age 17)

*(E*ditor's note: During the past year numerous talks have been made by our President, Dr. Cunningham, on the expediency of remaining in school and obtaining the full benefit of Davidson's educational facilities before entering the Armed Forces. We believe that the policy which the administration has followed in advising students has been wise, and it is evident that the interest of the Davidson students has been foremost in the minds of Dr. Cunningham and the other members of the faculty. The advice to each individual has been wholly unselfish on the part of the college, and the withdrawal of a number of students is the result of conditions beyond the control of the college or the students. The verse on the next few pages does not intimate mercenary tendencies within the administration, far from that, but it is simply the author's perversion of some of the facts in order to create an extremely satire-able situation.)

← *Styron is "almost certain" that he wrote this prefatory Editor's Note.*

Styron might have been prepared for writing satire, in part, by the rebelliousness of his nature: ". . . when I was quite young, and in school, or later in the Marine Corps, I realized how powerfully I was repelled by authority . . . ," the author recalled in an interview. He also confessed that he was often in minor trouble with teachers and other authority figures.

COLERIDGE

The Rhyme of the Ancient Mariner

*I*t is a College President,
And much surprised are we;
"By that tailored suit and Arrow tie,
What shalt thou say to me?"

He holds us with his faultless voice,
"Get all you can," quoth he;
Speak on, speak on, O President,
Eftsoons with smiles spake he.

Eftsoons: at once ➤

The students all sat in their seats:
They cannot choose but listen;
And as he spake in flowing words,
Their eyes, behold did glisten.

*Nathan, in Sophie's
Choice, is a talented carica-
turist: ". . . his gift was
not mimicry alone; what
emanated from him so drolly
was the product of dazzling
invention," the narrator,
Stingo, tells us, referring
to Nathan's southern
impersonations.*

"I urge of you emphatically
To stay in school," he cried;
"You shall be here quite long, you see;"
Forsooth the students sighed.

Day after day, day after day
We stayed, and had no notion
The V-1 would call us, yea,
To sail upon the ocean.

Army, Navy, everywhere
The students all did shrink,
Evacuate both East and West;
Morale began to sink.

Fill up that dormitory room
With five, or six, or more;
There goes a man to the E.R.C.,
Which leaves us now but four

*E.R.C.: Enlisted ➤
Reserve Corps*

The President, whose eye is bright,
And said "get all you can and more,"
Is gone and now the College Stud
Turned from Dean Bailey's door.

He went like one that hath been stunned
And is of sense forlorn,
A sadder and a drafted man,
He left last Tuesday morn.

SHAKESPEARE

Hamlet Soliloquizing

*T*o be or not to be: 'tis not the question;
But whether 'tis nobler to suffer the stress and strain
   of six more months,
Or to take arms like any other draftee
And end up a buck private. The E.R.C.,
No more; and by the E.R.C. to say
We end the deals and extended operations
The flesh is heir to, 'tis a consummation
Completely to be avoided. Get all you can;
All; perchance some more; ay, there's the J.O.;
For in that sleep of death called education
What things may come when we
Have shuffled off for the week-end,
Must give us pause: there's the respect
That makes calamity of a Phi Bete average;
But what limber would bear
The whips and scorns of a top sergeant
When he himself might a dealer make
With a bare bottle? Atch!

◄ In Styron's story "Love Day" (1985), Lieutenant Stiles mocks the "sham" decoy invasion he has been assigned to by performing his King Harry impression, hollering out lines from Henry V to his amused troops.

SHELLEY

Ozymandias

I met a traveler from the Students' Store
Who said: The office of the President
Is in Chambers. In it, through the door,
Sits a man who wished all the students well,
And told them all one day that before
They leave these old and hallowed walls to fight
They should remain and be well content,
For no Draft Board could ever cause them fright;
And he made in inspiring terms this speech:
"My name is J.R. Cunningham, President;
Get all you can, ye students, I beseech!"
Nothing beside remains. For after May,
When the students will Fort Benning reach,
The lonely campus stretches far away.

KIPLING

Tommy Atkins

*"Only one English poet →
escaped being a pederast,
and that was Kipling," pro-
nounces Captain Budwinkle,
an insipid military func-
tionary in Styron's 1972
satirical play* In the Clap
Shack. *Budwinkle then
recites his favorite lines:
"But the head and the hoof
of the Law / and the haunch
and the hump / is—Obey!"*

I went to Monday's Chapel talk to see wot
     I could see;
Cunningham 'e up an' sez, "They've called the
     E.R.C."
The faculty behin' their doors they
     laughed an' giggled fit to die,
I ousts right over to my room
     and to myself sez I:
O it's students this an' students that
     an' "we'll draft yer jus' the same,"
But it was "Thank yer, Mister Student,"
     before the Air Corps came,
Before the Air Corps came, my boys,
     before the Air Corps came,

O it was "Thank yer, Mister Student,"
 before the Air Corps came.

I went to Jackson's house one day, as meek as
 I could be,
'E sez to me, "Git out o' West, 'ere comes the
 A.A.C.;
Move yer things, pack yer stuff,
 you ain't got long to stay;
Find a place somewheres in town,
 you're drafted anyway!"
And it's students this an' students that,
 an' "students go away;"
But it was "we love yer, Mister Student,"
 before the Air Corps' stay,
Before the Air Corps' stay, my boys,
 before the Air Corps' stay,
O 'twas "we love yer Mister Student,"
 before the Air Corps' stay.

In Styron's novel The Long
March *(1952), Captain
Mannix focuses his "disgruntled sense of humor" on
the marine reserves when he
finds himself back in boot
camp. "Corporal, kindly
pass out the atom bombs for
inspection," he quips, in
parody of the tedious, banal
lectures on military doctrine
he is forced to attend.*

TENNYSON

Charge of the Light Brigade

*H*alf a year, half a year,
Half a year onward,
Into the E.R.C.
Went the Six Hundred;
"Stay here, get all you can,
We're with you, man for man,
You'll never see Japan!"
  Blissful Six Hundred.
Then came the A.A.C.,

← *There were 600 students
at Davidson in 1942
(before the influx brought
about by the A.A.C.), the
author explains.*

Can there some changes be?
Not though the students knew
Someone had blundered.
Theirs not to reason why
From East they quickly fly,
"No refund!" comes Jackson's cry.
        Crowded Six Hundred.

*Oppressed by the communal
living arrangement at the
Bachelor Officers' Quarters,
the narrator of Styron's
story "Marriott, the Marine"
(1971) is reminded "pain-
fully of college, of a dormitory, and I realized how
truly retrogressive my life
had become." ➤*

Army to right of them,
Navy to left of them,
4-F beyond them,
        All of them thundered.
"This room will hold four,
In a pinch, perhaps more,
Sleep there on the floor!"
        Dwindling Six Hundred.

When will their memory fade?
O what a sight they made!
        Nobody wondered.
Most are now gone for good,
They got all they could,
        Noble Six Hundred.

William Styron

Amy Tan at age 8. "Each morning before school," says Tan's character Waverly Jong in The Joy Luck Club, *"my mother would twist and yank on my thick black hair until she had formed two tightly wound pigtails."*

AMY TAN

*I*n Amy Tan's wildly successful first book *The Joy Luck Club* (1989), four Chinese-born mothers try to share their personal and cultural heritage with their four American-born daughters. One daughter, Jing-mei "June" Woo, responds to her mother's death by going to China to look for family there. Central to this collection of interrelated stories and to Tan's second book, *The Kitchen God's Wife* (a novel, 1991), is the significance of place—countries, cities, houses, landmarks—and its loss and discovery as well.

Lindo Jong, for example, names her daughter Waverly after the street in San Francisco where they lived. "I wanted you to think, This is where I belong," Lindo tells her daughter. "But I also knew if I named you after this street, soon you would grow up, leave this place, and take a piece of me with you."

In the childhood essay that follows, Tan discovers, loses, and rediscovers her own significant place: the Santa Rosa public library. Born in Oakland, California, in 1952, she wrote this tribute to her favorite haunt for a contest sponsored by a local citizens group. The winning entry, it was published along with other children's themes on the same topic in the Santa Rosa *Press Democrat*.

Amy Tan remarks:

> Upon re-reading this piece, "What the Library Means to Me," I am struck by the fact that my writing style has changed very little since I was eight years old. No doubt I was influenced by my father, a Baptist

minister. And so I tried to be as direct and as honest as possible, writing the way I talked. I wrote about emotions, the basics, happiness and sadness. I already had a fondness for metaphors, and in fact, those doors and windows are still pretty much the way I feel about reading fiction today. And I also brought up, as did my father at the end of a sermon, a pitch for money cloaked in the example of my own charitable giving. Although nowhere in my wildest eight-year-old imagination did I ever dream I could one day sell a book.

What the Library Means to Me
(1961, age 8)

Tan picks up the architecture-of-the-mind metaphor in The Joy Luck Club, *when Rose describes Old Mr. Chou, the guardian of dreams, as presiding over a door beyond which she finds herself in "a house without doors or windows."* ➤

Also in The Joy Luck Club, *Suyuan Woo returns to Shanghai in search of* ➤ *her family only to find that their house no longer exists. "I kept looking up to where the house used to be," she says. "And it wasn't a house, just the sky."*

*M*y name is Amy Tan, 8 years old, a third grader in Matanzas School. It is a brand new school and everything is so nice and pretty. I love school because the many things I learn seem to turn on a light in the little room in my mind. I can see a lot of things I have never seen before. I can read many interesting books by myself now. I love to read. My father takes me to the library every two weeks, and I check five or six books each time. These books seem to open many windows in my little room. I can see many wonderful things outside. I always look forward to go the library.

Once my father did not take me to the library for a whole month. He said, the library was closed because the building is too old. I missed it like a good friend. It seems a long long time my father took me to the Library again just before Christmas. Now it is on the second floor of some stores. I wish we can have a real nice and pretty library like my school. I put 18 cents in the box and signed my name to join Citizens of Santa Rosa Library.

Amy Tan

John Updike at about age 14 (at left, seated), with his Lutheran confirmation class. "I'm the little blurry fellow sitting in the row with the girls," Updike points out. "As you can see, I don't look happy."

JOHN UPDIKE

*J*ohn Updike's small-town childhood—short on glamor but rich in the daily magic of place, thought, and human interaction—underlies many of his nearly forty books of prose and poetry.

Born in 1932 in Shillington, Pennsylvania, Updike, an only child, took his boyhood pleasures passively, shyly—"burrowing in New York magazines and English mystery novels for the secret passageway out, the path of avoidance and vindication"—as he anticipated that day when he would do something worth admiring, something beyond his hometown's scope. And, in the bargain, he relates in his 1989 memoir *Self-Consciousness*, he would redress his father's meagerly rewarded career as a schoolteacher.

Updike confesses that one of the past selves that makes him cringe is the boy of 1945–48: the boy who wrote the mystery novel that follows. His family had moved from Shillington to an eighty-acre farm eleven miles away, and this rural isolation imposed, until he was old enough to drive, feelings of akwardness and exile. Avid reading provided his relief, as the young Updike continued to develop his "belief in print, in ink, in a sacred realm of publication," as he puts it in his memoir, that would "redeem" him.

He has managed to earn several million words' worth of redemption, beginning professionally with his contributions to *The New Yorker*, to whose sophisticated pages Updike aspired since early adolescence, and continuing with such prize-winning, best-selling contemporary literature as *The Centaur* (1963) and *Couples* (1968). He is best known for the famous Rabbit novels, which focus on a former high school basketball star—and the

America around him—at different periods of his life.

Updike's partial mystery novel written at age fourteen predicts his tremendous facility with language and his ambitious productivity, as well as an enduring fascination with misbehavior, befitting a boy with a "docile, good-child nature."

The author says of his contribution to this anthology:

> To my imperfect recollection, this was my first extended effort in fiction, except for some fables imitating Thurber's. It must have been composed in the summer, when I had the time; on the other side of one page is a poem signed "John Updike 8B," so I would place it in the summer between eighth and ninth grade, when I, with a March birthday, was fourteen years old. I had been a mystery-novel reader for some years—of Erle Stanley Gardner, Ellery Queen, Agatha Christie, John Dickson Carr.
>
> This is all there is; the plot collapses with the second murder, though I remember I had an idea of a secret staircase and someone walking down it backwards, leaving apparently upward footprints. Manuel Citarro, possibly, was meant to have "done it."
>
> The frightful fallibility of the creative process is here naked—the misspellings, the character misplacements, the repeatedly slippery details. Presently at work on my sixteenth novel, I recognize myself all too well in this pubescent perpetrator of dialogue, facial descriptions, and—very transparently—suspense. Seeking the clue-cluttered atmosphere of a classic detective puzzle, he created pure clutter and a glacial stasis of action.
>
> My editorial policy toward my struggling younger self has been that we should keep his misspellings, but where only a mistake in typing is involved, it should be silently corrected. He seems to have worked in some haste, and with a sticky machine.

Untitled mystery

(circa 1946, age 14)

After contemplating a child-hood photo of himself, the adult Updike describes feel-ing like the phantom cre-ation of the child's ambition to become an artist. "Now I wait apprehensively for his next command," he writes in "The Dogwood Tree: A Boyhood" (1962), "or at least a nod of appreciation, and he smiles through me, as if I am already transpar-ent with failure."

My employer, Manuel Citarro, pushed the letter across the desk at me. It was written in a large, mascueline hand, with no curly-cues and a firm down-stroke. "Mr. Citarro," it read, "I would like your presence over the week-end at my country home, White Haven. There will be three other guests besides yourself. The visit may have some interest professionly to you. Let me know if you can come.

WALTER HALDEMAN"

"Doesn't waste ink, does he," I remarked.

"That is what makes it so interesting," Manuel replied. "It is more like a command than an invation. Not one please, in the entire letter. The "interest professionally" sentance is indeed fascenating. It might mean anything. His wife might be unfaithful, his butler might be a pilferer, his dog might have fits, or his life might be in danger."

I chuckled. "Probably one of the first three. A big man like Walt Haldeman imagines he has to have the best of everything for anything, no matter how trifling. He probably calls in Adrian when his little girl wants a new doll-dress made."

Gilbert Adrian (1903–59), Hollywood costume and set ◂ *designer.*

"He doesn't have a little girl. And I disagree with you. I sense something big, important here, regard-less of his vague phraseology."

"Surely you're not going?"

"I am."

So it was that, later, Manuel Citarro, the famous detective and Thomas Mays, his obscure but deserv-ing secretary, stepped off of a grimy little train unto a grimier little railroad station called "White Haven." It was the station that was named after the home of Walter Haldeman, and not the other way around. White Haven station is about 30 miles, or 45 minutes, from New York City. The home White Haven is a mile from the station.

"You must be Mr. Sitarro," a slackmouthed young man adressed himself to my employer. He pronounced the "C" like "S."

"Yes, I am Mr. Kitarro."

"I was told to pick ya' up." He threw me a nasty look.

"This is my secretary, Thomas Mays," Citarro intervened. "He is with me."

"I wasn't told there'd be nobody else," he growled. He didn't like me very much.

"Well, I'm sure it's quite all right," Citarro snapped, "I must have my secretary, I'm sure that my hostess will understand." Then he became mellow and kindly, laying a hand on my shoulder. "Mays, here, is as important to me as my right hand." He waggled his right hand. "I could not do without him." I think he did that mainly to embarres me, for it was not the truth. I had been with Citarro for only three weeks and I could not feel that I was very important to him. It was my task to read his commoner fan mail, type a few letters, and chat with him occasionly. He was forever bustling in and out, doing things that I knew nothing about.

Nevertheless, the surly youth was subdued, if not overwhelmed. He led us to a shiny new automobile, and when we got in, he started the car. We drove on an asphalt lane, bordered by Maple Trees most of the way. It was a very pleasant and refreshing drive.

In my mind, "White Haven" had existed as a sprawling mansion, elaborately rich. "White Haven" turned out to be a cream-white block topped by a pointed grey slate roof, sitting admidst a dainty little garden. The house was made of wooden clapboards, and in its simplicity held a definate beauty. If I had been told that this refined and innocent home was going to house murder, I would have laughed rudely.

"Helllo, Mr. Citarro," a woman's voice cood. "We're so glad you could come." A buxom lady crossed the lawn and shook hands warmly with Citarro.

"Charming place you have here, Mrs.

Haldeman," returned my employer, with a deep bow after he had said hello.

Mrs. Haldeman showd her teeth. "Yes, isn't it. It's such a lovely location too."

Citarro smiled a very Latin smile and murmered, "But the home can never equal the beauty of its mistress."

Mrs. Haldeman looked at him in an odd way and said evenly, "You don't mean that. You're just acting Spanish." Citarro hesitated for a moment before he shrugged his shoulders and said, "Yes, it is true. My clients expect me to play the dashing conquisidor so I have gotten into the habit of doing it all the time, paying compliments, smiling, bowing."

She said, "Oh, I see you have brought your valet along." I blushed.

"He is not my valet," Citarro said sharply. "He is my secretary."

Mrs. Haldeman smiled again. "I hope that Mr ..."

"Mays," Citarro prompted.

"I hope that Mr. Mays will not mind sleeping on a cot. I'm very sorry, but our house isn't really as large as it should be, and all the rooms are filled up, so your secretary will have to sleep on a cot in your room."

"I'm very sorry that I shall make you the trouble," Citarro returned. "It is my fault entirely that this should happen. I should have asked first about conditions. I apoligise sincerely. Forgive me." Here he bowed deeply for the second time. "If you wish, I shall be only too happy to send Mays home."

"Oh, no, It is quite all right. Won't you come in."

Although Mrs. Haldeman had been extremely polite and gracious, I felt uncomfortable. It was the second time that day that the favorability of my presence had been doubted.

"Why didn't you let them know I was coming," I hissed at my employer as we walked along behind Mrs. Haldeman. "I feel about as welcome as a toad in between the bedsheets."

"Heavens, Tommy," he retorted, "don't be so disagreeable."

This hurt me, so I said nothing else. Instead I studied our hostess. She was an impressive woman. Her hair was practically white, with a few strips of black running through. She carried herself well, her carraige was that of a being who feels she is always right. At one time she had been beautiful, even now she was handsome. Her jaw was just a bit too square, too pronounced and her eyes were too grey and determined, they gave away the fact that here was a woman who got what she wanted. If I had been 40 years older, I would have thought of her as a member of the "old school."

The house inside was as simple in design as the outside. A wide hallway ran strait through the center of the house, with a door at each end. The stair way started about 20 feet from the front door, in the middle of the hall so that there were two smaller, but still ample halls on either side. "Certainly very neat and balanced" for such a fabulas tycoon as Walt Haldeman.

Mrs. Haldeman directed us into the first door to our right. The room was a large living, or drawing room. It was cleverly furnished in a way so that it would be comfortable yet looked slightly musty and antique, combining the new world of luxury and the old one of dignity and moderation. Reposed on the various pieces of furniture were three people, obviously engaged in the pastime of polite drawing-room conversation. Mrs. Haldeman introduced us. "This is Mr. Manuel Citarro, and his secretary, Mr. Mays. Mr. Citarro and Mr. Mays, this is my husband, Walter Haldeman." Automatically I classified them in my mind. Haldeman was "Rich Men Grown Old", solid, contented, dominated by his wife. "My sister, Grace. . ." I put her under "Sweet Old Paracites" probably never worked in her life, living off of her sister's character. "Mr. James Crayne. . ." "Sporting Old Chap" thin, intelligent looking, jolly good fellow. "And Mr. Merriwether Stone." And here I was stopped. A small, slight man, very delicate looking, with preposterously large brown eyes. They could not be called bovine, for they did not have that glazed look. They were clever, smart eyes. He made

In Updike's celebrated → story "Deaths of Distant Friends" (1982), old Miss Amy Merrymount, like Mrs. Haldeman, radiates a genteel self-possession. The narrator describes her "slender smooth beauty that sepia photographs remembered, the breeding and intelligence and, in a spiritual sense, ardor she still possessed."

me feel uneasy, so I hastily crammed him into Micellenaous and let it go.

It was an hour before dinner, and one of the party had not yet arrived, so Citarro and I joined the group in the drawing-room. "Dash it all, I wonder where Connie can have gotten to. She said she would come up by car after she did some things in New York. I could use the old rattletrap Packard, because she must have the new car for whatever it was she wanted to do. Probably meet some boy friend," Mr. Crayne was expounding to Walter Haldeman.

"Now, Jim, you mustn't be too hard on the kid, she's young and all that," Haldeman easily retorted.

It really wasn't necessary to reprimand Mr. Crayne, because all the time he was berating the absent Connie, there was a secretly amused light in his eyes. Nevertheless, he found it necessary to go on, even though he fooled no one. "This young generation," he snorted. "If only the girl's mother was here." Then a vague sorrow crept into his tone. "Connie was just a little tyke when Maggie died, she never knew her mother. Margaret was a lady, too. You didn't catch her going 70 miles an hour in a brand new automobile, or staying up until the next morning at some wild party. Sensation-crazy, that's what the young ones are."

"But hasn't the human race always been sensation crazy?" Merriwether Stone asked quietly. "Always asking for noveltys, for ways to risk their lives, for adventure. Everyone must work off his wild streak somehow. An office clerk might take dope, a married couple might work off their spirits by having fierce quarrels. The young generation, as you call it, may do seemingly alarming things in the eye's of their parents, but didn't those same parents alarm their parents years back. And when your children have children, those children will think their parents quite old fuddie-duddies. Come, Mr. Crayne, surely you can remember when you did things over your parents protesting bodies, but which now is a commonplace event in modern life. That is progress."

"Well, I remember my first automobile ride. I

← *Harry "Rabbit" Angstrom has inherited Thomas Mays's talent for the broad classification. Women, he muses in* Rabbit, Run *(1960), are "a different race." Foxy, in* Couples, *observes that every "marriage tends to consist of an aristocrat and a peasant."*

In the late '60s, youth confronts a whole new range of temptations. "It's not just cigarettes and a little feeling up. At fourteen now, they're ready to go," says Peggy Fosnacht, the mother of a teenager, in ← Rabbit Redux *(1971).*

Rabbit's father is less ➔ *philosophical about modern-day developments. Had he to face contemporary pressures as a younger man, he says in* Rabbit Redux, *"I'd no doubt just have put a shotgun to my head and let the world roll on without me."*

Antonio Maura (1853–1925), premier of Spain at several points in the early 1900s.

The author explains: "I ➔ *have no idea where I got the name of Governor Maura. My mother, the only writer I knew, was long absorbed in a never-published novel about Juan Ponce de Leon, the discoverer of Florida, and the house was full of books on Spain, especially in the reign of Ferdinand and Isabella. Hence, no doubt, my sleuth's Spanishness."*

didn't live with my parents, but, when I wrote them about it, they were so shocked they disinherited me for three months."

"Certainly," Merriwether Stone said, "Who knows but when your Connie is your age, 70 miles an hour will be the accepted rate of speed. That is that alarming phemominea known as progress."

My employer, Manuel Citarro, coughed a little cough, and looked about him carelessly. I knew that whenever he did that, he was about to talk about his favorite subject, himself. "You were speaking a moment ago about people being sensation crazy," he began. "I have noticed that tendency particualy strong in the American people."

"America is the most progressive of all nations," softly spoke Merriwether Stone.

"Yes, that is true also." Citarro spoke a little quickly, as if afraid the conversational lead would be wrested away from him. "I am a Spanierd, born in Spain. But I was taken away from my native country when I was three years old, in 1909. My father was a newspaper man who said some indiscreet things about the administration, under Maura. We came to Mexico, but my father was assisinated for saying indiscreet things about the Mexican administration a year later. An indiscreet man, my father. Anyway my mother died shortly after, and I was raised in an orphanage. When twenty-three, I came to America. I got a job in a factory, and probably would be there yet, had not some papers been stolen. I just applied a little common sense, and I relized immediately who had stolen them and how. Through my efforts, the criminal was arrested. I was surprised to find that I was gifted in deduction, so I set up a small detective agency.

"Now, here is the point of my story. I first called myself Mark Citers, Pvt. Investigator. Nobody came. Then a friend of mine told me to use my Spanish name. So I put out a second sign, Manuel Citarro, the Spanish Sleuth. My first customer was a fat lady by the name of Cranbury. I still remember that funny name, Cranbury. She came into my office a little exited and stared hard at me for several minutes. "It is true," she gasped at last, "That your a Spanierd detective." I thought that this was a resentment of the foreign birth. "Yes," I stammered, "it is true I was born in Spain, but I have lived in America for four years now, and I will be an American citizen as soon as I can." She was an extremely ugly old soul, but her face lighted up with a child-like look of wonder. Her business, it turned out was a stolen purse. I found it in her bureau drawer, hidden away under the sweaters. More curious people came, usually old women. I learned that there were certain things a Spanierd was expected to do. He must be handsome, have a mustache, and smoke tiny cigaretts in a long holder, he must speak with a slight accent, and he must throw a dagger. He also should be extremely charming to the ladies, paying florid compliments and bowing. I set about fulfilling these requirements. I was handsome already". Here I looked at him, appaled by this bland remark of conceit. But it was the truth, even now, although greying around the temples, he was very good-looking in a mascueline way. "But I did not have a mustache, so I grew one, I had always smoked a pipe, but I gave it up and smoked Turkish cigaretts in a long, delicate holder. I polished up my manners. I never could, however, bring myself to mar my English with Spanish. I even learned how to throw a dagger, and carried one under my arm in my sleeve, so I could demonstrate to my thrill-hungry customers. Watch." And he quickly drew out a small, intricatly decorated dagger and threw it at me. I had been trained to do this trick, so when he began talking about the requiremants of a Spanierd in America, I had rose from my seat and leaned against the wall. When he drew out his dagger, I quickly made a circle with my thumb and forefinger and laid my hand against the wall. It was in this circle that the dagger struck. It remained quivering in the wall. I had hardly expected that Citarro would dare do this cheap, melodramatic trick in a nice old house like this, for such intelligent people. It was all right to show off in

◄ *In* Rabbit Redux, *Rabbit vents a lot of this sort of resentment: "All these Greeks or Polacks or whatever are on the make,"* *he complains.*

his own office, for people who had come mainly to see a dashing Spanish sleuth. His office walls were marred by many dagger marks, and my fingers had many small scars from the times he was not quite accurate in his aim.

These people, however, were just as impressed as Mrs. Cranbury.

"Remarkable," Mr. Crayne exclaimed.

"By jove," cried Mr. Haldeman. "Superb shot." I had always thought that by jove was confined to English lords in books.

"Well," was all Mrs. Haldeman said, and I do not think that she was too pleased with the damage the wallpaper had suffered.

Mr. Stone, said nothing, but his eyes became a trifle brighter and bigger.

Citarro was rather sheepish. "I'm afraid," he said, "that I have been showing off, not to mention doing considerable damage. The mountebank in me comes out at the worst times. I was carried away by the wonder of myself. I apoligise." He bowed deeply.

"Oh, it's perfectly all right. It's not very often that we see a real Latin in full action. And as for that," Mrs. Haldeman gestured toward the slight mark the dagger had made, "We might have it encased and charge admission to see it."

Just then a lovely voice broke into the drawing room atmosphere. "What's this about daggers. Somebody done themselves in," the voice said. I looked up and saw a very lovely girl. Chesnut hair, dark brown eyes, an oval face, a slender figure. "Connie," Mr. Crayne exclaimed. "It's about time you got here. I've been here well over an hour. What took so long?"

"I got here as soon as I could, Daddy," she said sweetly.

"Hello, Connie," Mrs. Haldeman greeted. "Don't you mind him," she tossed her head in the direction of Mr. Crayne. "He's an old bear now and all he can do is grumble about the naughty young generation. Besides, he doesn't mean it, anyhow."

"Where do you get, that old bear stuff," snorted

Mr. Crayne amiably. "I got more life in me than a good many of these young cubs that can't use a foot for anything but pressing an accelerator."

"You're dead on your feet, Jim," smiled Mr. Haldeman. "And you know it. Now stop acting like a ham actor playing "Lord Elderbootly" in "The Unfaithful Children.""

That was the way it struck me, too. Everybody seemed to be playing a part, and slightly overdoing it. Here was Citarro acting Spanish, and Mr. Crayne acting the indignant but helpless elder. Mrs. Haldeman's sister couldn't be as quiet as she was, nobody could. Walt Haldeman seemed to have something on his mind, and tried to cover it up by being affable. And into this odd situation descended a remarkable young girl, Connie Crayne.

At dinner, everybody was talkative. I sat in between Miss Haldeman and Miss Crayne. I had planned to do a bit of talking with the lovely Miss Crayne, but my employer, Manuel Citarro, sat next to her, and held her interest. I turned to Miss Haldeman. She had a long, thin face, and her long straight nose together with this gave her a slightly equine look. She had charm, I relised, and a certain amount of beauty but not much force. She was about ten years younger than her older sister, and I thought that perhaps that was the reason she lived with her rich brother-in-law instead of being independent and free. By the time she was born, her sister would have been a big girl, so she would receive most of the attention. All through her childhood, her sister must have been helping her, showing her how to dance, getting her boy-friends, all the things a girl should do for herself. It would be only natural, therefore, when grown up she would come and live with her sister and the rich man her sister married. That type hardly ever married, they were afraid to.

It turned out she was writing a novel. That was not unusual. I never knew a woman like her who was not writing a novel. She took a great deal of pride in it, too, and outlined to me the entire plot.

◄ Within the social set of Couples, Updike's characters observe one another's role playing. ". . . Marcia had taken it upon herself to be dry and witty, when in fact, Janet knew, she was earnest and conscientious. . . ." Also, as Frank helps Marcia, his mistress, into her coat—an "innocent pantomime" laden with sexual energy—her eyes are described as rolling "Spanishly."

It was a shocking affair, about some poor girl, who when she became pregnant couldn't decide who the father was. Evidently she had several seducers on hand. From then I couldn't follow, but it finally ended up with the child in question an old and wretched bat dying in a prison, clad simply in a ragged skirt and a fearful past.

It was just at the end of the meal that Walt Haldeman announced, "How about getting a poker game together in about an hour."

"Walter," Mrs. Haldeman exclaimed in a shocked voice. "Poker for our week-end guests! Poker is not the game to play. If you must gamble, we can have two bridge games."

"But I despise bridge," he returned, in a whiny voice not unlike that of a disappointed adolescent. "Look, why can't you ladies have a bridge game, and let us men play poker. Bridge is a sissy game."

Mrs. Haldeman's smile was stern, though indulgent. "Yes, but there are only three women and five men."

Walt Haldeman blushed slightly and blurted, "Ennybody wanna go over to the other side?"

"Walter, that's intolerably rude," his wife screeched, and was about to say more when Manuel Citarro interrupted.

Other exotic ladies' men ➤ *to appear in Updike's fiction include Darryl Van Horne in* The Witches of Eastwick *(1984) and the Arhat in* S. *(1988).*

"If you don't mind, I would be only to happy to play bridge with the ladies. I, for some reason, can never learn the knack of poker, and I dislike the game heartily. But I fancy myself somewhat of a bridge expert, so I would much prefer the game to poker."

As a matter of fact, Citarro could play poker excellently.

"Oh, no, Mr. Citarro, we couldn't let you," Mrs. Haldeman said.

"But I insist."

"Yeah, really," sheepishly said Mr. Haldeman. "I was just kidding."

"I insist."

So Mr. Haldeman, Crayne, Stone and myself would meet in the Game room to play poker in an hour.

As we left the table, I saw Haldeman whisper something to Citarro, and Citarro followed him down the hall into his study. Probably the "interest professionly" touch, I thought and wished that I could go along, but Haldeman obviously didn't want company. In fact, he was rather furtive. The three ladies went in the drawing-room, Mr. Crayne went out into the garden. I wandered about in the garden for a while, then came back into the house. The library door was open, I walked in.

Merriwether Stone was sitting at a small table and playing chess with himself on a board inlaid in the table top.

"You can play that game better with two helping," I said.

He looked up quickly, as if startled. "Can you play," he asked.

I replied that I could. He invited me to sit down, and we soon had a game going.

"Must be very interesting work, being secretary to a famous Detective like Mr. Citarro," he remarked after a while.

I looked up. Merriwether Stone did not impress me as the kind of man who was interested by mystery stories and detectives. But he seemed to be sincere enough, and was looking at me somewhat like a little boy looks at a man who knows Roy Rogers.

"Yes," I said with a condescending air, "you get to see a great deal of interesting things."

"Really! Such as?"

I now was a bit flustered by this attention. "Well, I've only been with Mr. Citarro for three months. . ."

"If you are observant, you can notice many things in three months."

"Yes, that is so," I said. Merriwether Stone now was looking at me with very frank interest.

"To tell you the truth, I am a great reader of detective fiction." He said this as if he were making a great confession. "I'm really very interested how a real detective lives. Especially one so well-known as Citarro. I wonder if you could tell me a few things. Hard facts."

The author notes: "'Three weeks' back on page [424]. On page [430] he has had time to accumulate many scars. No doubt these discrepancies would have been ← ironed out in revision."

I felt good. "Well, I was hired right in the middle of the Horst case. . . ."

"Your move. Quite a sensational business, that case."

"Yes it was. Solving it established my employer for good. That was why he needed a secretary. So many people coming to see him and writing letters and whatnot."

"Tell me about the case. I read the newspapers, but you know the newspapers. I'd like some inside dope."

"I suppose you know, from the newspaper accounts..."

"Your move."

"Oh, yeah. I suppose you know, from reading the newspaper about the murder of old Jake Horst. Found with his skull bashed in with a poker. A man who wanted to get into his shop found him."

"Move."

"There was quite a stink about it in the newspapers, because everybody liked old Jake. And they all felt sorry for his wife, Wilma. A very gentle old soul with white hair and a timid look. Read the Bible a lot."

"Check."

Updike's teenage interest in dope finds renewed relevance in the late 1980s when Nelson Angstrom, Rabbit's only son, falls prey to cocaine in Rabbit at Rest *(1990).* ➤

"Jake left a good-sized fortune to his wife. She hired Citarro to find the killer. He mushed around a lot, squeezing all the publicity he could out of this case. It finally turned out that she was the murderer. Took dope. Needed money to buy the dope and killed Jake when she was nuts with the stuff."

"Very interesting. Check."

Thus encouraged, I continued, after, of course, moving my king. "I'll never forget the look on her face when they arrested her. She just turned kind of yellow and whispered real loud right in Citarro's face. "Judas! You'll pay for this." Then she screamed and made a lunge for his throat. This little old lady grabbed him and hung on and hung on. Then there was a shot, and she just collapsed on the floor. Citarro was holding a smoking gun."

"She died, didn't she? Your move."

"Yes. Almost institatously. Citarro felt terrible

about it. After that he quit carrying a gun. He has no weapon on him at all."

"He has that little knife, doesn't he? Check."

I scoffed. "Oh, that. That's just a joke. That's just to show the old ladies."

"Yes, but he could kill a man with it, couldn't he?"

This insistence annoyed me. "Yes I suppose it is possible. Of course, you can bite a man in the jugular vein and kill him that way too, but you would hardly classify your teeth as a deadly weapon."

He said quietly, "Maybe you wouldn't. Checkmate."

I was startled to find that I had lost the game, so I said, "It's twenty minutes until our poker game. Let's play another game of chess."

"All right."

As we arranged the pieces, he remarked, "Mr. Citarro must have a great deal of charm with customers. His sucess can't all be blamed on the Horst case."

"Yes, that's true. I've noticed that the same people always keep coming back and sometimes they bring friends with them. He certainly has some attraction. At first, only the thrill-seekers came, the silly old hens and the bald fat men, but now quite a few of the better class come."

"Your move."

I moved the pawn in front of my knight's bishop forward two.

"My, my," exclaimed Mr. Stone. "I've heard of it, but I never saw it done before." He slid his bishop across the board in a diagonal line with my exposed king. "Checkmate," he said happily. I looked at the board, and discovered that I had pulled the "Fool's Play," thus enabling the game to be played in three moves. It occurred to me that Mr. Stone liked winning very much.

He looked at me in an odd sort of way and said quietly, "You don't look like a stupid man to me, Mr. Mays. See if you can't be smarter then you were at these two chess games."

It was a remark that could not be answered. It

In his childhood account "The Dogwood Tree," Updike writes that he lost a playground contest by allowing himself to be distracted and tricked. The contest required children to race, pick out their own shoes from a large pile, put them on, and race back. When a voice in the crowd—disembodied and seemingly celestial—told him not to ◄ stop to tie his laces, he immediately raced back and was disqualified. "My world reeled at the treachery of that unseen high voice. . . ." Here Updike seems to be passing along this painful lesson to his narrator.

The author says: "Properly, 'Fool's Mate.' A neighbor in Shillington had taught me chess at the age of eleven, and for a time I was in love ◄ with the game."

◄ "He is absolutely in love with winning," Rabbit observes about his golf partner, Reverend Eccles, during one of their therapeutic games in Rabbit, Run.

astounded me so, that I probably couldn't have said anything if there was anything to say. I stalked out and slammed the door as loudly as I could without busting something. The little man had seemed so sincere when he said it. There was no malice or desire to hurt in it. He apparently meant it.

I found myself out in the hall, and not having anything better to do, I walked up the hall toward the front door. On my right, I heard the voice of Walt Haldeman. Being a very unscrupulous man at that moment, I stopped to listen. I heard the rather agitated, too-loud voice of Walt Haldeman. "If I'm murdered," it cried, "my wife will open an envelope I've given her. In it are named my murderer, and I know who it would be, and proof of that statement. If I die a natural death, the envelope will be burned. So you see, Mr. Citarro, I am quite safe, and have no fears. It is useless to think of such a thing." Then the voice of my employer. "Do not be too sure, Mr. Haldeman. Strange things have happened about murder." Then quite suddenly, the door flew open. My employer eyed me with obvious annoyance. "And what," he asked crossly and loudly, "Are you doing out here. Waiting for a bus?"

I looked my blandest. "Me?" I replied creduously. "I was just passing through to the front door. Say, isn't it about time for the card games to commence?"

"Yes, it is." Walt Haldeman came to the door. He looked a little pale, but slightly pleased with himself. "I think the ladies are all in the drawing-room. See if you can round up Stone and Crayne. Meet in the game room." I looked puzzled. "The game room," he explained, "is the furtherest room to the right at the end of the hall. Not much of a game room really. Just a few card tables and stuff. It has french Windows."

I found Merriwether Stone as I had found him before; playing chess with himself. "Is your opponant intelligent enough this time, Mr. Stone," was on the tip of my tongue to say, but I didn't. I told him that he was to go to the game room for our card game. I found Crayne on the porch.

Walt Haldeman was first dealer. He dealt the cards with a smooth, professional manner. It was easy to see that he was enjoying himself immensely. He took up his cards with the same degree of hapiness that a boy experiances when opening his Christmas presants. He loved the game a great deal, and was so happy about it that he could not keep the required strait face. When his cards were good, his eyes brightened slightly, and his mouth might quiver upwards slightly. When bad, his features contorted themselves subtly into a mask of annoyance. He tried to combat this by looking happy when he had a bad hand, but he was too obvious. A man who acts in poker is usually a poor player.

It showed up, too. By two hours, Walter Haldeman had dropped close to $200. The greater majority of it had been won by little Merriwether Stone, but the piles of Mr. Crayne and myself were noticable larger.

On the last hand, Merriwether Stone dealt. I got two threes, a nine, a queen and a king. I kept the king queen and the nine. I got two more threes. Lousy. I couldn't open. Mr. Crayne didn't, either. Haldeman did. He put ten dollars in. Merriwether Stone put $15 in.

"See you and raise you five," he said.

"Pass," I said.

"By me," Mr. Crayne meuttered.

Haldeman smiled slightly, and put all of his chips, exactly $325 worth, and a check for $680. "See you and raise you a thousand," he said. He looked triumphant.

Merriwether Stone was not perturbed. He put all his chips in, exactly $655 worth and a check for $345. "See you," he said.

Mr. Haldeman grew very pale. He had been bluffing, and his bluff had been called. I felt rather sorry for him, for he obviously couldn't come across. He was beaten. Merriwether Stone knew it, too. For the second time that night I was struck by the fact that he liked winning.

Mr. Haldeman laid down his hand. "Well, you

"When did I learn the rudiments of poker?" the author asks. "I can't remember. My parents and I used to play ← three-handed pinochle."

In Hugging the Shore *(1983), the author compares the terror of creating fiction—indeed of existing at all across the "abyss" of one's own life—with bluffing in a poker game holding "a nothing hand." ➤*

got me," he said at a pitiful attemp at cheerfulness. It consisted of two kings, an eight, a four, and a jack. Mr. Stone laid down his hand. His only counters were a pair of Aces.

I had thought that Merriwether Stone was sitting pretty with a powerful hand. I relized, now, that he was betting on nothing much more than Mr. Haldeman. But he won.

The ladies bridge game had been over for about half an hour. They had all gone up to bed, even Citarro. It was after 11. I poured my self a drink. All through the game we had occasionally been pouring ourselves drinks, until now the one bottle was empty and the other one was only half empty (or half full, for the benefit of the optimosts). "Mr. Stone," began Walt Haldeman shakily. "I would like to see you after the other two are gone." I was never one to disregard hints. Evidently Mr. Crayne wasn't either. We both left.

Manuel Citarro was at his desk, writing something very slowly and carefully. I walked over and peered over his shoulder. He turned quickly around and looked at me. "None of your business," he said.

"Okay, your the boss," I said. "I may be old-fashioned, but in all the detective stories I read the sleuth at least shows the Watson everything he's doing."

"Do you regard yourself as a Watson. I thought you were my secretary."

"I am." I guess I said it bitterly, for Citarro turned around and looked at me.

"Listen Tommy, I brought you along for the fun of it. I wanted you to come along so you came along. You've been reading too many mystery stories. I know that this is the ideal setting for a murder. Rich man's country home. Friends. He even has a detective here. But there isn't going to be a murder, so don't start imagining yourself as a Doctor Watson and start prying into my affairs. What I'm writing doesn't concern you. Neither does what Walt Haldeman says to me. I don't want to catch you listening in on my conversation again. Understand."

I didn't say anything. I climbed into my bed. The

cot was a very large and comfortable cot. I was laying there with my arms under my head when Citarro spoke.

"How much of that conversation did you hear," he asked.

I told him.

"Is that all?"

"Yes."

"Good."

Citarro was still writing when I dropped off to sleep.

Somebody was shaking me. "Wake up, wake up."

"Eh?"

I opened my eyes a little. The sun was streaming in through the closed window.

Somebody shook me again. Hard. I saw a blurred mass bending over me. It soon resolved itself into the likeness of my employer.

"Wha'?"

"WAKE UP, DAMMIT." Something hit me across the cheek.

I woke up. "What the devil is this. Can't I sleep around here?"

"Tommy," Citarro said. I noticed that he looked a little tired. "It's happened. Just like you said, Watson. Walt Haldeman was stabbed in the back last night. He's dead."

"WHAT? Good God?"

I hastily dressed and rushed downstairs. Everybody was in the game room. Miss Haldeman had fainted and was laying on the couch. The butler was looking very pale. "I—I've sent for the police and the doctor." He stammered to Mrs. Haldeman and walked out. She was bearing up under the strain extremely well. She had loved her husband, apparently, yet she showed enough character to relize that she must not break down.

She brightened a little when she saw Citarro. "Oh, Mr. Citarro. I'm so glad you're here. You must find the murderer. It was of course some prowler. The police will soon be here."

← *Since childhood, Updike confesses in his memoir* Self-Consciousness, *he's been a late sleeper, "preferring to let others get the world in order before I descend to it."*

"I sympathize greatly with you, Madame," Citarro replied. "And do not worry. The monster who did this will be found if I have to do it myself." He quickly added. "But the police are very effecient. I know the inspector myself."

Walt Haldemans body was slumped over in a chair, a little to the right and a large knife was stuck in his back, below and to the left of the nape of the neck. He was sitting in the most comfortable chair in the room, facing the French Windows and the garden. The French windows were closed. There were no signs of disorder or violence. A book he apparently had been reading was laid neatly on a small table at his side. There was very little blood.

The butler appeared in the doorway. "The police are here." Three men entered. One was Stephan Michal Claude—I recognized him from the dope case. He was a very thin man. He looked very bored. His face was long, his cheekbones high, and his mouth had a very tired expression. His eyes however conflicted with the half dead look of the other features. They were blue, and brightly alive. I knew that this man was intelligent and forceful, and he was a good policeman. A small, round pink man and a bearlike man accompnied him.

"Hello, Steve," greeted my employer. He spoke to Stephan Claude.

"What are you doing here, Citarro," Claude asked. He didn't betray any surprise, but he must have felt some.

"I'm a guest," Citarro retorted.

Claude smiled. "Like in the stories. The private dick is always around at a murder."

"I hope you aren't going to stand out here and shoot the bull all day," I put in indignantly.

Citarro laughed. "Poor Mays. He's so consientious. He's afraid we're going to let the wicked murderer get away."

I blushed furiously. "Well, it's all very well to laugh, but a man has been murdered and his wife and friends are in there waiting for the police, and

"Talk about self-referentiality! I can't seem to get over my excitement at being inside a mystery novel," says the author. ➤

all the police do is stand out in the hall."

Claude looked at me and said, "You have admirable sediments, my boy."

I said "Oh, shuttup."

Citarro clicked his tounge.

"How-do-you-do, Inspector," Mrs. Haldeman said evenly. "We've left the room just as it was when we discovered the body."

"Thank you, Madame," returned Stephan Claude. "I want to tell you how much we appreciate your coolness and presence of mind. I sympathise with you and admire you in your sorrow." A remarkable speech for a cop, I thought.

He turned from Mrs. Haldeman and said to the round pink man, "Check for prints, Palaferro. The usual places. Try the knife. I don't expect to find any, but you might as well try." Palaferro pulled several bottles and a brush out of his pocket, and dusted the doorknob with a fine powder. He went from there to the outer doorknob.

To the bearlike man: "Call up Doc Dennison, Lassert. Bring an ambulance."

"I'll show you the phone, sir," the butler offered. They went through the door.

Then he turned to the small group in front of him. "Now, then. Who found the body?"

Nobody answered.

"Somebody had to."

"Stephen—the butler—awakened me and told me that something was wrong with Mr. Haldeman. I imagine that he found the body," said Mrs. Haldeman at last.

Just then the butler came back.

"Did you discover the body," Inspector Claude asked.

"Why-er-yes."

"What happened?"

"I was coming down this morning and I happened to glance into the library and I saw him in here. I thought that perhaps he had fallen asleep last night and had not gone up to bed. I went in to wake him and I saw. . . ." Here he stopped short, and turned slightly green.

Claude said, "Who shut the French window and the other windows last night?"

"I did. I came in about one and he was lying very still in his chair. But he didn't have a knife in him. I'm sure."

"Did you speak to him?"

"No sir. When he fell asleep in his chair, he didn't want to be disturbed. He said that he had so much trouble falling asleep at night that when he did fall asleep, even if it wasn't in bed we were to let him alone."

"Were the windows open?"

"Oh yes. You see it was a very warm evening and they had had a bridge game in here, so the French windows were wide open."

"But you locked them."

"Yes, indeed, very securely."'

He turned around to the rest of the group. "Did anyone else see him after 12?"

No answer.

He turned to the butler. "Then you were the last person to see him alive."

The butler had become more ridgid and butler-like, recovering somewhat from the first shock. "Yes, I would imagine so."

"You could hear him breathing, or perhaps mumbling in his sleep?"

A frown crossed the butler's face. "Well, now that you say it, I don't recall anything like breathing. . . ." He was silent a moment. "But I do know that he moved. His right arm moved. It was lying on his chest like this." He placed his hand just below where his heart was. "And he moved it to the arm of the chair. I think he twitched, too."

"Were you in the room long?"

"Oh, no. Mr. Haldeman was a very light sleeper, and I had to move lightly and quickly or he would wake up. I just looked at him for a second or two,

"The first, it seems, of my many fictional insomniacs," says the author. ➤

then quickly closed the windows, and left."

"Where did you go after you left the game room. Straight to bed?"

"No. I closed the windows in the library next, then the drawing-room. I had already done the three rooms on the other side of the hall."

"What are the three rooms?" Inspector Claude had a dead look in his eyes, as if he didn't care, but was asking just to be polite.

"Why, in the front of the house, is Mr. Haldeman's study, then the dining room and the kitchen is in the back, across from this room—the game room."

"Game room?" he looked around the room.

Mrs. Haldeman broke in quickly and apoligatically. "It isn't much of a game-room," she said.

Claude didn't say anything, but turned to the butler. "Do you close the windows in the kitchen?"

"No. My wife, the cook, does that," the butler said quickly.

"Were there many windows to close?"

"Really, sir, is this so important."

"No."

The butler quickly answered. "Yes there were. It was a very muggy day."

"Okay. That's all I want to know." A very theatrical phrase, I thought.

The butler looked very pale. He turned the corners of his mouth down in an expression of distaste.

"One more question."

Stephen looked inquirenly.

"Did you kill Mr. Haldeman?"

A look of complete, unadulterated horror appeared on the dignified face of the butler Stephen. "L-L-Lord, no."

Mr. Claude, evidently unaware of the fact that he had given near heart-failure to an elder manservant, turned to the other people in the room. "What's this about the card game?"

Mrs. Haldeman explained. "Eight of us held a sort of card party. Us four," she made a vague gesture, which included herself, the two women, and

Citarro, "Had a bridge game. They," she waggled at me and Stone and Crayne, "and Mr. Haldeman played poker. He preferred poker," she added.

"Poker game, eh," Claude said. "Who won the most money?"

"I did," said Merriwether Stone.

"How much?"

"Not that it's any of your business, but I won well over eleven hundred dollars."

"That's quite a bit for a small game."

"Mr. Haldeman and I had a thousand dollar-pot in the last hand."

"Then Mr. Haldeman was the heavy loser."

"Oh, yes, by far."

"How much did he lose?"

Before Stone could answer, I burst into the conversation, much to my surprise. "Inspector, why on earth are you asking all these irrelevent questions? It's getting on my nerves."

There was a loud silence. I was ashamed of myself. "What's the matter with you," I thought. Inspector Claude looked at me, half amused, and said, softly, "What an odd thing to say. Will you please shuttup."

I blushed.

"Now, then, Mr. Stone, exactly how much did Mr. Haldeman lose? There's been a murder committed, and we don't have a motive. These may be one."

Merriwether Stone said, "But it isn't the heavy losers who are killed, it's the heavy winners."

Inspector Claude grinned. He seemed to be proud of Stone. "You're right there. But answer my question if you don't mind."

Merriwether Stone smiled, too. "He lost about twelve hundred. He was the only one who did lose."

"Really." He turned on me. "How much did you win?"

"About 45 dollars," I replied quickly.

"And you?" To Crayne.

"Twenty or so. Why?"

"Just curious." The huge policeman came back into the room. "Did ya' call?" Claude asked.

Like Thomas Mays, Harry Angstrom in Rabbit, Run *tends to assert himself impulsively and then regret it. With great arrogance, Angstrom sexually coerces his mistress, after which he finds he has lost "that strange floating feeling of high pride. Shame plunged in."* ➔

"Sure. He'll be here in about 15 minutes."

"I think I just heard Lewis and the boys ride up. Tell them to bring in the cameras. Make it snappy. And get Palaferro to take the knife now. I don't know where he got to."

Lassert grinned broadly. "He's out in the hall talking to some French cutie. Maid I guess."

"Get him and the cutie in here."

A red-faced individual in police uniform appeared in the doorway. Behind him I could see about three other uniforms and a plain suit.

"Hullo, Lewis," Claude greeted. He went out into the hall, and Lassert followed. I could hear a mumble of voices. The plain man who had just arrived took some cameras down the hall to the game room where the corpse of Walter Haldeman was sitting in a yellow leather chair. Lewis and the other three men also went down the hall in time. Lassert, Palaferro, and a small, dark haired girl in a maids outfit came into the room. "Find any prints, Palaferro?" Claude asked.

"Oh, sure, lots, on the doorknobs and around the room."

"Probably won't do us any good. They could be anybody's from the bridge game last night," Claude muttered, as if to himself. "Take the knife yet?" he asked Palaferro.

"Not yet. Wanted your O.K."

"See if there are any prints."

"Oke." Palaferro disappeared through the door.

Claude ignored the French girl who had just come in. Instead he asked the group who was the last person to see Haldeman alive.

"I imagine that I was," Merriwether Stone said meekly.

"When was this?"

"About 11:10—when the poker game was over."

"Did he want to speak to you about something?"

"Yeah."

"What was it?"

Merriwether Stone hesitated a moment before

Like Haldeman, Eastwick's mysterious newcomer Darryl Van Horne (The Witches of Eastwick) does not seem ➤ to possess the true capital to support his lofty standard of living.

The young author has ➤ apparently confused Stephan Michal Claude with lawyer Martain Stodge, who appears later.

he spoke. "He wanted to know if I could wait a little while before I cashed the check I won from him. He said that due to some mix-up, his bank didn't have the money right now."

"Did you consent?"

"Of course."

"Some mix-up at the bank, eh?" Inspector Martain Claude seemed a trifle more alert. "He told you more than that, didn't he? It doesn't sound very plausible."

Merriwether Stone shrugged his shoulders. "That's what he told me."

"How long did this take?"

"Not long. About 10 minutes, fifteen minutes at the most."

"How did Haldeman appear? Was he nervous? Apprehensive?"

"No," Stone said thoughtfully. "He was a little sluggish if anything."

"Then you went straight up to bed?"

"Yes."

"Did you hear anything that night? Suspicous?"

"I did hear several people walk past my door and out in the hall. I am a light sleeper. But I thought it was just people going. . ." He blushed slightly and stopped.

"No outcry?"

"No." He waggled his head slowly to give emphasis to his answer.

"Did anybody else hear anything out of the ordinary?" He spoke to the group.

Silence was his answer.

The doorbell rang. Someone ran up the hall and opened the door before the butler could get there. "Hello, Doc. C'min," the voice of Lewis, the policeman boomed. "Foller me." Claude half rose, as if going out to meet the coroner, but thought better of it, and sat down again.

He looked sternly at the French girl. "What is your name?" he asked.

"I-I-I am Jeanette, the maid."

"French?"

She smiled slightly. "No. I was born in Detroit."

Claude smiled, too. "How long have you been here."

"Two months."

"Are you the only maid?"

"Yes. But sometimes Mrs. Stephens, who is the cook, helps me—dusts and that sort of thing."

"How many other servants are there besides you and Mrs. Stephens and him." He tossed his head in the direction of the butler.

"We're the only ones. It isn't a very big home."

Mrs. Haldeman broke in. "We didn't need many. Besides we moved out here to live simply. Three servants were plenty." She leaned back with an air of a woman who has done her bit.

"I see," Inspector Stephen Claude said solemnly, although his eyes were twinkling. Evidently thirteen rooms besides the servant quarters and three servants would not have been regarded as simple living where he came from.

"Do you know of anything that might throw light on this—murder, Jeanette?" he asked of the maid. "Any noises or anything?"

"I did not get back until the morning," she replied. "You see it was my night off. And I spent the evening with my mother." She smiled.

"Exactly what time did you get. . ."

And so on and on went Inspector Stephen Michal Claude, asking for details, carefully retracing and checking, taking each person in their turn and ignoring the others. His expressionless eyes revealed nothing, except perhaps laughter, as he seemed to have a sense of humor notable for a policeman. It was well unto 1:30 before he stopped his questions. He had allowed the servants to leave an hour or so earlier so they could prepare lunch. Twice a policeman came into the room, and told him something, and each time he told us what it was. The first time it was the pink Palaferro, saying that there were no fingerprints on the knife, it had been wiped clean, and the ones

← Updike employs a similar joke near the end of his novel S., in which an intriguing Hindu holy man is revealed to be asthmatic Art Steinmetz, of Watertown, Massachusetts.

← In Couples, *Updike again refers to the rich person's philosophy on roughing it, when Janet Appleby explains that she and her friends love Tarbox for its lack of country clubs and servants. "It's so much more luxurious to live simply."*

on the doorknob were smudged, and it didn't really matter anyhow. He came just before we had lunch.

Claude turned to us. "I told Lewis to check all the doors and windows for pry marks or any other indications of a forced entry. If there were some, Lewis would have found them. He found none.

"This points to the probability of one of you either committing the murder or being the accomplice. Of course, Stephens may have accidently left one open. In any case, don't any of you leave this house. I'm going out to eat and report to headquarters. I'll be back at two thirty, to take your official statements." To me he said, "Can you take shorthand?"

I said I could.

"Very well. I want you to take down what is said this afternoon by these people." By way of explanation, he added, "My ordinary secretary went on a bender last night and didn't show up this morning." And he left.

Dinner was a very tense affair. Hardly anyone spoke, exept to mumble dinner requests like please pass the butter. The meal itself wasn't very good, and consisted mostly of things easy to prepare. What I had seen of the exitable Mrs. Stephens enabled me to create a mental visage of her going around the kitchen, sniffing into a soggy hankercheif, perhaps moaning to the maid. Mrs. Haldeman had gone up to bed right after Mr. Claude had made his little speech, and had had her dinner served to her up there.

It was 2:00 o'clock, and a half hour before that delightful person, Inspector Claude, was to reappear. I walked out into the garden. The sun was beating down furiously, and if a slight breeze had not been blowing, it would have been very hot. As it was, it was pleasantly warm, the kind of weather where you could enjoy the friendly glare of the sun, and still be cool. The garden was in full bloom, and a gentle fragrence surrounded me. Not enough to be called a smell, but definately there.

"Vision or image, → make up your mind," the older author advises his younger self.

I met Miss Catherine Crayne at a fork in the path, and I did not see her until she was about four feet from me. "Hullo," I said. I somehow felt pleased by her being there, and I felt more at home near to her than I did with forceful Mrs. Haldeman or her shadowy sister, or old Merriwether Stone.

"Hullo," she replied. We walked along the path, talking about the murder, and the people in the house, and how it was impossible that any of them could have committed the murder. "Why it's impossible. You can see that poor Mrs. Haldeman is all broken up, and her sister, well, wouldn't have the backbone to shoot a groundhog let alone her brother-in-law. And the Stone man, he's here for his first time."

"I know," I said stupidly. "It does seem incredible."

She continued with her defence of the guests. "I guess that in the eyes of Inspector Claude, even my father, and I guess you and me, are under suspicion." She laughed, a little tightly.

"You've forgotten four people," I said. "Mr. Stephens," I ticked them off on my fingers, "Mrs. Stephens, Jeanette, and that surly young man who drove me up here. Bertie something or other."

"Not Bertie, George, and his last name is Orgon."

"George Orgon," I laughed when I repeated the funny-sounding name.

"You forgot one person. That Spaniard, who you work for, the detective." She said seriously, "He could have done it."

"Oh, well now look," I said incrediously. "Citarro never even knew Haldeman. This was the first time he saw him. And besides, the very idea that he could commit a murder is preposterous. A famous detective like him. . . ."

"Well we have to include everybody."

"Of course you relize that the chances are none of them had anything to do with it. He probably let somebody in, and then something happened, and this unknown killed him."

"But then how did the door get closed. Or the window?"

◄ *In* Rabbit, Run *Harry Angstrom, the most movable of objects, finds a great many forces irresistible.* "Next to his mother Tothero had had the most *force*"— *so Rabbit describes his former basketball coach. Maternal forces appear especially powerful in Rabbit's universe.*

◄ *In* Couples, *Foxy is similarly taken aback by John Ong's name.* "You all have such funny names," *she says, to which Angela replies maturely:* "But aren't all names funny until you get used to them?"

"Maybe he was dead when the butler came around. He said he was asleep."

"But there wasn't any knife in him then. The butler surely would have noticed that."

*At some point within →
this conversation someone
has spoken twice in a row.*

"Well," she said quickly. "Let's leave this to the police. I don't think anyone of them did it either. I'm just arguing for the sake of arguing. But suppose they did. Heaven knows the facts point to it. Which one would you pick."

"Who do I choose from?" I was enjoying this

*This verbal intercourse →
with Miss Crayne seems
to have a vaguely sexual
dimension for Tommy.
Likewise, when Irene
and Frank engage in an
affectionate argument in
Couples, Carol points
out that the debate is a
form of "sex for Irene."*

immensely.

She ticked them off on her fingers. "One. Mrs. Haldeman. Two. Grace Haldeman, her sister. Three. My Father. Four. Merriwether Stone. Five. Manuel Citarro. Six. Stephens. Seven. Mrs. Stephens. Eight. Jeanette. And Nine. George Orgon."

"You forgot you and me."

"Well, if it is one of us, and it's me, we certainly won't say it's me, of course. We will be putting on an act. I don't think it's you. You're too innocent."

I was offended at this. "Listen here, young woman, I'll have you know that at collage I was known as "The Collage Casanove." I would have elaborated on this if she hadn't interrupted.

"Okay. Youre a wild and wooly customer. I don't think you did it. And I know I didn't do it. Do you think I did it?"

I was very quick about saying "No, of course not."

We sat down on a bench propped up against a small, white building at the far end of the garden.

*"One thing I had →
certainly observed about
mystery novels was that
they contained lists. How
to get away from the lists
I hadn't yet figured out,"
observes the author.*

"Let's go through the list," she suggested.

"Mrs. Haldeman," she announced, as if she named an object to be auctioned off.

"Mr. Haldeman," I said slowly, "was a very rich man. He would leave it probably to his wife, with perhaps a small amount to his sister-in-law. Money is always an important factor."

"In the detective novels it is, because it sounds so logical and probable. But how often do you read of a murder being commited for an inheritance? For every big money murder you will find a hundred commited for a few dollars, usually in fear of discovery. And you will find two hundred sex slayings, or crime passionales. I don't think there are very many people who can murder in cold blood, as the cliche goes. But in fear, or hate. . ." She stopped, with a meanful shrug.

"Yes, there is a good deal in what you say. But we cannot overlook the chance of any motive. Besides, she had the opportunity."

"Everybody did. It wouldn't be hard to sneak past the doors quietly. The floors are good, and don't squeak much."

"Then we have to take it from a purely motive standpoint. Mrs. Haldeman, there is money, or perhaps some other reason. Perhaps Mr. Haldeman was unfaithful, or beat her, or wanted to divorce her. In the course of a husband-wife relationship, there are hundreds of opportunities for a murder motive to crop up."

"Mrs. Haldeman has a strong character," Catherine mused. "It is not impossible for her to kill someone. She is a forceful and determined woman."

"Wait," I cried. "I just thought of something. It's impossible that Mrs. Haldeman could have done it. I heard a conversation between my employer and the dead man, just the tail end of it." I told her about what I heard through the study door. "Do you see? He said he left a note to his wife telling her the name of his murderer. He knew that he might be murdered, and he knew who would be the murderer. If the murderer was his wife, why address the note to her telling who it was to her if she was the one."

"Yes, but then why address it to her at all, why not to the police?"

"I guess he thought the police would open it even if he died a natural death, just to see what was the evidence inside. But, anyhow, this knocks Mrs. Haldeman completely out of the picture."

She muttered to herself, under her breath, "I wonder if she has it now." She looked at me, with a frown of puzzlement on her face, then said aloud.

← *Updike writes often on the subject of domestic discord. Strident, righteous Felicia Gabriel (*The Witches of Eastwick*) has long been planting seeds of rage in her husband, Clyde, until one Scotch-soaked night, the newspaper editor kills her with a fire poker.*

"Not necessairly. Suppose that Mr. Haldeman thought that one person was going to murder him, but that person didn't do it at all. I know it sounds involved, but it's possible. Then this note would be accusing the wrong person. Then Mrs. Haldeman could have done it, and he would still have the note addressed to her, but he wouldn't be accusing her."

"It's so ridiculous," I said, "that it might be possible. Not," I added hastily, "that that remark makes any sense."

She grinned. "We certainly are getting a lot of weird possibilities for a pair of amateurs."

Then after a moment, she went on, "Well, then, let's take up the next victim. Miss Grace Haldeman."

"I think we can do away with her. As you said, she has no guts at all. Even if she had a wonderful motive, she couldn't murder."

"She always resisted → simple concurrence, and would nimbly take a contrary position, as if to make life, for herself and her partner in dialogue, more interesting." So the narrator describes his mother's conversational flirtatiousness, in Updike's 1992 story "His Mother Inside Him."

She said, "I don't agree with you there. Anyone can murder if given enough reason. And murder is a weapon of the weak, rather than the strong. She might easily have murdered if given enough reason. I'll admit she's not the type of two gun Westerner who kills at the draw of a gun. Suppose you had lived off of your brother-in-law for years, never had to earn your own living, and wouldn't know how to if you did have to. All you had to do was to be charming to guests, and maybe help a little with the planning of the guest lists and entertainment. Otherwise you could write, or etch, or do nothing at all. You didn't have to. Then suppose, for some reason, your brother-in-law was going to send you out of his house, into the world. Alone. And leave you drift out there. You would be terrified. Don't you think that then you could murder, without half relizing what you were doing? Self-preservation is a very wicked institution."

"Yes, but that's purely theoritical. What reason would Haldeman have for throwing his sister-in-law out? Maybe when his wife first suggested that her sister come and live with them, he might have refused. Or maybe if she got on his nerves, he might have broken and thrown her out a year or so after she came. But heavens, the sister must have been living with them now for many years."

"Almost thirty, to be exact."

"And," I continued. "If he hadn't gotten used to her after thirty years, he still wouldn't have thrown her out then, after bearing it so long. Besides, I didn't notice any sort of friction between the two."

"They were very fond of each other. She rather admired him, and he basked in her admiration. But suppose something turned up. Suppose she had been a prostitute before she came, or suppose she had been robbing him of all his money, or something."

"You said she has been here for thirty years. She can't be much over forty five. She'd have to be a pretty young prostitute at fifteen. And, for the second, she didn't need money."

"Suppose she gambled. Some people do. And that type always likes money, and if a person like her who never knew the lack of it really needed it bad, she wouldn't hesitate to steal for it."

"Or murder."

"What?"

"Why, if you want to continue along this supposing line, she might have murdered him for an inheritance. He would probably leave her something. And even if he didn't, I imagine Mrs. Haldeman would be a pretty soft touch for her kid sister."

"As a matter of fact, Mr. Haldeman made out a very sizable insurance policy to her. He made a will leaving everything to his wife. Then after he made it, Mrs. Haldeman said that he should leave something to Grace. So instead of making a new will, he simply made her beneficiary of an insurance policy he was taking out at the time. For something like $50,000, I think."

"Say, how do you know all this?" I asked.

"My father told me. He was an old friend of the family. Still is, for that matter."

"So far, we've done nothing but suppose. And we've given everybody perfectly probable motives.

"When I write. . . .," Updike once told The Paris Review, *"I think of the books on library shelves, . . . years old, and a countryish teen-aged boy finding them, and having them speak to him."* A boy, we can presume, not unlike the one who composed these pages.

Who's next?"

She blushed slightly, "My father, John Crayne."

"Well, you know more than I do. Does he have a motive?"

"Not a money motive." She stopped here, as if she was going to say something else.

"Any other kind," I probed.

She spoke slowly. "My father was always in love with Mrs. Haldeman. He worshipped her. At one time he was sure she was going to marry him. But at the last minute, she married a young broker, Walter Haldeman. Father was very broken up about it. A month or so, after the marriage, he married a chorus girl, Magaret du Chaucier. It took them five years to have me. I imagine they were very happy together, but not in love. She died when I was three years old. Since then he's played the comic part of the forgotten, but persistant suitor. He and Mr. Haldeman got along well, and Father has never made any passes, or anything, at Mrs. Haldeman. But he's always been there, a favorite guest of the Haldemans'." She sighed. Her father's sad love affair found sympathy in her, to all appearances.

Hoping to comfort her, in my own stupid way, I said, "Yes but it's very improbable that this thirty year old romance would result in revenge now. Besides, your father struck me as being a very nice, conservative man, who would take being jilted in a calm and stoical manner."

"I hope so. But father broods a lot over things. He loved Belle Haldeman something terific. And maybe, after all this, he would go crazy in a mild sort of way and imagine Walter Haldeman as the only obstacle to his happiness and think that if he were dead, he could have Marybelle."

"Is her real name Marybelle?"

"Yes, it is."

"Say, look. Don't think for one minute that a thirty year old romance is a motive for a murder. It's ridiculous. And if your father would have no other reason, like money. . ."

"Father is a very rich man."

"All right, then. We'll think of your father as extremely improbable. Who's next?"

"Mr. Merriwether Stone."

"He's an odd customer. There's more to him than meets the eye. You never saw him before."

"No he's a total stranger. He seems rather intelligent and nice, though."

"Well, since we know nothing about him, we can't pass judgement on him."

"If you want to count Citarro, he's possible."

"Technically yes," I said, accenting the yes so that I inferred that it was ridiculous to even mention him. "How about the servants? They all could have, I suppose, exept Jeanette, of course."

"Why exclude Jeanette?" she asked.

"She was away all night last night, it was her day off. She spent the night at her mother's."

"Her mother's, eh?" Catherine asked in a sarcastic tone, with a sniff, indicating that she didn't think any such thing. "If she slept at all last night, it wasn't at her mother's."

"What makes you think that?" I asked, my eyes wide open in a pretendance of innocence.

She didn't say anything, but turned her head slightly to the left, away from me. At last she said, "This Spanish detective of yours—Citarro—he's quite nice, isn't he? I mean handsome and courteous and—well, attractive." For some reason this unforseen interest in the charms of my employer annoyed me.

"Yes, I suppose so," I said crossly, then added, "to women."

She was silent a little while, then said absently, "How old is he? He looks around forty."

"He's 45 exactly."

I got up. "I imagine we've been out here some time. We'd better get on back to the house. I'm supposed to take notes for Claude this afternoon."

She got up, and turned around toward the white gardener's shed in doing so. She looked at the wall

← Jill, the Porsche-driving, half-orphaned, worldly wise lass in Rabbit Redux, *shares Catherine Crayne's penchant for mental sparring. One senses that, like Rabbit, Tommy is in over his head.*

with a startled expression. "What on earth. . ." she said softly.

I looked at the white wall. On it, in letters an inch high, evidently cut in by a knife, was a word. Somehow that one word seemed more sinister than the body of Walt Haldeman, a bloody knife in his back. Catherine took in her breath sharply, and I stared, my mouth open. The word was "DEATH."

A voice nearby called, "Tommy. Miss Crayne. There you are. Inspector Claude wants you, Tommy. He wants you to hurry, too." It was Manuel Citarro.

I gestured toward the carved word on the wall. "Look," I said.

He looked. His eyebrows drew themselves together and his green eyes became harder and brighter. "What the devil. This is silly." In a louder voice he said to me, "This is preposterous. Who on earth would want to carve the word death on gardening house walls? It isn't done in real life, maybe in books, but not here." He was silent a moment, then turned to me and Catherine. "This is obviously the work of the murderer. He must be crazy."

Catherine said haltingly, "Perhaps a child did this, when playing."

Citarro stepped over to the carving, and looked at it intently. "No, this was done recently, within the past week."

"Well, shouldn't we tell Inspector Claude. . ." Catherine asked.

"You'd better let me tell him," Citarro said quickly, "Don't you tell him, I'll tell him. Let's go up to the house now."

We walked through the garden in silence. Inspector Claude was waiting for us. "Where in hell, have you been," he asked. "It's almost three. C'mon with me. You two," he said to Citarro and Catherine, "go in the drawing-room and wait to be called."

I followed Claude down the hall, into the dead man's study, which he had converted into kind of an office. "Sit there," he said, indicating a chair in the darkest corner of the room. "Here's your equip-

"The lurking sense → of death has figured strongly in Updike's fiction," writes Robert Detweiler in his 1984 critical appraisal of Updike's career. Even The Poorhouse Fair, Updike's first novel, written when he was just 25, was inspired by his childhood "fascination with the incomprehensible fact of death," concludes Detweiler.

ment." He gave me a pad and a pencil. "Think you can take as fast as they give it out?"

I said I thought I could.

"Okay." To the policeman Lassert, who had been standing near the door. "Fetch the Mrs. in." Without a word, Lassert left, and returned [in] a half minute with Mrs. Haldeman in tow.

"Sit down," Claude commanded. "I'd like to ask a few questions about what you did last night, from dinner on. They will be taken down, and typed up into a statement. Then, if it meets your approval, you'll sign. For the records, you know." Evidently satisfied with the effect of his verbal combination of the emphatic and the vague, he commenced his painstating, careful questioning.

It would be a waste of paper to record all that was said in those four hours of interrogation. Hardly anything of importance was said that I didn't know or hadn't guessed.

Mrs. Haldeman said that right after dinner, she had gone into the drawing room with the other two ladies and talked until around 8:15, when she had gone upstairs to make up, and finally she and Stephens had put the card tables in position, got out the liquor, and prepared for the game. At 11 o'clock, when the game was over, she went straight up to bed, and slept soundly through the night.

Miss Haldeman's story was identical with her sister's, except she had taken until the game to make up and she had slept fitfully all night, and had thought she had heard someone creep past her door. ("What time was this?" "I imagine it must have been a little after two, I vaguely remember, the clock hands pointing to two." "Did the floorboards squeak?" "Yes, and I heard a faint sound, like the rustle of cloth.")

Miss Catherine Crayne saw nothing, heard nothing, told nothing.

Merriwether Stone went into the library right after dinner, played chess with himself. ("It's not very often that I meet such a skilled opponent.") At about 7:45, or fifteen minutes after dinner, I came in. We played two games. ("Who won?" "I did." "You do a lot of winning, don't you?" "I try to.") He played poker until about 11:20, talked with Mr. Haldeman for a few minutes, then went to bed. No, he had not heard anything or anyone, but he was a light sleeper and probably would have if a board had squeaked or any other noise had been. ("It's a shame the floors are so well built.")

Manuel Citarro came in in an airy mood: "Greetings, Stephan, how are all the little Flatfeets?" He had gone to bed right after the bridge game. ("You know me, Steve, always ready for beddy-bye.") And had heard nothing ("If I heard anybody go past my door, which is at the end of the hall, it would mean either the murderer walked down past my door and walked back again, or else leaped over the bannister.") I thought that he was going to tell Claude about the carving on the building, but he didn't.

Stephens, the butler, ate his dinner in the pantry, and had read a book until 12. He repeated his story about the window closing and the sleeping Mr. Haldeman. He was positive on his story, ("Certainly, he didn't have a knife in his back. Gawd, I'm not quite that blind!") ("Yes, I'm sure I shut *all* the windows. For three years now, I've been shuttin' windows in this house, and I never missed a one. And I'm sure that last night was no diffrunt. Sir.") He had gone to bed directly after he had closed the windows. His version of the morning's discovery was not changed. Immediately after he had found Haldeman, he had notified Mrs. Haldeman.

Mrs. Stephens was hysterical, unitelligible, and frantic in about equal parts. She had retired to her quarters almost immediately after dinner. She had read a while, then fell asleep.

Jeanette was appropiately coy. Not until Claude asked her where she had really been did she become natural. ("Oh, hell, here.") She wrote an address in a scummy section of New York. When she had gone, Inspector Claude was amused.

George Orgon came last. He had nothing to say, ("Gawdam coppers, I wuznt even here yesterday,

Gawdam it.") After he had met us at the station, he had gone to his home, about 12 miles away. He worked as a part time gardner on Tuesdays, Thursdays, and Saturdays. Today was Saturday. He had an alibi for Thursday night.

When Orgon had gone, he [Claude] turned to me, and asked, "Well, buddy, how about you? What did you do, last night?" I told him. He seemed satisfied. After pondering a moment or two, he asked "Do you notice anything funny about these stories?"

I had to admit they seemed all right to me. "Don't you notice anything contradictory about any of them?" Claude said slowly. "He paused a moment, then took my tablet and pencil away from me, turned it over to a clean sheet. And began to scribble on it. After a while, he handed it back to me.

On it he had drawn a rough diagram of the upstairs. He handed it back to me expectently. "See?"

I had to admit I didn't see.

He was impatient. "Look. Grace Haldeman says she heard somebody creep past her door. Look at the diagram. Her room is at the farthrest end of the hall. How could anybody go past her door? It's like Citarro said a while ago. They either would have to do it deliberately, or jump over the banister.

"Furthermore, Merriwether Stone says that if there were anybody out there he would have heard them. It's a shame the floors are so well built. Well, then, how could have she have heard squeaky footsteps?

"Lassert, get er in here—No wait. Before we do that, let's go up and see something." To me he said, "You stay here. I might want you to take something down." Lassert and he went out the door, and I could hear them going up the stairs. In a minute I could hear them walking around the entire upstairs hall. They would walk up and down close to the wall, then around in circles. They did this, for five minutes, and not once did I hear a floorboard squeak. At last they came down. Claude came into the study, and Lassert followed him a little later with Miss Grace Haldeman.

"Sit down, please," Claude commanded. "Miss Haldeman," He began, so severely, that he reminded me of a strict school teacher reprimanding his favorite pupil. "A while ago you stated that you heard someone out in the hall in front of your door. It has just occurred to me that your room is at the far end of the hall, and no one would have any concievable reason for passing there."

"I didn't mean," said Miss Haldeman quickly, "in front of my door, I meant out in the hall, possibly on the landing."

"Yes, but, Seargant Lassert and I were just up there, and we stamped around for fully five minutes, and not once did a floorboard squeak."

Miss Haldemans composure had begun to crack a little, and she appeared a trifle worried. "I can't," she said, "help that. I know what I heard and I shall stick by it. And if you're accusing me of lying. . ."

"Now, now, Miss Haldeman," Claude soothed hastily. "No one is accusing you of lying. I simply think you might be misstakin."

She was now quite indignant. "I know that I am not misstakin. I know what I heard was not a mistake. It was squeaky footsteps and the rustle of cloth. I'm positive."

Inspector Claude was about to say something, but he didn't. Instead he shrugged and muttered, "Very well." She left, and I thought her bearing, although it may have been my imagination, was arrogant.

"Lassert." Inspector Claude's voice was like a sharp knife cutting through butter.

Lassert turned and raised his eye brows. "What?"

"She's fibbing."

Undoubtedly the young author meant Walter Haldeman. →

After dinner, Martain Stodge came. He was the lawyer for Walter Stone. He explained he wouldn't have come so soon, if it were not for an odd thing. He did not elaborate on the "odd thing." He was a short, stubby man about fifty. His black bushy eyebrows met and became a solid line which formed a boundry between his squarish scalp and low forehead, and the massive, crude cut features set in a face like the bottom half of a circle.

The black eyes flicked across me like they were skimming a dull part of a book. They rested on Mrs. Haldeman. She greeted him cordially, and he conveyed his sympathy with a polish conflicting with his cave man appearance.

"You may wonder why I did not wait until later to read the will. All this is highly irregular. In fact, the will is incidental."

"Well, what is this important bit of news, all this has been a dreadful strain on me. . ."

"Yes, yes, of course," Stodge said, oozing understanding at every pore. "I imagine you will want to know in private. . ."

"Nonsense," she snapped. "Every one of these people is under suspicion for murder. They will also hear what you have to say. Come into the drawing-room."

Everybody else was in the drawing-room already, with the exeption of the servants. Mrs. Haldeman closed the door behind her. Martain Stodge seemed embarressed, and addressed all his remarks to Mrs. Haldeman, standing up.

He cleared his throat. "Mr. Haldeman," he began. "Left every cent he had to you, Mrs. Haldeman." He hesitated. "The odd part though," he resumed, "is that he didn't have any money." He emphisized the remark by adding, "He was broke."

A short silence followed. Everyone there looked surprised, exept one. I think you all knew the fabulous story of Walt Haldeman's sucess. He was one of the few sucessful speculators of Wall Street. He started out when he was 21, when he stole money from a bank, put it all into a certain shaky stock, the stock zoomed up almost tripling in value in a week. He sold just before it took a downward zoom that ended in bankruptcy. He quickly paid the bank off, quit his job, and descended unto Wall Street a rich young man. His sucess was phenomoninal. He possesed an uncanny judgement of men and companys, and a true instinct for a sound thing. He only mar-

← In response to the Great Depression, Updike and his parents shared his maternal grandparents' house in Shillington. His father's "favorite nightmare was poverty," writes the author in "The Dogwood Tree." But even though his family struggled, Updike did not feel deprived. As he puts it in Self-Consciousness: "There was no stinting on paper and pencils and cardboard to feed my 'creativity.'"

ried once. It was supposed that he was worth over eight million when he retired from the scene, much to the general relief of Wall Street.

And here was a bushy haired lawyer telling us he possessed not a penny. Only Mrs. Haldeman seemed unperturbed. "Yes, I know," she said, an ironic smile playing with her mouth. "For months we have been living on credit. It was all we could do to keep up appearances. The real reason we moved from the city to the country wasn't because we wanted to get away from it all. We both loved the city. It was that we wouldn't be expected to entertain so much out here, and we could get away from having too many servants. I think I called it roughing it. In reality it was econimizing."

I asked a question which ordinairly I would have thought exceedingly rude and in poor taste. "Yes," I blurted, "But how did your husband lose his money?"

She turned to look at me with an overly polite air. "Is it," she asked coldly, "any of your business?" She added, "Does it really matter?"

I felt my neck and ears getting hot, and red. "Sorry," I mumbled.

Manuel Citarro said to Mrs. Haldeman, after giving me the benefit of a very dark and suitably Mediterreanain scowl, "You must excuse Tommy. He is a damn fool."

She said, "I relize that."

Everybody was polite enough not to laugh or scold out loud, but I felt that both tendencies were present among the company.

Mr. Stodge broke the silence, by remarking absently, "He gave me this to give to you if he were murdered. Here." He gave her a long, white envelope, that bulged with many things contained. "He gave it to me about a week ago. Last Wednesday."

Mrs. Haldeman looked at the letter. On the envelope was written something. She looked a moment, then casually turned it over. "It is some memo from my husband. Nothing important, I am afraid, to anyone exept me." But I knew different. I had seen part of Walter Haldeman's message on the envelope. And

"The need not to look ➤ foolish is one of youth's many burdens. . . ." Updike writes in Self-Consciousness.

two of the words were "contains," and "murderer."

She turned to Martain Stodge. "Well, Mr. Stodge, you have told me nothing I already didn't know, but thanks anyhow, for coming out and taking the trouble to inform me of this obviously startlying piece of information. Thank you." She shook hands with him in a ladylike way. He left.

I whispered to Citarro what I had seen on the envelope. He seemed highly exited. "What," he whispered loudly and hoarsly. "That must mean that envelope has something to do with the murderer."

Mrs. Haldeman, with a short speech of apolagy, announced that she was going to lie down. She left the room, and Citarro, trying to appear casual, followed her. Not knowing what else to do, I followed him.

Out in the hall, he called "Mrs. Haldeman." She turned, her eyebrows raised, and asked what he wanted.

"That envelope you have," he said, "has the name of the killer in it, doesn't it?"

She hesitated a moment, then said shortly, "No, it doesn't. What ever gave you that idea?" She made as though to head for the stairs.

"No, wait," Citarro said firmly. "I know it does. Mr. Haldeman told me that when and if he was murdered, a letter was to be given to you containing the name of his murderer, and proof. That," he waved his hand toward the envelope in her hand, "must be it."

She was silent for a few moments, then said reluctently, "If it were, what about it?"

"Just this. If you know who the murderer is, you will be the next target. If you open and read what is inside that envelope, your life is in danger. I know murderers. I've worked with them, and I've worked against them. A person who will commit one murder, will not hesitate to commit a second. A murderer is always dangerous, and I think that this one is clever, besides."

"This wisdom comes straight from Agatha Christie, I believe," the ← author notes.

She remained silent.

Citarro continued. "So it is up to you to give me or Inspector Claude that envelope, unopened. Please. Then in your ignorance you will be safe."

Mrs. Haldeman said, "Nonsense" and walked up the stairs. We heard her door close upstairs. Citarro turned to me. "Call Inspector Claude, Tommy. Quick."

I rang the operator for Police, and a moment later I heard a voice say, "Police Headquarters." I asked to be connected with Inspector Claude. "Just a minnit." A minute or so later I heard the flat voice of Inspector Claude. "Yeah?" I told him who I was. "You're Citarro's Friday, aren't you?" I said that I was Mr. Citarro's secretary. When he asked me what I wanted, I told him that Citarro thought you ought to come up. I related to him about the visit of the lawyer, and about the white envelope and our opinions toward it. He said, "Okay. I'll be up." And there was a big click at the other end of the line, indicating that the other party had hung up.

Citarro was back in the drawing-room, joining in conversation being held there. The people in the room were nervous and upset, but were adopting the attitude, well we might as well enjoy ourselves. They talked of politics, philosiphy, and anything but the recent murder. Mr. Crayne was the calmest one of the lot, and it was he who kept the conversation going. Every now and then, he would pause to draw a hankerchief out of his pocket and would blow his nose. I relized that he had a sinus condition.

In five minutes, Inspector Claude came. Citarro and I went to the door. Ignoring the questioning glances of the others, we led Claude into the hall, but not into the drawing room. Claude came along. "Well, now, Citarro, what's this about the murderer?" he asked, adding, "seen some carving on the wall?"

Citarro snapped his fingers, "By damn, that reminded me. We do have some carving on the wall." He told Claude about the word on the gardening shed. Claude seemed interested, but not particularly alarmed. "That's just plain silly," he scoffed. "We must be dealing with a nut."

"Maybe you want to see it. I'll get Miss Haldeman to show it to you. You can take a flashlight."

Updike found some of →
his earliest vocational inspi-
ration in a book of James
Thurber cartoons, given to
him at the age of 11 at his
request. As he recalls in
Hugging the Shore, *"the*
volume spoke to me of . . .
sophistication, of amusing
adult misery. . . ."—quali-
ties that the 14-year-old
Updike seems intent on
evoking here.

"Miss Crayne" →
is meant here.

"Yes, but I came here for something about an envelope, didn't I?"

"Well, look. Tommy and me will stay here and chat with the company, and also be here in case Mrs. Haldeman wishes to reveal the name of the killer while you're looking at the thing."

"Yes, but Citarro. Don't you think it would be wiser to take it off of her now? Hell, we're the police."

"No, no. You can't," said Citarro quickly, "it won't do any good. I don't think the killer can do anything. Don't worry. I'll be here."

Inspector Claude's eyes narrowed. "Say, who got me up here? Was it old lady Haldeman? Or was it you?"

"Yes, it was. Y'see, Claude, something's wrong here. Unless I have lost my nose for likely situations, there's going to be a killing here very soon. And I want you around." To me he said "Tommy, fetch Miss Crayne." I brought her out of the game room, where everybody was, and told her what she was to show Mr. Claude. She nodded and agreed. So she and Claude went out into the garden. It was still light, enough to see by, since it did not get dark until around 9:15 Daylight Saving.

The group in the drawing-room had moved. Mr. Crayne was in the game room, engaged in a bit of Solotaire. Merriwether Stone was at the side of the house, smoking. Miss Haldeman was talking to the cook in the kitchen about something, probably concerning the preparation of the meals. She was as much mistress of the house as Mrs. Haldeman.

Citarro and I went into the game room to chat with Mr. Crayne. I noticed then what sort of a person he was. He before [had] always been chatting with someone when I had seen [him and] gave the effect of being an extra in a play, with only a few important lines to say. Now, alone, he was a strong, fine figure of a man. His lean, tan face possesed youth, even though the hair around his temples was white. The grey eyes were steady and keen, and his mouth gave the impression of being about to break into a smile. He was, I thought, like a middle-aged boy of twenty. This was

"I want stories to startle and engage me within the first few sentences," Updike wrote in his introduction to The Best American Short Stories 1984, *"and in their middle to widen or deepen or sharpen my knowledge of human activity. . . ."*

the man, I thought, who has been loving Marybelle Haldeman for 30 years.

He greeted us in a jovial mood. "Greetings. I hope this will teach you detectives to stay away from respectable people. They get killed right away." He wasn't taking the murder of Walter Haldeman very hard, I thought.

"Don't worry. After this I'll go up and be a hermit in the Alps." Citarro grinned back.

"I pity the poor skiiers."

The conversation drifted into more conventional channels. We talked of the grand old house in which we were at the present, and other topics of which people who have nothing in common talk. The butler, Stephen, came into the room. He was stiff and butlerlike. "Mrs. Haldeman says that she wants Mr. Claude to come up at once. She knows he is here. She says it is extremely urgent and he is to come at once." He paused, then looked at us. "Where is he?" he asked.

Out in the garden, muttered Citarro, and leaped to his feet. "The woman's in danger. I'll go up. Tommy, go out and fetch Claude." He started for the door. . .

"She asked," the butler said fridgidly, "For the police."

"Damn, man," Citarro shouted, "I'm better [than] the police!" He stormed toward the door. A moment later he was gone.

I ran after him. The hall was empty. Instead of going back into the game room, I went into the garden at the back of the house and walked down the path toward the tool shed. Claude and Catherine were studying the carving on the wall.

"Claude," I said. "Citarro wants you up at the house. Mrs. Haldeman called for the cops a moment ago and Citarro went up to her room. It probably has something to do with the murder."

He didn't waste any time. He ran. I followed him, keeping up as best I could. Catherine walked, slowly.

We went though the back door into the hall. Citarro was coming down the stairs. Merriwether

Stone came through the game room door out into the hall, followed by Mr. Crayne. Citarro seemed a little out of breath.

"Something the matter," he said gravely. "Her door is locked, and although I knocked and called both, she doesn't answer." There was a feeling of alarm that went through the little group. Citarro hesitated a moment, then said, "Come on, all of you if you wish." Everyone wished. All five of us went up the stairs. We all wanted to run up as fast as we could, but no one did.

Claude stopped at her door. He rapped lightly with the back of his hand. "Mrs. Haldeman," he called, "It's Inspector Claude. Open up please." No one answered. He tried again, knocking harder this time. Silence was his answer. He looked around, his impassive face even more impassive. "I think that maybe we had better break the door down, if it is certain that she didn't come down at all. . ."

"I don't think she did, Claude," Citarro said.

Claude looked around. "O.K." By this time Baily had arrived. "C'mon, let's bust the door down."

Claude was not a very powerful man, but Citarro was strong and so was Baily. After four unsuccessful tries, the door panel began to splinter. They threw their shoulders against the door, and the panel broke. Claude reached inside, turned the knob, and the door opened.

Marybelle Haldeman was lying in bed. The clothes she wore at dinner were still on, and she was on top of the covers. A knife was stuck in the side of her neck. Blood was all over the pillow and was still flowing. The knife was very familiar. It was the little throwing knife of Manuel Citarro.

Claude made a peculiar noise with his tongue. Citarro swore softly, under his breath. The rest of us stood still for a moment. Then Claude walked over to a small table aside of the bed. On it were a great many ashes. He poked through them with his forefinger. They were all black, and in tiny pieces, as the unknown burner had purposely crushed

As a boy, Updike imagined art—drawing and writing both—as a "method of riding a thin pencil line out of Shillington, out of time altogether, into an infinity of unseen and even unborn hearts. He pictured this infinity as radiant," he writes of his younger self, in "The Dogwood Tree." "How innocent!" And yet, he continues, these boyhood images have not been supplanted in adulthood.

them. A little bit away from the pile was a very small piece of paper, oblong in shape, and burnt around the edges. On it was am in dang . . . y murderer is M . . . . . and that was all.

Inspector Claude held it between the tip of his forefinger and his thumb and regarded it sourly. "Well, we have a clue, anyhow."

"The murderer's name begins with M," I said.

"Not necissairly," Claude returned. "You forget all of the common forms of address: Mr., Missus, and Miss. He might even have been going to say My brother or My aunt, or something like that." He looked around the room, then sighed deeply. "Baley," he said. "Call the boys, we have another murder on our hands

THINGS TO DO IN REWRITE

Have somebody show Mays, Stone and Citarro around house. Secret staircase. Have fact brought out that Crayne is old admirer of Mrs. Haldeman. Show more background and character emphasis.

XXXV

O   On it he had drwan a rough diagram of the upstairs.
He handed it back bme expectently. "See?"

.I had to admit I didn' see.

He was impatient. "Look. Grace Haldeman says she
heard somebody creep past her door. Look at the diagram.
Her room is at the farthrest end of the Hall. How could
anybody go past her door? IT's like Citarro said xxmmm-
a whaile ago. They either would have to do it deliberately,
or jump over the bannister.

"Furthermore, Merriwether Stone says that if there were anybody out there he
would have heard them. It's a shame the floors are so well built. Well, then, how
could have the Hald an heard squeakly footsteps?"

"Lassert, get er in here- -No wait. Before we do that, Let's go up and see
something." To me he said, You stay here. I might want you to take something down."
Lassert and he went out he door, and I could hear them going up the stairs. In a minut
I could hear them walking aroung the entire upstairs hall. They would walk up an down,
close to the walls, then around in circles. They did this, for five minutes, and not
once id i hear a floorboard squeak. At last they camw down. Claude came into the
study, and Las ert followed him a little later with Miss Grace Hal dman.

"Sit down, please." Claud commanded. "Miss Haldeman," He began, so severely,
that he remimned me of a strict school teacher reprimanding his favorite pupil,
"Awhile ago you stated that you heard someone out in the hall in front of your door.
It has just occurred to me that your room is at the far end of tge hall, and no one
would have any conceivable reason for passign there. "

"I didn't mean," hxxxx said Miss. Haldman quickly, "In frotn of my door, I eanst
out in the hall, possible on the landing."

"Yes, but, Seargant Lassert and I were just up there, and we stamped around for
f lly five minutes, and not once did a floorboard squeak."

Miss Hald mans composure had begun to crack a little, and she appeared a trifl
worried. "I cant," She said, help that. I know what i Heard an I shall stick by it.

Updike added this clarifying sketch to the upper right corner of page 36 of his manuscript.

THE RABBIT AND THE BOYS

The boy in the blue shorts yelled excitedly. "Look, look! A pink rabbit!
A pink rabbit! Two other boys ran up. "Look! A pink rabbit! the first boy repeated.

"Where?? asked a boy with red hair and too many freckles.

"There!" screamed the boy in the blue shorts. "Right over there," he yelled, gesturing wildly.

The rabbit quivered and looked as if he was going to spring.

"Chee!" said the boy in tattered overalls. "Hey, gang! Over here!"

Soon at least ten boys were assembled, gazing at the rabbit. "Gosh. I
bet we'd make a lot of money if we'd catch 'im." said one voice. "We cud charge
admission to look at im." observered another. "A million dollars, I betcha."
exclaimed a third. "At least a billion!" differed a rather small blonde kid.
"A trillion!" "A zillion" "A frillion!" screamed the many headed. "Stop!"
thundered the boy in the blue shorts. "First we gotta ketch 'im. Skinny, go
home and get your Pop's fishing net. Somebuddy else get a box to put 'im in."

The plan was met with unanimious approval. Skinny was despatched on his errand,
and three others went for boxes. "Oh, boy!" hollered one emoninail youngster,
"Will we ever be rich!" " A billion dollars eachm I bet!" said one. "Naaa. A gollion."
This staret a rather heated contreversy, and by the time the box and net had arrived, the bidding had gone up to 'a billion-billion-trillion-zillion-rillion-
hillion dollars.

Soon, however, harsh words were forgotten, hysteric screamings abandonded,
and the boys were slowly creeping up on the rabbat, who had remained perfectly
still during the activitys of young blood.

"Boy! " whispered one small boy, overcome with emotion. "Think of it!
A pink rabbat." At this, the rabbit jerked his head, and looked strait at the
speaker.

"A pink rabbit?" it said in a low, deep voice. "Don't be silly. There is
no such thing!" There was one hidious silence, in which the boys stared,
horrified, dumb-struck. Then, with one ear peircing scream, they broke ranks.
Scrambling, yelling, running the boys went home with rapidity rarely equalled
in the locality.

"When the last one was out of sight, the rabbit sighed, cloded his eyes,
and ƥƥƫ/ prepared to take a nap on the cool clean grass. "That always gets
'em," he chuckled softly.

                    THE END

John Updike

Gore Vidal in 1943, as pictured in his Exeter graduation yearbook.

GORE VIDAL

Gore Vidal, who was born Eugene Luther Vidal in 1925 in West Point, New York, and raised in the environs of Washington, D.C., has described certain years of his youth as "sequestered" and "remote from any reality." In contrast, the Phillips Exeter Academy in New Hampshire, where he composed the two stories below, seemed to Vidal "as like the real world as it is possible for a school to be." He told one interviewer in 1979 that it was at Exeter that he began his identity as both a novelist and a politician, going on to say: "and I've never ceased to be, more or less, what I was at fourteen."

Instead of going to college, in 1946 he published his first novel, *Williwaw* ("written when I was nineteen and easily the cleverest young fox ever to know how to disguise his ignorance and make a virtue of his limitations"). His third novel, *The City and the Pillar* (1948), was described by one scholar in 1982 as "certainly the most significant novel on the subject [of homosexuality] written by an American." In addition to his role as an outspoken critic of society, politics, and letters, Vidal is most widely known for his "American chronicle": six novels cited for their entertaining and demystifying treatment of U.S. history, including *Burr* (1973), *1876* (1976), and *Hollywood* (1990).

The infamous *Myra Breckinridge* (1968) and its 1974 sequel *Myron* were once described by the author as his most unique and immortal creations. Rendered in high camp style, the novels are about two personalities warring for control over a single body through a series of psychical, and sometimes physical, sex changes. Passive Myron is transformed into megalomaniacal Myra, whose mission (or curse) leads her to violate "your average hundred-percent all-American stud," with the aim of altering her victim's sexual identity.

Vidal's juvenile piece about a werewolf attacking and transforming his friend, delightful in its own right, is a perhaps significant precursor to *Myra Breckinridge* and *Myron*.

Mostly About Geoffrey
(1942, age 17)

The manuscript of this story was found in the men's room of the Colby Theatre in Colby, Maryland. As the author has never been discovered, we hereby feel safe in printing the following tale for what it is worth.

It was on Thursday, the 8th of August, that my bosom friend Geoffrey told me he was a were-wolf. I must say that I, though surprised, took it rather well. "Were-wolf, you say?" I remarked casually. I made a desperate attempt to sound intelligent, but somehow failed. So I sat there and waited for him to answer.

Geoffrey was a calm, efficient kind of person with a legalistic turn of mind. There was little of the actor about him; if he said he was a were-wolf he was a were-wolf and that was that.

"Yes," said Geoffrey, carefully choosing his words, "I think, in fact I know, I am one. The other day at the Claytons' I was bitten by a wild-looking dog. As it later turned out, the beast was not a dog but a wolf that had strayed into the back garden. According to ancient lore it seems that he who is bitten by a were-wolf becomes one himself. . . ."

"But," I interrupted, "how do you know this . . . this creature was a were-wolf? It didn't change into anyone, did it?"

"I wish," said Geoffrey petulantly, "you'd let me finish my story. I presume the animal was a were-wolf, because

Myra tries to reclaim control of the body she shares with her alter ego, in Vidal's novel Myron. Shortly after making her grand entrance, Myra declares: "Now let the enfolding night ring once again . . . with the ululations of the werewolf. . . ." →

last night when the moon was full I changed into a wolf."

I sat there woodenly for a moment, and looked at him. He was calm; there was a look of oppressive sanity in his eyes, and a feeling of comfortable security in his receding hair line. This was not a mad man, and yet it could not be a were-wolf. I giggled in a hideously strangled voice, and said something like "well, what a funny world it is." I am not at my best in a crisis.

Geoffrey went to the window, and gazed pensively at the nearby woods. I probably should have stated before that we were in his home near the town of Colby, Maryland. Colby is a rustic sort of hamlet set amidst some legend-filled woods. The townspeople are kindly, old-fashioned, and perhaps a little mad.

Standing before the window Geoffrey seemed substantial enough. Without turning around he said, "I think you had better leave here before night fall. The moon will be full again tonight."

I had an insane desire to tell him that I was going to turn into a chipmunk; fortunately I stifled it. At last I said, "I think I had better stay here with you tonight. After all you'll need someone to keep you from eating things like . . . like babies."

Geoffrey wheeled around, his eyes bulging. "Christ, what I'd give for a plump baby!"

Five minutes later I was heading for the most crowded place in Colby, namely the Colby Theatre. I felt safe here, until I discovered that the movie starred Boris Karloff in one of his more vicious roles. I am afraid I was not in the proper mood to enjoy this picture; in fact, I did not stay long enough to find whether I would like it or not.

Just before night fall I decided to return to Geoffrey's house. I suppose I felt it was my duty to be with him.

He was seated quietly in his study when I arrived. He rose when he saw me. "Sorry I bothered you," he said. His voice possessed just the right shade of contrition. Together we sat down before the newly-lit fire.

"The moon will be full in three hours," he remarked cozily, picking up a book.

"The doubleness *of things,"* as Vidal puts it in Two Sisters *(1970),* has long been a vital element in his fiction. ➔

"How nice," I said, with studied calm.

We sat there chatting in a desultory fashion for about an hour. Finally I asked him what he planned to do with the rest of his life. "You know you can't go on being both a man and a wolf. People would talk."

He laughed unpleasantly. "What cure would you suggest my taking?" I told him that there was nothing to get nasty about, and added that he did not show the proper spirit. There was an uncomfortable silence.

Geoffrey stood up abruptly, and began to pace the floor. I was becoming intensely nervous. Several times he went to the curtained windows. Each time he halted before them for a moment, and then restlessly moved on. I began to wonder why I had come back. Gloomily I thought of my position should Geoffrey really become a wolf.

Finally he went to the window by his desk; there was determination in his gait. Slowly he pushed back the curtains, and the wind shrieked in. The moon was full in the black sky above the woods.

He gave a cry of delight; and I quickly placed the friendly contours of a large couch between us. Then the incredible happened. Geoffrey began to gasp in the best were-wolf fashion. He seemed to shrink . . . to bunch up. After a moment of what seemed intense pain he turned and faced me. I noticed with horror that he was covered with dark fur.

Incapacitated in the hospital after being struck by a car, Myra (Myra Breckinridge*) begs for some female hormones when she begins turning back into Myron. "I'm sprouting hair in all directions," she complains.* ➔

"How do you feel?" I asked, trying to make conversation.

"Like hell," he replied. I noted that he mumbled a great deal, and had trouble with his diction.

Then a ridiculous thing happened: he stopped changing. I am not acquainted with the various stages of were-wolfdom, but I am quite sure that one does not stop in the middle of the transformation, and remain looking more like a bearded drunk than a wolf. Anyway, that's what happened to Geoffrey.

"I feel an awful fool," he mumbled, and I detected a blush of shame beneath the hirsute growth of his face.

"You look an awful fool," I said, with considerable asperity, for I felt reasonably safe. Anyone as ineffective as Geoffrey looked could not be dangerous. He did look hideous, though, and I felt I should take no liberties with him.

Sadly he huddled himself into a chair; the semi-claws he had for hands beat the air vainly. "It worked last night," he kept repeating.

"Do you think if you tried very hard you could change completely?" I asked curiously.

"Fat chance," he said, but he did grunt a little. It was no use.

"Well, you're not a very effective were-wolf," I said gaily. He looked at me furiously; I had hurt him to the quick. Then to my terror he got out of his chair, and came walking slowly toward me, his semi-tusks slobbering. "So I'm not a very effective were-wolf, am I?" His voice was threatening; he snarled once or twice. Hastily I retreated to the fire-place, and grabbed a poker.

"Come any closer and I'll club you!" I said. He came a great deal closer, and suddenly, when he was about two feet from me, he jumped. There was a brief scuffle in which he bit my arm, and I killed him; the creature turned back into Geoffrey on the floor.

Suddenly I wondered if the police would call me a murderer; it was obvious that they would not believe in my were-wolf story. Panic-stricken I dropped the poker and ran into the town again, leaving a trail of blood behind me. For safety I fled into the men's room of the Colby Theatre.

I have been sitting here for an hour now writing this story on a roll of toilet paper. I can hear the police cars and ambulances outside in the street. But I don't think they will catch me, for I have a feeling that I am going to turn into a wolf. Geoffrey did bite me. Well, I have come . . ."

Here the roll of toilet paper ends. Just as incidental intelligence the "Colby Daily" in an issue dated the 9th of August told a brief story to the effect that a mad dog has emerged from the men's room of the Colby Theatre. It was not caught.

In Myra Breckinridge, *Myra/Myron is surprised to learn that during her/his hospital convalescence, she/he had bitten the night nurse's* ◄ *arm "to the bone."*

Vidal uses a similar structural device, also for comic effect, in Myra Breckinridge. *Most of the narrative is presented as Myra's journal, which Myron finds near the novel's end. "What an extraordinary document!" Myron exclaims.*

New Year's Eve
(1943, age 17)

"Well, only two more hours to go and it's another year!" exclaimed the Colonel jovially. In the garishly lighted Officers' Club the small party at his table agreed with him. The electric light bulbs in the ceiling were unshaded and it hurt to look up. A small band from the nearby town was grinding out monotonous music. "Too much noise," thought the young Lieutenant at the Colonel's table.

There were many other officers in the club besides those in the Colonel's party. With the officers were their wives or if not wives girls from the town. They were all either dancing, or grouped into parties around the wood tables covered with confetti and the litter of dinners already eaten. "Far too many people," thought the Colonel's wife, squeezed between her husband and the young Lieutenant.

The six guests of the Colonel were trying to be gay and yet listen to the Colonel's stories at the same time. One bottle of champagne had been emptied; it stood now among the used dishes and confetti and champagne glasses. The Colonel noticed it.

"More champagne, waiter!" he shouted. His red face under thinning gray hair shone with opulence, with good will. He was very flushed, and his wife thought, "I do hope he doesn't drink too much. He's such a damned bore when he does." She felt the eyes of the young Lieutenant upon her. Somehow she was pleased.

He was looking at her. "I wonder how old she is," he was thinking. "Forty, forty-five? Certainly not over forty-five anyway." He watched her as she talked to the others at the table. She was making elaborate gestures with her hands, and he knew she was conscious of his watching. She was still handsome. She was somewhat heavy, but tall enough to carry it well. Her hair was only slightly gray and much of it was still black. There was a little sag about her mouth, but when she smiled, as she did too often, it vanished.

"Have some more, my dear," said the Colonel and he filled her glass. His hand shook and some of the champagne splattered onto the table cloth. "He's getting there fast," she thought, and she smiled brightly at him and thanked him.

"You know, I came up through the ranks . . ." The Colonel was still talking loudly. "He's off," she thought, but she was not annoyed; rather she felt detached. She glanced at the Lieutenant. He was not at all bad-looking. She felt that he would he bald and stout in ten years, but then in ten years what would anyone be like? "He's somewhat like a sheep," she thought, "but such a nice sheep."

"If it wasn't for my wife here . . ." The Colonel nodded at her, and the others looked glassily at her. He was telling them of his life and his wife. "His life and his wife." She repeated the words to herself. They were a pattern, a pattern that rhymed. That's all anything was, she thought, a god-damned pattern that rhymed or should rhyme. She wished he would stop talking. She said something and looked pleadingly at him, but he was too drunk to notice or to care.

"I wonder if I'll be like that when I'm fifty," thought the Lieutenant. It was not much of a question, though, for he knew that he could never be like that . . . a middle-aged bore. The Lieutenant knew that he was ineffably charming. Already the wine had taken effect and he was feeling elated and very wonderful. He watched the Colonel's wife. He wondered about her.

"Marriage is the greatest institution there is," said the Colonel. She shuddered when he said this, for she knew that he would say it again and again. It was one of those trite little sayings that he was fond of. "Blissful institution," she thought to herself, and the words in her brain were like ice freezing her. She would never be young again. She would go on living like this celebrating new years. Celebrating them! God! Celebrating what? Celebrating getting old and lonely and useless. Welcoming the sterile emptiness of new years that would be so very much alike. She wondered, almost panic-stricken, where the time had got to.

"Waiter! More champagne!" roared the Colonel. He poured it into her glass until the glass was full. She drank it quickly. The bubbles made tears come to her eyes. She could forget about herself when drunk—that was the beauty of drinking—to forget, just simply to forget. She felt the Lieutenant close beside her. He felt warm with an animal warmth. She pushed closer to him and he did not move away. Her heart beats began to quicken. "I'm a fool, a fool . . ."

"There's no fool like an old fool," said the Colonel. He laughed too loudly; he had been telling a story about somebody who did something-or-other amusing. The Lieutenant wiggled uncomfortably. "She's probably old enough to be my mother," he thought. He was a very wonderful person indeed, and she was old and spent. Her leg pushed against his leg; he did not move. It was a very amusing situation.

"I remember back in 1916, last war, you know . . ." said the Colonel. "That's all we can do," she thought, "remember when. When New Year's Eve was something more than memory." The Lieutenant's wriggling brought her back. He stood up and asked her to dance. They went out onto the dance floor among the crowd. Couples were swaying back and forth beneath multi-colored streamers. The band was noisier than ever. She pressed close to the Lieutenant, and she could feel the buttons of his coat press into her as he breathed.

"You'd never believe that she's forty-seven . . ." said the Colonel to the table at large. He was very proud of her. She caught the words and was furious, but then she relaxed and no longer cared. The Lieutenant waltzed well, and she felt as though she were floating, almost as though she were young. The

Vidal's short story "Three Stratagems" (circa 1956) conveys a similar, somewhat grim, sense of amusement at the romantic mismatch between age and youth. On Key West, Michael hopes to take advantage of his own youth to entice the older, wealthier "fools," whom, he imagines, see him as a "beloved angel" able to "exorcise the graceless shadow of the years." →

dance stopped, and they paused breathless and bright-eyed. They smiled at each other. Together they went into the long room where the bar was. Here was a great crowd, mostly of men. They were forced back into a corner. Someone shoved her against him. He looked down at her through a champagne mist. He kissed her full upon the lips.

The music had begun to play again. The tune was "Night and Day," sultry and moving. She was carried away by the music, by the champagne, by . . . She clutched him to her. For a moment she was blind to all else, and then she saw that he was sober now. He did not move, and she felt cold again.

"Only two minutes to go!" roared the Colonel as they came back. The Lieutenant was pale and silent. She seemed gay and vivacious as she took her place at the table. Suddenly the lights went out and some one shouted, "Happy New Year!" The Colonel leaned over the table and kissed her. "Happy New Year, old girl," he whispered. She smiled at him and said, "Happy New Year."

As in "Three Stratagems," Vidal moves the middle-aged would-be lover toward the brink of foolishness and then back to a state of dignity.

Gore Vidal

Tobias Wolff at about age 15.

TOBIAS WOLFF

Tobias Wolff has already provided readers with a striking portrait of his childhood in the 1989 memoir *This Boy's Life*. Born in Birmingham, Alabama, in 1945, but often uprooted across the country, young Wolff responded to his somewhat chaotic upbringing by continually reinventing himself. He adopted the name Jack (after Jack London), spun yarns in long pen-pal letters, and fabricated elements of his prep school applications. In confessional, he once offered someone else's misdeeds rather than his own.

The childhood described in *This Boy's Life* straddles mischief and delinquency. In one chilling recollection, the preteenage Wolff sights passers-by through his loaded Winchester rifle, relishing his power over them, until so overcome with the need to shoot, he kills a squirrel. He is immediately, if briefly, remorseful. In this elegantly written memoir, however, even his more ignoble childhood exploits are transformed by the grace of his telling, and it is clear that Wolff, in these intervening years, has in a sense mastered the art and spirit of confession.

Much as Wolff the boy wrestled with right and wrong (and what he could get away with), so do the characters in his much-celebrated fiction, which includes the short-story collections *In the Garden of the North American Martyrs* (1981) and *Back in the World* (1985) and the 1984 novella *The Barracks Thief*. He credits his father and mother—as well as his older brother, the writer Geoffrey Wolff—for the example they set as storytellers. Wolff remembers writing tales as early as age six, and in school he would write stories for friends' assignments, he told one interviewer, adding: "I don't know exactly at what time the idea hardened in me to become a writer, but I certainly never wanted to be anything else."

The poem "Death," written when Wolff was fifteen, could be seen as an effort to create a little order in his often tumultuous youth. As its mannered style might suggest, Wolff was engaging in a bit of the posturing that he often relied on in his early years. After all, one of the epigraphs to *This Boy's Life* quotes Oscar Wilde: "The first duty in life is to assume a pose. What the second is, no one has yet discovered."

When he was perhaps 13, the author wrote a short story about two Yukon wolves locked in mortal combat. Though the story is lost, wolves make a later appearance in the adult author's short story "Poaching" (1979). In it a young boy, whose parents have split up, wishes for a pet wolf. When his somewhat overbearing father argues that a wolf would be too dangerous, the boy counters: "He would protect me. . . . He would love me."

Death

(circa 1961, age 15)

The Pessimist has cautioned me, has whispered low
In my ear to warn me of that vague, black-hooded
    knight,
Who steals through the darkness, coming for me . . .
Coming to extirpate my life, and to carry me down,
Into his Black Castle.
There to blind me with eternal darkness,
To bind me for time immeasurable in the dank,
    hideous, clay
And twist my soul in an infinite agony of dispair . . .
This the Pessimist would have me know of Death.

The Optomist—he has proclaimed in tones loud and
    clear,
That the whole of humanity might hear,
Proclaimed that the successor of life is a fair-haired
    Apollo
Who hovers resplendently over . . . waiting . . .
To sweep me gently away on wings of light gold to
    his abode,
His green mountain of eternal happiness;
There to give my eyes true sight,
To surround me with timeless beauty

And bathe my soul forever in the tranquil waters
  of peace . . .
The Optomist . . .

And the Realist . . . states flatly that Death
Is simply that condition which follows the cessation
  of life . . .
A condition, he declares; not a blindness or light,
Neither suffering nor happiness . . .
And, he further assures me, it neither steals through
  the Shadows
Nor does it soar lightly above,
But inevitably arrives . . . and is just there . . . and
  is nothing.

Such have I been told . . .
By one, death seems a limitless paroxysm; another,
A never-ending dream of love and contentment,
While a third asserts the presence of an incessantly
  closing door
Which, when closed, shuts me up forever . . . in
  painless, unlit
Nothingness . . .
I side with none; each is so involved in his own edicts
That he lives the death which he predicts.

◄ Not long before composing this poem, Wolff, seeking a way to improve his situation, wanted to apply to prep schools. Faced with the prospect of sending out a transcript heavy with C's, he opted for "giving up— being realistic, as people liked to say, meaning the same thing," he writes in This Boy's Life. *"Being realistic made me feel bitter. It was a new feeling, and one I didn't like, but I saw no way out." (After getting his hands on some blank transcript forms and school letterhead, however, he was able to enhance his applications, filling them with what he saw as the truth of his hidden self. He was accepted at The Hill School, in whose literary magazine this poem first appeared.)*

Tobias Wolff

APPENDIX

Sources, Permissions, and Photo credits

The bibliographic matter that follows is not intended to be comprehensive; it includes only those sources that have particularly informed this work.

I. INTRODUCTION

Authors of historical juvenilia referred to in the introduction are listed in many cases under the anthologies in which they were found. Contemporary juvenilia, whether or not they are referred to in the introduction, are listed under the individual authors in Part II of this appendix.

Austen, Jane, and Charlotte Brontë. *The Juvenilia of Jane Austen and Charlotte Brontë*. Ed. Frances Beer. New York: Penguin, 1986.

Bailey, John. *Introductions to Jane Austen*. London: Oxford University Press, 1931.

Branch, Edgar Marquess. *The Literary Apprenticeship of Mark Twain: With Selections from His Apprentice Writing*. Urbana: University of Illinois Press, 1950.

Braybrooke, Neville, ed. *Seeds in the Wind: Early Signs of Genius*. 1989. Reprint. San Francisco: Mercury House, 1990. Juvenilia from poets and some prose writers, the majority of them British, since the mid-1800s, with a few still living today. Includes samples from Virginia Woolf and Evelyn Waugh.

Chekhov, Anton. *Letters of Anton Chekhov*. Ed. Avrahm Yarmolinsky. New York: Viking, 1973.

De la Mare, Walter. *Early One Morning in Spring: Chapters on Children and on Childhood as It Is Revealed in Particular in Early Memories and in Early Writings*. London: Faber & Faber, 1935. Part III mixes many samples of juvenilia, primarily those belonging to the titans of British poetry, with de la Mare's own broad-reaching and poetic commentary. Discusses and/or includes juvenilia from Samuel Taylor Coleridge, Abraham Cowley, Lewis Carroll, Marjory Fleming, Edgar Allan Poe ("To Helen"), Alexander Pope ("Ode on Solitude" and play), Percy Bysshe Shelley, Robert Louis Stevenson, Alfred Tennyson, and others.

Fitzgerald, F. Scott. *The Apprentice Fiction of F. Scott Fitzgerald: 1909–1917*. Ed. John Kuehl. New Brunswick, N.J.: Rutgers University Press, 1965. Includes "A Luckless Santa Claus," "The Trail of the Duke," and thirteen other Fitzgerald stories written from age thirteen to twenty-one.

Flaubert, Gustave. *Early Writings*. Trans. (with introduction) Robert Griffin. Lincoln: University of Nebraska Press, 1991.

Godwin, Gail. "How to Be the Heroine of Your Own Life." *Cosmopolitan,* March 1988.

Grey, J. David, ed. *Jane Austen's Beginnings: The Juvenilia and* Lady Susan. Ann Arbor: University of Michigan Research Press, 1989. Scholarly essays, including contributions by Donald Stone and A. Walton Litz.

Hemingway, Ernest. *Ernest Hemingway's Apprenticeship: Oak Park, 1916–1917.* Ed. Matthew J. Bruccoli. Washington, D.C.: Microcard Editions, 1971. The author's high school publications, including "Judgment of Manitou."

Kupferberg, Tuli, and Sylvia Topp, comp. *First Glance: Childhood Creations of the Famous.* Maplewood, N.J.: Hammond, 1978. Includes about one hundred entries, mostly from previous generations, representing all fields. Among the authors included are Anton Chekhov, W. E. B. Du Bois, Ben Franklin, Anaïs Nin, Sylvia Plath, and Edgar Allan Poe (letter).

Livingston, Myra Cohn. *The Child as Poet: Myth or Reality?* Boston: Horn, 1984.

Marecki, Joan E. "Bowles, Paul (Frederick)." *Contemporary Authors New Revision Series.* Vol. 19. Detroit: Gale Research, 1987.

Pickard, Samuel T. *Hawthorne's First Diary.* 1897. Reprint. New York: Haskell House, 1972.

Plath, Aurelia. Introduction. *Letters Home.* By Sylvia Plath. New York: Harper & Row, 1975.

Randall, Harry, comp. *Minor Masterpieces: An Anthology of Juvenilia by Twelve Giants of English Literature.* Alden, Mich.: Talponia Press, 1983. Includes Evelyn Waugh.

Shanks, Lewis Piaget. *Flaubert's Youth, 1821–1845.* 1927. Reprint. New York: Arno Press, 1979.

Stallworthy, Jon, ed. *First Lines: Poems Written in Youth, From Herbert to Heaney.* New York: Carcanet, 1987. Fifty-eight entries, mostly from poets of earlier generations. Includes Edgar Allan Poe ("To Helen") and Alexander Pope ("Ode on Solitude").

II. BY AUTHOR

Following each author's name, readers will find a list of the author's childhood works included in this volume (if they were published previously), the adult works of the author that were used in our preparation, secondary sources also used in the preparation of this volume, as well as photo information. Additional source material was obtained through direct correspondence with the authors.

Isaac Asimov

"Little Brothers." Boys' High *Recorder* (student literary magazine of Boys' High School, Brooklyn, N.Y.), Spring 1934. Copyright 1934 by Isaac Asimov. Reprinted by the author's permission.

Asimov, Isaac. "The Callistan Menace"(written when Asimov was eighteen). *The Early Asimov: Or, Eleven Years of Trying.* New York: Doubleday, 1972 .

——. *The Early Asimov.*

——. *In Memory Yet Green: The Autobiography of Isaac Asimov, 1920–1954.* New York: Doubleday, 1979.

——. "Stranger in Paradise." *The Complete Robot.* New York: Doubleday, 1978.

——. "The Ugly Little Boy." *Other Worlds of Isaac Asimov.* Ed. Martin H. Greenberg. New York: Avenel, 1987.

Fiedler, Jean, and Jim Mele. *Isaac Asimov.* New York: Frederick Ungar, 1982.

Adult photo by Alex Gotfryd, courtesy of Doubleday. Childhood photos courtesy of Isaac Asimov.

Margaret Atwood

Margaret Atwood's juvenilia appear by the author's permission. Copyright 1993 by Margaret Atwood.

Atwood, Margaret. *Bodily Harm.* 1981. Reprint. New York: Bantam Books, 1983.

——. *The Edible Woman.* Boston: Little, Brown,1969.

——. *The Handmaid's Tale.* 1985. Reprint. New York: Fawcett Crest, 1987.

——. "The Man from Mars." *The World of the Short Story: A Twentieth Century Collection.* Ed. Clifton Fadiman. 1986. Reprint. New York: Avenel, 1990.

——. *You Are Happy.* New York: Harper & Row, 1974.

Oates, Joyce Carol. "Margaret Atwood: Poems and Poet." *New York Times Book Review,* 21 May 1978.

Photos courtesy of the author.

Louis Auchincloss

"The Futility of Prophesy." Groton School (Groton, Mass.) *Third Form Weekly,* 21 Dec. 1931, 3–5. Copyright 1931, 1993 by Louis Auchincloss. Reprinted by the author's permission.

Auchincloss, Louis. *The Cat and the King.* Boston: Houghton Mifflin, 1981.

——. *Diary of a Yuppie.* Boston: Houghton Mifflin, 1986.

——. *The Rector of Justin.* Boston: Houghton Mifflin, 1964.

——. *A Writer's Capital.* Minneapolis: University of Minnesota Press, 1974.

Bryer, Jackson R. *Louis Auchincloss and His Critics: A Bibliographical Record.* Boston: G. K. Hall, 1977.

Dahl, Christopher C. *Louis Auchincloss.* New York: Frederick Ungar, 1986.

Photos courtesy of the author.

Amiri Baraka

"The Statue." *The Acropolis* (student literary magazine of Barringer High School, Newark, N.J.), Spring 1951: 2, 18. Copyright 1951, 1993 by LeRoy Jones/Amiri Baraka. Reprinted by the author's permission.

Baraka, Amiri. *The Autobiography of LeRoi Jones.* New York: Freundlich, 1984.

——. "The Death of Horatio Alger." *Three Books by Imamu Amiri Baraka.* New York: Grove, 1975.

——. *The LeRoi Jones/Amiri Baraka Reader.* Ed. William J. Harris in collaboration with Amiri Baraka. New York: Thunder's Mouth Press, 1991.

——. "Two Writers' Beginnings." *Washington Post Book World,* 19 Nov. 1989, 5.

Photo as an adult by Risasi-Zachariah Dais copyright 1991, courtesy of Amiri Baraka. Photo as a teenager from *The Acropolis,* courtesy of Barringer High School.

Madison Smartt Bell

Madison Smartt Bell's juvenilia appear by the author's permission. Copyright 1993 by
    Madison Smartt Bell.

Bell, Madison Smartt. "Barking Man." *Barking Man and Other Stories.* New York: Ticknor
    & Fields, 1990.

——. *Soldier's Joy.* New York: Ticknor & Fields, 1989.

Photos courtesy of the author.

Roy Blount, Jr.

"Dear Diary by Joe Crutch." Decatur, Ga., High School *Scribbler* (newspaper), Dec.
    1957–Feb. 1959. Also in *The Scribbler:* "Robot Goes Berserk: 87 Perish as Monster
    Roams Streets," 23 Apr. 1959; "Roy's Noise," 12 Sep. 1958; "Science Fair Is Miserable
    Flop," 1 Apr. 1958; "Signs of Spring," 15 Apr. 1958. "You Ought to Be in Football."
    The National Beta Club *Journal* (Spartanburg, S.C.), April 1959: 14–15. Reprinted by
    the author's permission. Copyright 1957, 1958, 1959, 1993 by Roy Blount, Jr.

Blount, Roy, Jr. *About Three Bricks Shy of a Load: A Highly Irregular Lowdown on the Year the
    Pittsburgh Steelers Were Super but Missed the Bowl.* Boston: Little, Brown, 1974.

——. *First Hubby.* New York: Villard, 1990.

——. *Not Exactly What I Had in Mind.* Boston: Atlantic Monthly Press, 1985.

——. "Trash No More." *Crackers: This Whole Many-Angled Thing of Jimmy, More Carters,
    Ominous Little Animals, Sad-Singing Women, My Daddy and Me.* New York: Knopf, 1980.

——. *What Men Don't Tell Women.* Boston: Little, Brown, 1984.

——. "Women in the Locker Room!" *What Men Don't Tell Women.*

Brown, Jerry Elijah. *Roy Blount, Jr.* Boston: Twayne, 1990.

Photo as an adult by Slick Lawson, courtesy of Roy Blount, Jr. Photo as a teenager by
    John Baker (*Scribbler* staff photographer), courtesy of Roy Blount, Jr.

Vance Bourjaily

"Jack and Jill." *The Bowdoin Quill* (student publication, Bowdoin College, Brunswick,
    Me.) 46, no. 2 (1942): 65–66. Copyright 1942, 1993 by Vance Bourjaily. All of Vance
    Bourjaily's juvenilia appear by the author's permission, and, in the case of "Jack and
    Jill" and *Not to Confound My Elders,* by permission of the Special Collections depart-
    ment of the Bowdoin College Library, which holds the complete typescript of *Not to
    Confound My Elders.* Copyright 1993 by Vance Bourjaily.

Bourjaily, Vance. *Confessions of a Spent Youth.* New York: Dial Press, 1960.

——. *The Hound of Earth.* 1955. Reprint. New York: Dial Press, 1964.

——. Interview. With Matthew J. Bruccoli. *Conversations with Writers.* Vol. 1. Detroit:
    Gale Research, 1977.

——. *The Man Who Knew Kennedy.* New York: Dial Press, 1967.

——. *Old Soldier.* New York: Donald I. Fine, 1990.

——. Untitled essay. *Contemporary Authors Autobiography Series.* Vol. 1. Detroit: Gale
    Research, 1984.

Aldridge, John W. "Vance Bourjaily: The Two Worlds of Skinner Galt." *After the Lost
    Generation: A Critical Study of the Writers of Two Wars.* New York: McGraw-Hill, 1951.

Smith, Logan Pearsall. *Trivia*. London: Constable, 1918.

Stringfellow, Howard. "Vance Bourjaily." *Dictionary of Literary Biography*. Vol. 2. Detroit: Gale Research, 1978.

Photo as an adult courtesy of Vance Bourjaily; other photos courtesy of Robin Bourjaily. Solo studio portrait from youth by Edward Vantine. Group studio portrait from youth by Aime Dupont.

Paul Bowles

"Poor Aunt Emma" and the lyrics from "Le Carré" are excerpts from *Without Stopping*, copyright © 1972 by Paul Bowles. First published by The Ecco Press in 1985 (pp. 32, 36). Reprinted by permission. "Bluey: Pages from an Imaginary Diary." *View*, no. 3, series 3 (1943): 81–82. "Entity." *transition*, no. 13 (Summer 1928): 219–20. (The previous number of *transition* included Bowles's poem "Spire Song.") "The Lady of Peace" (part of "Aunt Pete"). *Exquisite Corpse*, April 1983: 8. "A White Goat's Shadow." *Argo: An Individual Review*, 1, no. 2 (Dec. 1930): 50–51 (Bowles's first published piece of fiction). Copyright 1928, 1930, 1943, 1972, 1983, 1993 by Paul Bowles. All of Paul Bowles's juvenilia appear by the author's permission.

Bowles, Paul. "A Distant Episode." *Collected Stories 1939–1976*. Santa Rosa: Black Sparrow Press, 1986.

——. "The Hyena." *Collected Stories*.

——. "In the Red Room." *The Best American Short Stories of the Eighties*. Ed. Shannon Ravenel. Boston: Houghton Mifflin, 1990.

——. "Journal, Tangier 1987–1988." *Our Private Lives: Journals, Notebooks, and Diaries*. Ed. Daniel Halpern. New York: Vintage, 1990.

——. *The Sheltering Sky*. 1949. Reprint. New York: Vintage, 1990.

——. *Without Stopping: An Autobiography*. 1972. Reprint. New York: Ecco Press, 1985.

Photo as an adult by Suomi La Valle, courtesy of The Ecco Press. Juvenile photos of Paul Bowles supplied by the Photography Collection, Harry Ransom Humanities Research Center, The University of Texas at Austin. Reprinted by permission. Toddler photo by W. C. Rowley.

William S. Burroughs

"Personal Magnetism." *John Burroughs Review* (John Burroughs School, St. Louis, Mo., literary magazine), Feb. 1929. (This story was later found by Ted Morgan, who included it in his biography of Burroughs, pp. 39–40; see below.) Copyright 1929, 1993 by William S. Burroughs. Reprinted by permission of the author.

Burroughs, William S. *Junky*. 1953 (as *Junkie* by "William Lee"). Reprint. New York: Penguin, 1977.

——. "My Purpose Is to Write for the Space Age." *William S. Burroughs at the Front: Critical Reception, 1959–1989*. Ed. Jennie Skerl and Robin Lydenberg. Carbondale: Southern Illinois University Press, 1991.

——. *Naked Lunch*. 1959 (as *The Naked Lunch*). 25th Anniversary Edition. New York: Grove Press, 1984. Includes an introduction by Jennie Skerl.

——. "The Name Is Burroughs." *The Adding Machine*. New York: Seaver Books, 1986.

——. *Queer*. New York: Viking, 1985.

Grauerholz, James. Introduction. *Interzone*. By William S. Burroughs. New York: Viking, 1989.

Lydenberg, Robin and Jennie Skerl. "Points of Intersection: An Overview of William S. Burroughs and his Critics." *William S. Burroughs at the Front*.

Morgan, Ted. *Literary Outlaw: The Life and Times of William S. Burroughs*. New York: Henry Holt, 1988.

Skerl, Jennie. *William S. Burroughs*. Boston: Twayne, 1985.

Fred Chappell

"And with Ah! Bright Wings." *The Archive* (student literary magazine of Duke University), Feb. 1955: 5–10. Courtesy of William R. Perkins Library, Duke University. Copyright 1955, 1993 by Fred Chappell. Reprinted by permission of the author.

Chappell, Fred. *The Fred Chappell Reader*. New York: St. Martin's Press, 1987. Includes *Dagon*, parts of *I Am One of You Forever* and of *It Is Time, Lord*, "Linnaeus Forgets," "Moments of Light," "Mrs. Franklin Ascends," "Notes Toward a Theory of Flight," "Thatch Retaliates," and an afterword essay by the author.

——. Interview. With Irv Broughton. *The Writer's Mind: Interviews with American Authors Volume III*. Ed. Irv Broughton. Fayetteville: University of Arkansas Press, 1990.

Carolyn Chute

Chute, Carolyn. *The Beans of Egypt, Maine*. New York: Ticknor & Fields, 1985.

——. *Letourneau's Used Auto Parts*. 1988. Reprint. New York: Harper & Row Perennial Library, 1989.

Pear, Nancy. "Chute, Carolyn." *Contemporary Authors*. Vol. 123. Detroit: Gale Research, 1988.

Judith Ortiz Cofer

Cofer, Judith Ortiz. "American History." *Iguana Dreams: New Latino Fiction*. Ed. Delia Poey and Virgil Suarez. New York: Harperperennial, 1992.

——. "Fever." *Puerto Rican Writers at Home in the USA*. Ed. Faythe Turner. Seattle: Open Hand, 1991.

——. "The Life of an Echo." *Puerto Rican Writers at Home in the USA*.

——. *The Line of the Sun*. Athens: University of Georgia Press, 1989.

——. "Old Women." *Puerto Rican Writers at Home in the USA*.

——. *Silent Dancing: A Partial Remembrance of a Puerto Rican Childhood*. Houston: Arte Público Press, 1990.

"Cofer, Judith Ortiz." *Hispanic Writers*. Detroit: Gale Research, 1991.

Photo as an adult by John Cofer, courtesy of the author. Photo as a teenager courtesy of the author.

Pat Conroy

"To Randy Randel" was first published in the 1962 Beaufort, S.C. High School yearbook. Copyright 1962, 1993 by Pat Conroy. All of Pat Conroy's juvenilia appear by the author's permission.

Conroy, Pat. "Colonel Dad." *Washingtonian,* April 1991.

——. *The Prince of Tides*. 1986. Reprint. New York: Bantam, 1991.

——. *The Water Is Wide*. 1972. Reprint. New York: Bantam, 1987.

Photos courtesy of the author.

Michael Crichton

Michael Crichton's juvenilia appear by the author's permission. Copyright 1993 by Michael Crichton.

Crichton, Michael. *The Andromeda Strain*. New York: Knopf, 1969.

——. "Climbing Up a Cinder Cone: A Visit to Sunset Crater Makes a Novel Side Trip in Arizona." *New York Times,* 17 May 1959. (Crichton's first travel piece, published at age sixteen).

——. *Jurassic Park*. New York: Knopf, 1990.

——. *Rising Sun*. New York: Knopf, 1992.

——. *The Terminal Man*. New York: Knopf, 1972.

——. *Travels*. New York: Knopf, 1988. (Includes the essay "Quitting Medicine.")

Harvard photo by Robert Gifford. Photo as an adult by Bruce McBroom. All photos courtesy of Michael Crichton.

Stephen Dixon

Stephen Dixon's piece of juvenilia appears by the author's permission. Copyright 1993 by Stephen Dixon.

Dixon, Stephen. *Garbage*. New York: Cane Hill Press, 1988.

——. "Milk Is Very Good for You." *14 Stories*. Baltimore: Johns Hopkins University Press, 1980.

Friedman, Alan H. "Prose that Expands the Arteries." Rev. of *Frog,* by Stephen Dixon. *New York Times Book Review,* 17 Nov. 1991.

Mandelbaum, Paul. "Dangerous Obsessions." *Johns Hopkins Magazine,* Apr. 1989. (Many of the introductory remarks and side notes are adapted from this profile of the author.)

Photo as an adult copyright by Meredith Waddell, courtesy of Stephen Dixon. Photo as a teenager courtesy of Stephen Dixon.

Rita Dove
Rita Dove's juvenilia appear by the author's permission. Copyright 1993 by Rita Dove.

Dove, Rita. *Through the Ivory Gate.* New York: Pantheon, 1992.

"Dove, Rita (Frances)." *Contemporary Authors: New Revision Series.* Vol. 27. Detroit: Gale Research, 1989.

Photo as an adult by Fred Viebahn, courtesy of Rita Dove. Childhood photos courtesy of Rita Dove.

Clyde Edgerton
"An Afternoon in the Gym." *The Southern Drawl* (Southern High School literary magazine, Durham, N.C.), Dec. 1960. "Buzzard Gets Bird's-eye View of Three-Man Adventures: Chick, Clyde, Burton Lose Themselves in True Woodsman Style." *Southern Script* (Southern High School newspaper), 27 May 1960, 2. Copyright 1960, 1993 by Clyde Edgerton. Reprinted by the author's permission.

Edgerton, Clyde. *The Floatplane Notebooks.* 1988. Reprint. New York: Ballantine, 1989.

——. *Killer Diller.* 1991. Reprint. New York: Ballantine, 1992.

——. *Raney.* 1985. Reprint. New York: Ballantine, 1986.

——. *Walking Across Egypt.* 1987. Reprint. New York: Ballantine, 1988.

Photos courtesy of the author.

Stanley Elkin
"Malice in Wonderland." *The Green Caldron* (University of Illinois, Department of Rhetoric publication), Apr. 1949: 5–6. Copyright 1949, 1993 by Stanley Elkin. Reprinted by the author's permission.

Elkin, Stanley. *Early Elkin.* Flint, Mich.: Bamberger Books, 1985.

——. "In Darkest Hollywood." *Harper's,* Dec. 1989.

——. *The Six-Year-Old Man.* Flint, Mich.: Bamberger Books, 1987.

Apple, Max. "Having Their Last Good Time." Rev. of *The Magic Kingdom* by Stanley Elkin. *New York Times Book Review,* 24 Mar. 1985.

Emerson, Ken. "The Indecorous, Rabelaisian, Convoluted Righteousness of Stanley Elkin." *New York Times Magazine,* 3 Mar. 1991.

Photo as a teenager courtesy of Stanley Elkin. Photo as an adult copyright 1986 by Mariana Cook, courtesy of Stanley Elkin.

George Garrett
George Garrett's juvenilia appear by the author's permission. Copyright 1993 by George Garrett.

Garrett, George. *Death of the Fox.* New York: Doubleday, 1971.

——. "Noise of Strangers" (originally "Cold Ground Was My Bed Last Night"). *An Evening Performance.* 1985. Reprint. New York: Penguin, 1986.

——. *Poison Pen; or, Live Now and Pay Later.* Stuart Wright, 1986.

——. "A Record as Long as Your Arm." *An Evening Performance.*

Dillard, R. H. W. *Understanding George Garrett.* Columbia: University of South Carolina Press, 1988.

Photos courtesy of the author.

Ellen Gilchrist

Ellen Gilchrist's juvenilia appear by the author's permission. Copyright 1993 by Ellen Gilchrist.

Gilchrist, Ellen. *Falling Through Space: The Journals of Ellen Gilchrist.* Boston: Little, Brown, 1987.

——. "Rich." *In the Land of Dreamy Dreams.* Boston: Little, Brown, 1981.

——. "The Time Capsule." *Light Can Be Both Wave and Particle.* Boston: Little, Brown, 1989.

Yardley, Jonathan. "Knockout 'Victory': The Best Stories Yet from Ellen Gilchrist." *Washington Post,* 12 Sept. 1984.

Photo as an adult by Jerry Bauer, courtesy of Little, Brown. Photo as a teenager courtesy of Ellen Gilchrist.

Gail Godwin

Gail Godwin's juvenilia appear by the author's permission. Copyright 1993 by Gail Godwin.

Godwin, Gail. "Becoming a Writer." *The Writer on Her Work.* Ed. Janet Sternburg. New York: Norton, 1980.

——. "Becoming the Characters in Your Novel." *The Writer,* June 1982.

——. "A Diarist on Diarists." *Our Private Lives: Journals, Notebooks, and Diaries.* Ed. Daniel Halpern. New York: Vintage, 1990.

——. "Dream Children." *Dream Children.* New York: Knopf, 1976.

——. *Father Melancholy's Daughter.* New York: Morrow, 1991.

——. *The Finishing School.* New York: Viking, 1985.

——. "Journals: 1982–1987." *Our Private Lives.*

——. "My Lover, His Summer Vacation." *Dream Children.*

——. "Notes for a Story." *Dream Children.*

——. "Some Side Effects of Time Travel." *Dream Children.*

——. "The Southern Belle." *Ms.,* July 1975.

——. *A Southern Family.* New York: Morrow, 1987.

——. "The Uses of Autobiography." *The Writer,* Mar. 1987.

Hill, Jane. *Gail Godwin.* New York: Twayne, 1992.

Photo as an adult by Jerry Bauer, courtesy of Gail Godwin. Photos from youth courtesy of Gail Godwin.

Allan Gurganus

"Dare to Be Different" (drawing). Rocky Mount, N.C. High School *Blackbird,* 1 Nov. 1963. Reprinted by the author's permission. Copyright 1963, 1993 by Allan Gurganus. Allan Gurganus's piece of juvenilia appears by the author's permission. Copyright 1993 by Allan Gurganus.

Gurganus, Allan. "Adult Art." *White People.* New York: Knopf, 1991.

——. "Garden Sermon: Being the History of a History, Notes from a Journal about How to Keep a Long Long Project Alive. Or:—What I Did with My Summer Vacation." From "Two Essays for Aloud." *Iowa Review,* 19, no. 1 (1989).

——. "Minor Heroism." *New Yorker,* 18 Nov. 1974. (Included in *White People.*)

——. *Oldest Living Confederate Widow Tells All.* New York: Knopf, 1989.

Prince, Tom. "Mouth of the South." *New York,* 21 Aug. 1989.

Reed, Susan, with David Hutchings. "He's 42, She's 99—Together They Make the South Rise Again." *People,* 18 Sept. 1989.

Photo as an adult copyright by Marion Ettlinger, courtesy of Allan Gurganus. Photo as a teenager by Paul Nagano, courtesy of Allan Gurganus.

Mark Helprin

"Lightning North of Paris." *A Dove of the East and Other Stories.* 1975. Reprint. San Diego: Harcourt Brace Jovanovich, 1990. Copyright 1975, 1993 by Mark Helprin. Reprinted by permission of the author.

Helprin, Mark. "The Schreuderspitze." *The World of the Short Story: A Twentieth Century Collection.* Ed. Clifton Fadiman. 1986. Reprint. New York: Avenel, 1990.

——. *A Soldier of the Great War.* 1991. Reprint. New York: Avon, 1992.

——. *Winter's Tale.* San Diego: Harcourt Brace Jovanovich, 1983.

Alexander, Paul. "Big Books, Tall Tales." *New York Times Magazine,* 28 Apr. 1991.

Photos courtesy of the author.

John Hersey

John Hersey's piece of juvenilia appears by the author's permission. Copyright 1991 by John Hersey.

——. "God's Typhoon." *Fling and Other Stories.* New York: Knopf, 1990.

——. *Hiroshima.* New York: Knopf, 1946, 1985 (Hersey returned to Japan years later to follow up on the six survivors featured in *Hiroshima* and published an updated version of the book in 1985).

——. "Homecoming." *New Yorker,* 10 May 1982, 17 May 1982, 24 May 1982, 31 May 1982. This four-part series provides an autobiographical account of the author's childhood in Tientsin (as well as his modern-day observations of that city and China).

——. *A Single Pebble.* 1956. Reprint. New York: Bantam, 1982.

Sanders, David. *John Hersey Revisited.* Boston: Twayne, 1990.

Photos courtesy of the author.

Charles Johnson

"50 Cards 50." *The Evanstonian* (Evanston, Ill., High School newspaper), 3 Feb. 1966. "Man Beneath Rags." *Evanstonian,* 19 Nov. 1965. "Rendezvous." *Evanstonian,* 3 June 1966. The ongoing "Wonder Wildkit" strip also appeared in *The Evanstonian.* "Individuality, not collectivity, is vehicle for attaining equality." *The Daily Egyptian* (Southern Illinois University), 1968. *The Daily Egyptian,* Johnson's college student newspaper, also published his King drawing in 1968. Reprinted by the author's permission. Copyright 1965, 1966, 1968, 1993 by Charles Johnson.

Johnson, Charles. *Being and Race: Black Writing since 1970*. 1988. Reprint. Bloomington: Indiana University Press, 1990.

——. *Middle Passage*. 1990. Reprint. New York: Plume, 1991.

——. "Popper's Disease." *The Sorcerer's Apprentice*. New York: Atheneum, 1986.

Photo as an adult copyright by Jerry Bauer, courtesy of Charles Johnson. Photo as a teenager by Charles Johnson.

Stephen King

Stephen King's piece of juvenilia appears by the author's permission. Copyright 1993 by Stephen King.

King, Stephen. *Carrie*. New York: Doubleday, 1974.

——. *Danse Macabre*. New York: Everest House, 1981.

——. *It*. New York: Viking, 1986.

——. "Word Processor of the Gods." *Skeleton Crew*. 1985. Reprint. New York: Signet, 1986.

Magistrale, Tony. *Stephen King: The Second Decade*. New York: Twayne, 1992.

Photo as an adult by Tabitha King, courtesy of Stephen King. Childhood photo courtesy of Stephen King.

Maxine Hong Kingston

"In My Opinion." *The Edison Hi-Lite* (student newspaper, Edison Senior High School, Stockton, Calif.), 24 Jan. 1957. Reprinted by the author's permission. Copyright 1957, 1993 by Maxine Hong Kingston. Maxine Hong Kingston's juvenilia appear by her permission. Copyright 1993 by Maxine Hong Kingston.

Kingston, Maxine Hong. *Tripmaster Monkey: His Fake Book*. 1989. Reprint. New York: Vintage, 1990.

——. *The Woman Warrior: Memoirs of a Girlhood Among Ghosts*. 1976. Reprint. New York: Vintage, 1977.

Photo as an adult courtesy of Random House. Photo as a teenager from *The Edison Hi-Lite,* courtesy of Maxine Hong Kingston.

W. P. Kinsella

"These Changing Times." *Civil Service Bulletin* (a magazine issued by Kinsella's employer at the time, the Alberta government), 1955. The author's first published story, it is reprinted by his permission. Copyright 1955, 1993 by W. P. Kinsella. "The Custom," previously unpublished, also appears by his permission. Copyright 1993 by W. P. Kinsella.

Kinsella, W. P. *The Iowa Baseball Confederacy*. 1986. Reprint. New York: Ballantine, 1991.

——. "Reports Concerning the Death of the Seattle Albatross Are Somewhat Exaggerated." *The Further Adventures of Slugger McBatt*. Boston: Houghton Mifflin, 1988.

——. "Weasels and Ermines." *Born Indian*. Ottawa: Oberon Press, 1981.

Johnson, Anne Janette, and Jean W. Ross. "Kinsella, W(illiam) P(atrick)." *Contemporary Authors: New Revision Series*. Vol. 21. Detroit: Gale Research, 1987.

Photo as an adult by Scott Norris, courtesy of W. P. Kinsella. Photo as a teenager courtesy of W. P. Kinsella.

Ursula K. Le Guin
The author's juvenilia appear by her permission. Copyright 1993 by Ursula K. Le Guin.
Le Guin, Ursula K. *The Dispossessed: An Ambiguous Utopia.* New York: Harper & Row, 1974.
——. *The Language of the Night: Essays on Fantasy and Science Fiction.* Ed. Susan Wood. 1979. Reprint. New York: Berkley Publishing Group, 1985.
Attebery, Brian. "Ursula K. Le Guin." *Dictionary of Literary Biography.* Vol. 8, part I. Detroit: Gale Research, 1991.
Photo as an adult copyright by Marian Kolisch, courtesy of Ursula K. Le Guin. Childhood photo courtesy of Ursula K. Le Guin.

Madeleine L'Engle
Madeleine L'Engle's included juvenilia first appeared in school literary journals and are reprinted by her permission. Copyright 1929, 1932, 1933, 1993 by Madeleine L'Engle.
L'Engle, Madeleine. *A Circle of Quiet.* 1972. Reprint. New York: Harper & Row, 1984.
——. *Dare to Be Creative* (Nov. 16, 1983 lecture at the Library of Congress). Washington, D.C.: Library of Congress, 1984.
——. *A Severed Wasp.* 1982. Reprint. New York: Farrar, Straus, and Giroux, 1987.
——. *A Wrinkle in Time.* 1962. Reprint. New York: Dell, 1973.
Photo as an adult by Steve Vinik, courtesy of Madeleine L'Engle. Childhood photos courtesy of the Wheaton College (Ill.) Special Collections.

Jill McCorkle
Jill McCorkle's juvenilia appear by the author's permission. Copyright 1993 by Jill McCorkle.
McCorkle, Jill. "Crash Diet." *Crash Diet.* Chapel Hill, N.C.: Algonquin, 1992.
——. "Gold Mine." *Crash Diet.*
——. "Man Watcher." *Crash Diet.*
——. "Sleeping Beauty, Revised." *Crash Diet.*
——. *Tending to Virginia.* Chapel Hill, N.C.: Algonquin, 1987.
Photos courtesy of Jill McCorkle.

Norman Mailer
"The Martian Invasion." *First Glance: Childhood Creations of the Famous.* Ed. Tuli Kupferberg and Sylvia Topp. Maplewood, N.J.: Hammond, 1978. Proofread against this version. Copyright 1978, 1993 by Norman Mailer. Reprinted by permission of the author.
Mailer, Norman. *Advertisements for Myself.* New York: G. P. Putnam's Sons, 1959. (This compilation includes two stories and a novella from Mailer's Harvard days, written when he was eighteen to twenty: "The Greatest Thing in the World," "Maybe Next Year," and "A Calculus at Heaven.")

——. *Harlot's Ghost.* New York: Random House, 1991.

——. "The Warren Report." Profile of Warren Beatty. *Vanity Fair,* Nov. 1991.

——. *Why Are We in Vietnam?* New York: G. P. Putnam's Sons, 1967.

Kellman, Steven G. "Mailer, Norman." *Contemporary Authors: New Revision Series.* Vol. 28. Detroit: Gale Research, 1990.

Manso, Peter. *Mailer: His Life and Times.* New York: Simon and Schuster, 1985.

Merrill, Robert. *Norman Mailer.* Boston: Twayne, 1978.

Mills, Hilary. *Mailer: A Biography.* New York: Empire Books, 1982.

Thompson, Toby. "Mailer's Alpha and Omega." *Vanity Fair,* Oct. 1991.

Photo as an adult copyright 1991 by Nancy Crampton, courtesy of Random House. Childhood photo courtesy of Barbara Wasserman.

Bobbie Ann Mason

"The Afternoon Before the Morning." *Stylus* (University of Kentucky literary magazine), 1960: 33–39. Copyright 1960, 1993 by Bobbie Ann Mason. Reprinted by permission of the author.

Mason, Bobbie Ann. *In Country.* New York: Harper & Row, 1985.

——. "Nancy Culpepper." *Shiloh and Other Stories.* New York: Harper & Row, 1982.

——. "The Rookers." *Shiloh.*

——. *Spence + Lila.* New York: Harper & Row, 1988.

Photo as an adult by Thomas Victor, courtesy of Bobbie Ann Mason. 1960 photo courtesy of Bobbie Ann Mason.

Susan Minot

Susan Minot's three untitled pieces of juvenilia appeared originally in the literary magazine of her boarding school (Concord Academy, Concord, Mass.). Reprinted by permission of the author. Copyright 1973, 1993 by Susan Minot.

Minot, Susan. *Monkeys.* New York: Dutton/Lawrence, 1986.

——. "Lust." *Lust & Other Stories.* Boston: Houghton Mifflin/Lawrence, 1989.

——. "Sparks." *Lust.*

——. "The Swan in the Garden." *Lust.*

Pryor, Kelli. "The Story of Her Life: Writer Susan Minot Begins a New Chapter." *New York,* 12 June 1989.

Photo as an adult copyright 1991 by Huger Foote, courtesy of Susan Minot. Photo as a teenager courtesy of Susan Minot.

Gloria Naylor

"Hidden Wealth?" *The Star* (literary magazine of Andrew Jackson High School, Cambria Heights, N.Y.), Spring 1967. Copyright 1967, 1993 by Gloria Naylor. Reprinted by permission of Sterling Lord Literistic, Inc. and the author.

Naylor, Gloria. Interview. With Kay Bonetti. Columbia, Mo.: American Audio Prose Library, 1988.

——. *Mama Day.* New York: Ticknor & Fields, 1988.

——. *The Women of Brewster Place.* 1982. Reprint. New York: Penguin, 1983.

Photo as an adult copyright 1984 by Donna DeCesare, courtesy of Gloria Naylor. Photo as a teenager courtesy of Gloria Naylor.

Joyce Carol Oates

"A Long Way Home." *Will o' the Wisp* (literary magazine of Williamsville Junior-Senior High School, Williamsville, N.Y.), 1956. Copyright 1956, 1993 by Joyce Carol Oates. Appears by permission of the author. Courtesy of Syracuse University Library, Special Collections.

Oates, Joyce Carol. "Facts, Visions, Mysteries: My Father, Frederic Oates." *Family Portraits: Remembrances by Twenty Distinguished Writers*. Ed. Carolyn Anthony. New York: Doubleday, 1989.

——. "Family." *Heat and Other Stories*. New York: Dutton, 1991.

——. "House Hunting." *Heat*.

——. "How I Contemplated the World from the Detroit House of Correction and Began My Life Over Again." *The Wheel of Love and Other Stories*. New York: Vanguard Press, 1970.

——. *Marya: A Life*. New York: Dutton, 1986.

——. *The Rise of Life on Earth*. New York: New Directions, 1991.

——. "The Seasons." *Raven's Wing*. New York: Dutton, 1986.

——. "Where Are You Going, Where Have You Been?" *The Wheel of Love*.

Milazzo, Lee, ed. *Conversations with Joyce Carol Oates*. Jackson: University Press of Mississippi, 1989. (A collection of interviews and profiles.)

Photo as an adult by Brian J. Berman, courtesy of Joyce Carol Oates. Photo at age twenty courtesy of Joyce Carol Oates.

Tillie Olsen

Tillie Olsen's juvenilia appear by the author's permission. The typescripts are kept at the Berg Collection of English and American Literature in the New York Public Library. Copyright 1993 by Tillie Olsen.

Olsen, Tillie. "I Stand Here Ironing." *Tell Me a Riddle*. 1961. Reprint. New York: Delta, 1989.

——. "Tell Me a Riddle." *Tell Me a Riddle*.

——. *Silences*. New York: Delacorte Press, 1978.

——. *Yonnondio: From the Thirties*. 1974. Reprint. New York: Dell, 1975.

Atwood, Margaret. "Tillie Olsen: Silences." *Second Words: Selected Critical Prose*. 1982. Reprint. Boston: Beacon Press, 1984.

Olson, Ted. "Words to Be Graven on Sandstone." *A Stranger and Afraid*. New Haven: Yale University Press, 1928.

Pearlman, Mickey, and Abby H. P. Werlock. *Tillie Olsen*. Boston: Twayne, 1991.

Photos courtesy of Tillie Olsen.

William Styron

"Get All You Can: A Parody in Verse." *Scripts 'N Pranks* (school literary magazine, Davidson College, N.C.), May 1943: 6–7. Copyright 1943, 1993 by William Styron. Reprinted by permission of the author.

Styron, William. *Darkness Visible: A Memoir of Madness.* New York: Random House, 1990.

——. Interview. With John Baker. *Conversations with Writers II.* Vol. 3. Ed. Matthew J. Bruccoli. Detroit: Gale Research, 1978.

——. *In the Clap Shack.* New York: Random House, 1973.

——. *The Long March.* New York: Random House, 1952.

——. "Love Day." *Esquire,* Aug. 1985.

——. "Marriott, the Marine." *Esquire,* Sept. 1971.

——. *Set This House on Fire.* New York: Random House, 1960.

——. *Sophie's Choice.* New York: Random House, 1979.

——. *This Quiet Dust and Other Writings.* New York: Random House, 1982.

Coale, Samuel. *William Styron Revisited.* Boston: Twayne, 1991.

West, James L. W., III, ed. *Conversations with William Styron.* Jackson: University Press of Mississippi, 1985. (Interviews and a profile.)

Photo as an adult copyright by Stathis Orphanos, courtesy of Random House. Photo as a teenager courtesy of William Styron.

Amy Tan

"What the Library Means to Me." The Santa Rosa *Press Democrat,* 1961. Copyright 1961 by the Santa Rosa *Press Democrat.* Reprinted by permission of the author.

——. *The Joy Luck Club.* New York: G. P. Putnam's Sons, 1989.

Photo as an adult by Robert Foothorap Company 1991, courtesy of Amy Tan. Childhood photo courtesy of Amy Tan.

John Updike

John Updike's piece of juvenilia is published here by his permission. Copyright 1993 by John Updike.

Updike, John. *Couples.* New York: Knopf, 1968.

——. "Deaths of Distant Friends." *The Best American Short Stories of the Eighties.* Ed. Shannon Ravenel. Boston: Houghton Mifflin, 1990.

——. "The Dogwood Tree: A Boyhood." *Assorted Prose.* New York: Knopf, 1979. (An earlier version of this boyhood account appears as a chapter in *Five Boyhoods.* Ed. Martin Levin. New York: Doubleday, 1962.)

——. "His Mother Inside Him." *New Yorker,* 20 Apr. 1992.

——. *Hugging the Shore: Essays and Criticism.* New York: Knopf, 1983.

——. Interview. With Charles Thomas Samuels. *Writers at Work: The Paris Review Interviews.* Fourth Series. Ed. George Plimpton. New York: Viking, 1976.

——. Introduction. *The Best American Short Stories 1984.* Ed. John Updike with Shannon Ravenel. Boston: Houghton Mifflin, 1984.

——. *Rabbit at Rest.* New York: Knopf, 1990.

——. *Rabbit Redux.* New York: Knopf, 1971.

——. *Rabbit, Run.* 1960. Reprint. New York: Fawcett Crest, 1990.

——. *S.* New York: Knopf, 1988.

——. *Self-Consciousness: Memoirs.* New York: Knopf, 1989.

——. *The Witches of Eastwick.* New York: Knopf, 1984.

Detweiler, Robert. *John Updike.* Boston: Twayne, 1984.

Photo as an adult by Martha Updike, courtesy of John Updike. Childhood photo courtesy of John Updike.

Gore Vidal

"Mostly About Geoffrey." *Phillips Exeter Review,* 10, no. 1 (1942): 7–9. "New Year's Eve." *Phillips Exeter Review,* 10, no. 2 (1943): 3–4. The stories are reprinted by permission of the author and the trustees of Phillips Exeter Academy. Copyright 1943, 1993 by Gore Vidal.

Vidal, Gore. Interviews. *Views from a Window: Conversations with Gore Vidal.* Ed. Robert J. Stanton and Gore Vidal. Secaucus, N.J.: Lyle Stuart, 1980.

——. *Myra Breckinridge* and *Myron.* 1968. 1974. Reprint. New York: Vintage, 1987.

——. "Norman Mailer: The Angels Are White." *Norman Mailer: The Man and His Work.* Ed. Robert F. Lucid. Boston: Little, Brown, 1971. (Includes Vidal's comment, quoted in the introduction to his chapter in this volume, about having been the "cleverest young fox. [. . .]")

——. "Three Stratagems." *A Thirsty Evil: Seven Short Stories.* 1956. Reprint. New York: Signet, 1958.

——. *Two Sisters: A Memoir in the Form of a Novel.* Boston: Little, Brown, 1970.

Kiernan, Robert F. *Gore Vidal.* New York: Frederick Ungar, 1982.

Photo as an adult copyright by Jane Bown, courtesy of Random House. Gore Vidal's 1943 yearbook photo courtesy of Phillips Exeter Academy.

Tobias Wolff

"Death." *The Record* (magazine of The Hill School, Pa.), Spring 1962. Copyright 1962, 1993 by Tobias Wolff. Reprinted by the author's permission.

Wolff, Tobias. Interview. "Wolff, Tobias (Jonathan Ansell)." With Jean W. Ross. *Contemporary Authors.* Vol. 117. Detroit: Gale Research, 1986.

——. "Poaching." *In the Garden of the North American Martyrs.* New York: Ecco Press, 1981.

——. *This Boy's Life: A Memoir.* New York: Atlantic Monthly Press, 1989.

Photo as an adult by Jerry Bauer, courtesy of Atlantic Monthly Press. Photo as a teenager courtesy of Tobias Wolff.